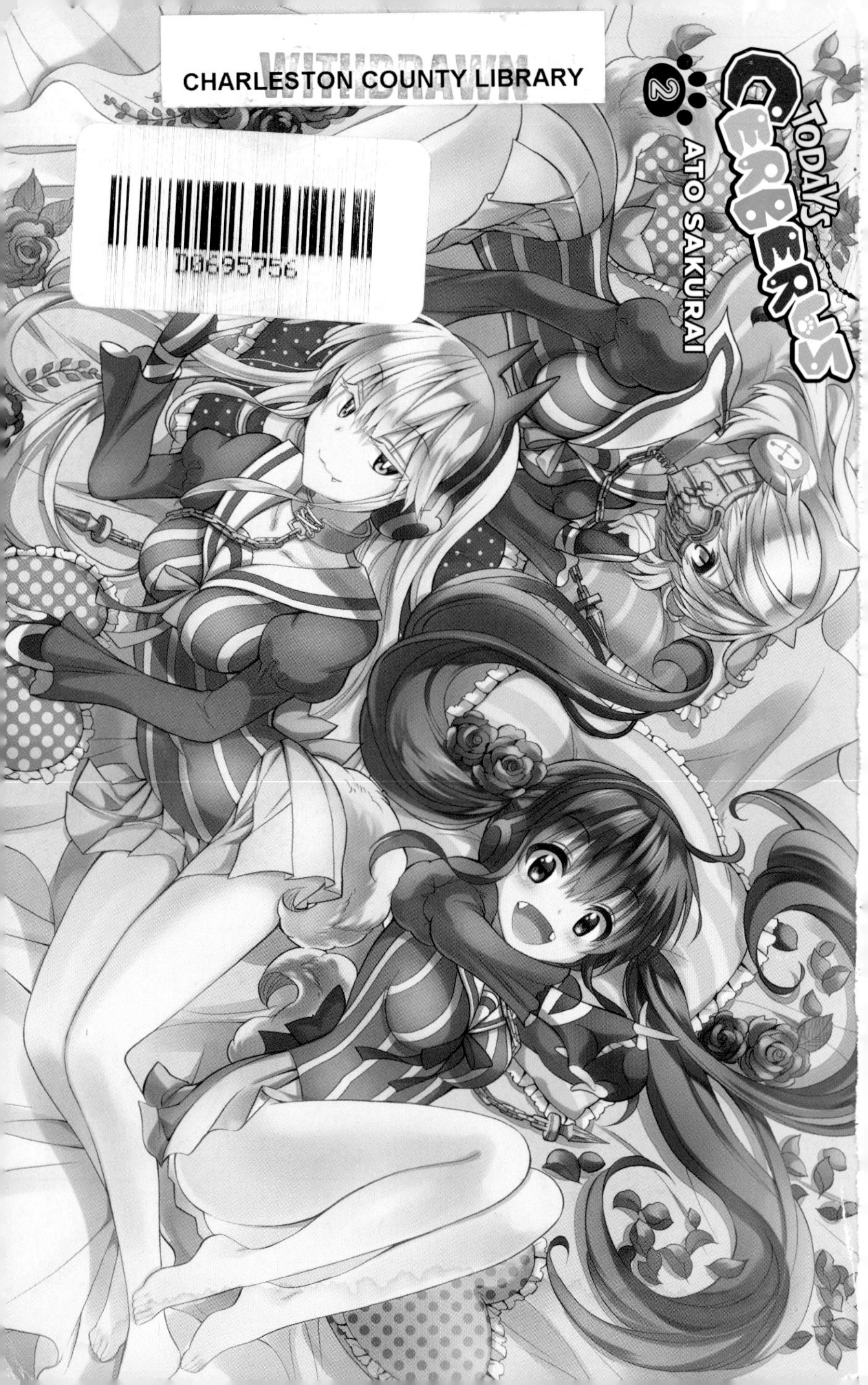
TODAY'S CERBERUS
2
ATO SAKURAI

CONTENTS

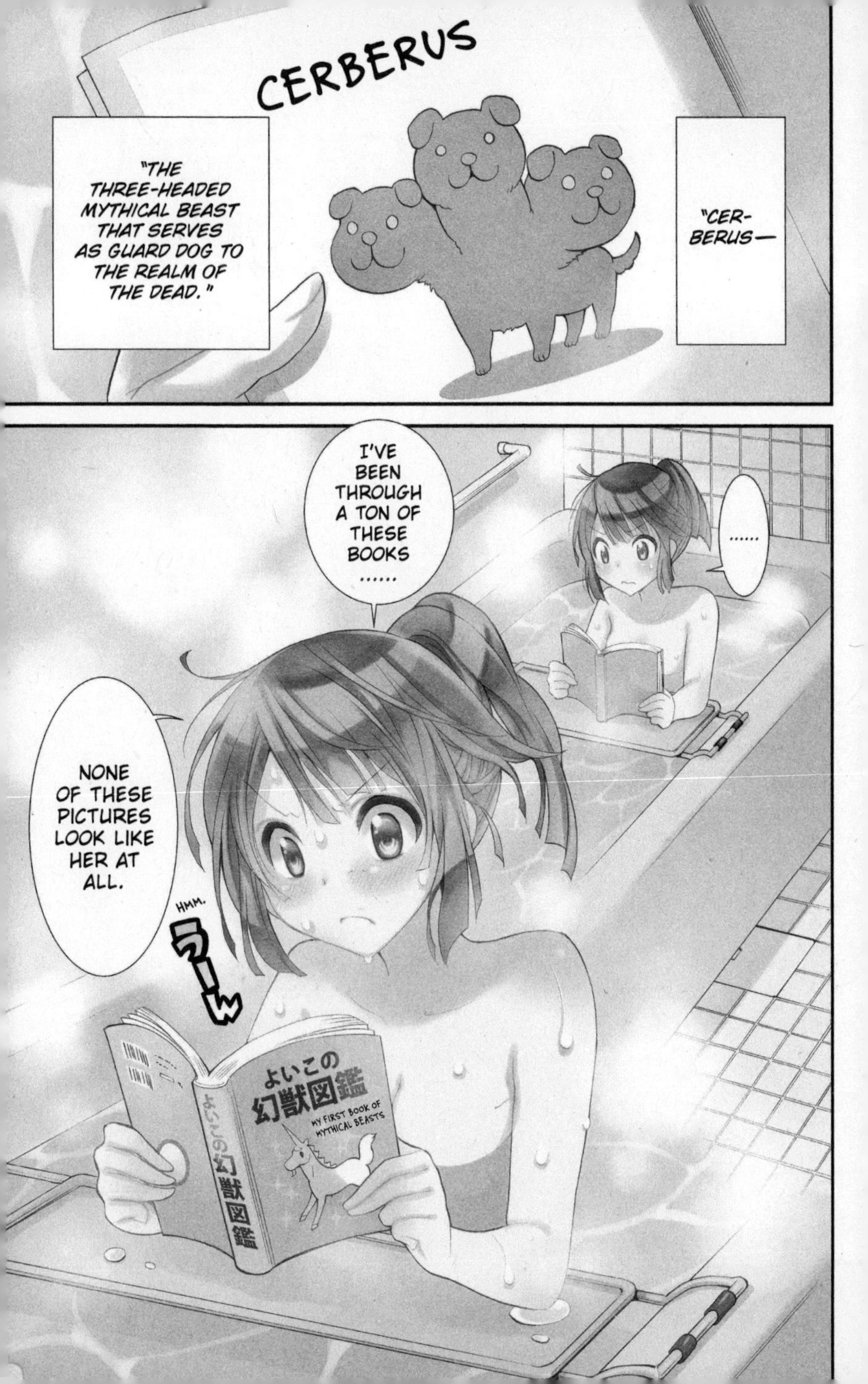
CERBERUS
"CER-BERUS—
"THE THREE-HEADED MYTHICAL BEAST THAT SERVES AS GUARD DOG TO THE REALM OF THE DEAD."
......
I'VE BEEN THROUGH A TON OF THESE BOOKS ....
NONE OF THESE PICTURES LOOK LIKE HER AT ALL.
HMM.
うーん
よいこの幻獣図鑑
MY FIRST BOOK OF MYTHICAL BEASTS
よいこの幻獣図鑑

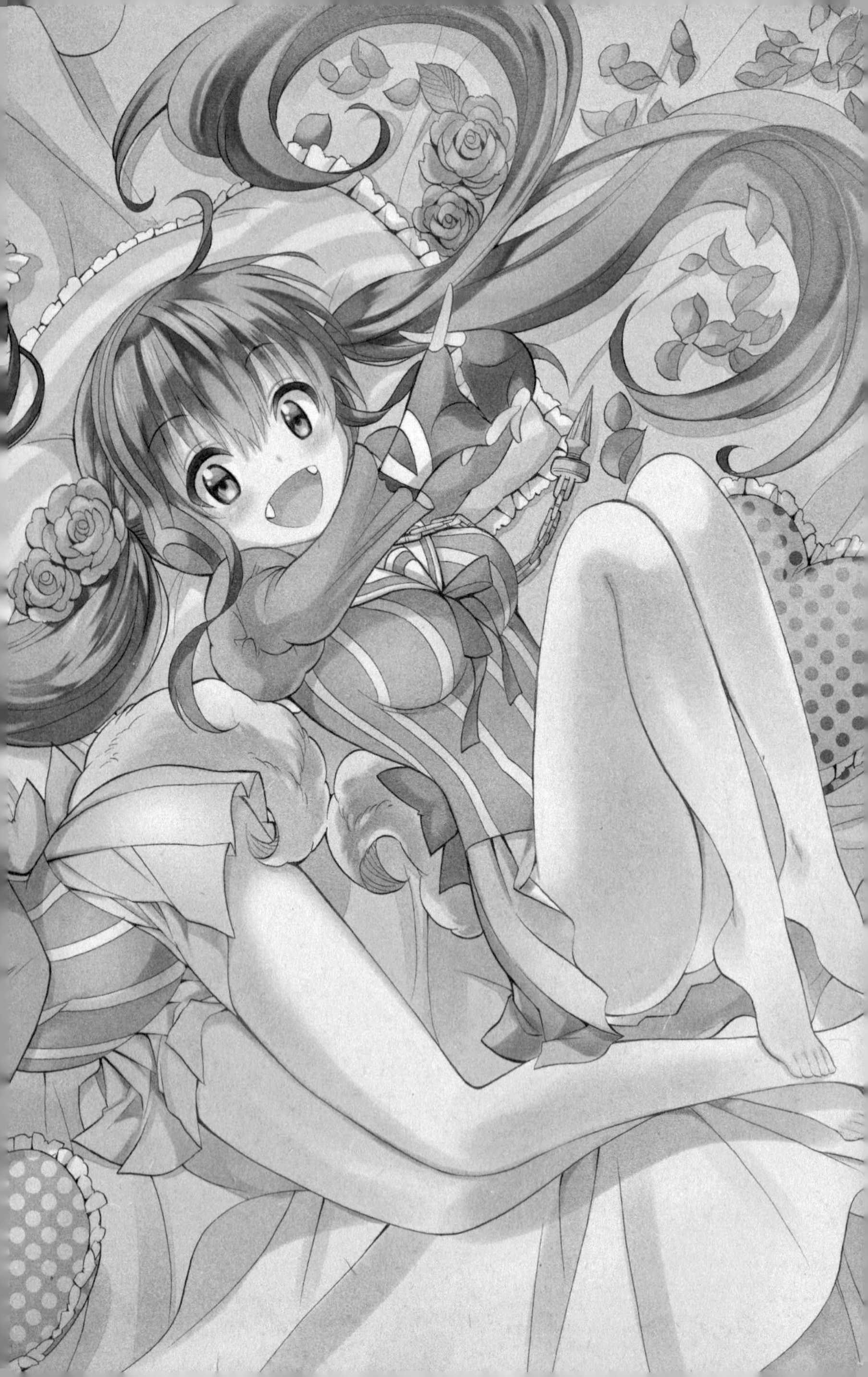

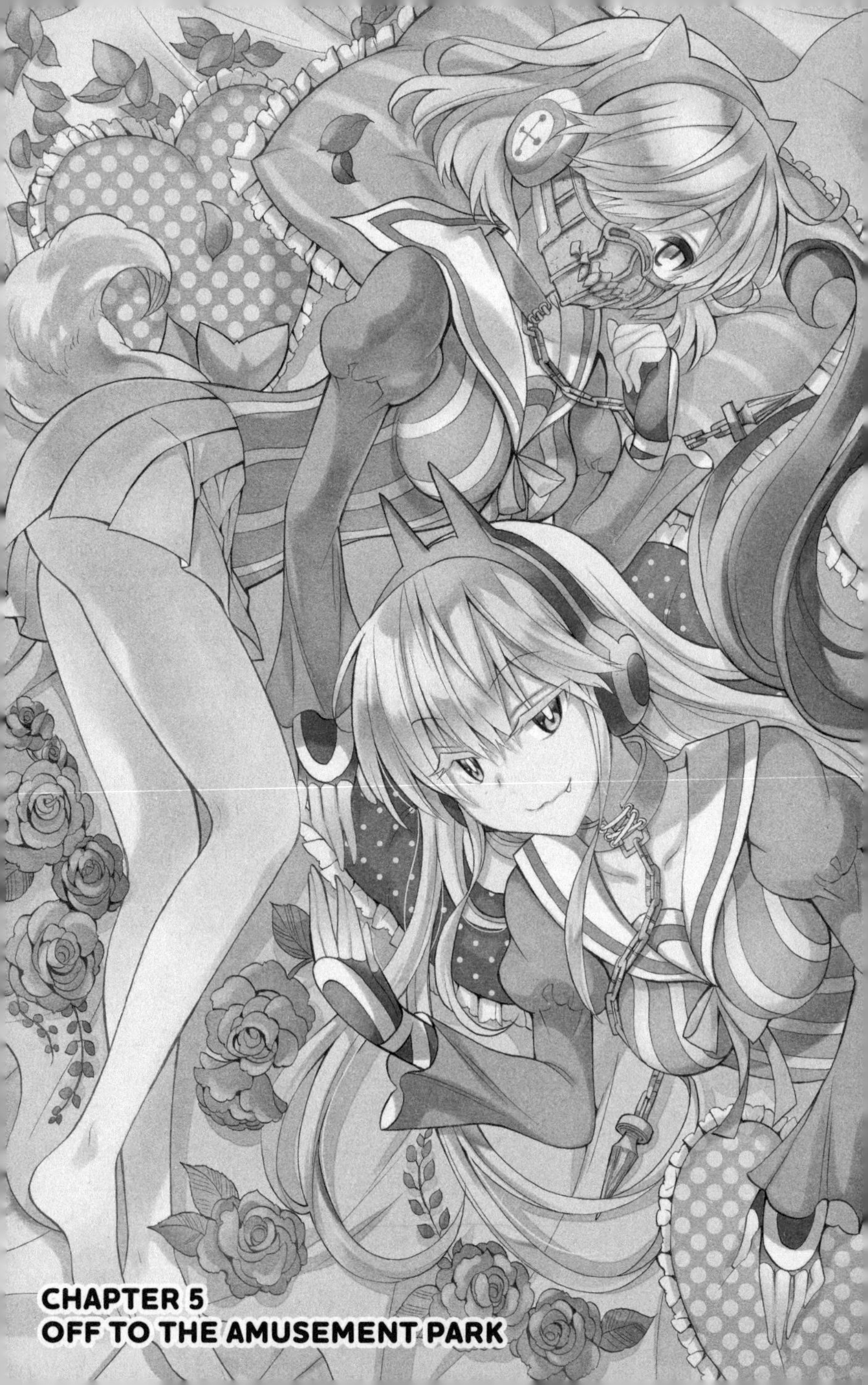

CHAPTER 5
OFF TO THE AMUSEMENT PARK

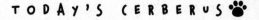
TODAY'S CERBERUS 🐾

I'M...I'M GOING CRAZY HERE...

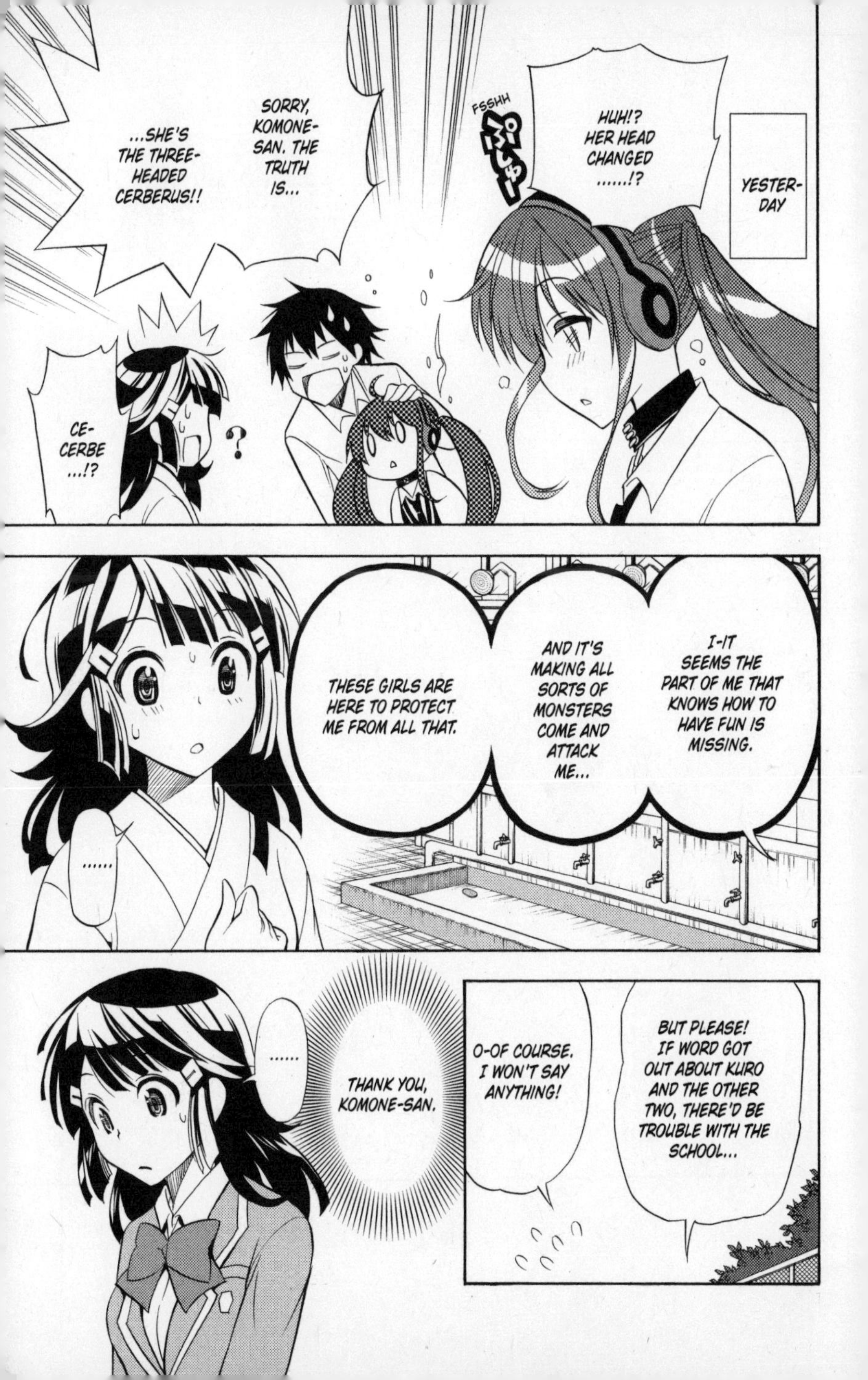
YESTER-DAY
HUH!? HER HEAD CHANGED ......!?
FSSHH
SORRY, KOMONE-SAN. THE TRUTH IS...
...SHE'S THE THREE-HEADED CERBERUS!!
CE-CERBE ...!?
I-IT SEEMS THE PART OF ME THAT KNOWS HOW TO HAVE FUN IS MISSING.
AND IT'S MAKING ALL SORTS OF MONSTERS COME AND ATTACK ME...
THESE GIRLS ARE HERE TO PROTECT ME FROM ALL THAT.
......
BUT PLEASE! IF WORD GOT OUT ABOUT KURO AND THE OTHER TWO, THERE'D BE TROUBLE WITH THE SCHOOL...
O-OF COURSE. I WON'T SAY ANYTHING!
THANK YOU, KOMONE-SAN.
......

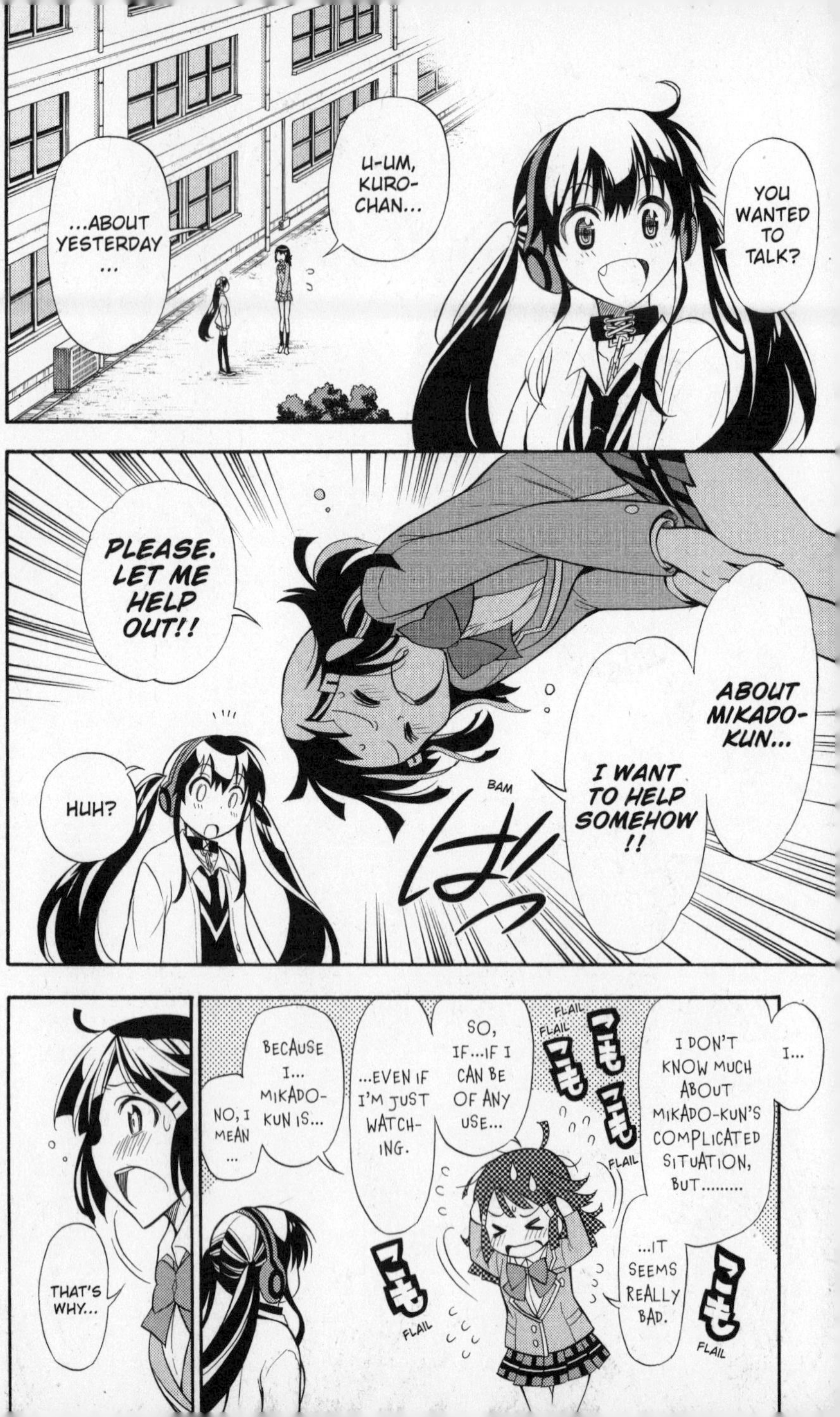
YOU WANTED TO TALK?
U-UM, KURO-CHAN...
...ABOUT YESTERDAY ...
ABOUT MIKADO-KUN...
I WANT TO HELP SOMEHOW !!
BAM
はっ
PLEASE. LET ME HELP OUT!!
HUH?
I...
I DON'T KNOW MUCH ABOUT MIKADO-KUN'S COMPLICATED SITUATION, BUT.........
...IT SEEMS REALLY BAD.
FLAIL
FLAIL
FLAIL
SO, IF...IF I CAN BE OF ANY USE...
...EVEN IF I'M JUST WATCHING.
BECAUSE I... MIKADO-KUN IS...
NO, I MEAN ...
FLAIL
FLAIL
THAT'S WHY...

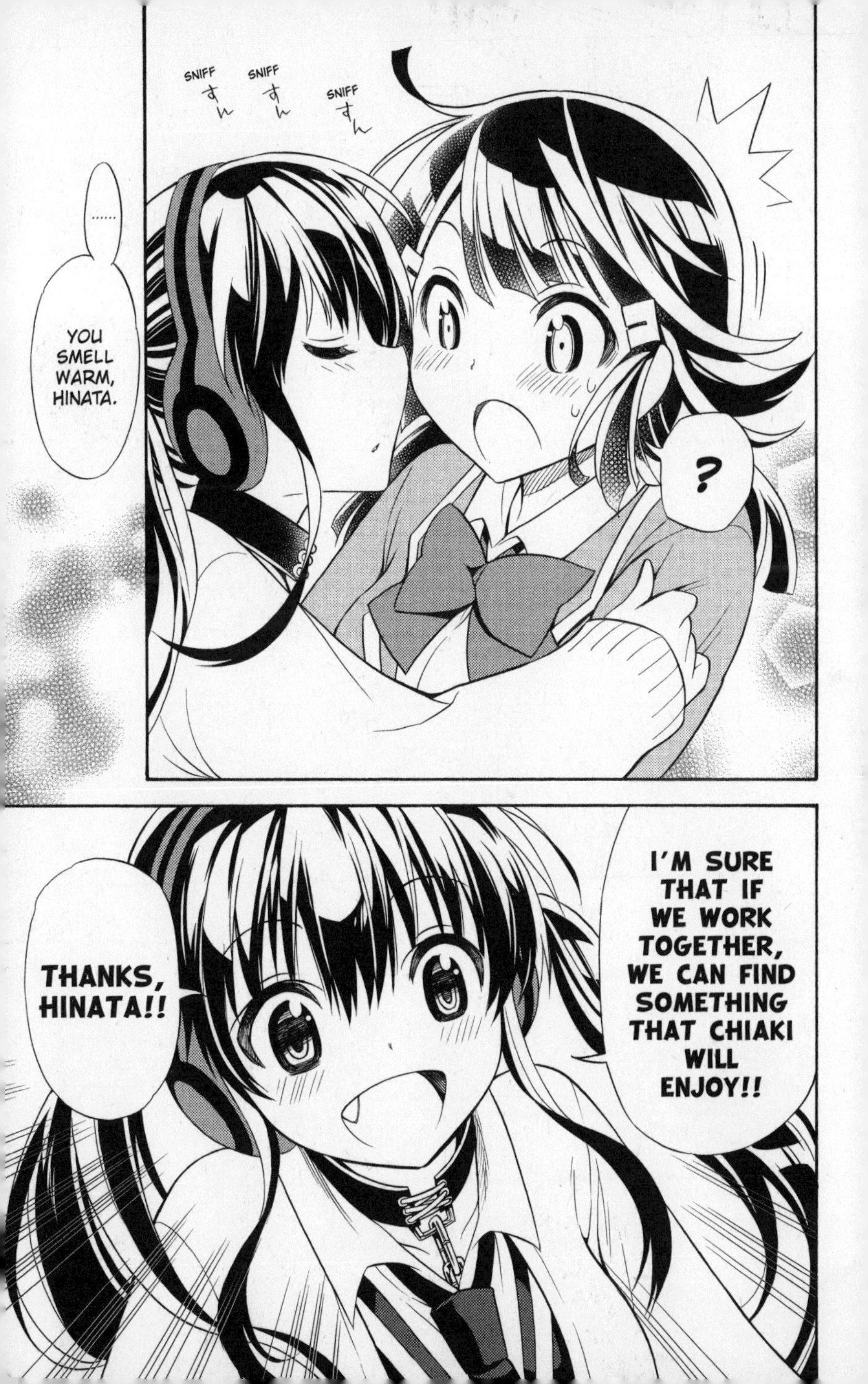
SNIFF すん
SNIFF すん
SNIFF すん
......
YOU SMELL WARM, HINATA.
?
I'M SURE THAT IF WE WORK TOGETHER, WE CAN FIND SOMETHING THAT CHIAKI WILL ENJOY!!
THANKS, HINATA!!

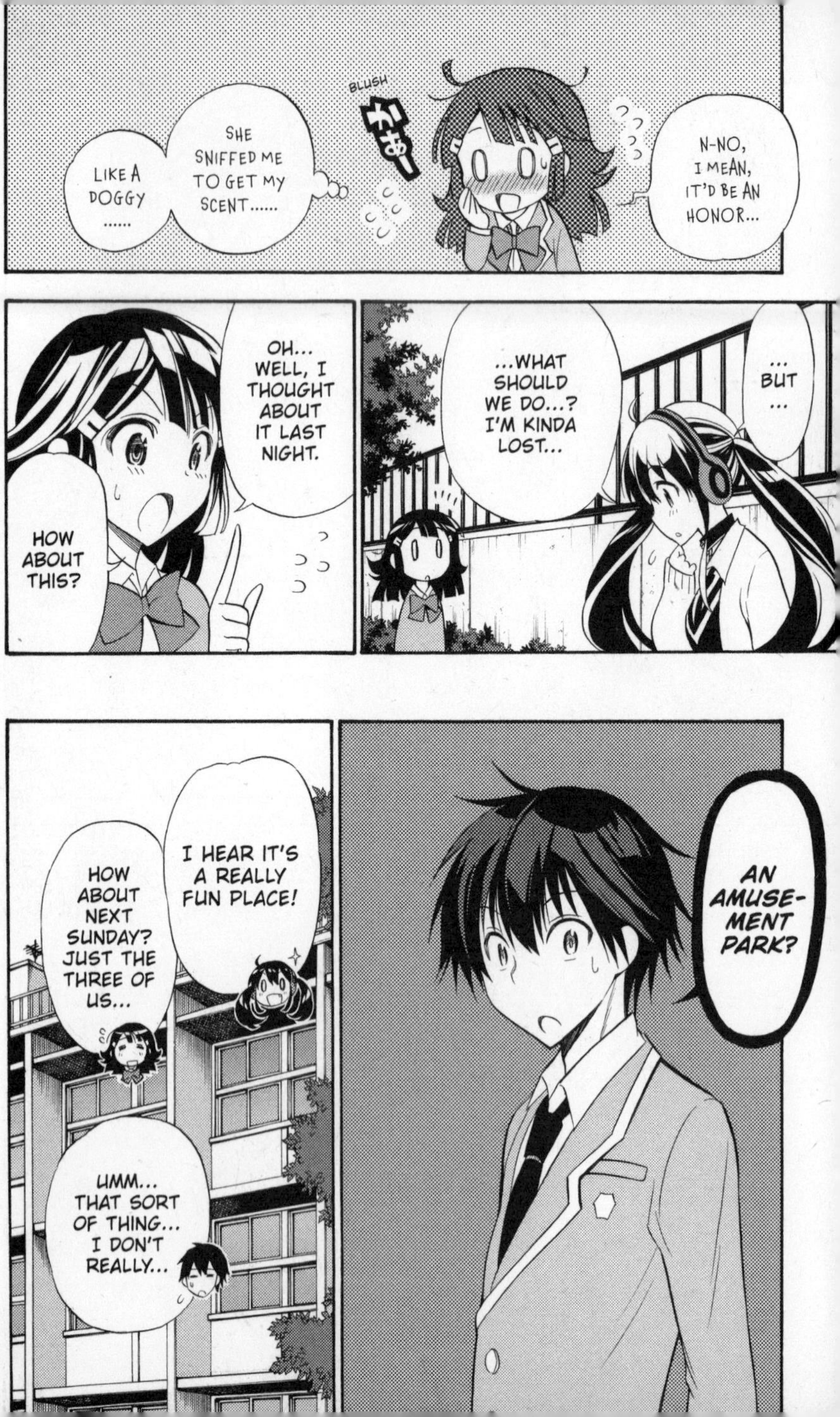
N-NO, I MEAN, IT'D BE AN HONOR...
BLUSH
SHE SNIFFED ME TO GET MY SCENT......
LIKE A DOGGY ......
... BUT ...
...WHAT SHOULD WE DO...? I'M KINDA LOST...
OH... WELL, I THOUGHT ABOUT IT LAST NIGHT.
HOW ABOUT THIS?
AN AMUSEMENT PARK?
I HEAR IT'S A REALLY FUN PLACE!
HOW ABOUT NEXT SUNDAY? JUST THE THREE OF US...
UMM... THAT SORT OF THING... I DON'T REALLY...

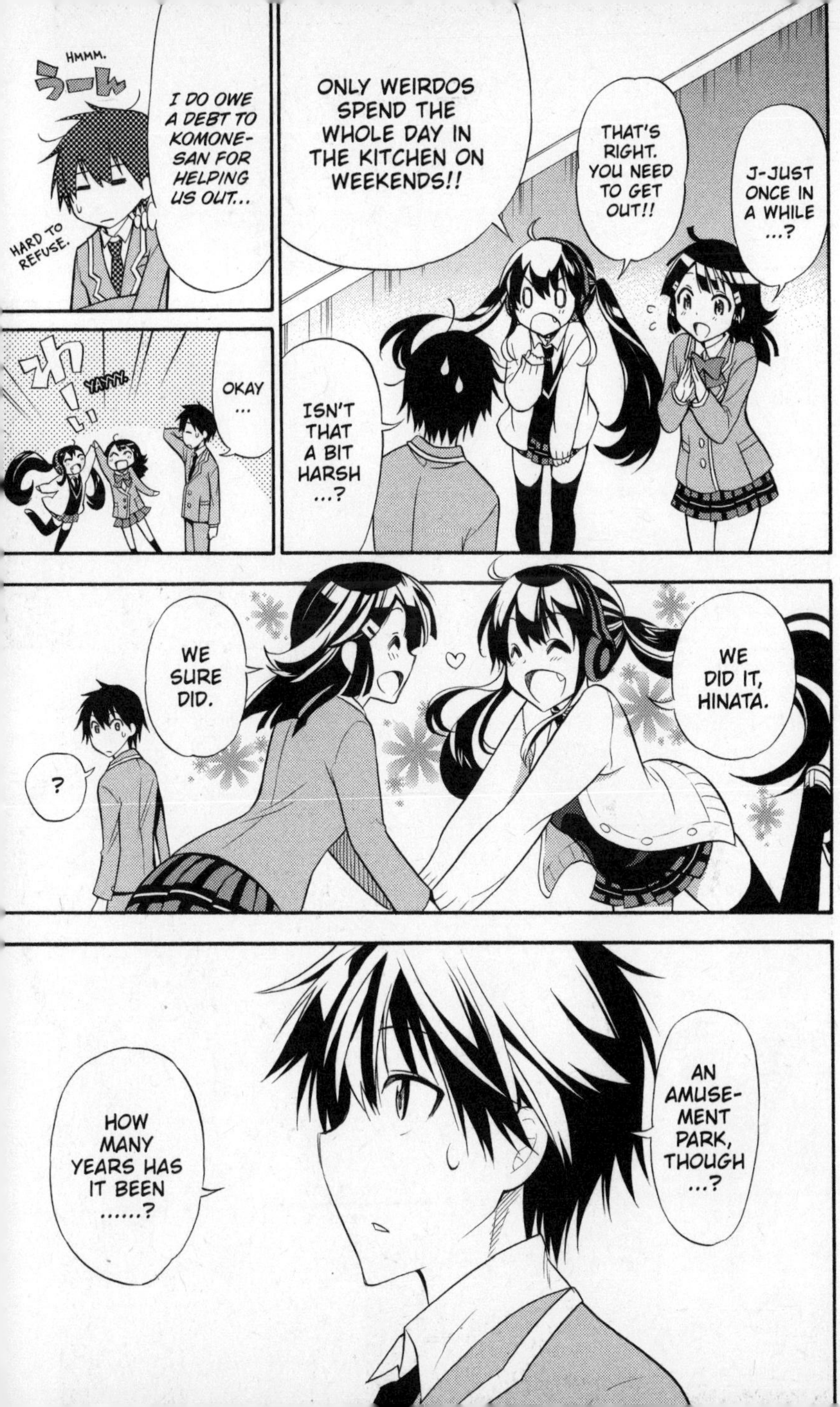
J-JUST ONCE IN A WHILE ...?
THAT'S RIGHT. YOU NEED TO GET OUT!!
ONLY WEIRDOS SPEND THE WHOLE DAY IN THE KITCHEN ON WEEKENDS!!
ISN'T THAT A BIT HARSH ...?
I DO OWE A DEBT TO KOMONE-SAN FOR HELPING US OUT...
うーん
HMMM.
HARD TO REFUSE.
OKAY ...
YAYYY.
WE DID IT, HINATA.
WE SURE DID.
?
AN AMUSEMENT PARK, THOUGH ...?
HOW MANY YEARS HAS IT BEEN ......?

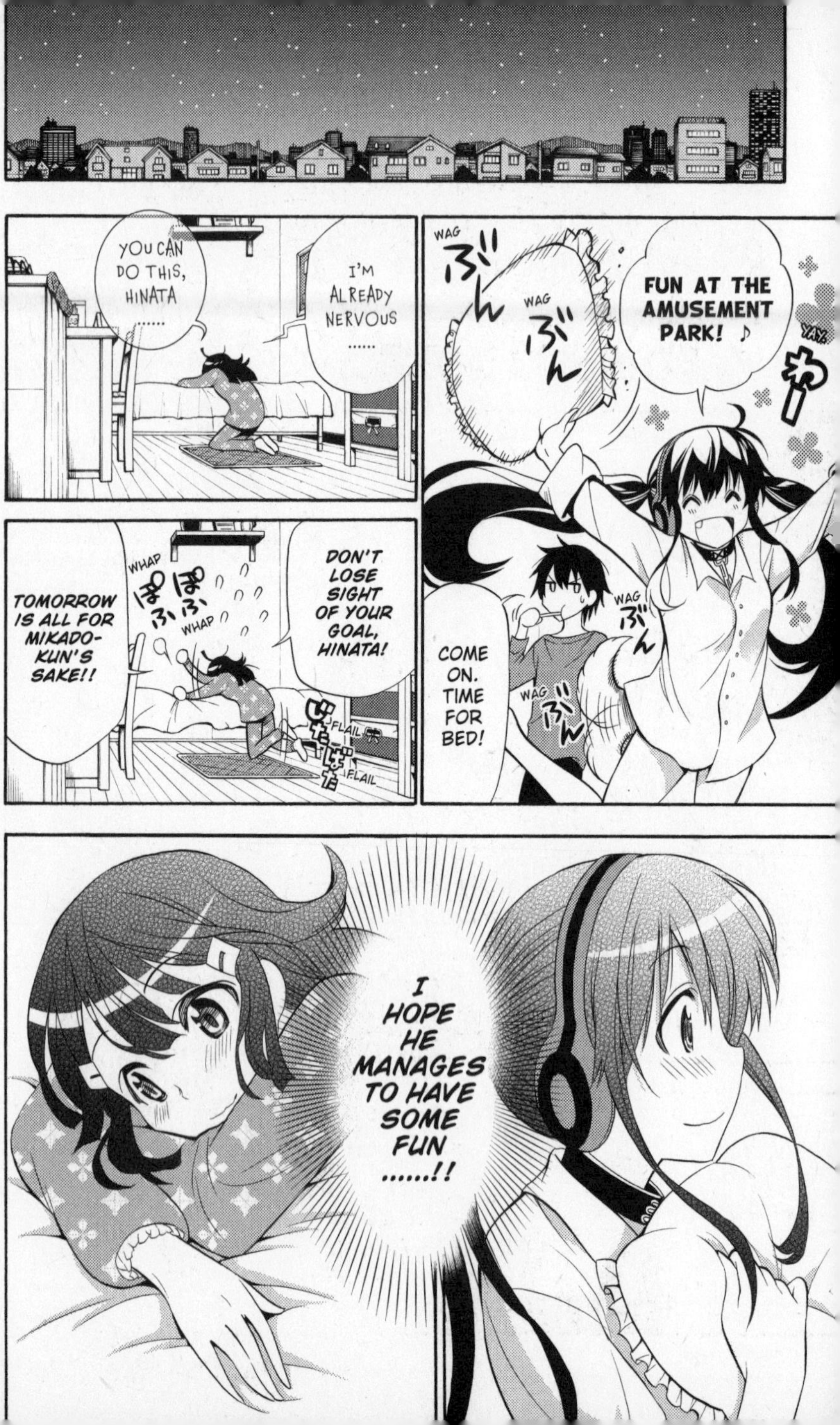

WAG
ぶん
WAG
ぶん
FUN AT THE AMUSEMENT PARK! ♪
YAY
わー
WAG
ぶん
WAG
ぶん
COME ON. TIME FOR BED!
YOU CAN DO THIS, HINATA ......
I'M ALREADY NERVOUS ......
DON'T LOSE SIGHT OF YOUR GOAL, HINATA!
WHAP
ぽふ
WHAP
ぽふ
TOMORROW IS ALL FOR MIKADO-KUN'S SAKE!!
FLAIL
じた
FLAIL
ばた
I HOPE HE MANAGES TO HAVE SOME FUN ......!!

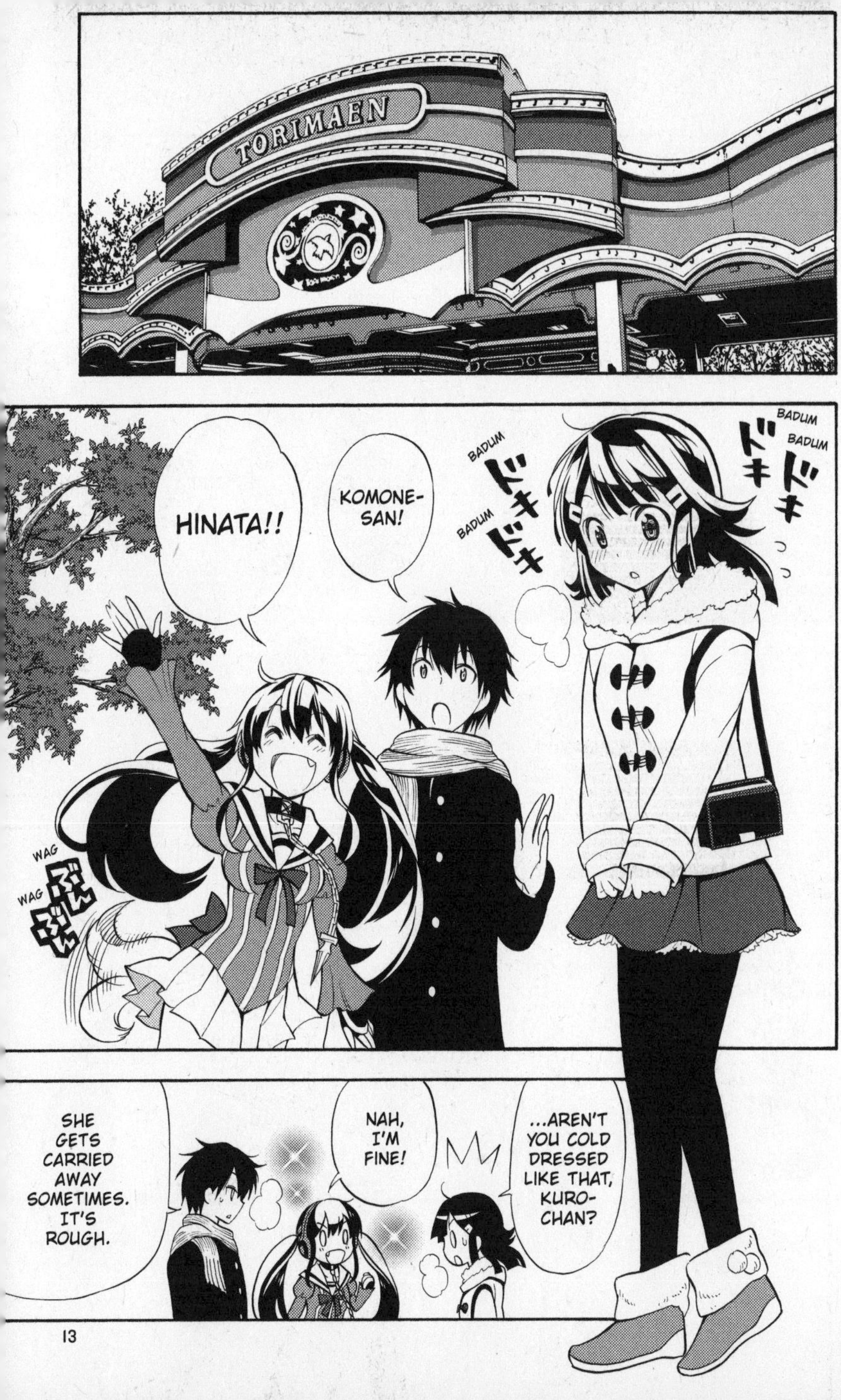
TORIMAEN
BADUM BADUM
BADUM BADUM
KOMONE-SAN!
HINATA!!
WAG WAG
...AREN'T YOU COLD DRESSED LIKE THAT, KURO-CHAN?
NAH, I'M FINE!
SHE GETS CARRIED AWAY SOMETIMES. IT'S ROUGH.

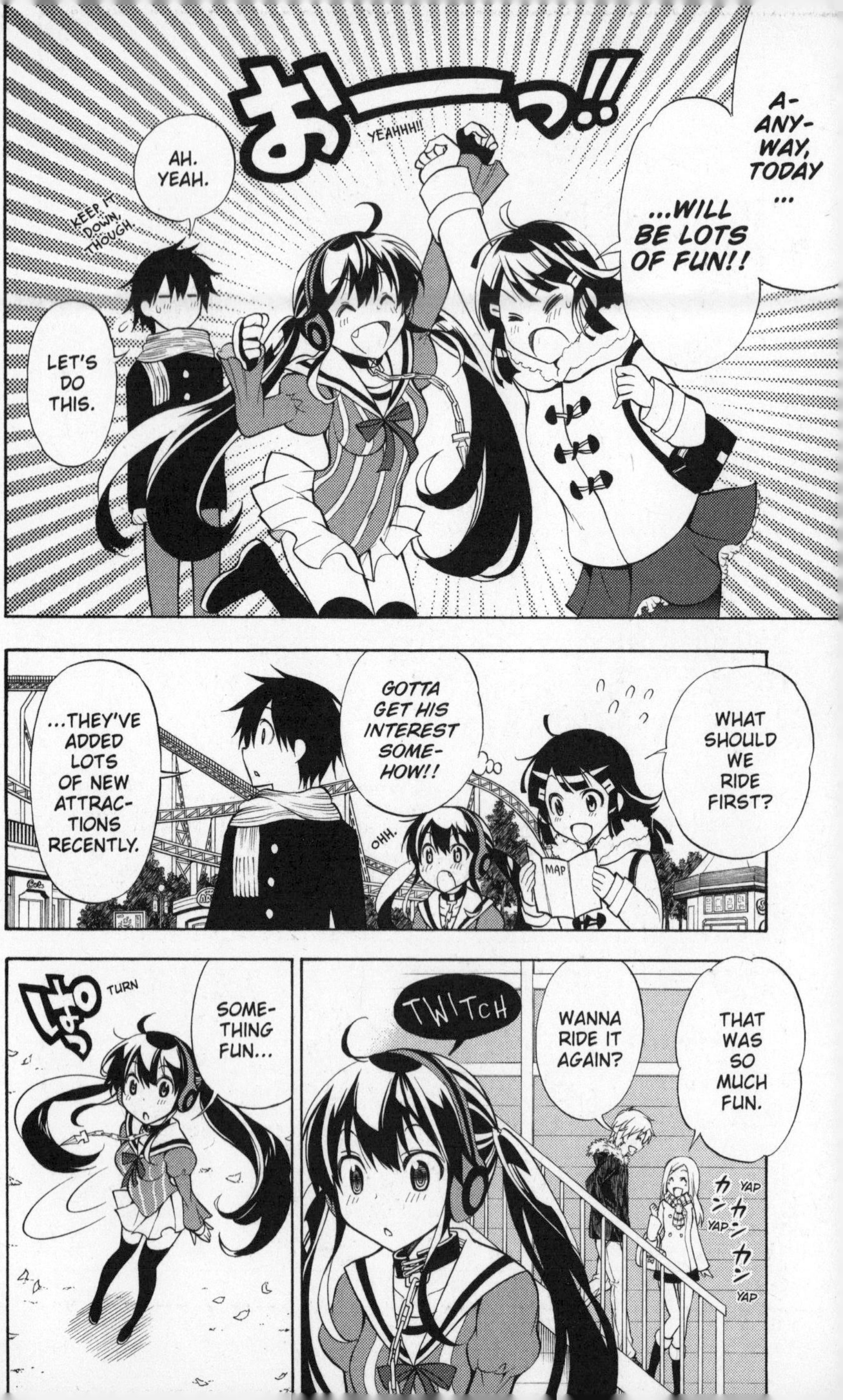
A-ANYWAY, TODAY...
...WILL BE LOTS OF FUN!!
おーっ!!
YEAHHH!!
AH. YEAH.
KEEP IT DOWN, THOUGH.
LET'S DO THIS.
WHAT SHOULD WE RIDE FIRST?
MAP
GOTTA GET HIS INTEREST SOMEHOW!!
OHH.
...THEY'VE ADDED LOTS OF NEW ATTRACTIONS RECENTLY.
THAT WAS SO MUCH FUN.
カンカンカン
YAP
YAP
YAP
WANNA RIDE IT AGAIN?
TWITCH
SOMETHING FUN...
TURN

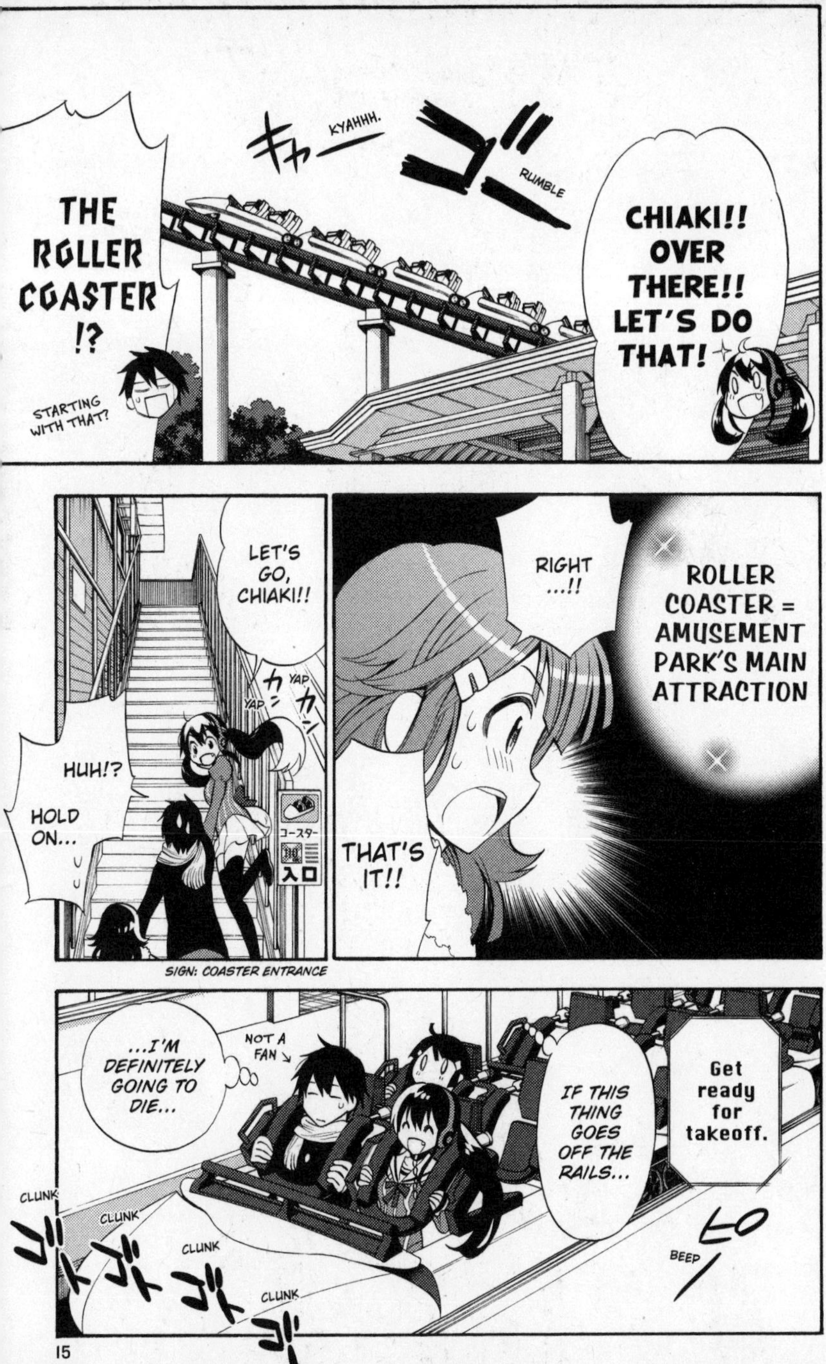
CHIAKI!! OVER THERE!! LET'S DO THAT!
RUMBLE
KYAHHH.
THE ROLLER COASTER!?
STARTING WITH THAT?
ROLLER COASTER = AMUSEMENT PARK'S MAIN ATTRACTION
RIGHT ...!!
THAT'S IT!!
LET'S GO, CHIAKI!!
YAP
YAP
HUH!? HOLD ON...
コースター
入口
SIGN: COASTER ENTRANCE
BEEP
Get ready for takeoff.
IF THIS THING GOES OFF THE RAILS...
NOT A FAN
...I'M DEFINITELY GOING TO DIE...
CLUNK
CLUNK
CLUNK
CLUNK

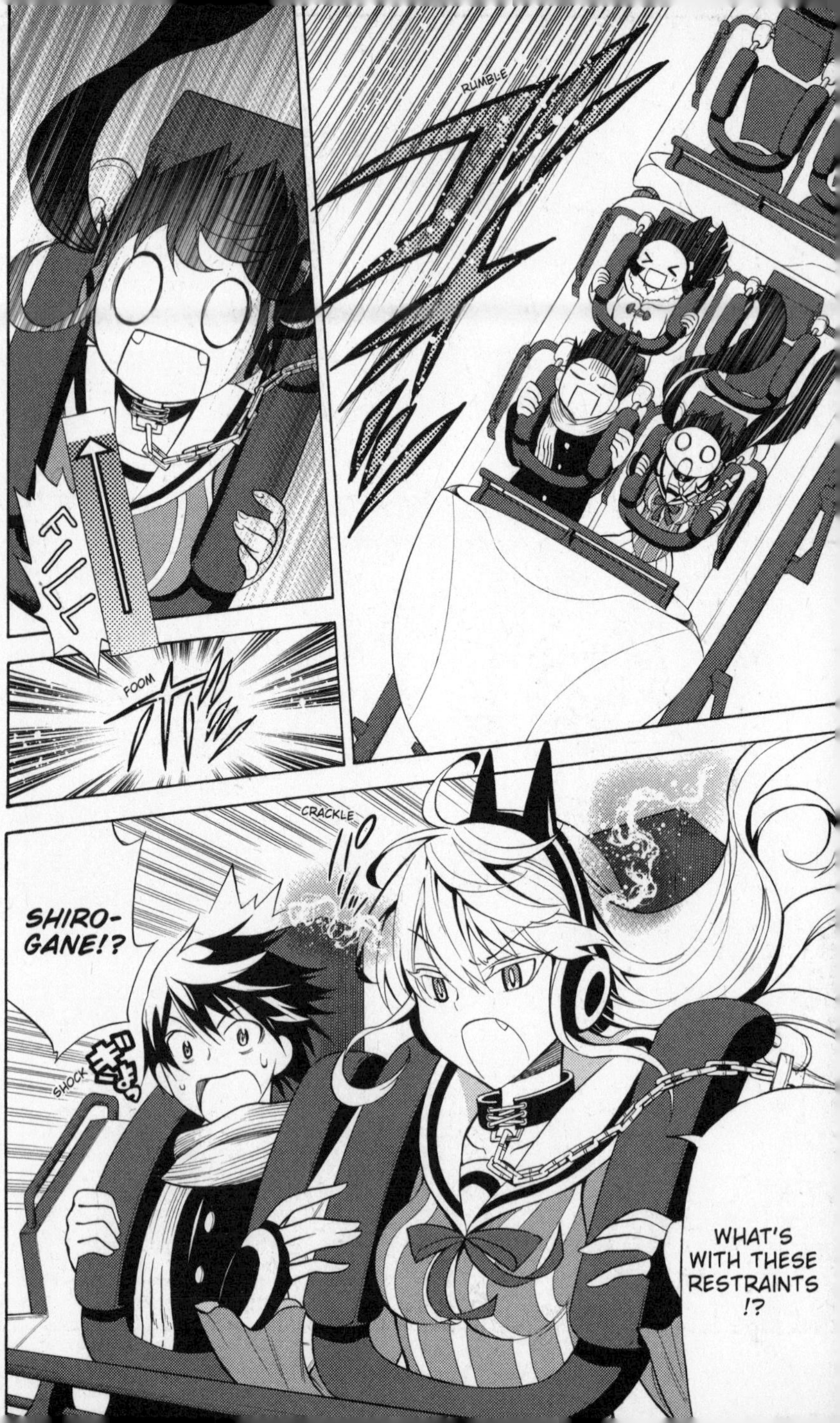
RUMBLE
FILL
FOOM
CRACKLE
WHAT'S WITH THESE RESTRAINTS !?
SHIRO-GANE!?
SHOCK

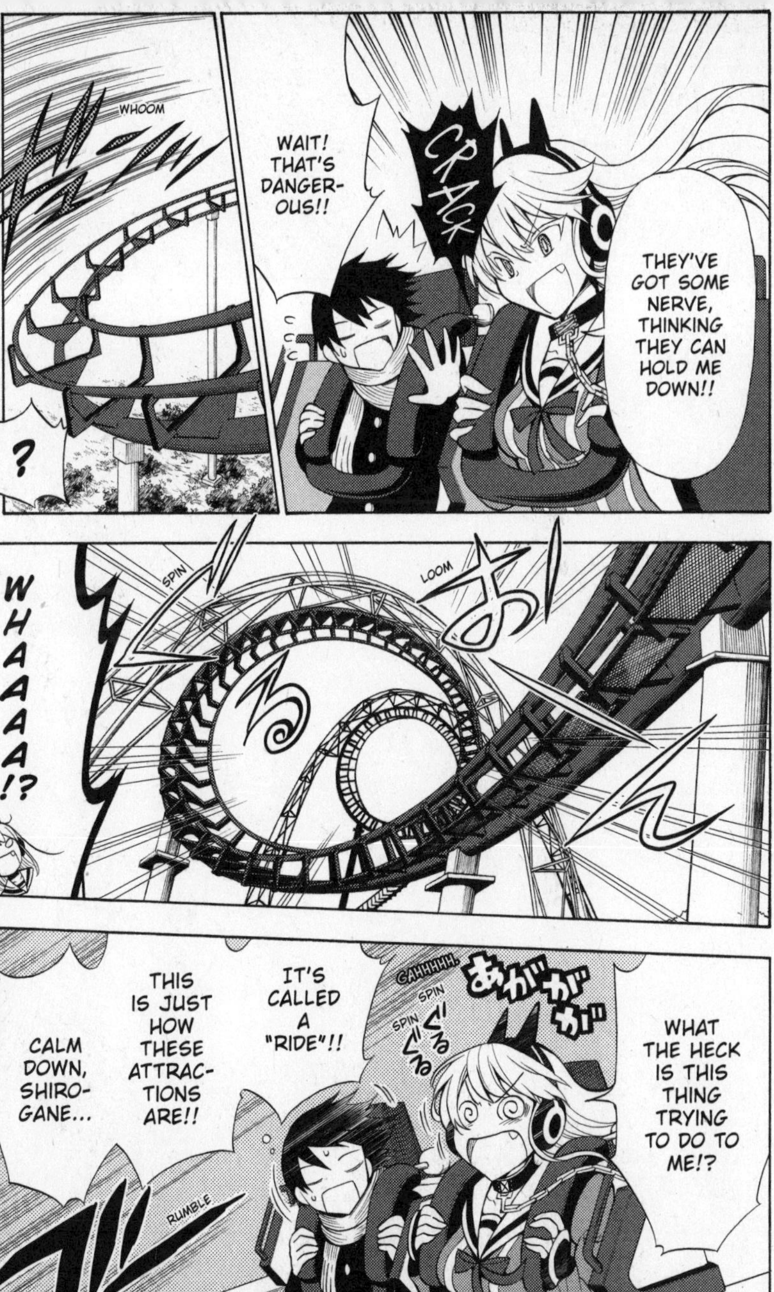
CRACK
THEY'VE GOT SOME NERVE, THINKING THEY CAN HOLD ME DOWN!!
WAIT! THAT'S DANGER-OUS!!
WHOOM
?
LOOM
SPIN
WHAAAAAA!?
WHAT THE HECK IS THIS THING TRYING TO DO TO ME!?
GAHHHHH
SPIN
SPIN
IT'S CALLED A "RIDE"!!
THIS IS JUST HOW THESE ATTRAC-TIONS ARE!!
CALM DOWN, SHIRO-GANE...
RUMBLE

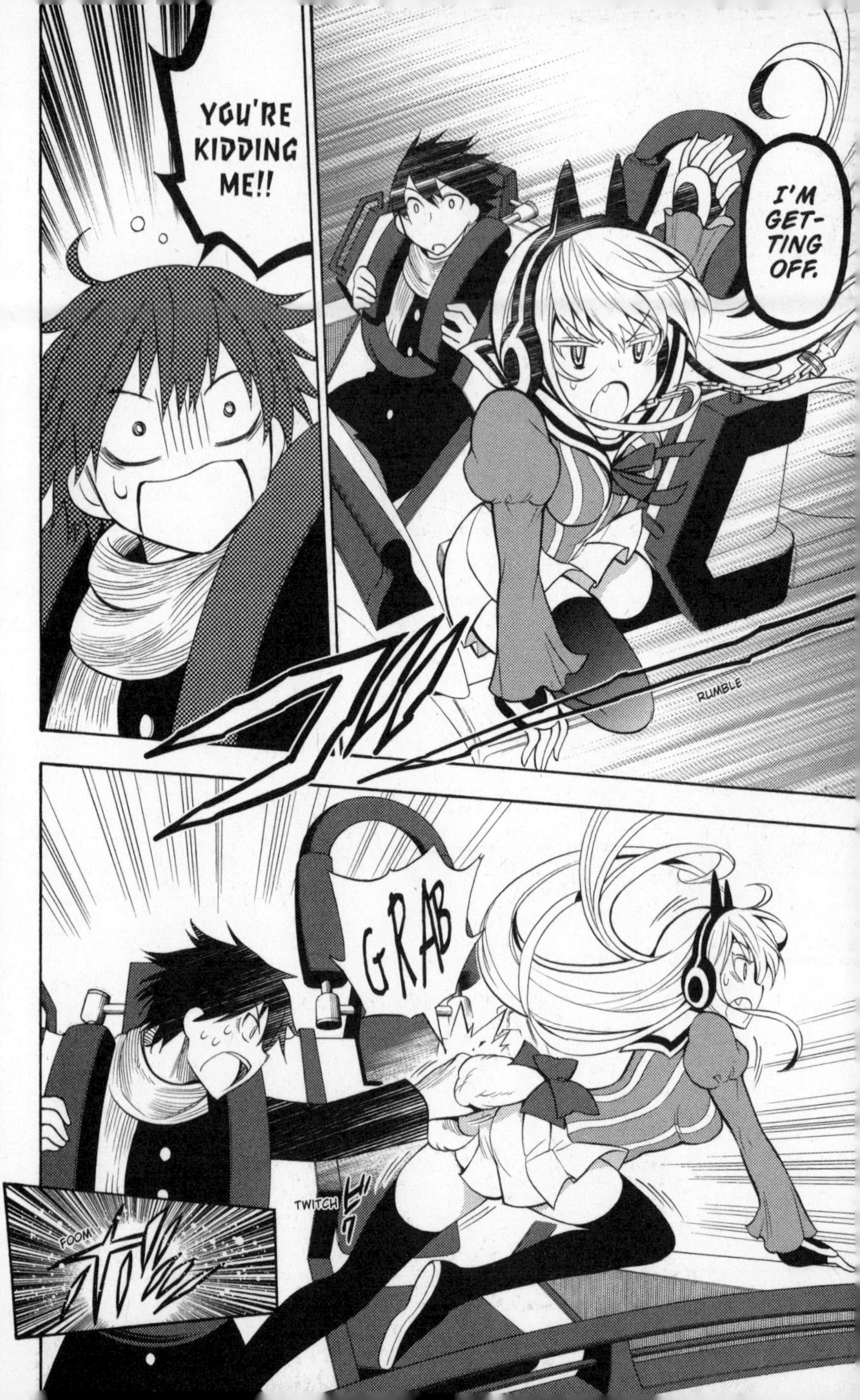
I'M GET-TING OFF.
RUMBLE
YOU'RE KIDDING ME!!
GRAB
TWITCH
FOOM

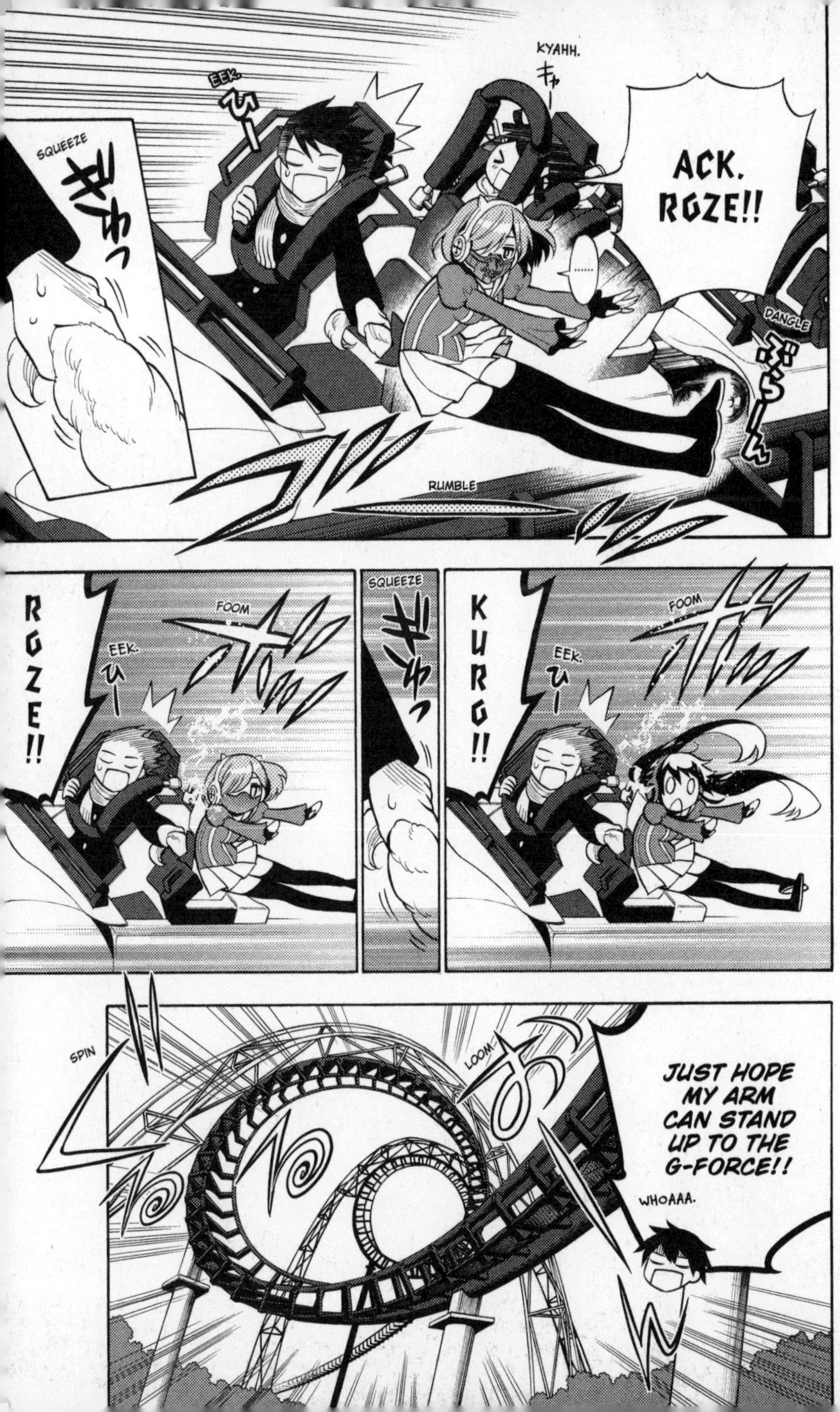
KYAHH.
キャー
ACK. ROZE!!
EEK.
ひー
SQUEEZE
ぎゅっ
......
DANGLE
ぶらーん
RUMBLE
KURO!!
FOOM
EEK.
ひー
SQUEEZE
ぎゅっ
ROZE!!
FOOM
EEK.
ひー
JUST HOPE MY ARM CAN STAND UP TO THE G-FORCE!!
LOOM
WHOAAA.
SPIN

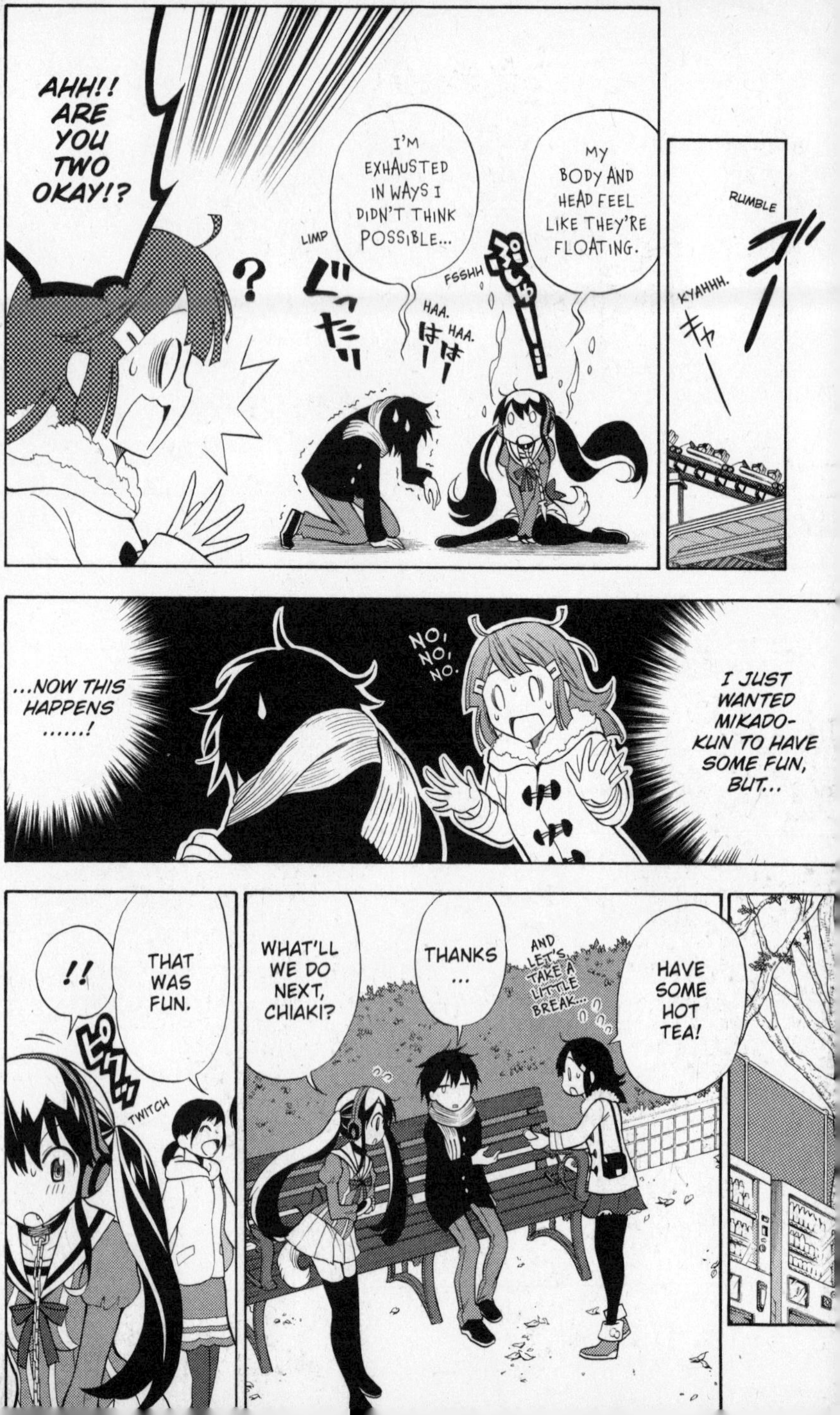
RUMBLE
KYAHHH.
MY BODY AND HEAD FEEL LIKE THEY'RE FLOATING.
FSSHH
I'M EXHAUSTED IN WAYS I DIDN'T THINK POSSIBLE...
HAA. HAA.
LIMP
AHH!! ARE YOU TWO OKAY!?
?
I JUST WANTED MIKADO-KUN TO HAVE SOME FUN, BUT...
NO, NO, NO.
...NOW THIS HAPPENS ......!
HAVE SOME HOT TEA!
AND LET'S TAKE A LITTLE BREAK...
THANKS ...
WHAT'LL WE DO NEXT, CHIAKI?
THAT WAS FUN.
!!
TWITCH

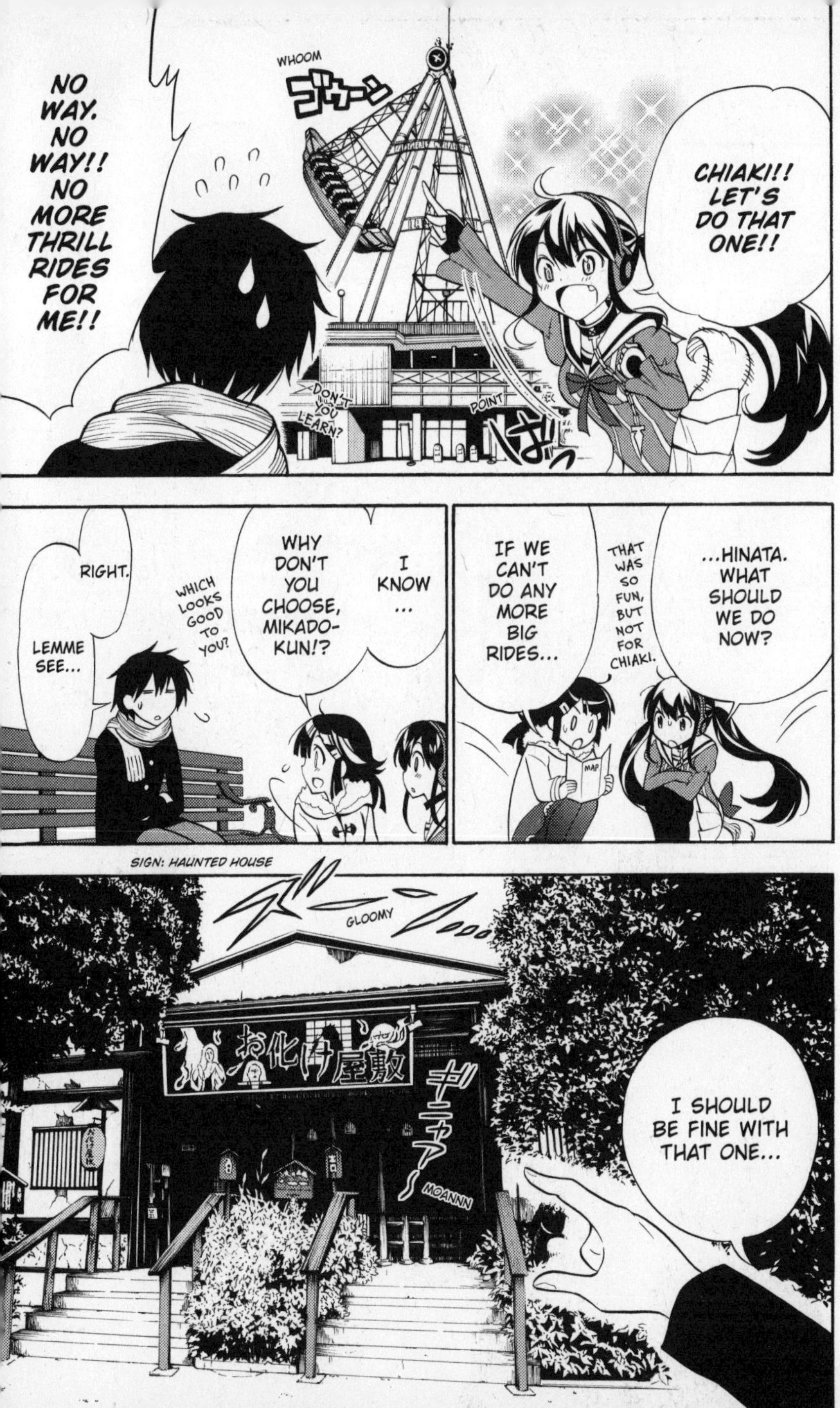
WHOOM
CHIAKI!! LET'S DO THAT ONE!!
POINT
DON'T YOU LEARN?
NO WAY. NO WAY!! NO MORE THRILL RIDES FOR ME!!
...HINATA. WHAT SHOULD WE DO NOW?
THAT WAS SO FUN, BUT NOT FOR CHIAKI.
IF WE CAN'T DO ANY MORE BIG RIDES...
I KNOW ...
WHY DON'T YOU CHOOSE, MIKADO-KUN!?
WHICH LOOKS GOOD TO YOU?
RIGHT.
LEMME SEE...
SIGN: HAUNTED HOUSE
GLOOMY
I SHOULD BE FINE WITH THAT ONE...
MOANNN

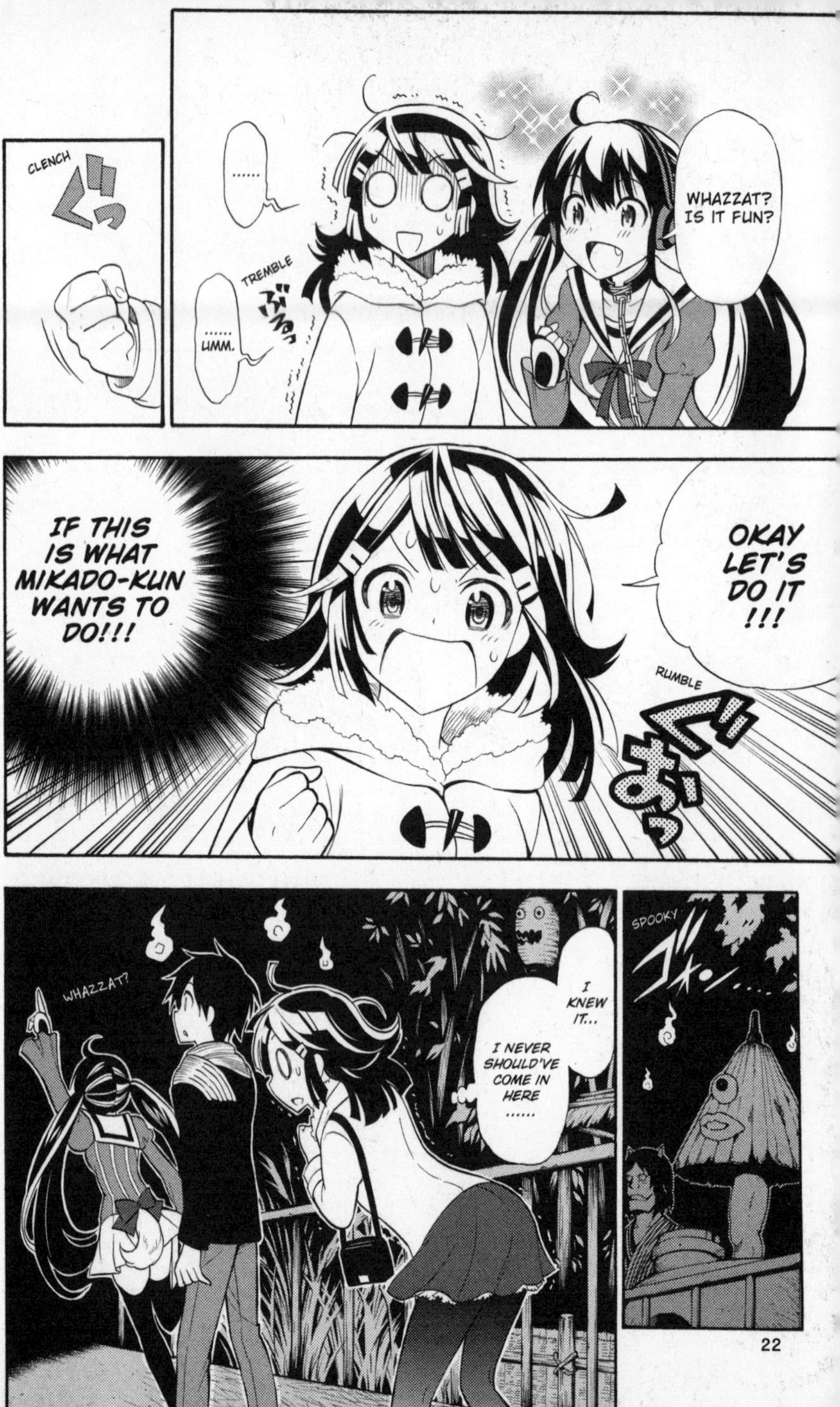
WHAZZAT? IS IT FUN?
......
TREMBLE
...... UMM.
CLENCH
OKAY LET'S DO IT !!!
IF THIS IS WHAT MIKADO-KUN WANTS TO DO!!!
RUMBLE
SPOOKY
I KNEW IT...
I NEVER SHOULD'VE COME IN HERE ......
WHAZZAT?

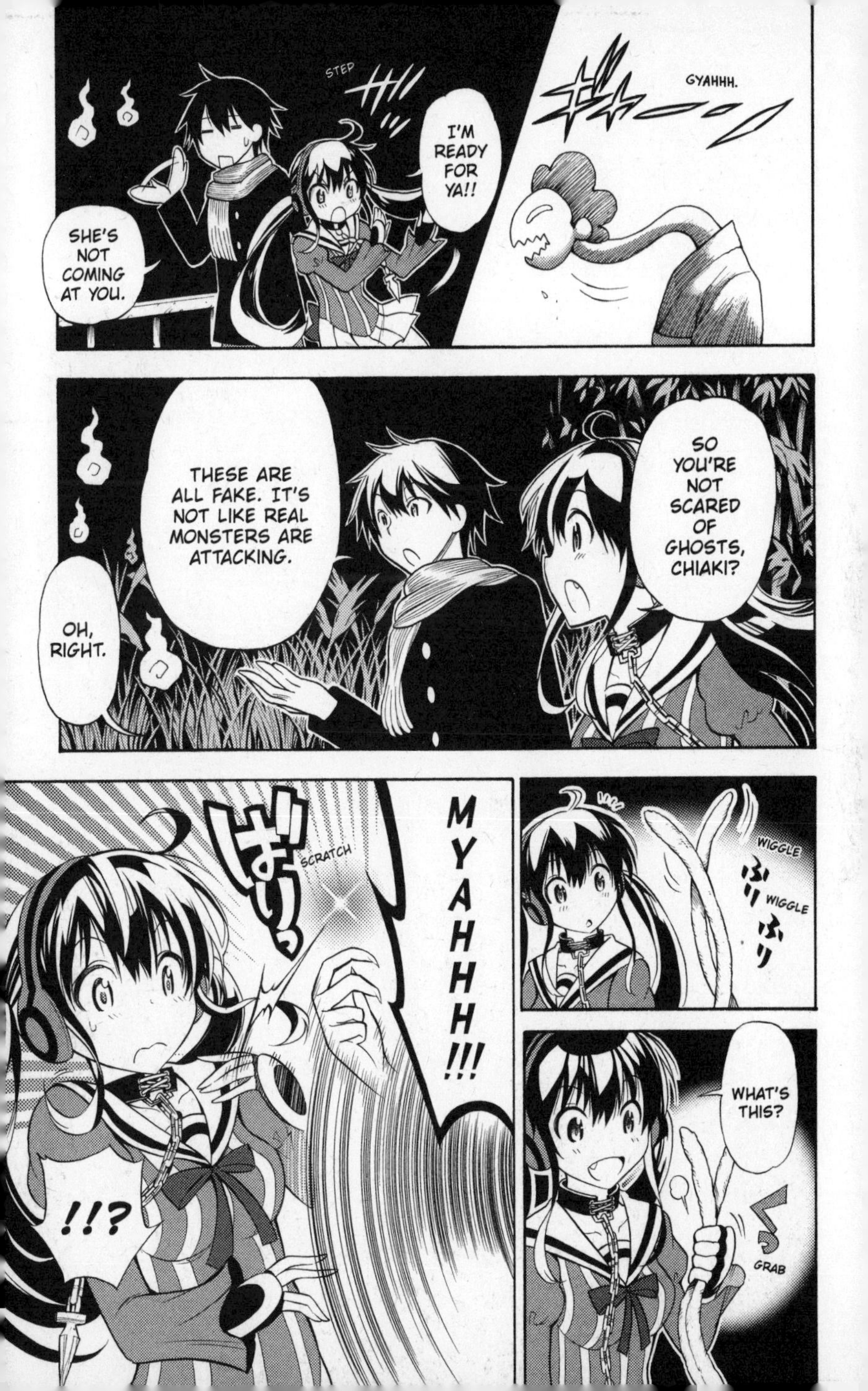
GYAHHH.
STEP
I'M READY FOR YA!!
SHE'S NOT COMING AT YOU.
SO YOU'RE NOT SCARED OF GHOSTS, CHIAKI?
THESE ARE ALL FAKE. IT'S NOT LIKE REAL MONSTERS ARE ATTACKING.
OH, RIGHT.
WIGGLE
WIGGLE
WHAT'S THIS?
GRAB
SCRATCH
MYAHHHH!!!
!!?

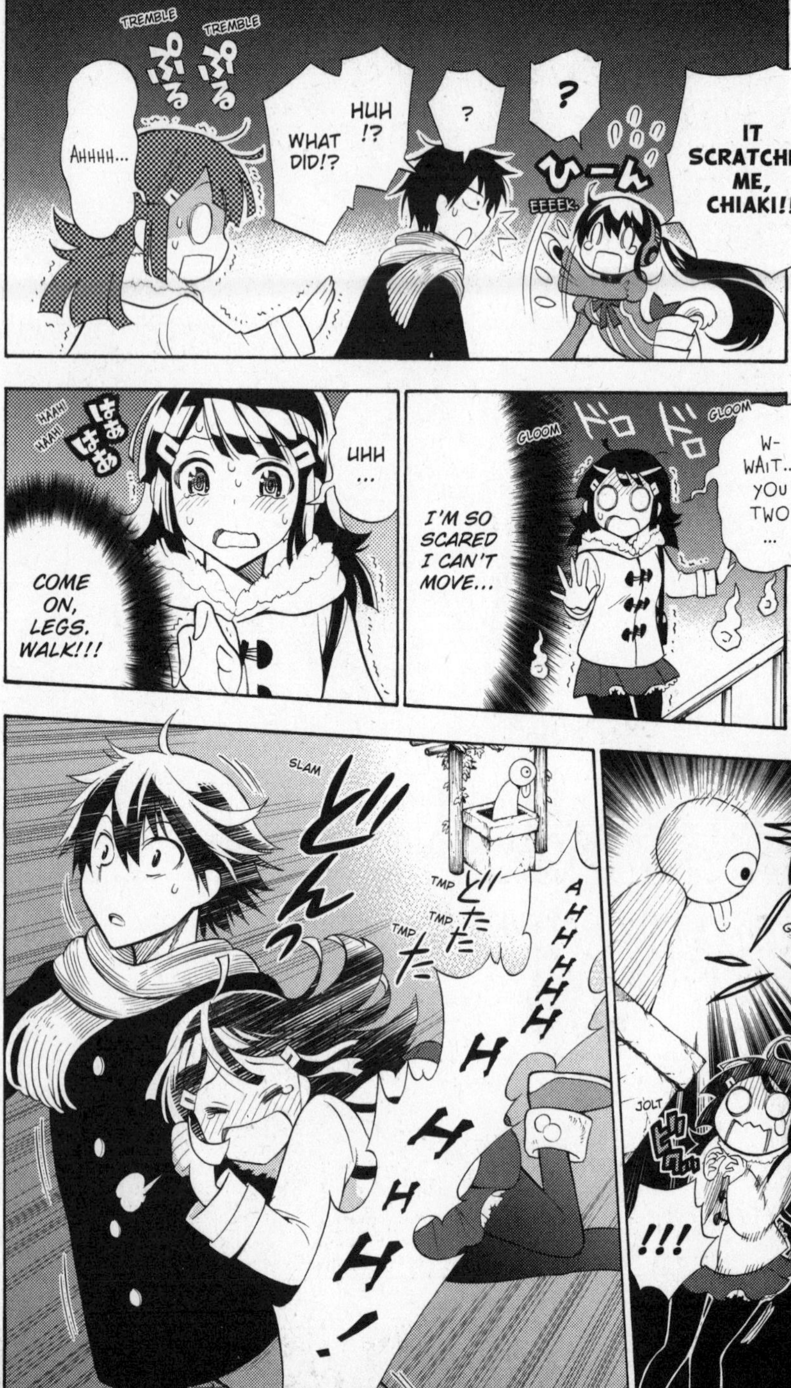
IT SCRATCHED ME, CHIAKI!!
ひーん
EEEEK.
?
?
HUH!?
WHAT DID!?
ぷるぷる
TREMBLE TREMBLE
AHHHH...
ドロドロ
GLOOM GLOOM
W-WAIT... YOU TWO...
I'M SO SCARED I CAN'T MOVE...
UHH...
はぁはぁ
HAAH! HAAH!
COME ON, LEGS. WALK!!!
GYAHHH.
JOLT
!!!
AHHHHHHHHHHHH!
どたたた
TMP TMP TMP
どんっ
SLAM

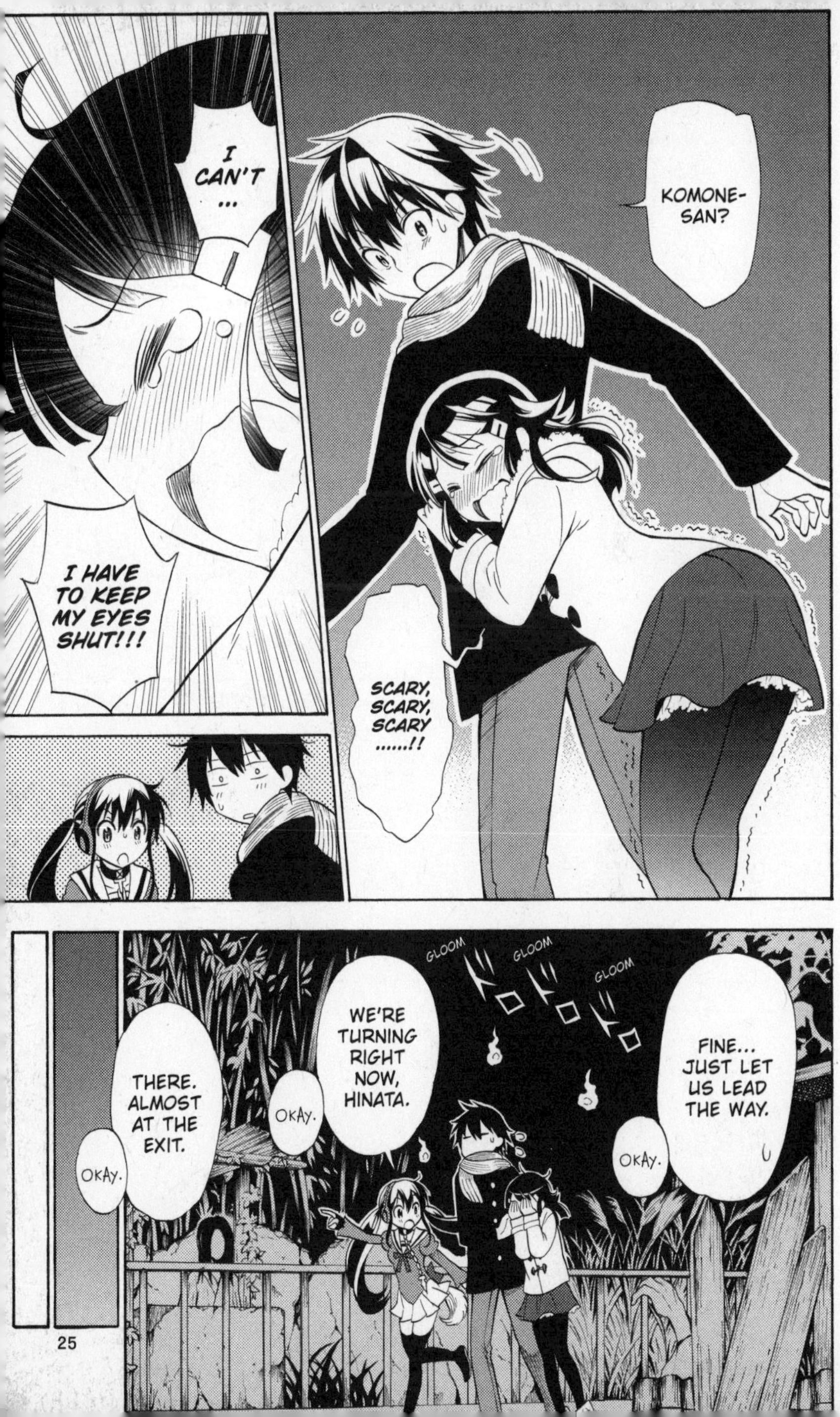
KOMONE-SAN?
SCARY, SCARY, SCARY ......!!
I CAN'T ...
I HAVE TO KEEP MY EYES SHUT!!!
FINE... JUST LET US LEAD THE WAY.
OKAY.
GLOOM
GLOOM
GLOOM
WE'RE TURNING RIGHT NOW, HINATA.
OKAY.
THERE. ALMOST AT THE EXIT.
OKAY.

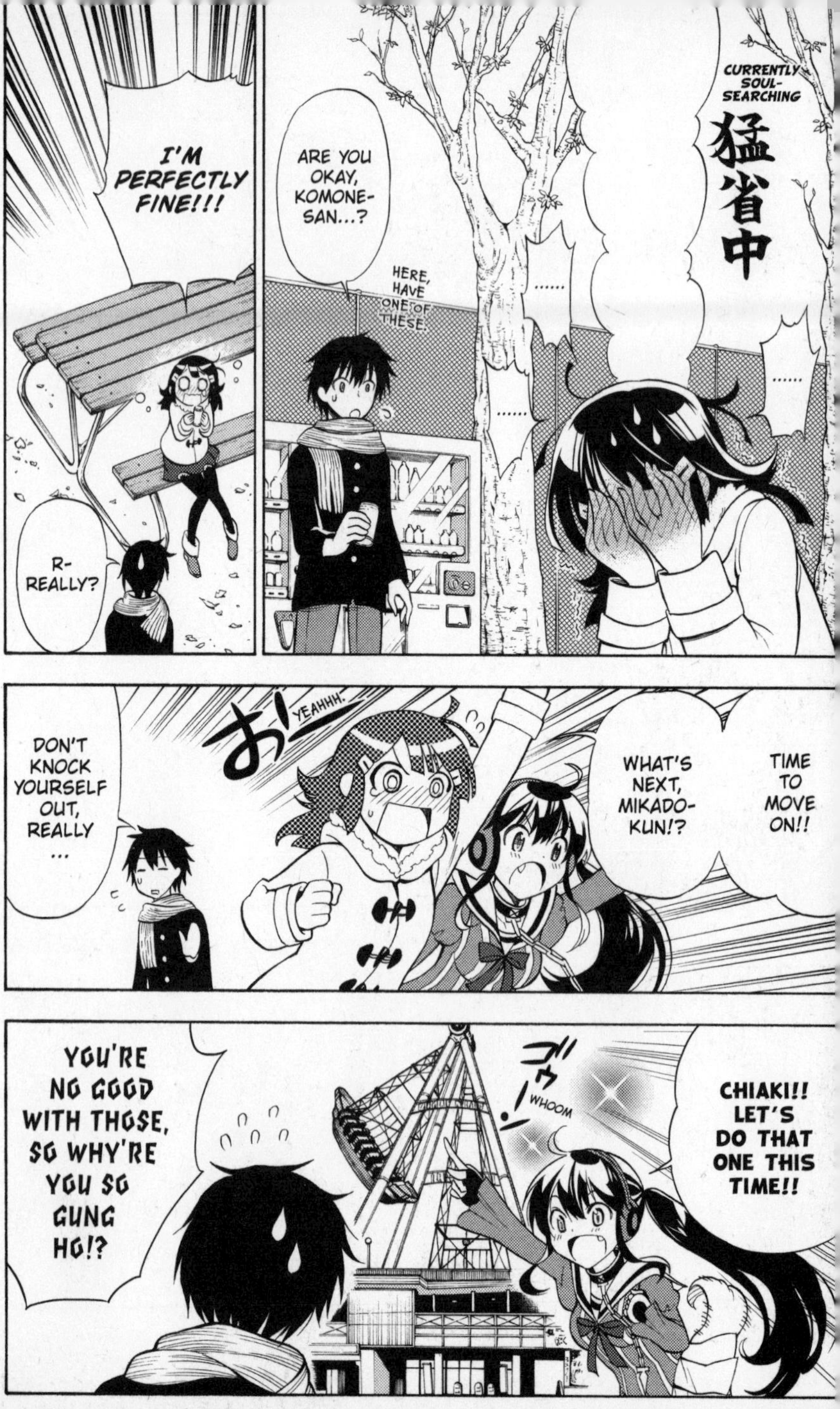
CURRENTLY SOUL-SEARCHING
猛省中
......
......
......
HERE, HAVE ONE OF THESE.
ARE YOU OKAY, KOMONE-SAN...?
I'M PERFECTLY FINE!!!
R-REALLY?
TIME TO MOVE ON!!
WHAT'S NEXT, MIKADO-KUN!?
お！ YEAHHH.
DON'T KNOCK YOURSELF OUT, REALLY ...
CHIAKI!! LET'S DO THAT ONE THIS TIME!!
ゴウン WHOOM
YOU'RE NO GOOD WITH THOSE, SO WHY'RE YOU SO GUNG HO!?

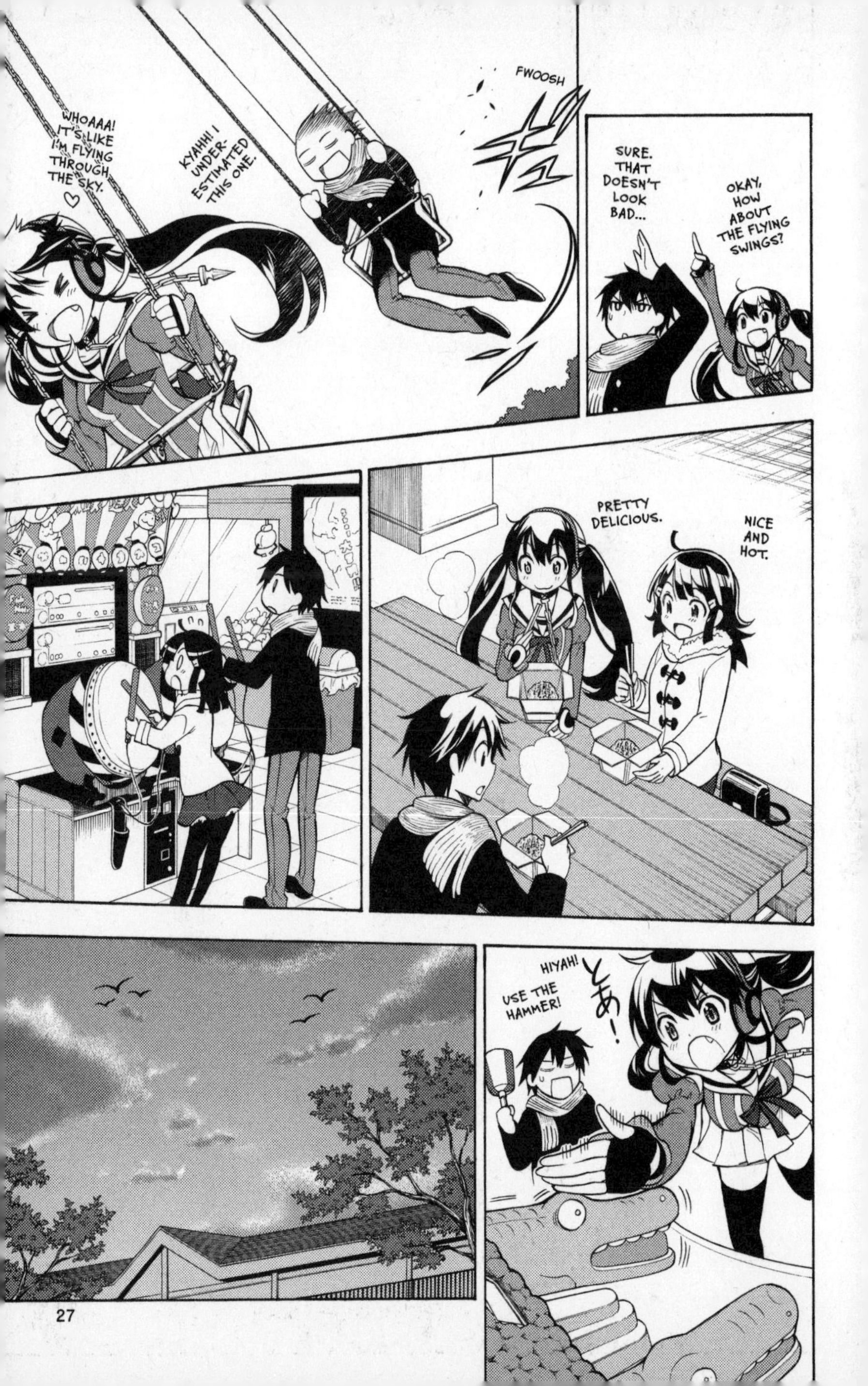
OKAY, HOW ABOUT THE FLYING SWINGS?
SURE. THAT DOESN'T LOOK BAD...
FWOOSH
KYAHH! I UNDER-ESTIMATED THIS ONE.
WHOAAA! IT'S LIKE I'M FLYING THROUGH THE SKY. ♡
NICE AND HOT.
PRETTY DELICIOUS.
とあ!
HIYAH!
USE THE HAMMER!

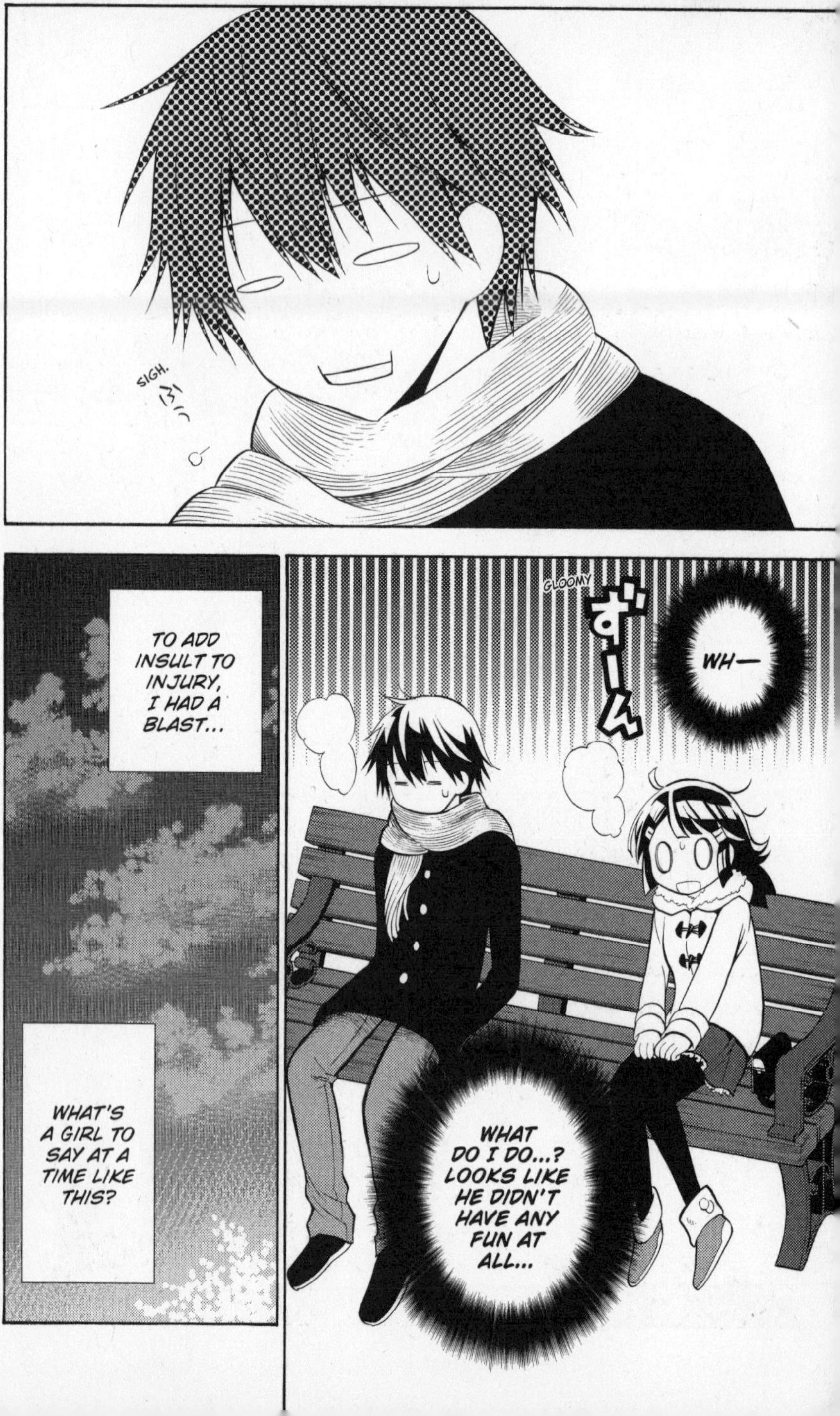
SIGH.
ふぅ
GLOOMY
ずーん
WH—
WHAT DO I DO...? LOOKS LIKE HE DIDN'T HAVE ANY FUN AT ALL...
TO ADD INSULT TO INJURY, I HAD A BLAST...
WHAT'S A GIRL TO SAY AT A TIME LIKE THIS?

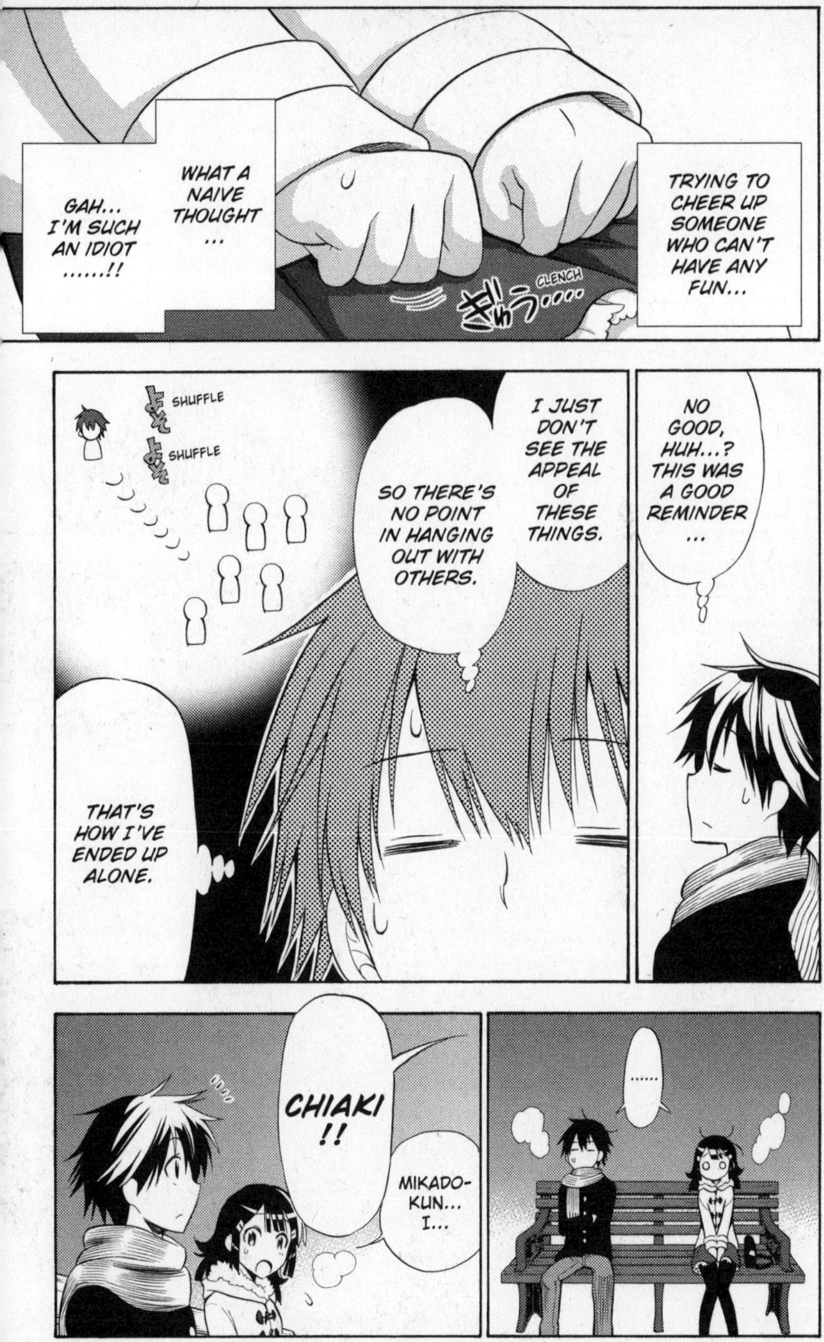

TRYING TO CHEER UP SOMEONE WHO CAN'T HAVE ANY FUN...
WHAT A NAIVE THOUGHT...
GAH... I'M SUCH AN IDIOT......!!
CLENCH
NO GOOD, HUH...? THIS WAS A GOOD REMINDER...
I JUST DON'T SEE THE APPEAL OF THESE THINGS.
SO THERE'S NO POINT IN HANGING OUT WITH OTHERS.
SHUFFLE
SHUFFLE
THAT'S HOW I'VE ENDED UP ALONE.
......
CHIAKI!!
MIKADO-KUN... I...

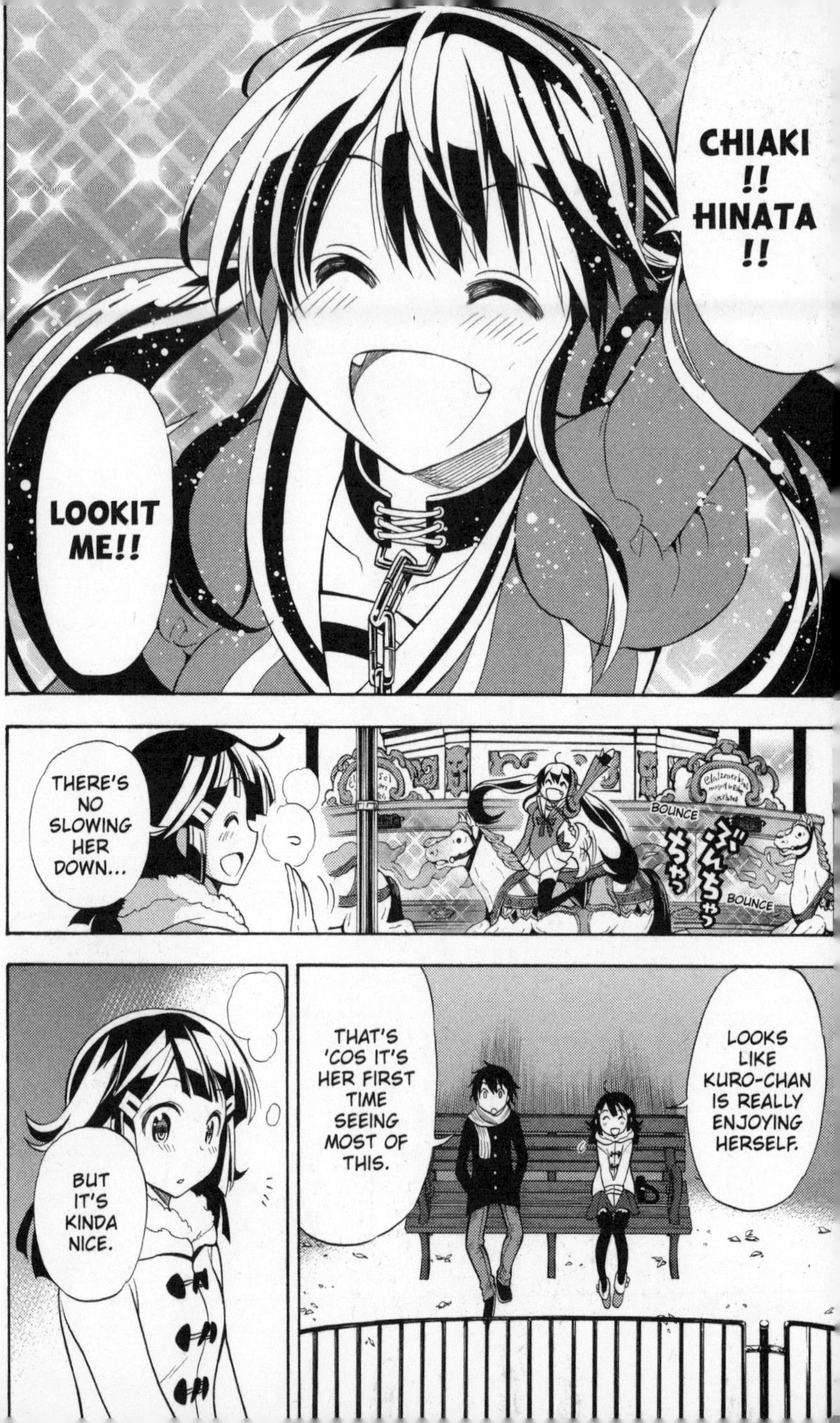
CHIAKI!! HINATA!!
LOOKIT ME!!
ずんちゃっ
ちゃっ
BOUNCE
BOUNCE
THERE'S NO SLOWING HER DOWN...
LOOKS LIKE KURO-CHAN IS REALLY ENJOYING HERSELF.
THAT'S 'COS IT'S HER FIRST TIME SEEING MOST OF THIS.
BUT IT'S KINDA NICE.

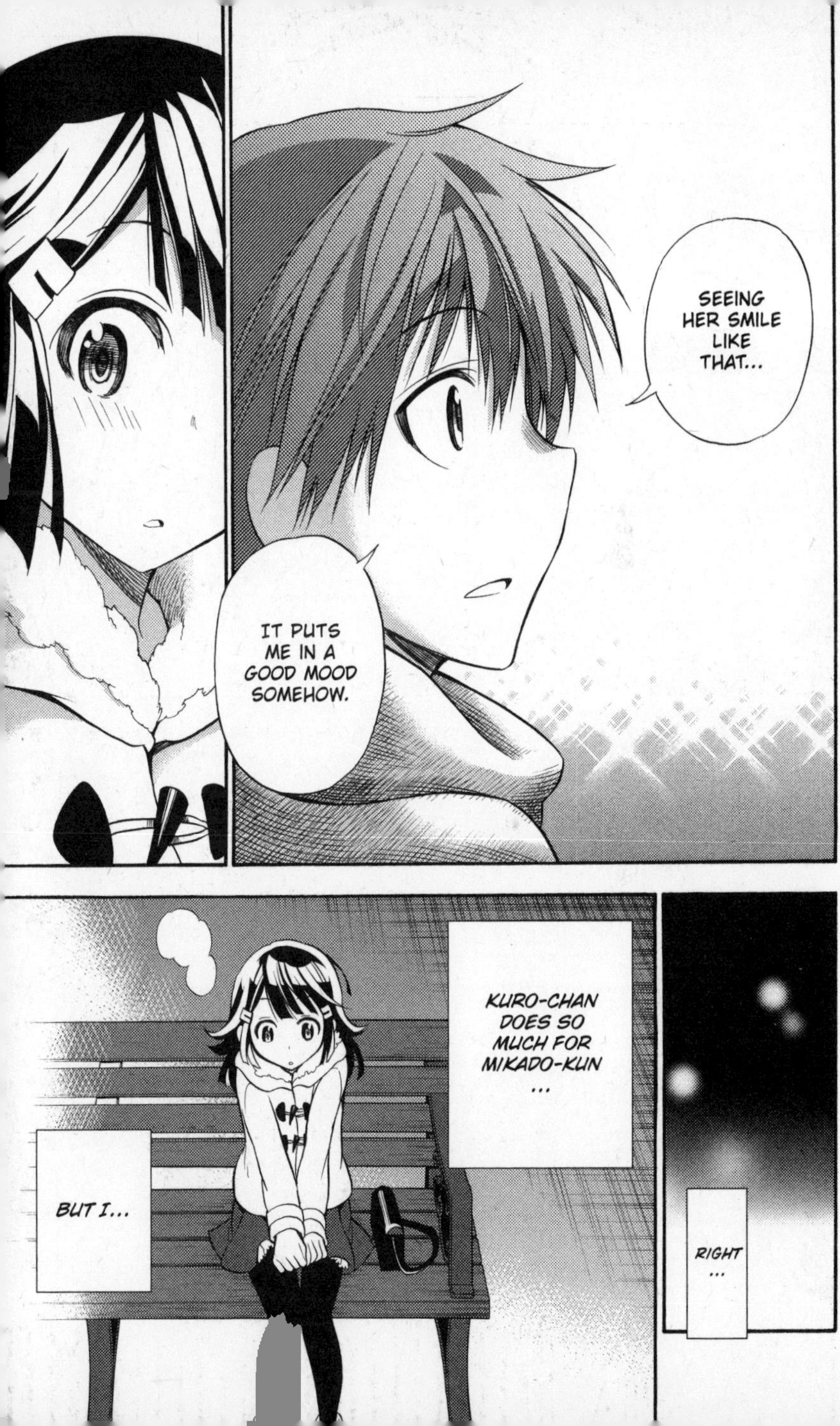
SEEING HER SMILE LIKE THAT...
IT PUTS ME IN A GOOD MOOD SOMEHOW.
RIGHT...
KURO-CHAN DOES SO MUCH FOR MIKADO-KUN...
BUT I...

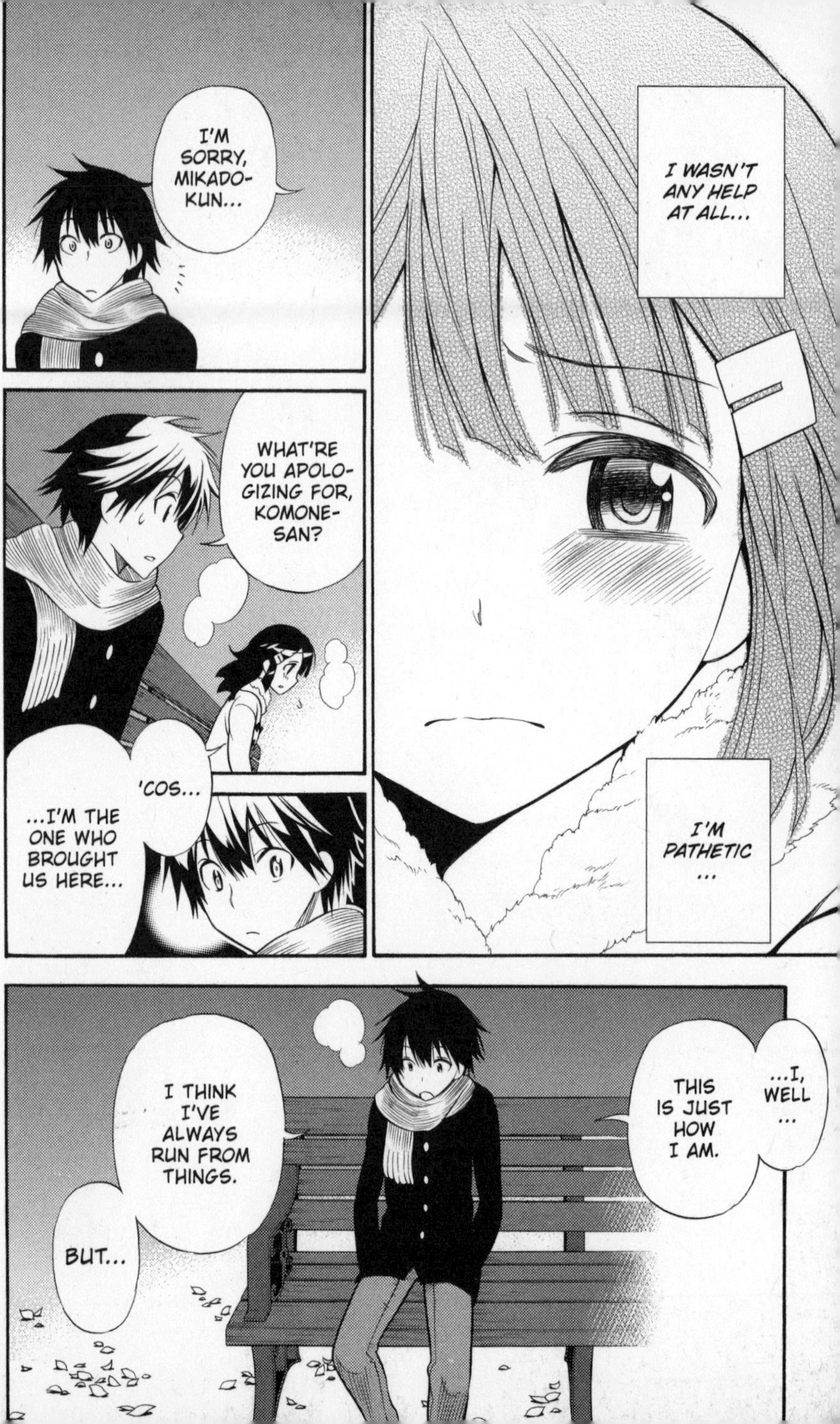
I WASN'T ANY HELP AT ALL...
I'M PATHETIC ...
I'M SORRY, MIKADO-KUN...
WHAT'RE YOU APOLOGIZING FOR, KOMONE-SAN?
'COS...
...I'M THE ONE WHO BROUGHT US HERE...
...I, WELL ...
THIS IS JUST HOW I AM.
I THINK I'VE ALWAYS RUN FROM THINGS.
BUT...

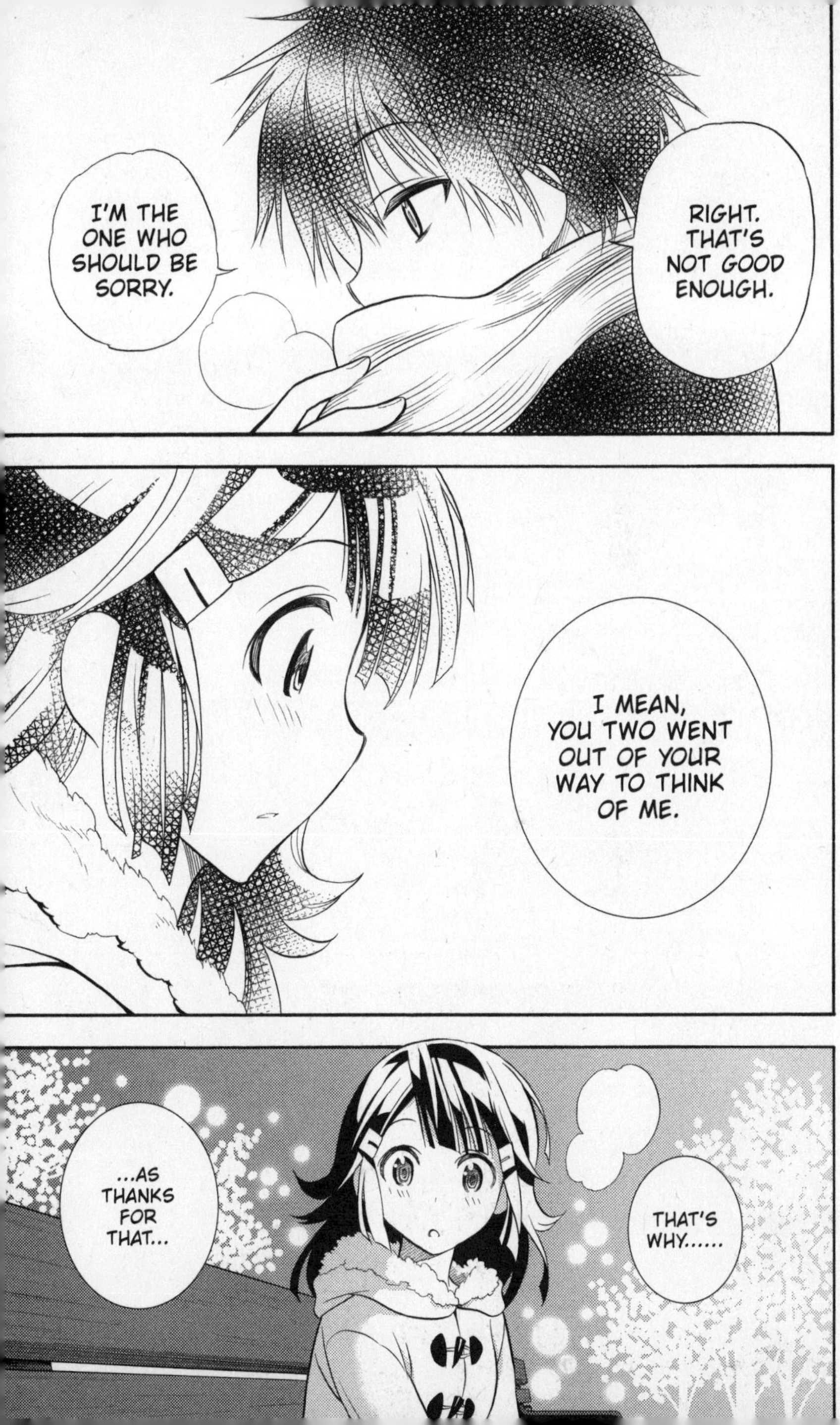
RIGHT. THAT'S NOT GOOD ENOUGH.
I'M THE ONE WHO SHOULD BE SORRY.
I MEAN, YOU TWO WENT OUT OF YOUR WAY TO THINK OF ME.
THAT'S WHY......
...AS THANKS FOR THAT...

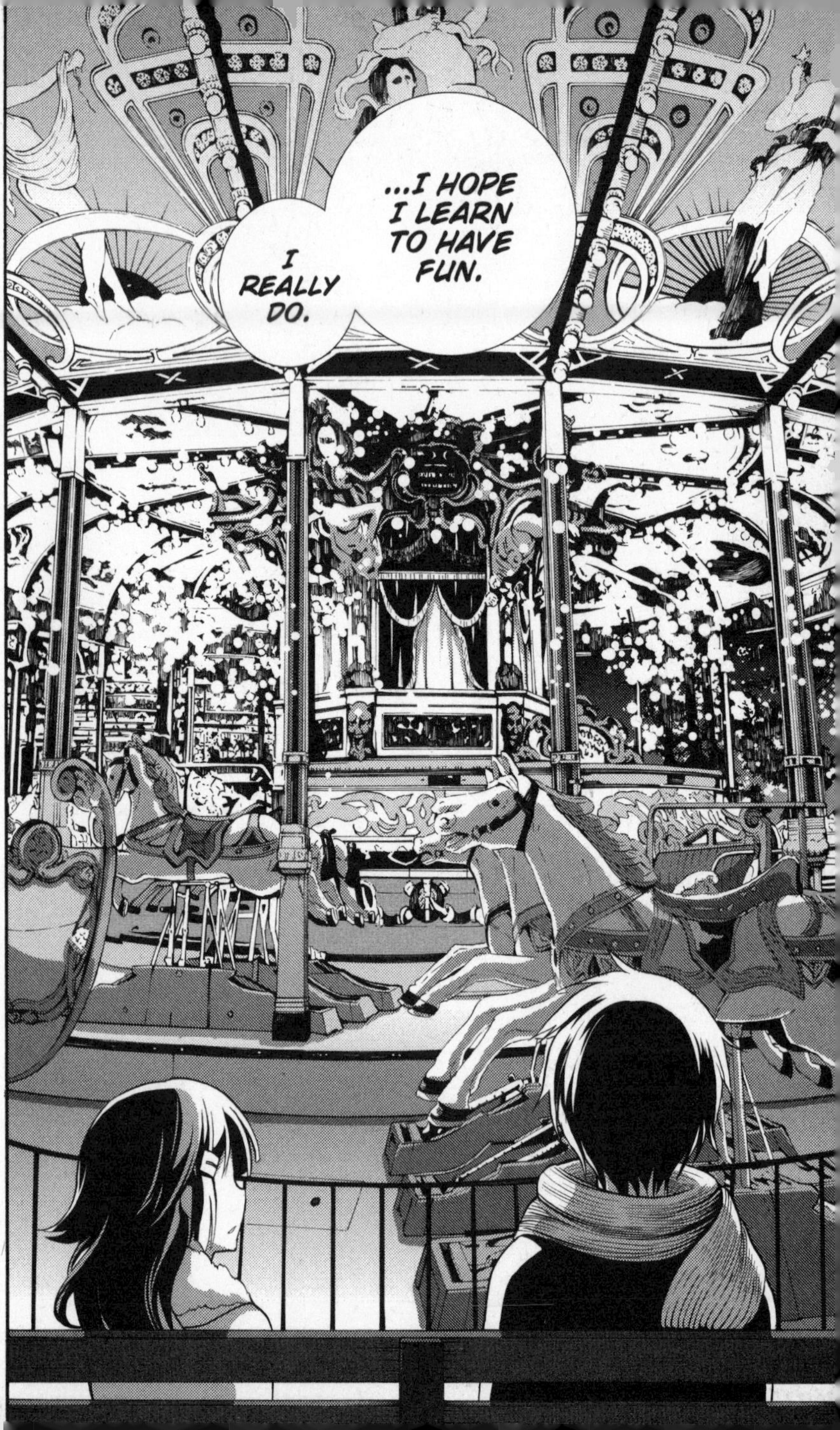
...I HOPE I LEARN TO HAVE FUN.
I REALLY DO.

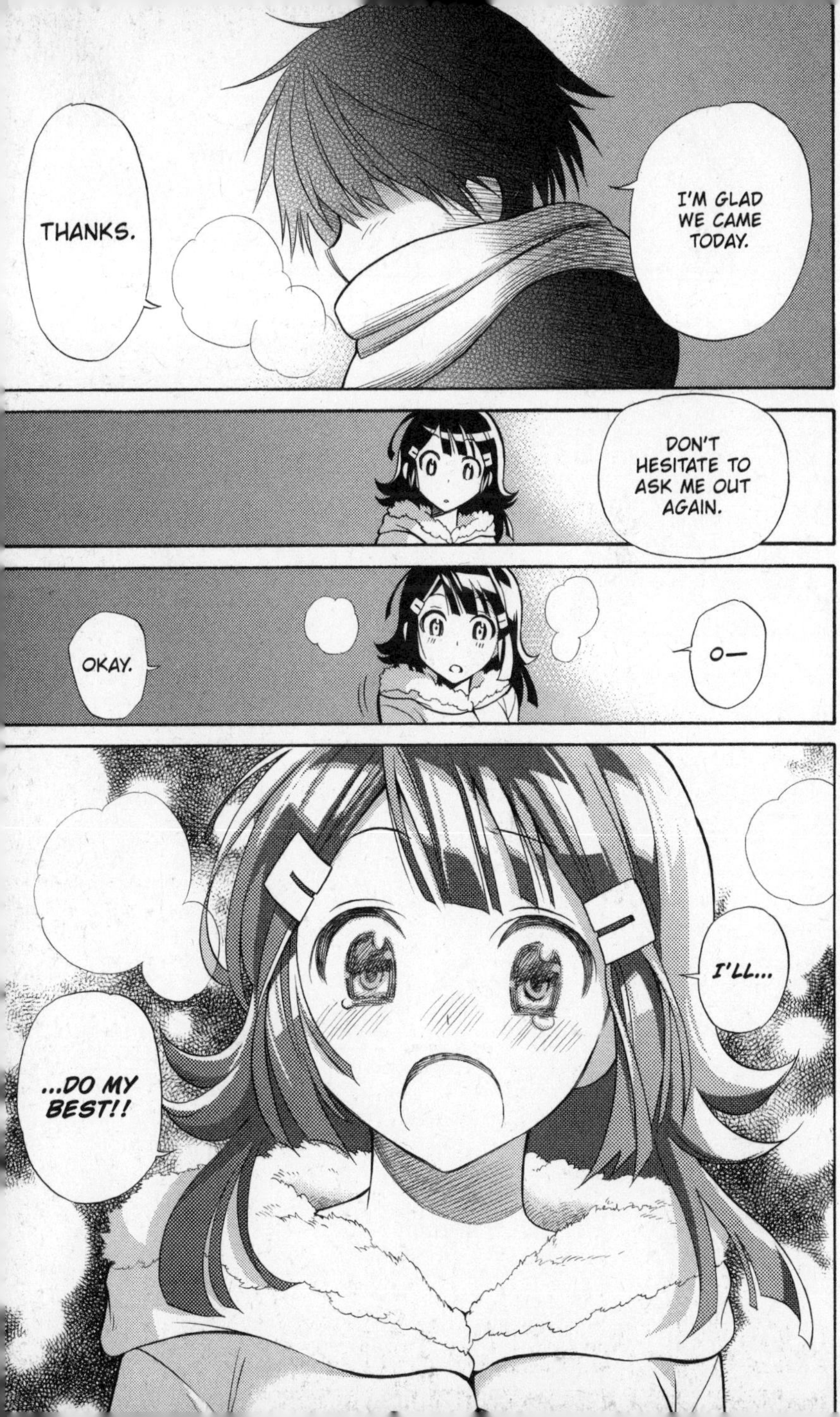
I'M GLAD WE CAME TODAY.
THANKS.
DON'T HESITATE TO ASK ME OUT AGAIN.
O—
OKAY.
I'LL...
...DO MY BEST!!

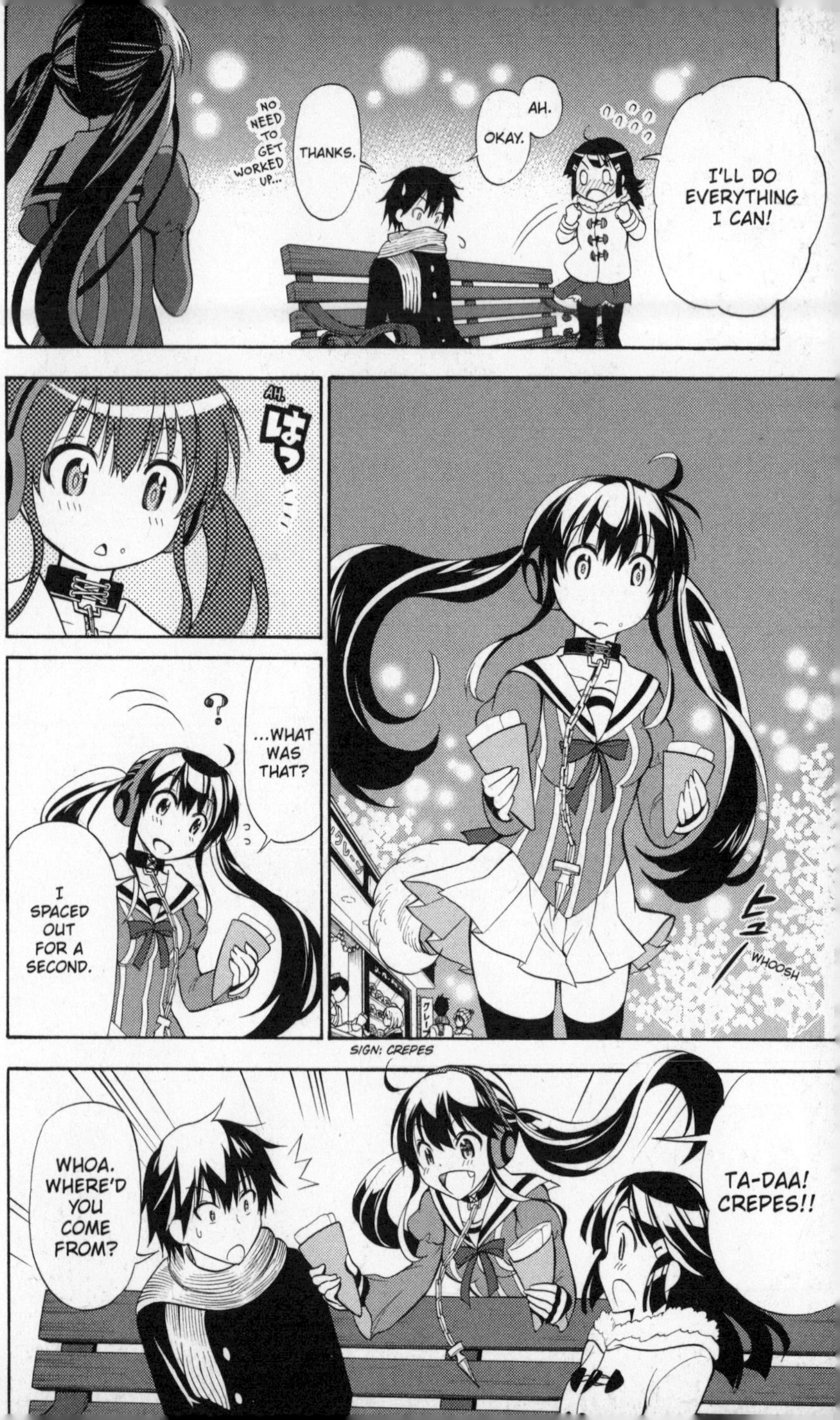
I'LL DO EVERYTHING I CAN!
AH.
OKAY.
THANKS.
NO NEED TO GET WORKED UP...
ヒュ
WHOOSH
SIGN: CREPES
はっ
AH.
...WHAT WAS THAT?
I SPACED OUT FOR A SECOND.
TA-DAA! CREPES!!
WHOA. WHERE'D YOU COME FROM?

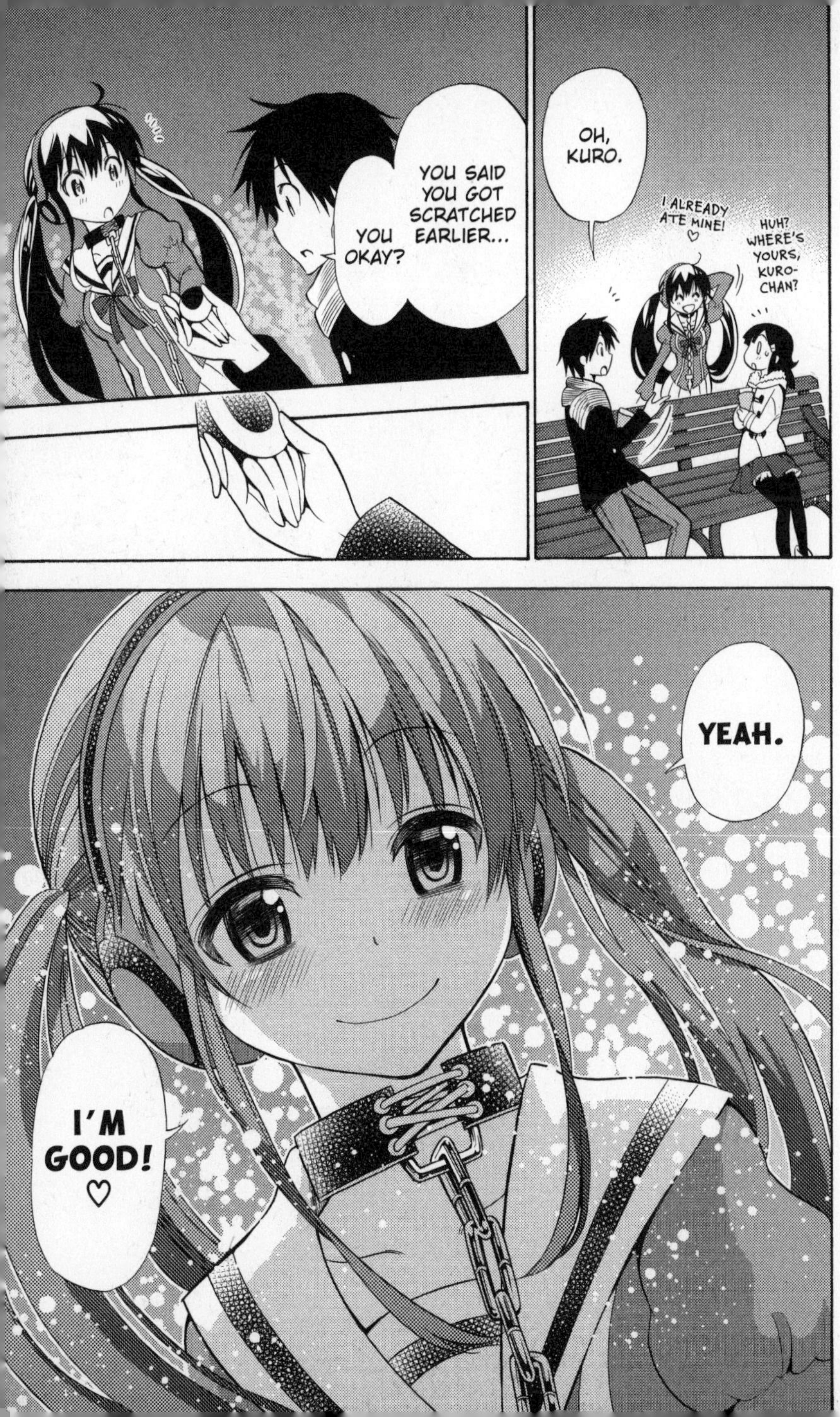
HUH? WHERE'S YOURS, KURO-CHAN?
I ALREADY ATE MINE! ♡
OH, KURO.
YOU SAID YOU GOT SCRATCHED EARLIER...
YOU OKAY?
YEAH.
I'M GOOD! ♡

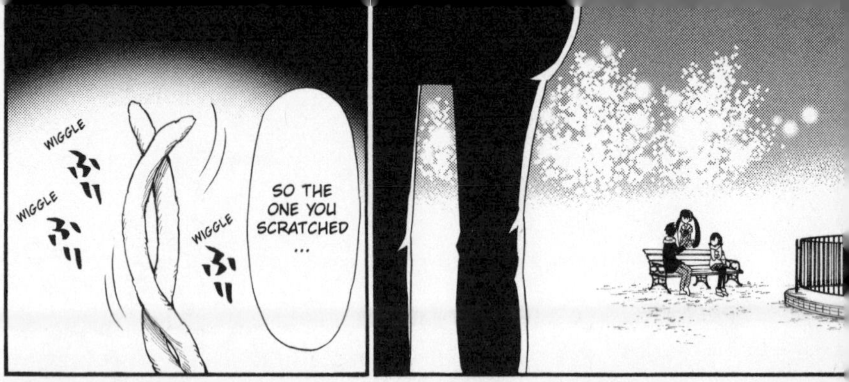
SO THE ONE YOU SCRATCHED ...
WIGGLE
ふり
WIGGLE
ふり
WIGGLE
ふり

SIGN: CREPES

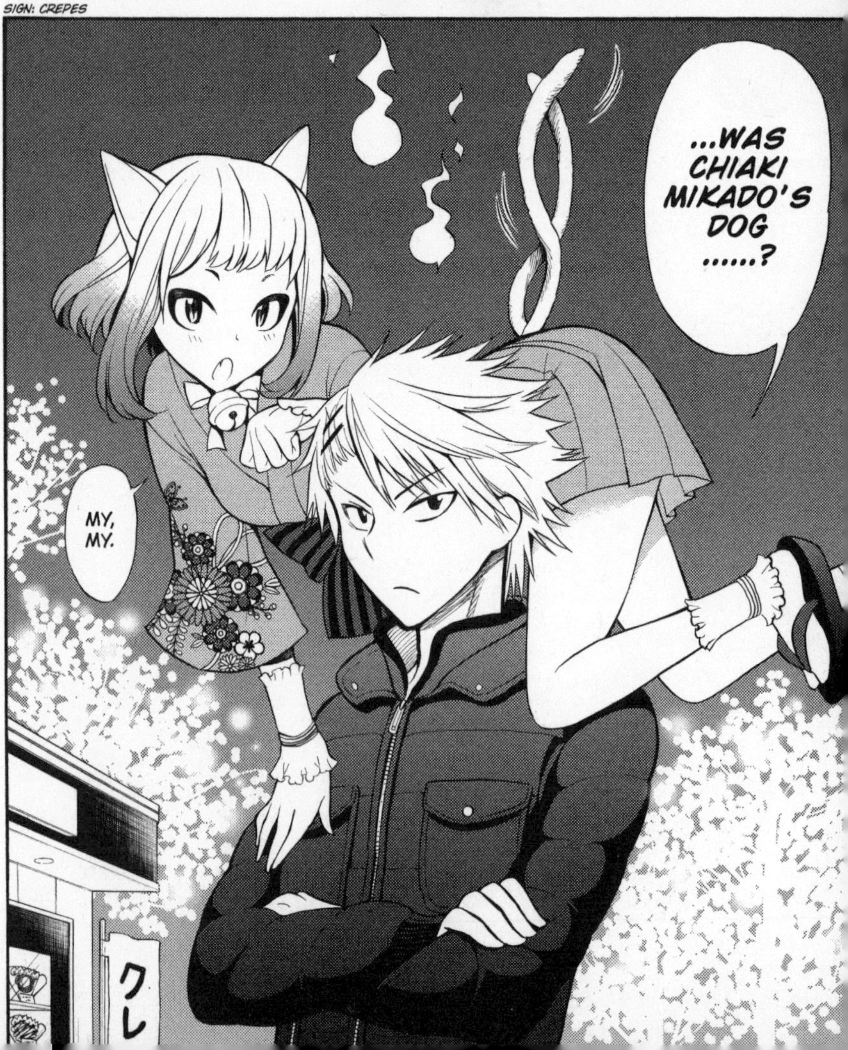
...WAS CHIAKI MIKADO'S DOG ......?
MY, MY.
クレ

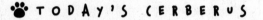

🐾 TODAY'S CERBERUS

WHAT FUN.

ROLLER COASTER.

TODAY'S CERBERUS

Q:
WHY GET SCARED WHEN YOU CAN EXORCISE REAL DEMONS?

W-WELL... THE GHOSTS IN A HAUNTED HOUSE... I CAN'T DETECT THEIR PRESENCE AT ALL. THEY JUST POP OUT OF NOWHERE. AT LEAST WITH REAL GHOSTS, I CAN FEEL THEM COMING.

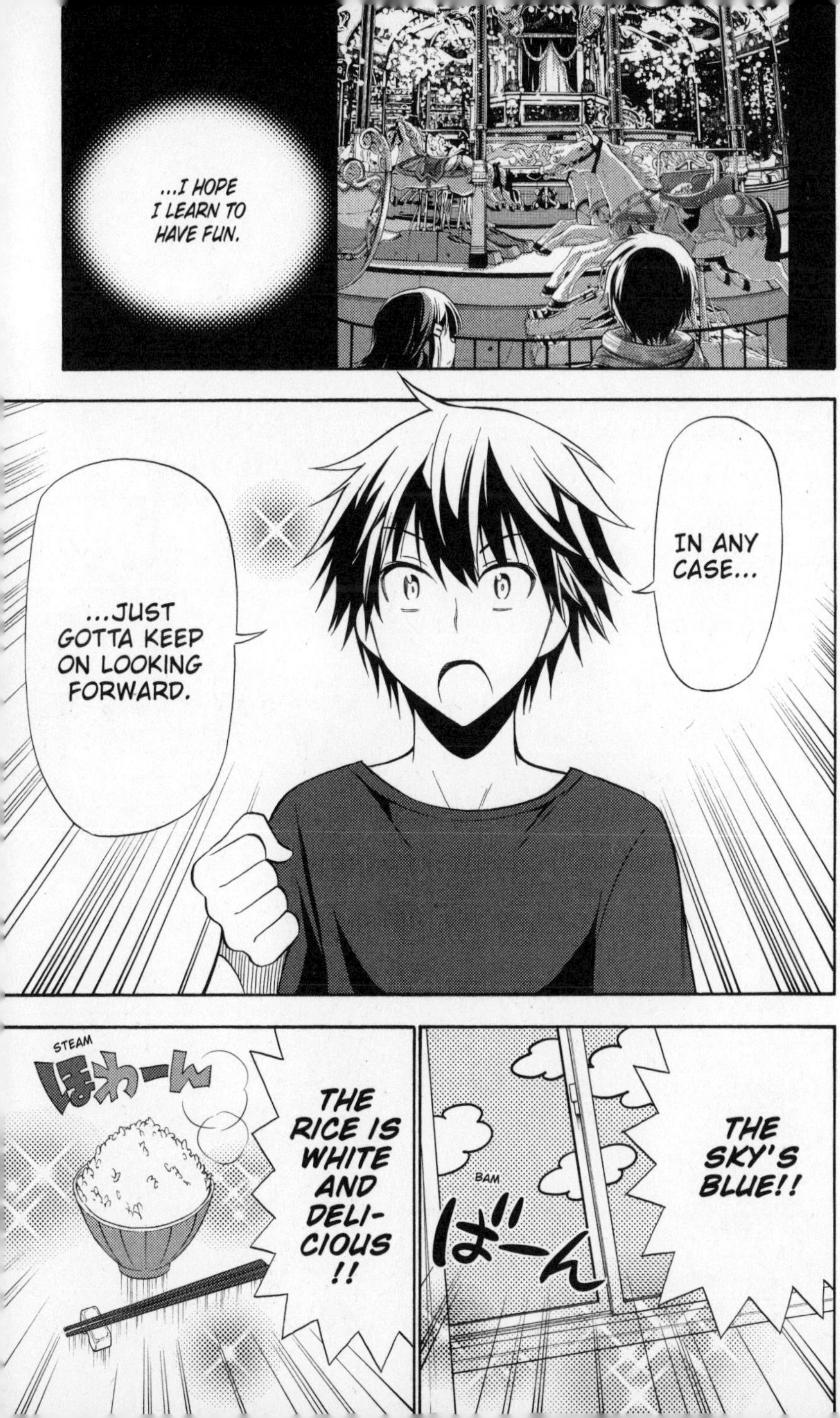
...I HOPE I LEARN TO HAVE FUN.
IN ANY CASE...
...JUST GOTTA KEEP ON LOOKING FORWARD.
THE SKY'S BLUE!!
BAM
ばーん
THE RICE IS WHITE AND DELICIOUS!!
STEAM
ほわーん

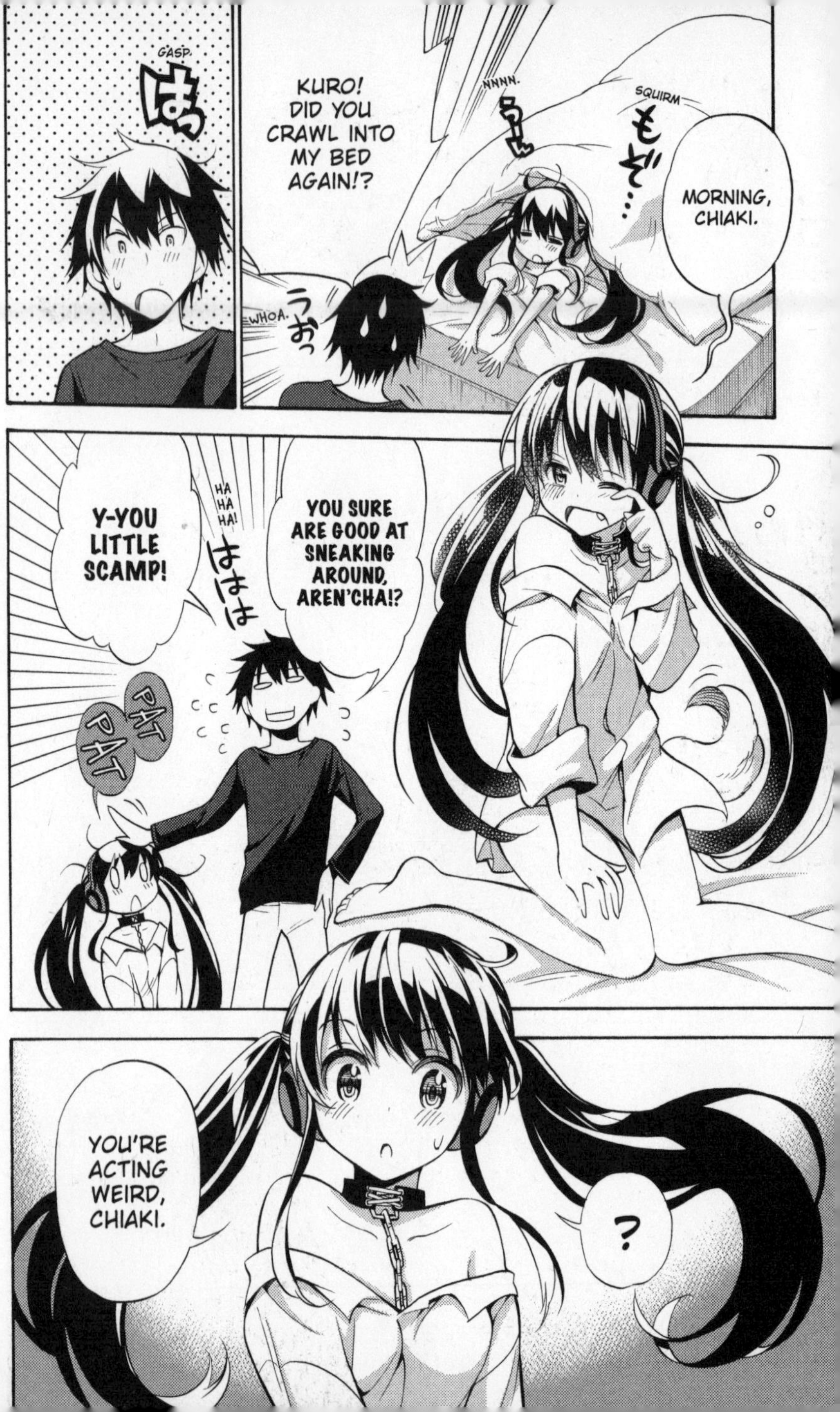
SQUIRM
もぞ…
MORNING, CHIAKI.
NNNN.
うーん
KURO! DID YOU CRAWL INTO MY BED AGAIN!?
WHOA.
うおっ
GASP.
はっ
YOU SURE ARE GOOD AT SNEAKING AROUND, AREN'CHA!?
HA HA HA!
ははは
Y-YOU LITTLE SCAMP!
PAT PAT
?
YOU'RE ACTING WEIRD, CHIAKI.

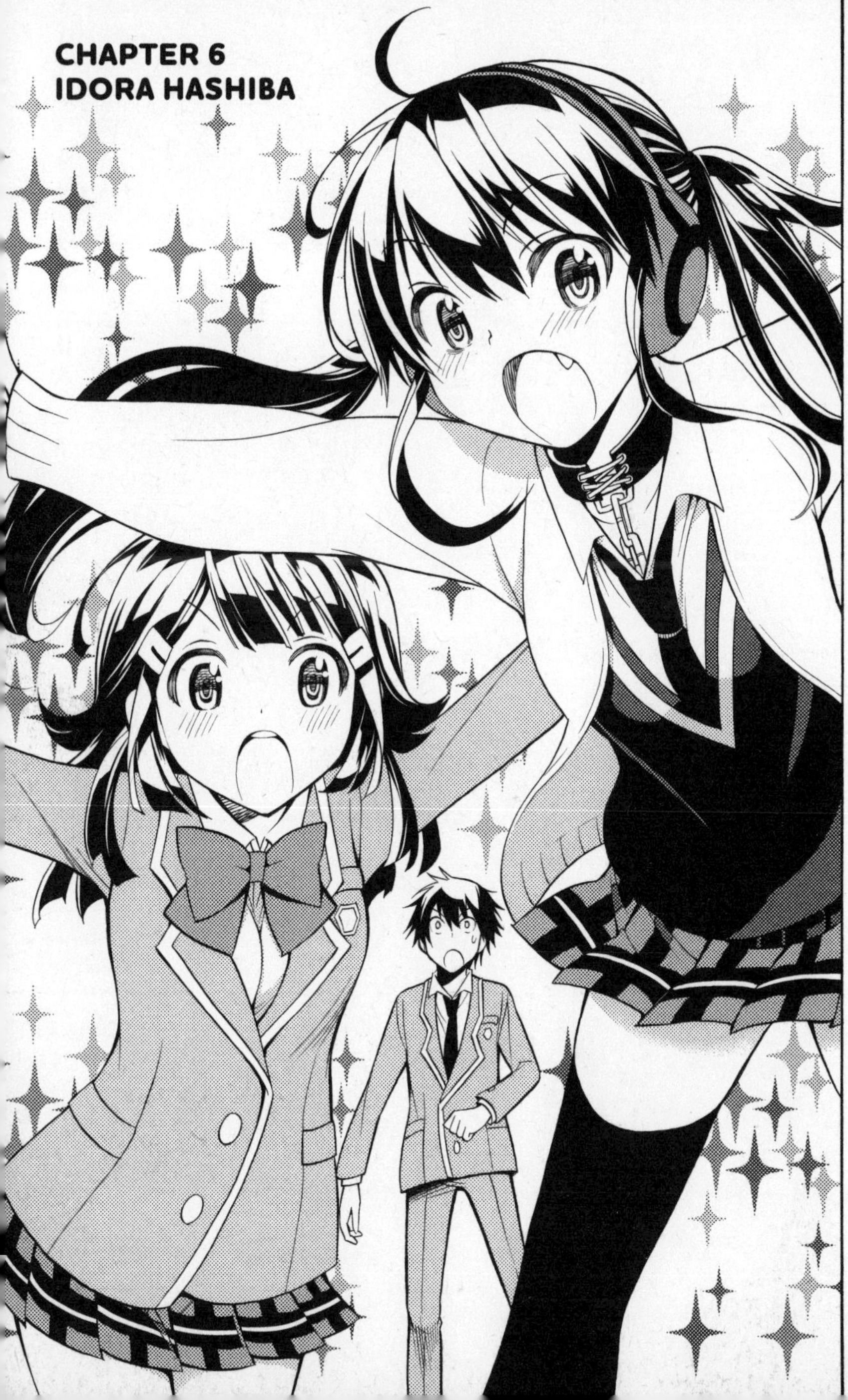
CHAPTER 6
IDORA HASHIBA

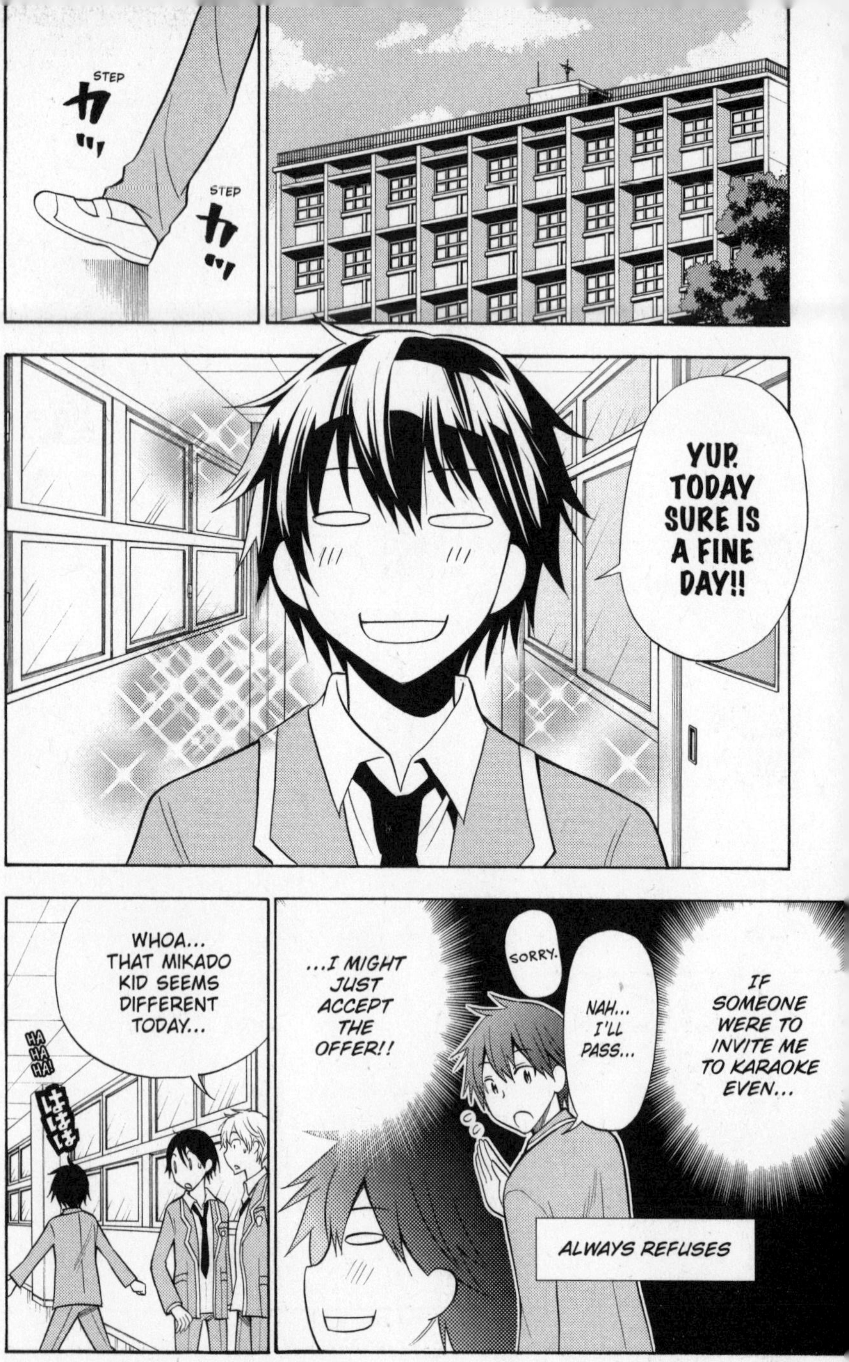
STEP
カッ
STEP
カッ
YUP. TODAY SURE IS A FINE DAY!!
IF SOMEONE WERE TO INVITE ME TO KARAOKE EVEN...
SORRY.
NAH... I'LL PASS...
ALWAYS REFUSES
...I MIGHT JUST ACCEPT THE OFFER!!
WHOA... THAT MIKADO KID SEEMS DIFFERENT TODAY...
HA HA HA!
はははは

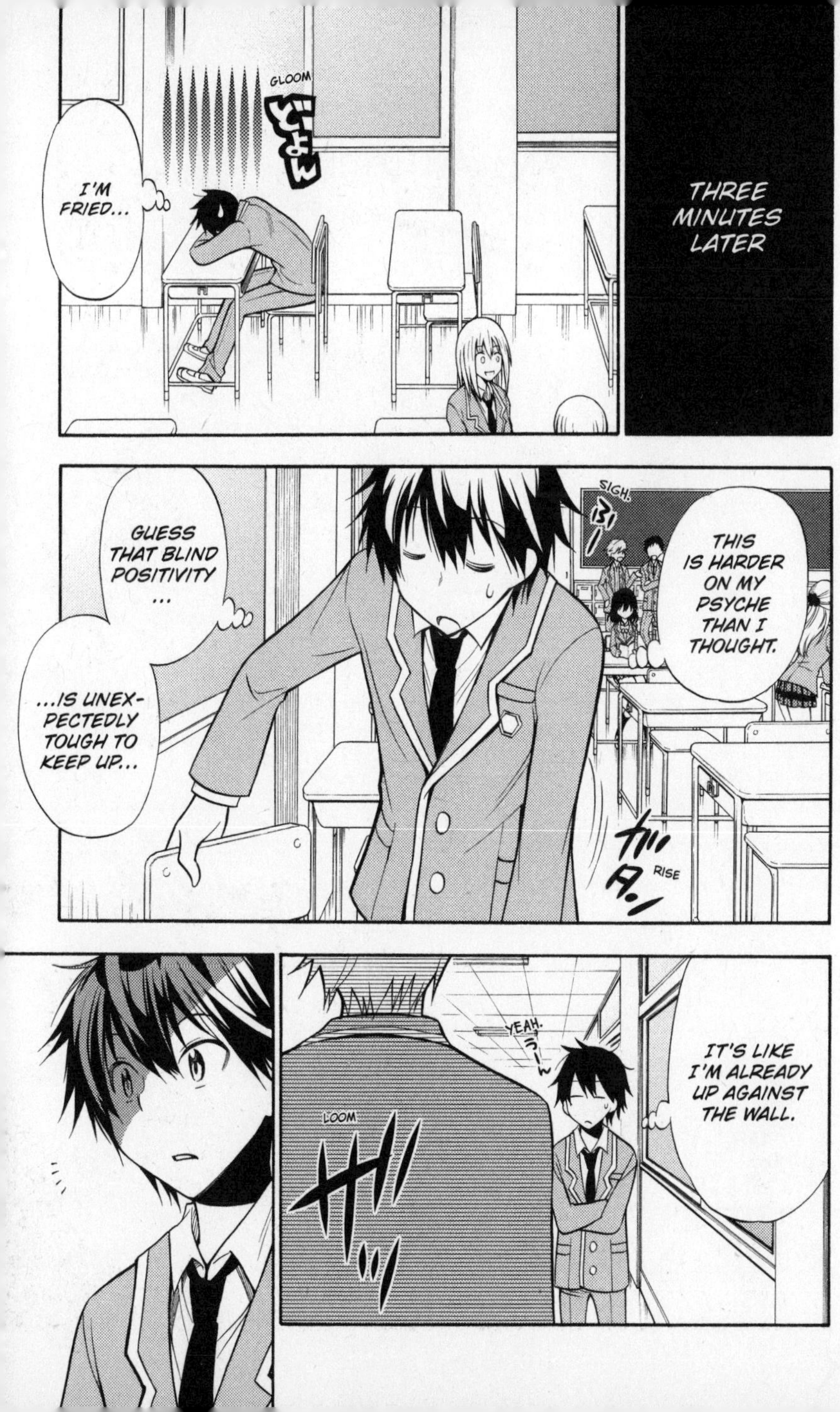

THREE MINUTES LATER
GLOOM
どよん
I'M FRIED...
SIGH.
ふー
THIS IS HARDER ON MY PSYCHE THAN I THOUGHT.
GUESS THAT BLIND POSITIVITY...
...IS UNEXPECTEDLY TOUGH TO KEEP UP...
ガタッ
RISE
IT'S LIKE I'M ALREADY UP AGAINST THE WALL.
YEAH.
うーん
LOOM
ザッ

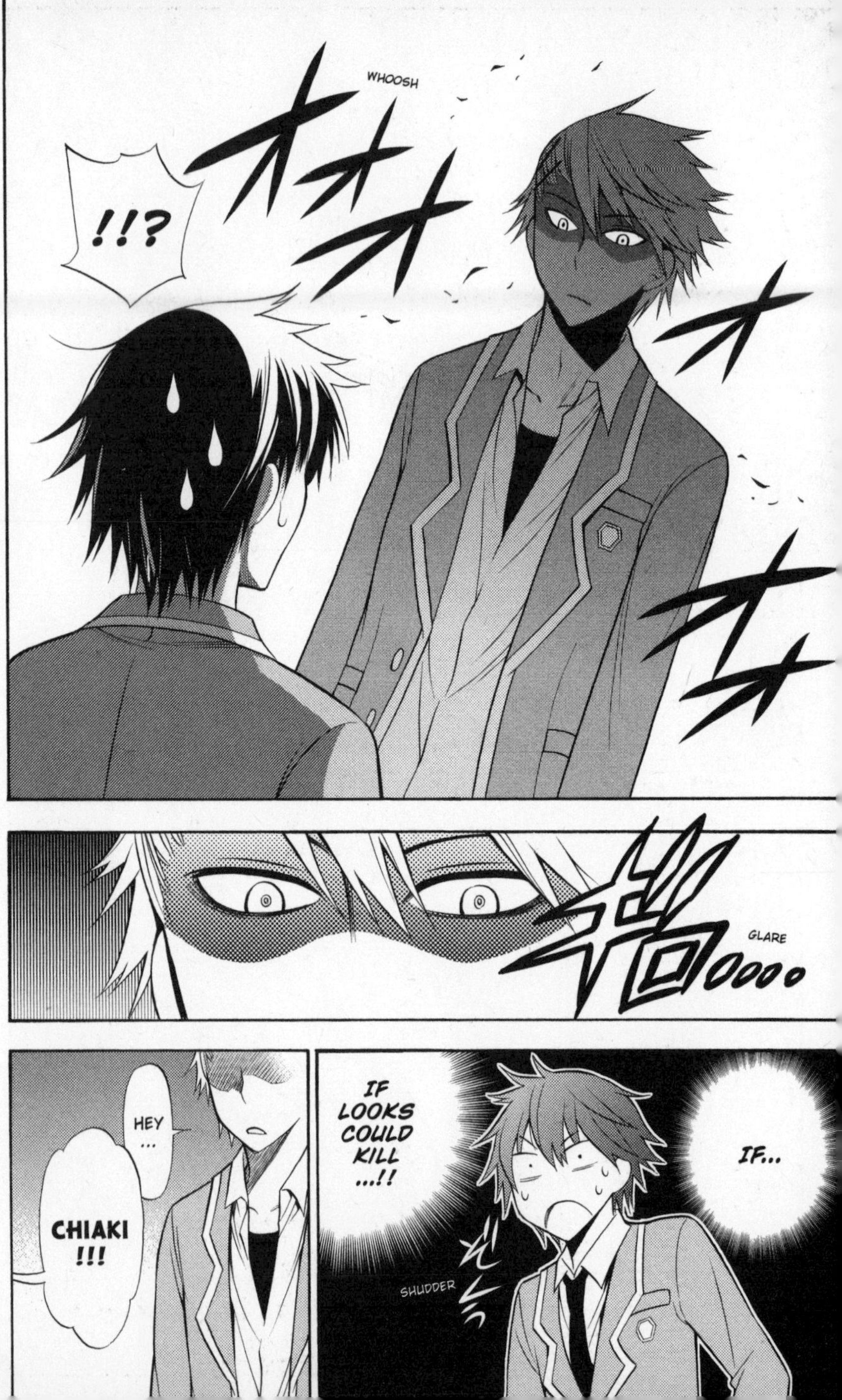
WHOOSH
!!?
GLARE
IF...
IF LOOKS COULD KILL ...!!
SHUDDER
HEY ...
CHIAKI !!!

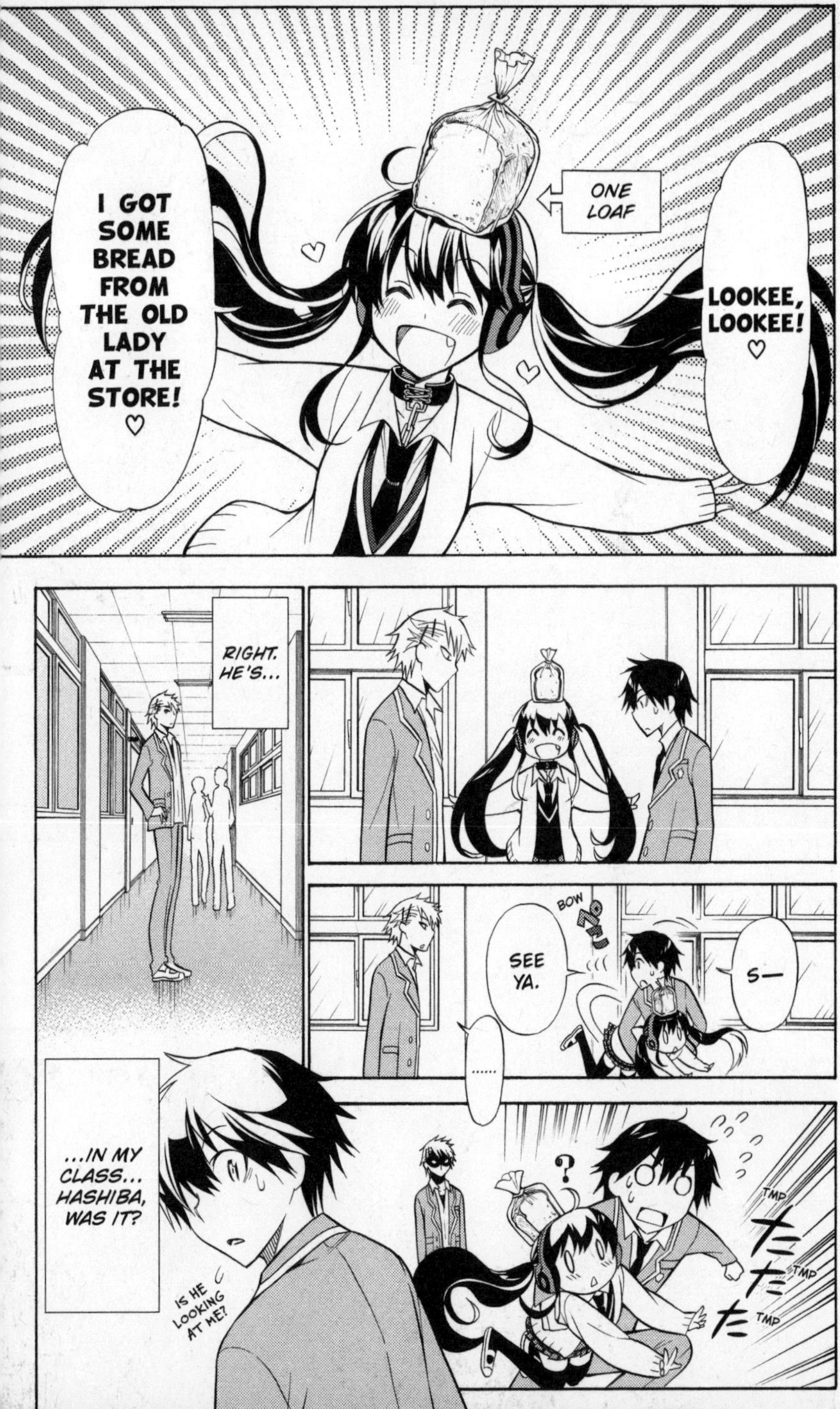
LOOKEE, LOOKEE! ♡
ONE LOAF
I GOT SOME BREAD FROM THE OLD LADY AT THE STORE! ♡
S—
BOW
SEE YA.
......
RIGHT. HE'S...
TMP TMP TMP
?
...IN MY CLASS... HASHIBA, WAS IT?
IS HE LOOKING AT ME?

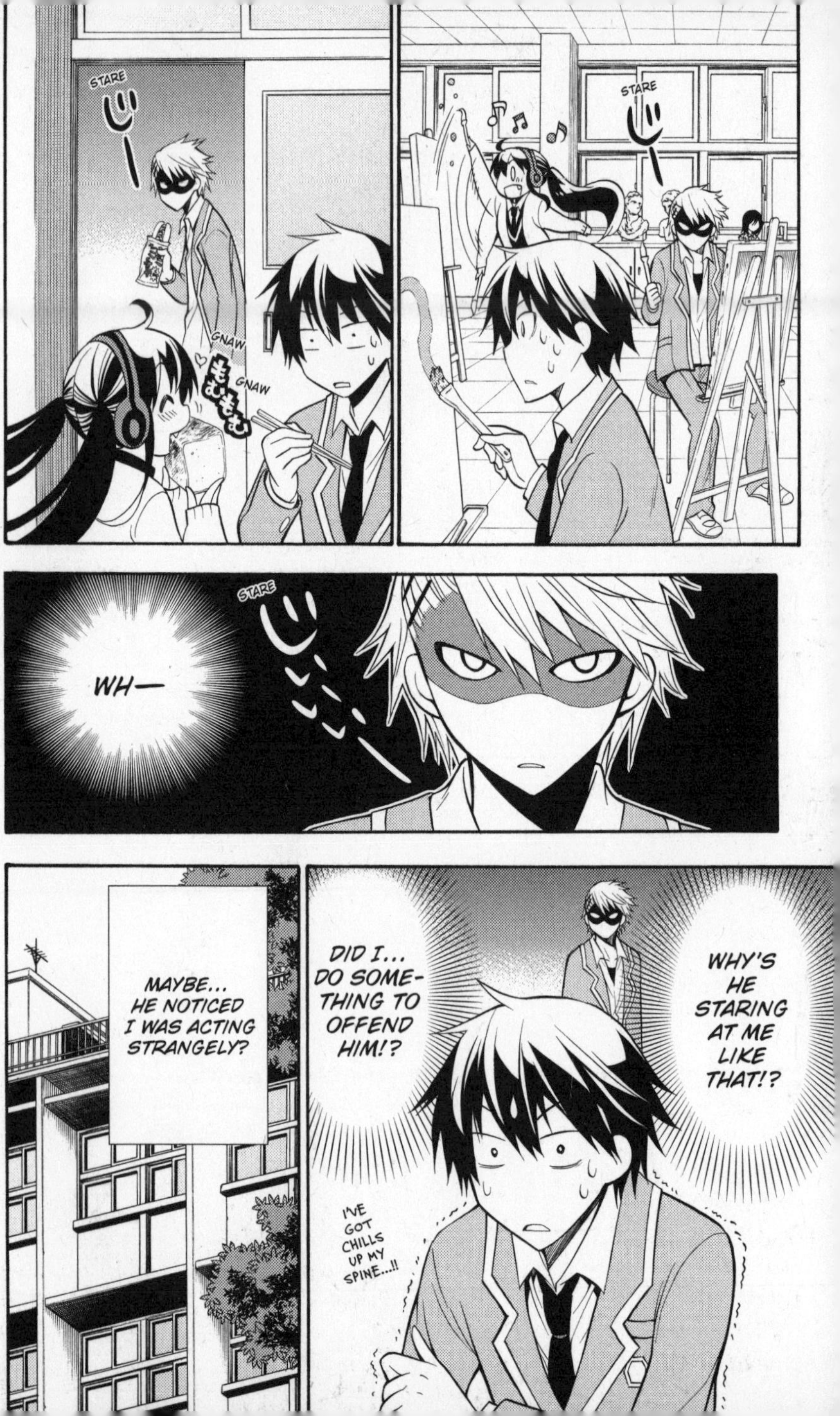
STARE
じー
STARE
GNAW
GNAW
もむもむ
STARE
じーー
WH—
WHY'S HE STARING AT ME LIKE THAT!?
DID I... DO SOME-THING TO OFFEND HIM!?
I'VE GOT CHILLS UP MY SPINE...!!
MAYBE... HE NOTICED I WAS ACTING STRANGELY?

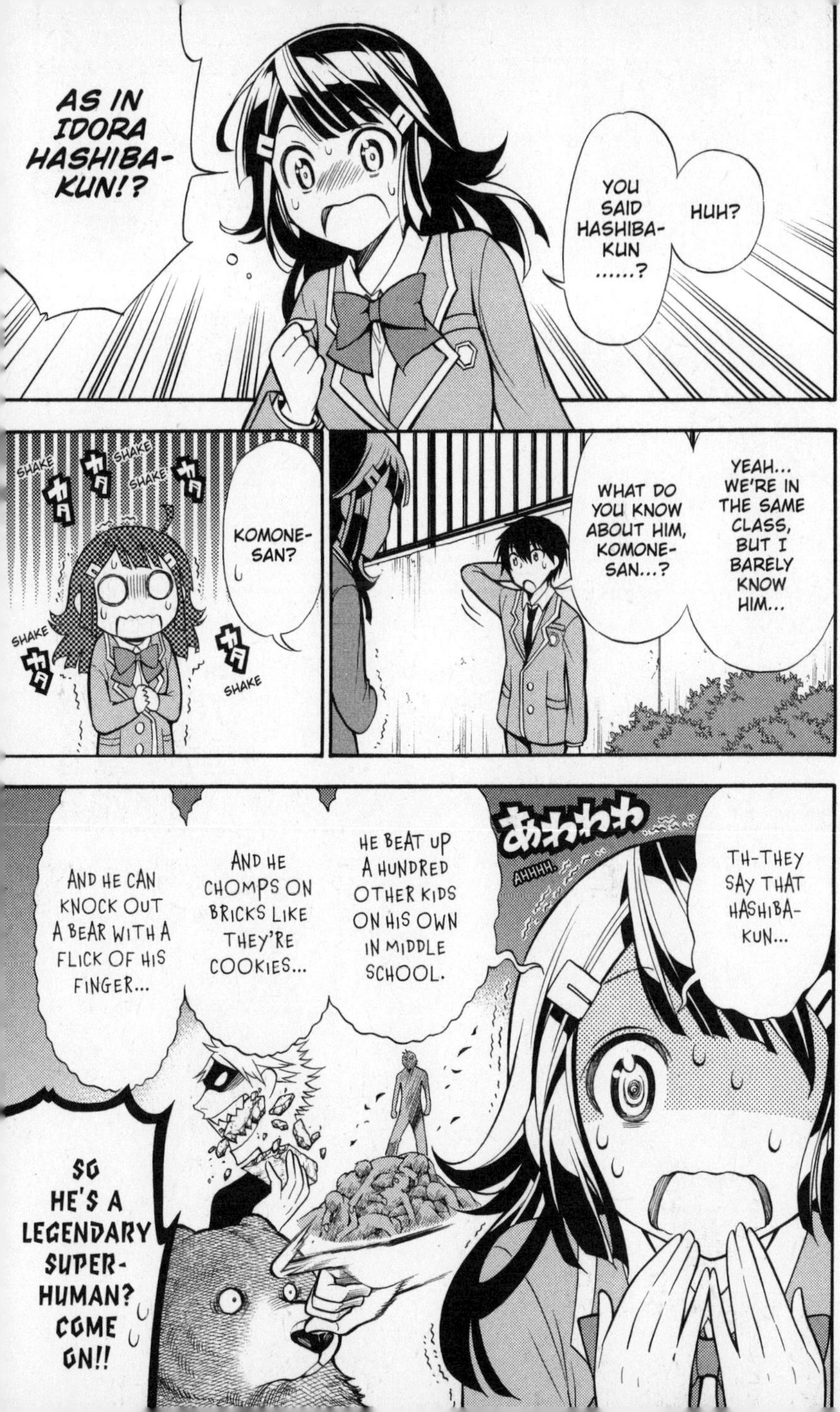
HUH?
YOU SAID HASHIBA-KUN......?
AS IN IDORA HASHIBA-KUN!?
YEAH... WE'RE IN THE SAME CLASS, BUT I BARELY KNOW HIM...
WHAT DO YOU KNOW ABOUT HIM, KOMONE-SAN...?
KOMONE-SAN?
カタ SHAKE
カタ SHAKE
TH-THEY SAY THAT HASHIBA-KUN...
あわわわ
AHHHH.
HE BEAT UP A HUNDRED OTHER KIDS ON HIS OWN IN MIDDLE SCHOOL.
AND HE CHOMPS ON BRICKS LIKE THEY'RE COOKIES...
AND HE CAN KNOCK OUT A BEAR WITH A FLICK OF HIS FINGER...
SO HE'S A LEGENDARY SUPER-HUMAN? COME ON!!

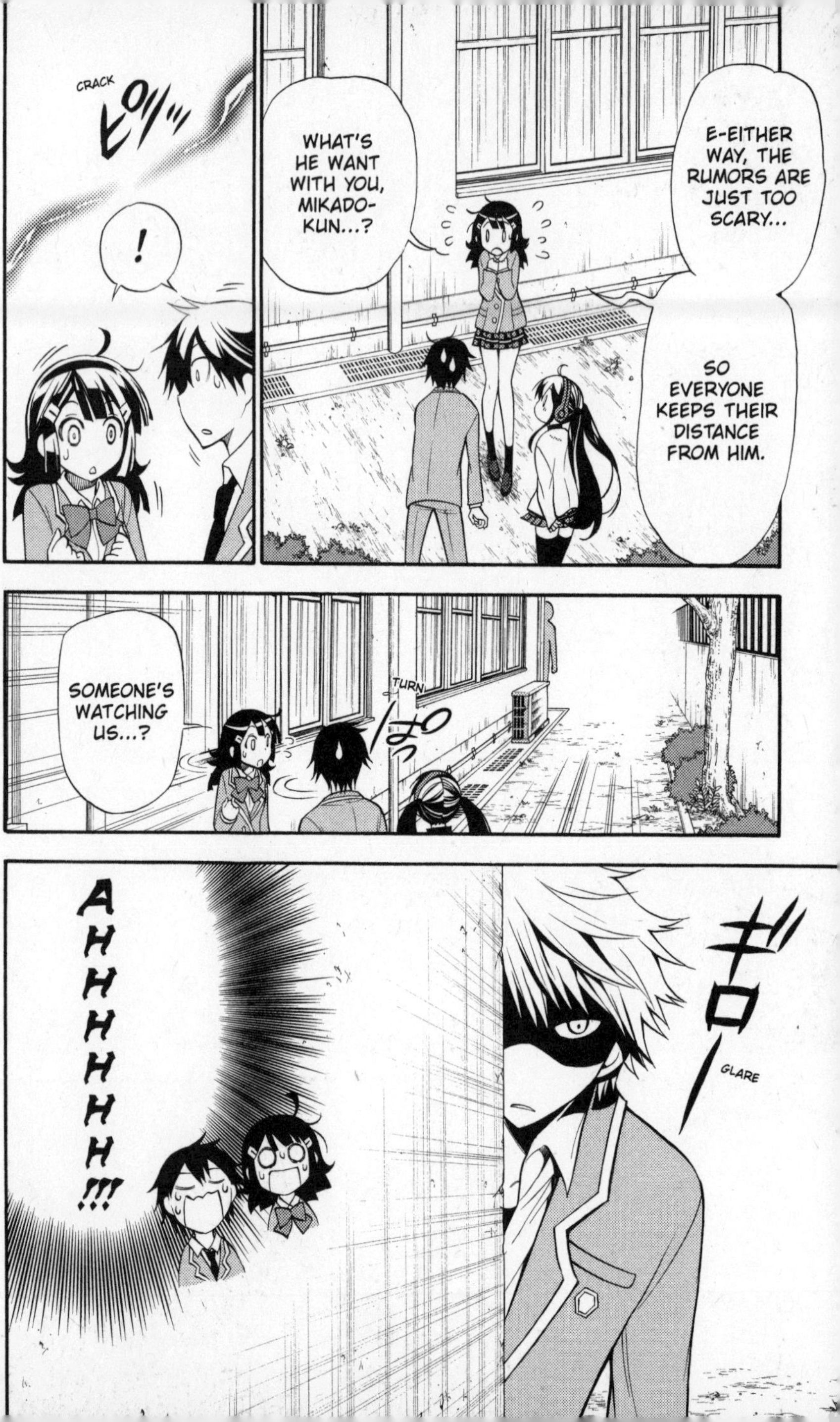
E-EITHER WAY, THE RUMORS ARE JUST TOO SCARY...
SO EVERYONE KEEPS THEIR DISTANCE FROM HIM.
WHAT'S HE WANT WITH YOU, MIKADO-KUN...?
CRACK
!
TURN
SOMEONE'S WATCHING US...?
GLARE
AHHHHHHH!!!

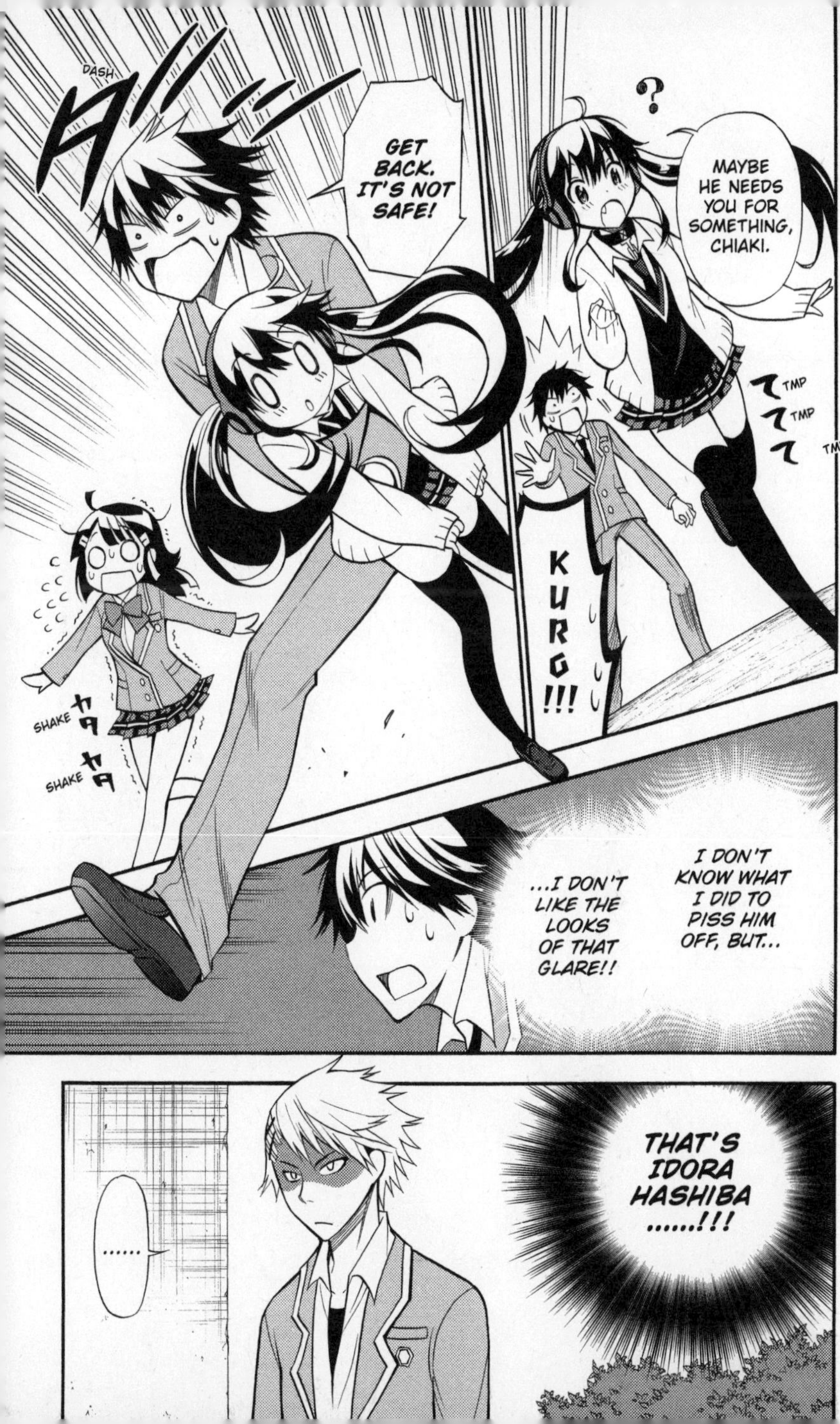
?
MAYBE HE NEEDS YOU FOR SOMETHING, CHIAKI.
TMP
TMP
TMP
KURG!!!
DASH
GET BACK. IT'S NOT SAFE!
SHAKE
SHAKE
I DON'T KNOW WHAT I DID TO PISS HIM OFF, BUT...
...I DON'T LIKE THE LOOKS OF THAT GLARE!!
THAT'S IDORA HASHIBA......!!!
......

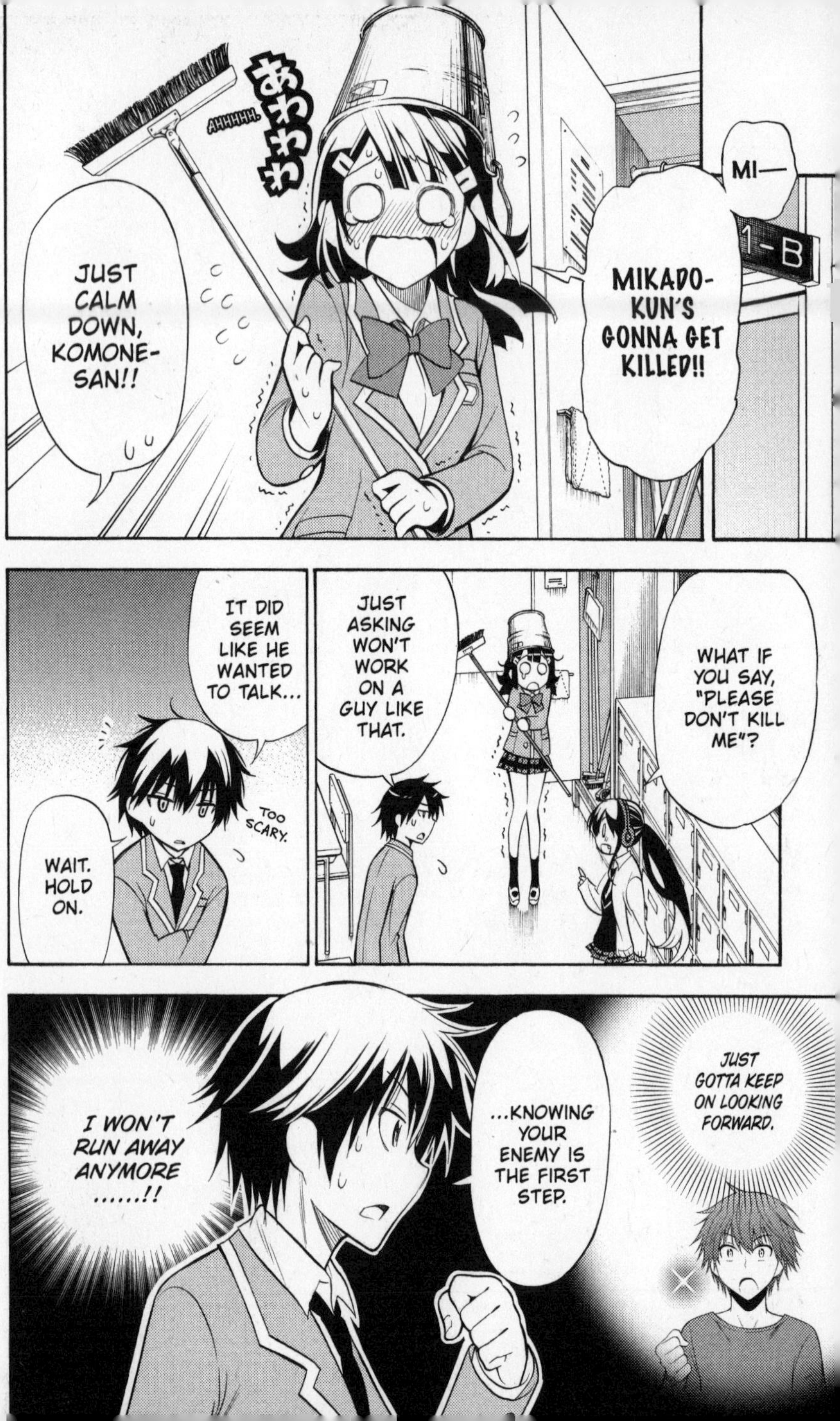
MI—
MIKADO-KUN'S GONNA GET KILLED!!
あわわわ
AHHHHH.
JUST CALM DOWN, KOMONE-SAN!!
WHAT IF YOU SAY, "PLEASE DON'T KILL ME"?
JUST ASKING WON'T WORK ON A GUY LIKE THAT.
IT DID SEEM LIKE HE WANTED TO TALK...
TOO SCARY.
WAIT. HOLD ON.
JUST GOTTA KEEP ON LOOKING FORWARD.
...KNOWING YOUR ENEMY IS THE FIRST STEP.
I WON'T RUN AWAY ANYMORE ......!!

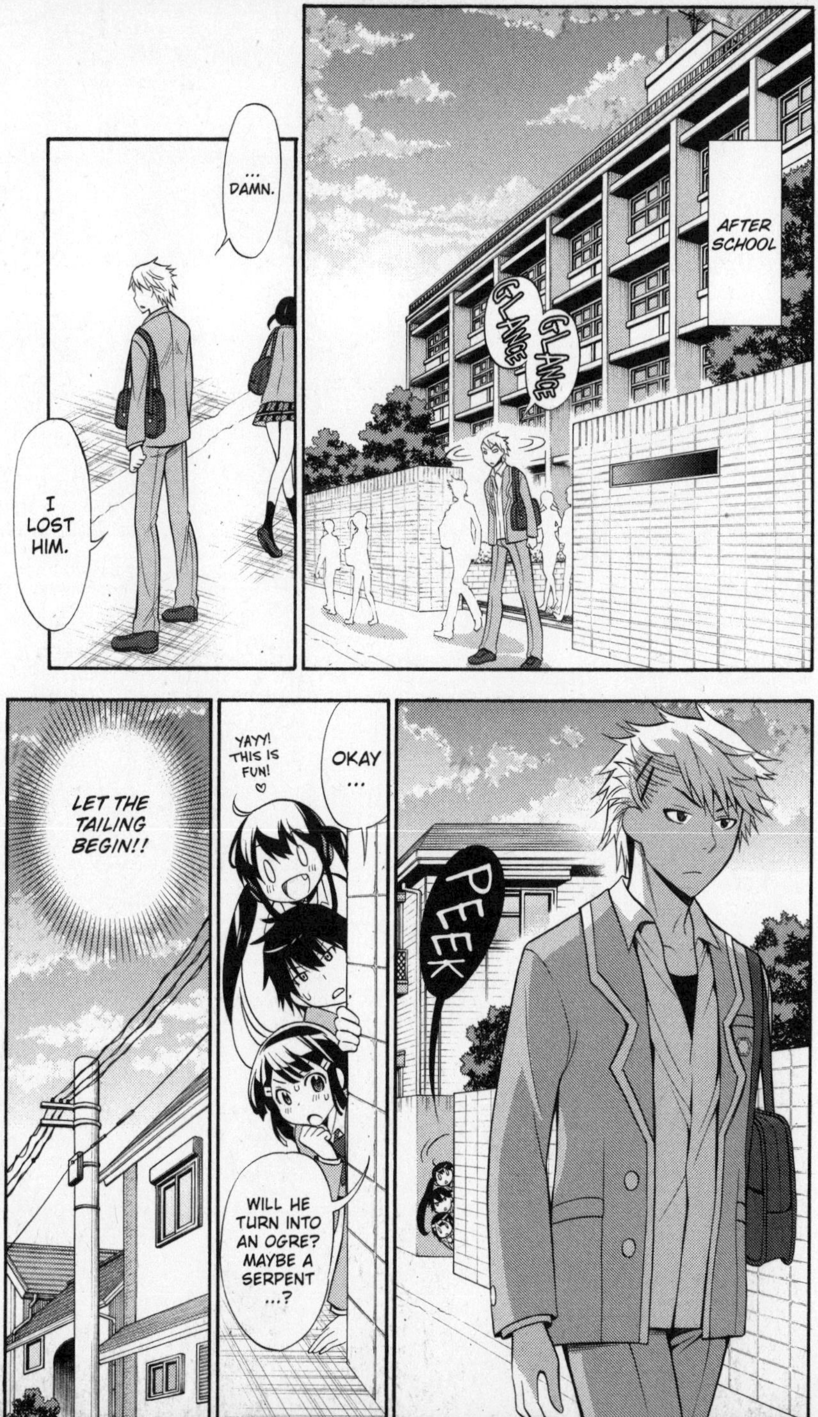
AFTER SCHOOL
GLANCE GLANCE
... DAMN.
I LOST HIM.
PEEK
OKAY ...
YAYY! THIS IS FUN! ♡
WILL HE TURN INTO AN OGRE? MAYBE A SERPENT ...?
LET THE TAILING BEGIN!!

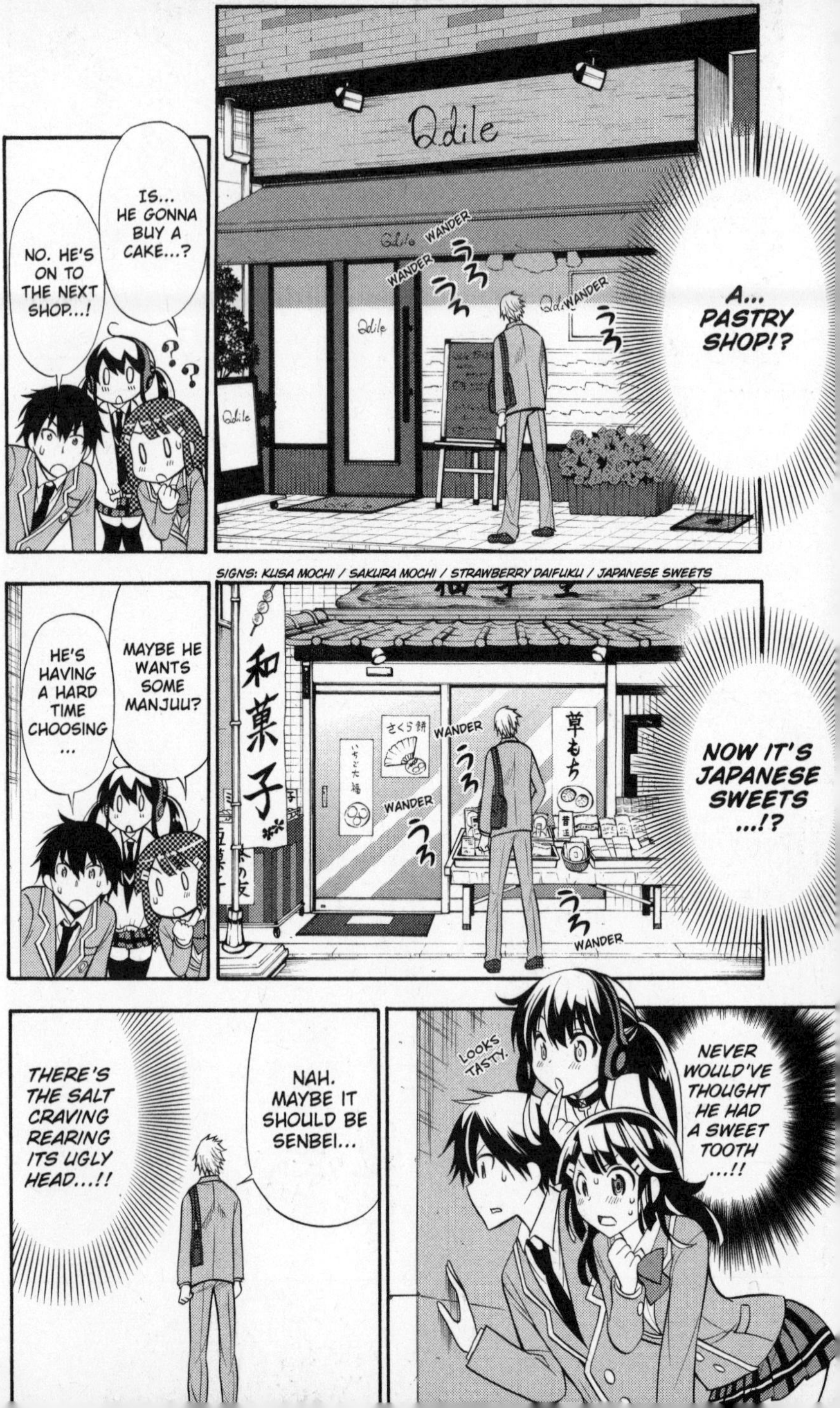
A... PASTRY SHOP!?
Qdile
WANDER
WANDER
WANDER
IS... HE GONNA BUY A CAKE...?
NO. HE'S ON TO THE NEXT SHOP...!
SIGNS: KUSA MOCHI / SAKURA MOCHI / STRAWBERRY DAIFUKU / JAPANESE SWEETS
NOW IT'S JAPANESE SWEETS ...!?
草もち
さくら餅
いちご大福
和菓子
WANDER
WANDER
WANDER
MAYBE HE WANTS SOME MANJUU?
HE'S HAVING A HARD TIME CHOOSING ...
NEVER WOULD'VE THOUGHT HE HAD A SWEET TOOTH ...!!
LOOKS TASTY.
NAH. MAYBE IT SHOULD BE SENBEI...
THERE'S THE SALT CRAVING REARING ITS UGLY HEAD...!!

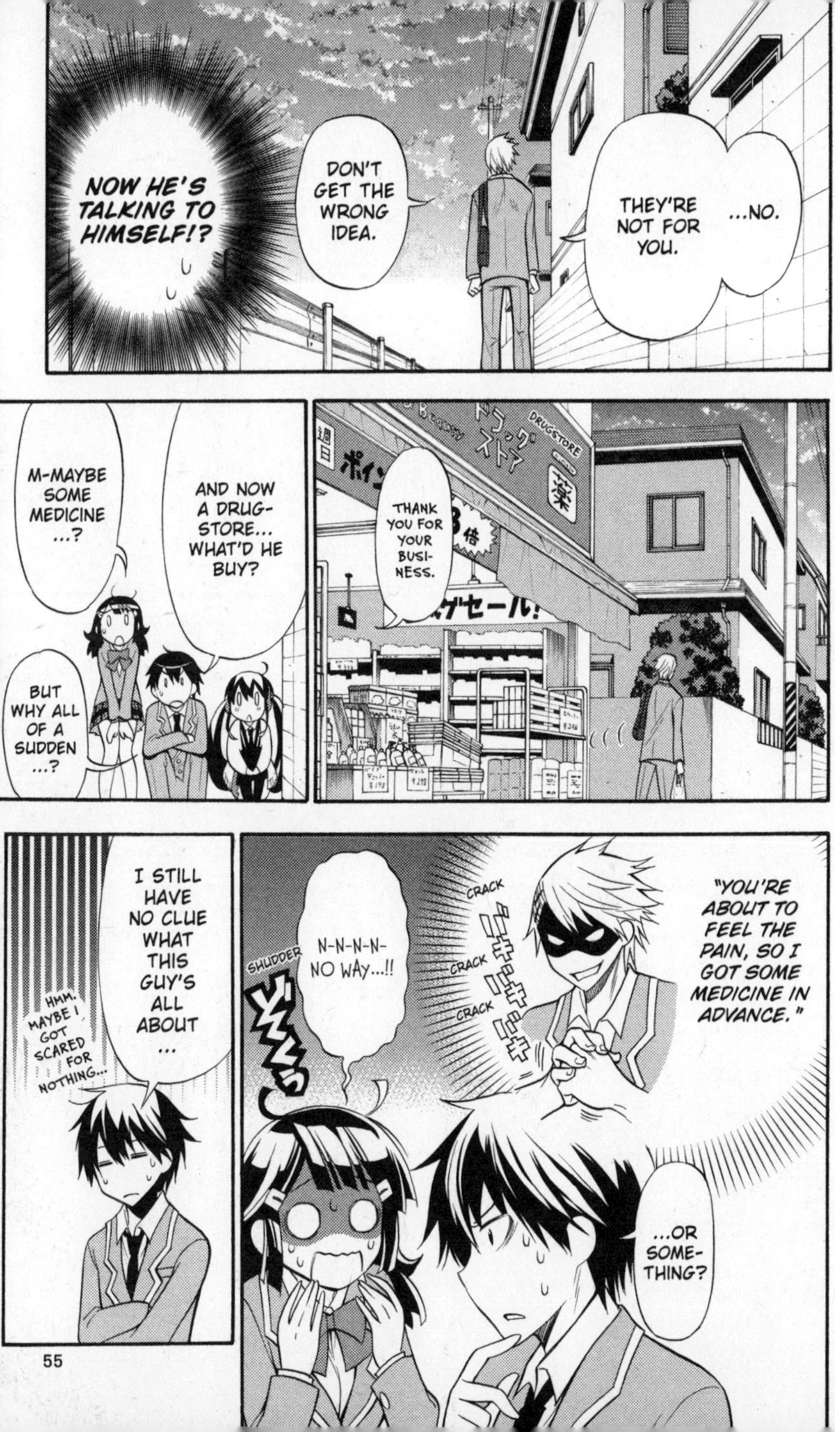
...NO.
THEY'RE NOT FOR YOU.
DON'T GET THE WRONG IDEA.
NOW HE'S TALKING TO HIMSELF!?
DRUGSTORE
THANK YOU FOR YOUR BUSI-NESS.
AND NOW A DRUG-STORE... WHAT'D HE BUY?
M-MAYBE SOME MEDICINE ...?
BUT WHY ALL OF A SUDDEN ...?
"YOU'RE ABOUT TO FEEL THE PAIN, SO I GOT SOME MEDICINE IN ADVANCE."
CRACK
CRACK
CRACK
N-N-N-N-NO WAY...!!
SHUDDER
...OR SOME-THING?
I STILL HAVE NO CLUE WHAT THIS GUY'S ALL ABOUT ...
HMM. MAYBE I GOT SCARED FOR NOTHING...

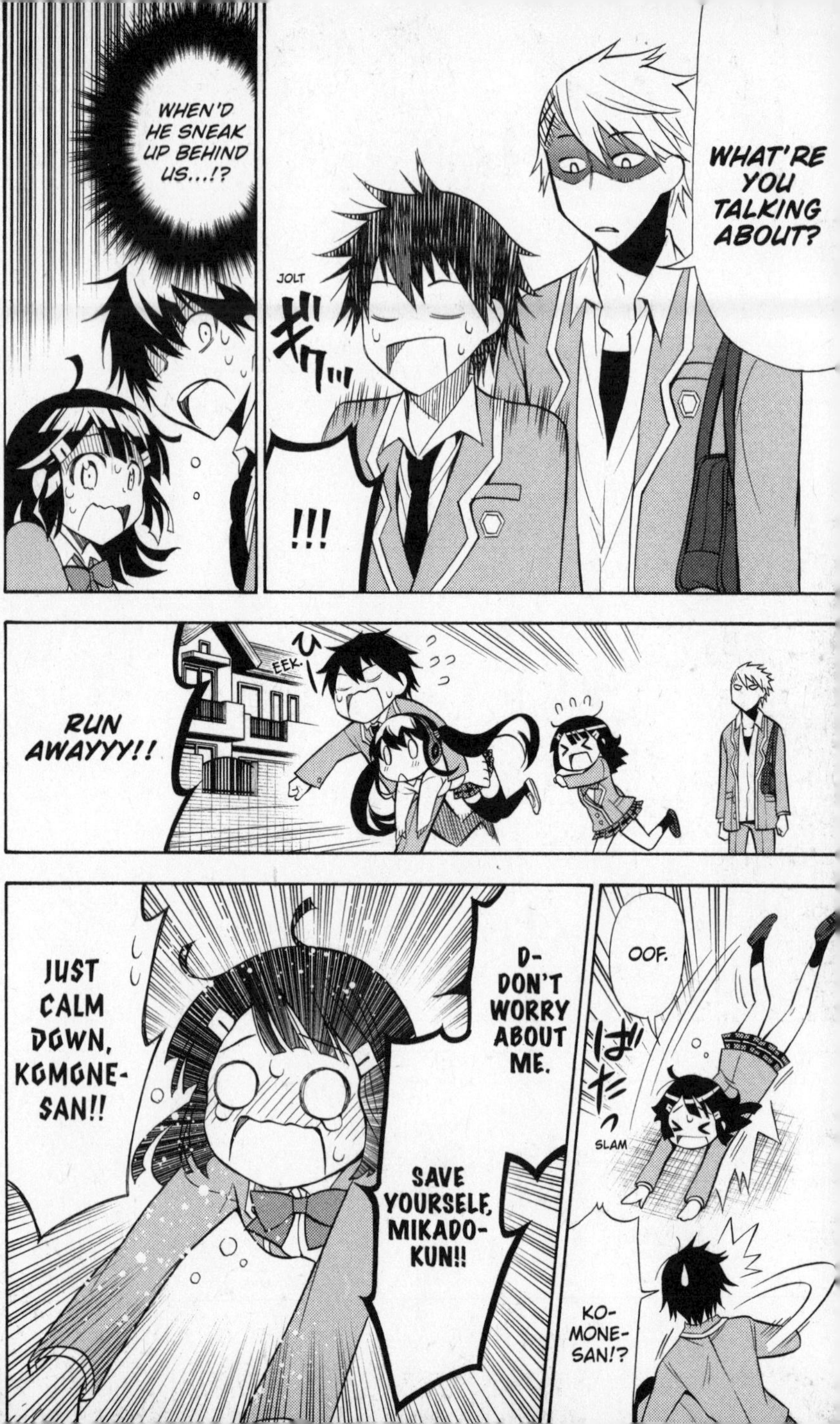
WHAT'RE YOU TALKING ABOUT?
JOLT
!!!
WHEN'D HE SNEAK UP BEHIND US...!?
EEK.
RUN AWAYYY!!
OOF.
SLAM
KO-MONE-SAN!?
D-DON'T WORRY ABOUT ME.
SAVE YOURSELF, MIKADO-KUN!!
JUST CALM DOWN, KOMONE-SAN!!

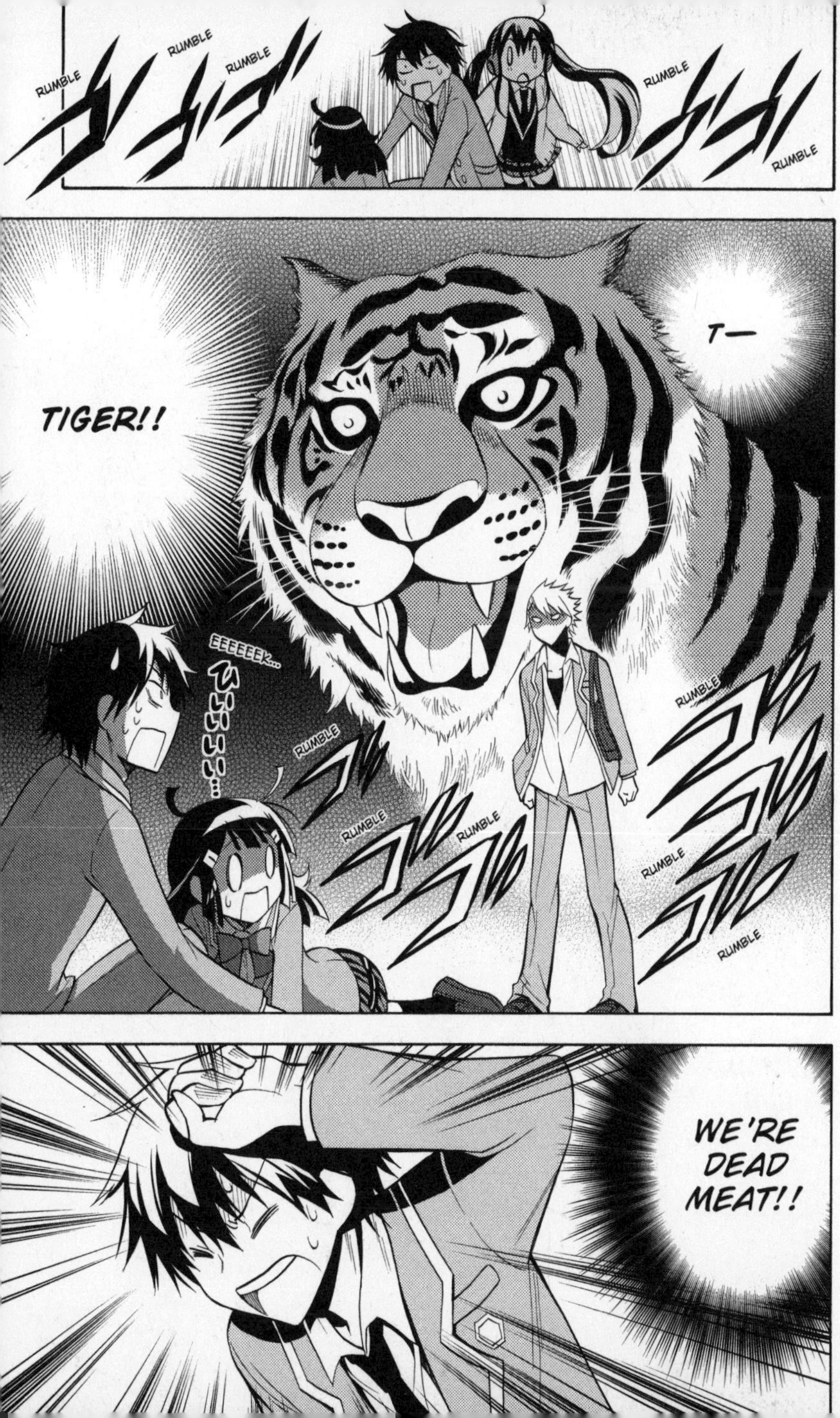
RUMBLE
RUMBLE
RUMBLE
RUMBLE
RUMBLE
T—
TIGER!!
RUMBLE
RUMBLE
RUMBLE
RUMBLE
RUMBLE
EEEEEEK...
ひぃぃぃぃぃ…
WE'RE DEAD MEAT!!

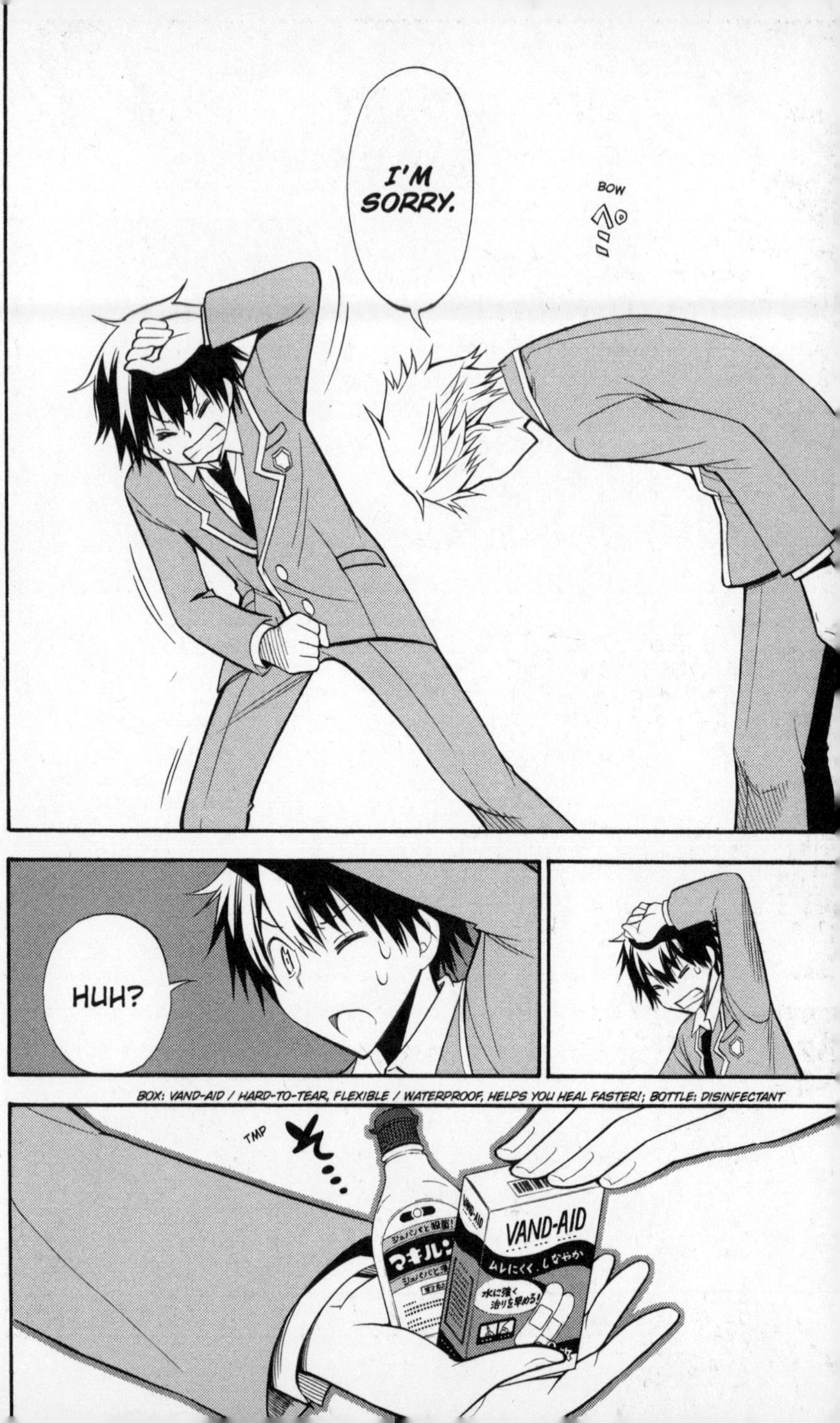
I'M SORRY.
BOW
HUH?
BOX: VAND-AID / HARD-TO-TEAR, FLEXIBLE / WATERPROOF, HELPS YOU HEAL FASTER!; BOTTLE: DISINFECTANT
TMP
VAND-AID
ムレにくく、しなやか
水に強く
治りを早める!
マキルン

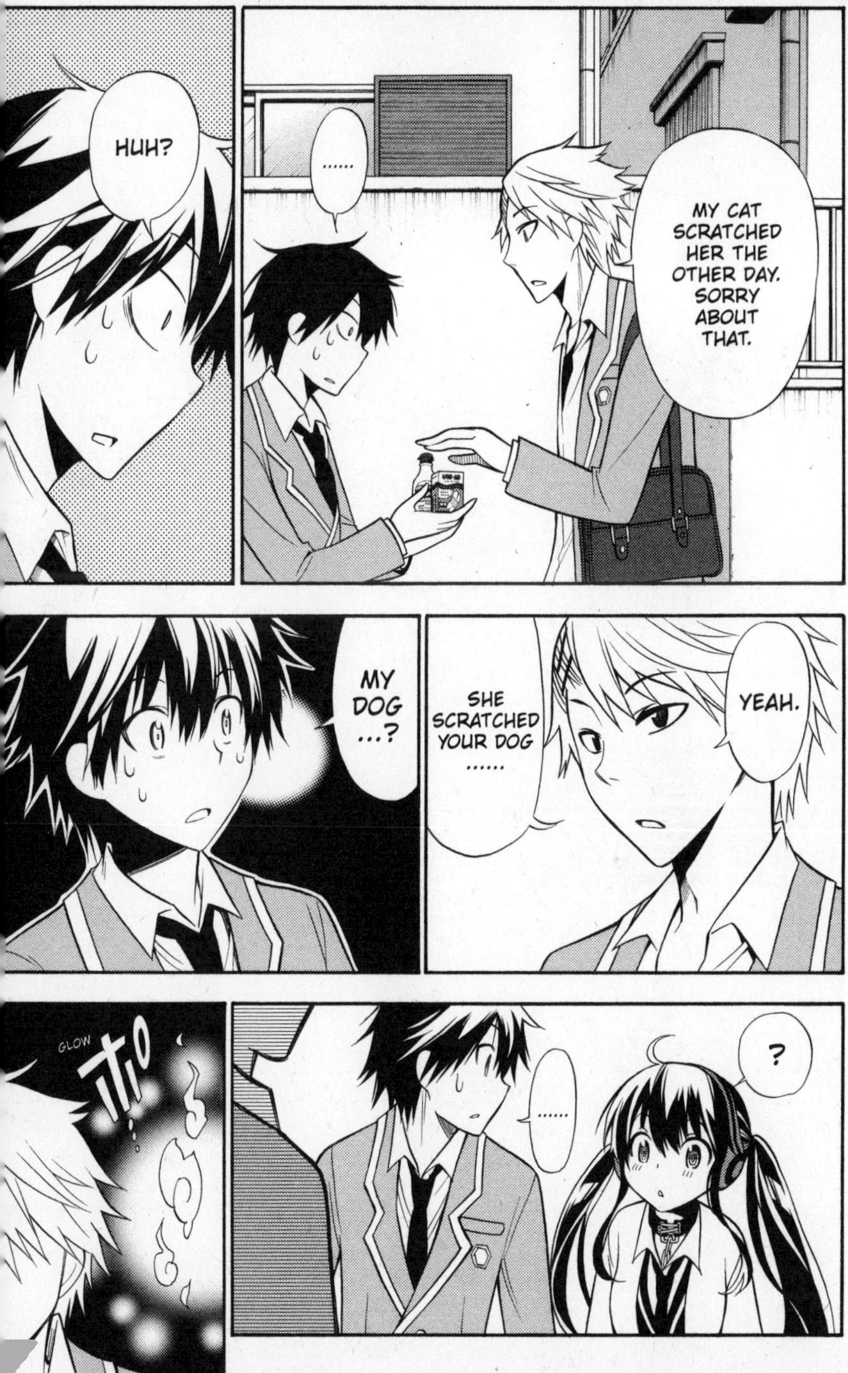

MY CAT SCRATCHED HER THE OTHER DAY. SORRY ABOUT THAT.
......
HUH?
YEAH.
SHE SCRATCHED YOUR DOG ......
MY DOG ...?
?
......
GLOW

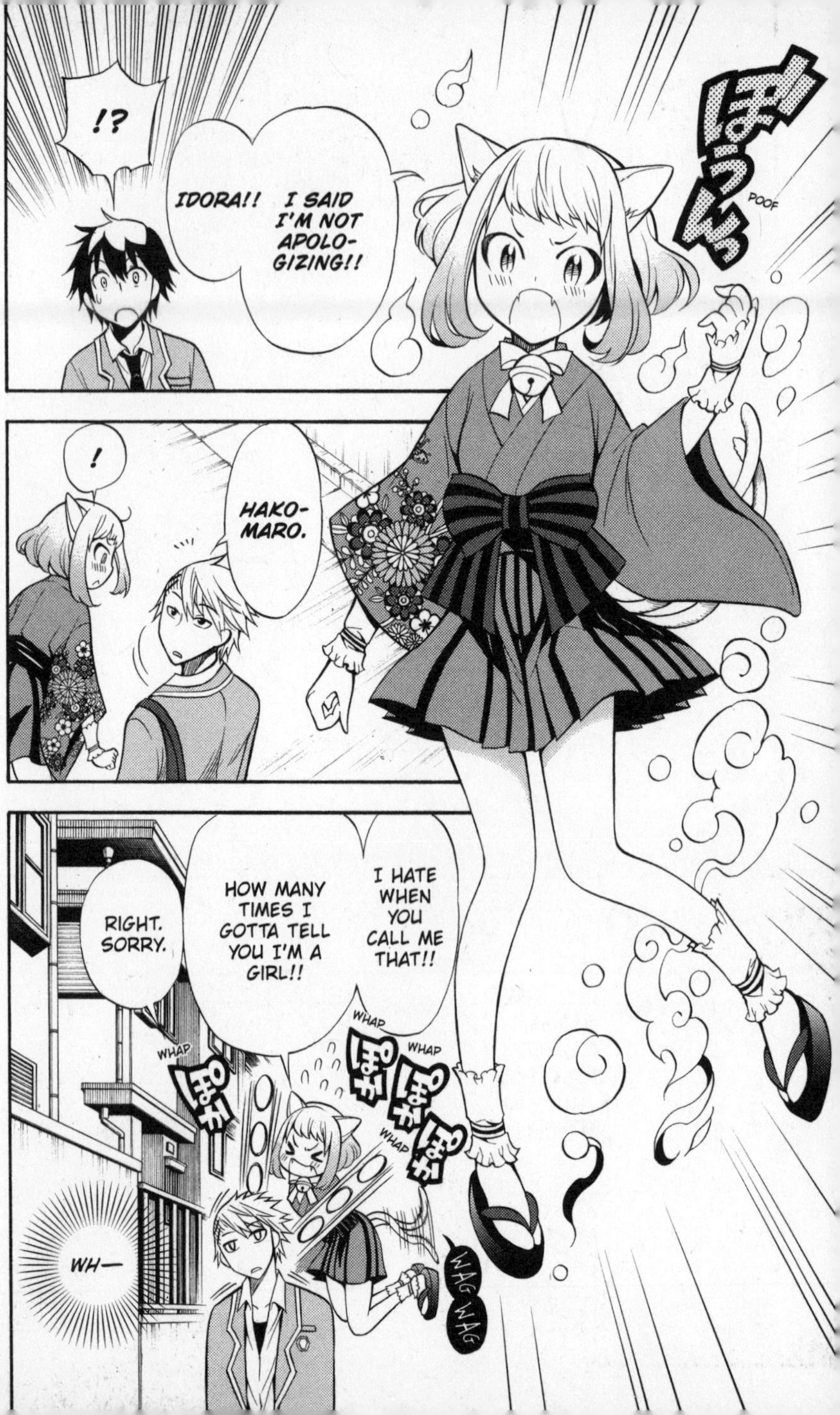
ぽうん
POOF
IDORA!! I SAID I'M NOT APOLO-GIZING!!
!?
HAKO-MARO.
!
I HATE WHEN YOU CALL ME THAT!!
HOW MANY TIMES I GOTTA TELL YOU I'M A GIRL!!
RIGHT. SORRY.
ぽか WHAP
ぽか WHAP
ぽか WHAP
ぽか WHAP
WAG WAG
WH—

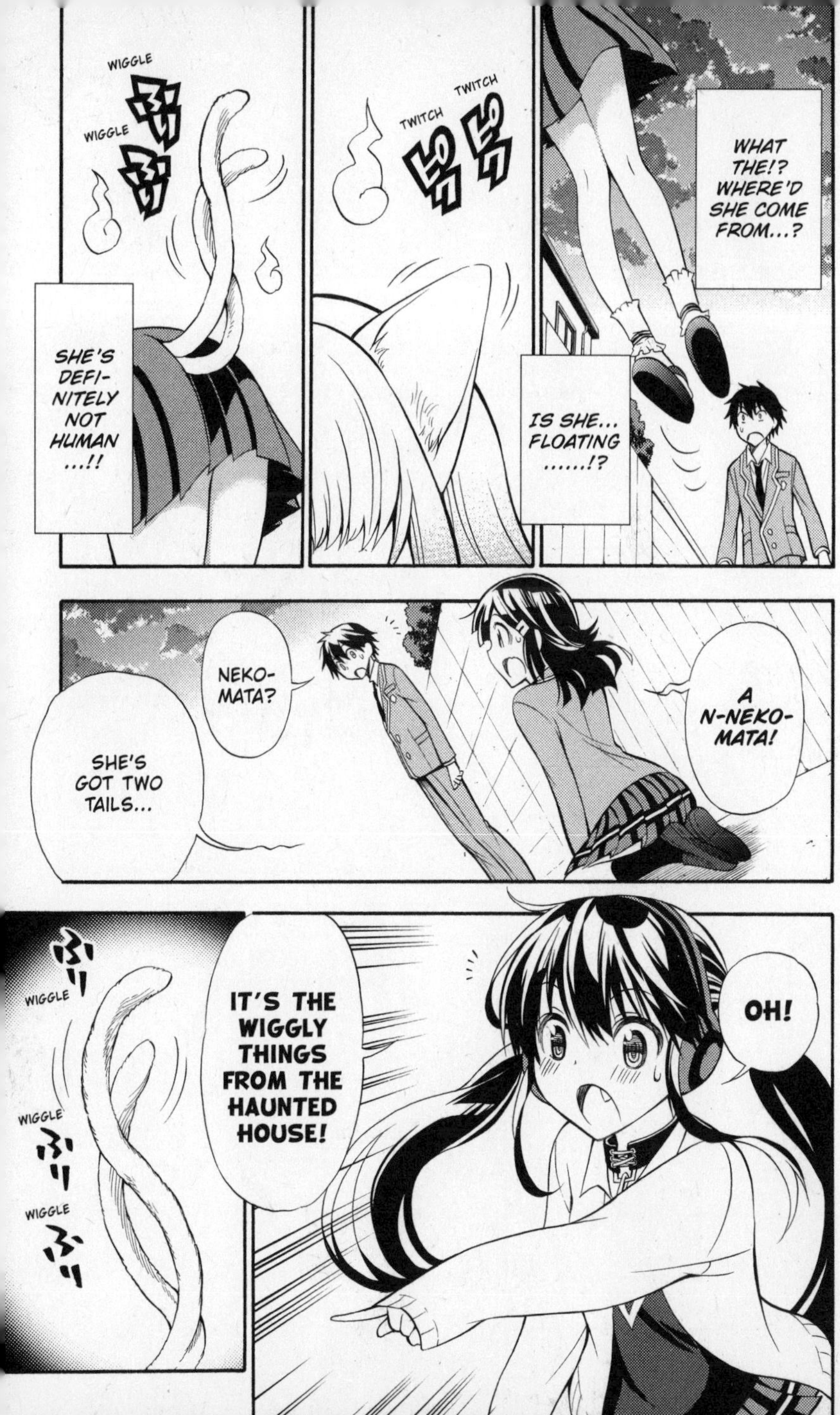
WHAT THE!? WHERE'D SHE COME FROM...?
IS SHE... FLOATING ......!?
TWITCH
TWITCH
WIGGLE
WIGGLE
SHE'S DEFI-NITELY NOT HUMAN ...!!
A N-NEKO-MATA!
NEKO-MATA?
SHE'S GOT TWO TAILS...
OH!
IT'S THE WIGGLY THINGS FROM THE HAUNTED HOUSE!
WIGGLE
WIGGLE
WIGGLE

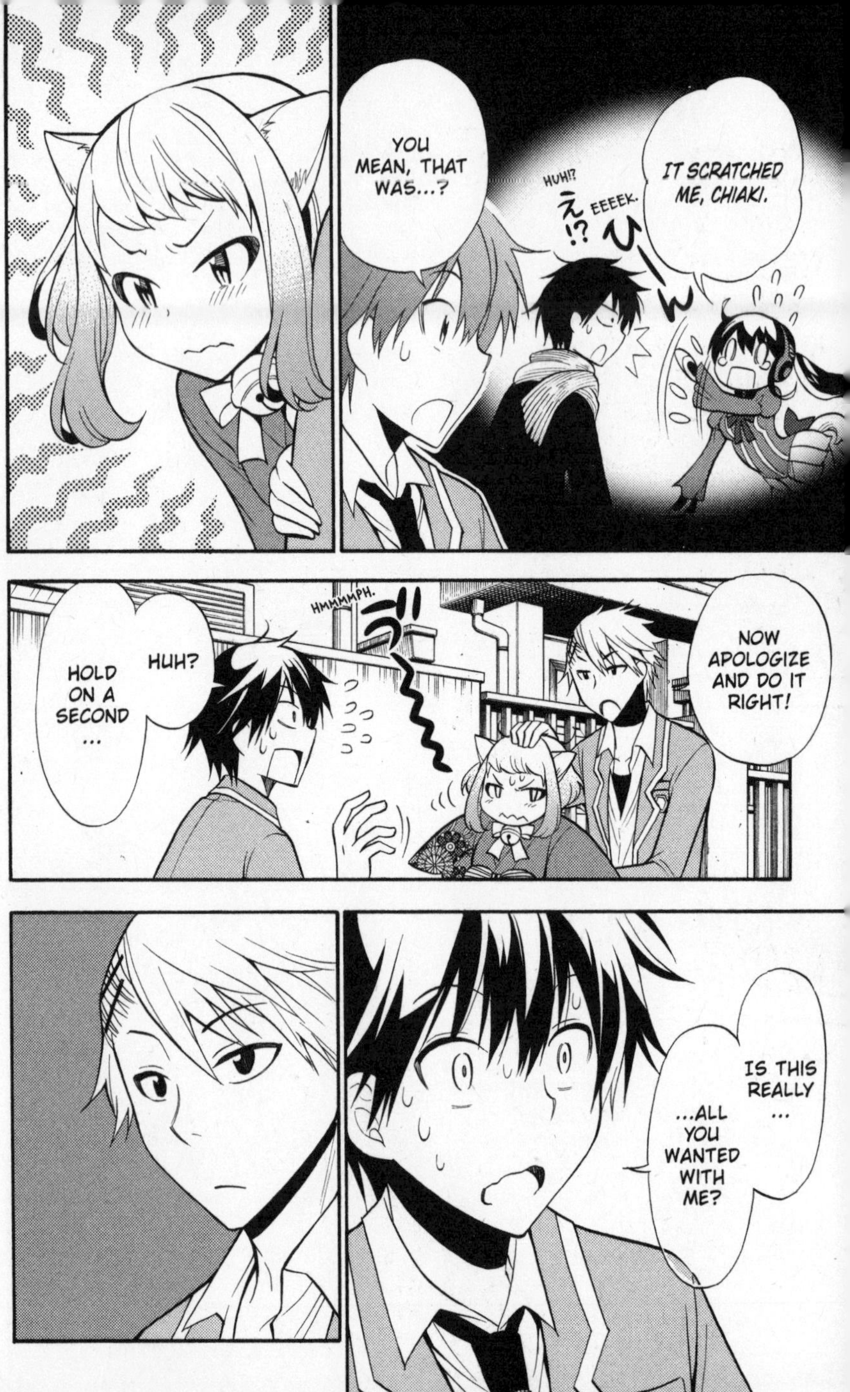
IT SCRATCHED ME, CHIAKI.
EEEEK.
HUH!?
YOU MEAN, THAT WAS...?
NOW APOLOGIZE AND DO IT RIGHT!
HMMMMPH.
HUH?
HOLD ON A SECOND ...
IS THIS REALLY ...
...ALL YOU WANTED WITH ME?

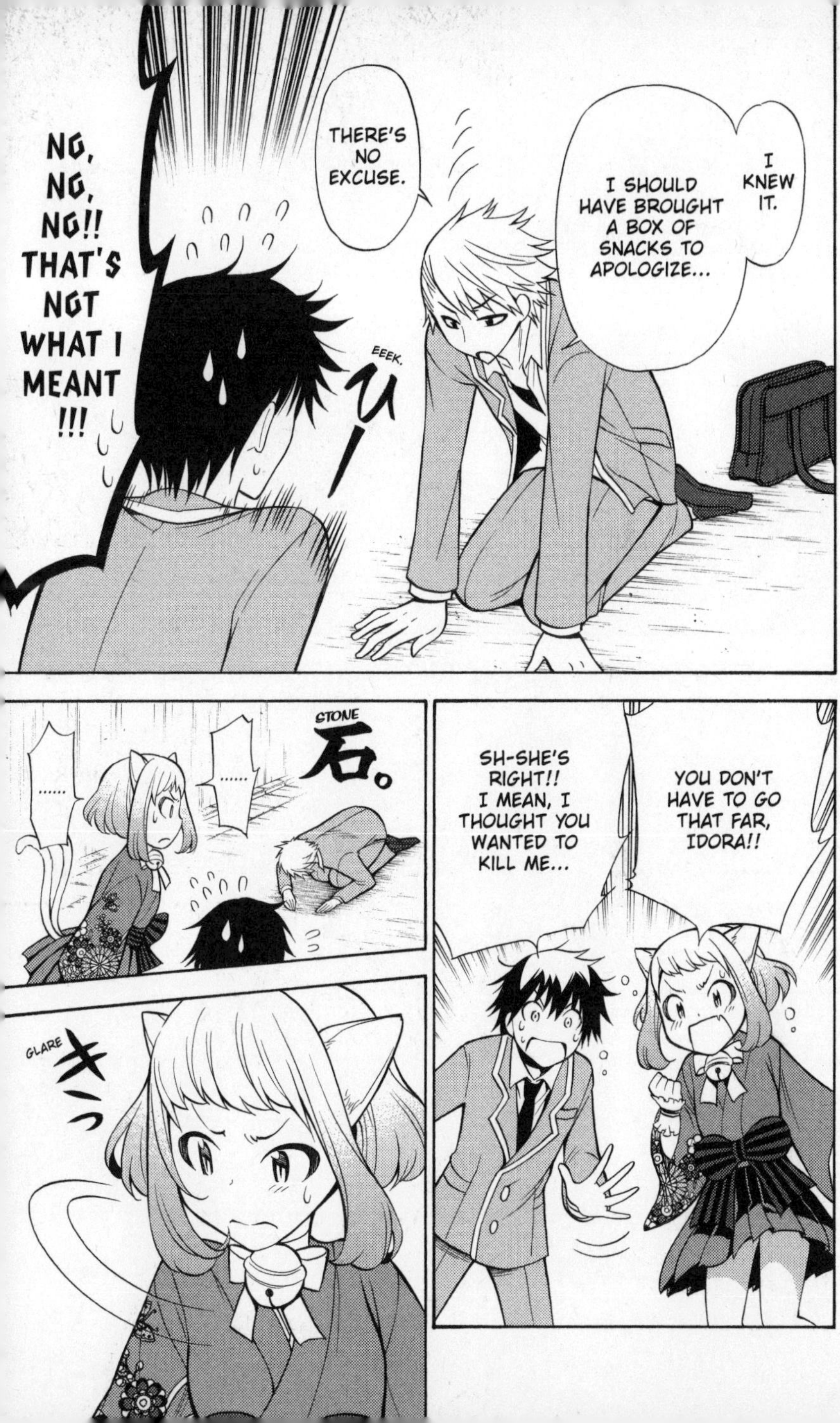
I KNEW IT.
I SHOULD HAVE BROUGHT A BOX OF SNACKS TO APOLOGIZE...
THERE'S NO EXCUSE.
EEEK.
ひー
NO, NO, NO!! THAT'S NOT WHAT I MEANT!!!
YOU DON'T HAVE TO GO THAT FAR, IDORA!!
SH-SHE'S RIGHT!! I MEAN, I THOUGHT YOU WANTED TO KILL ME...
STONE
石。
......
......
GLARE
キッ

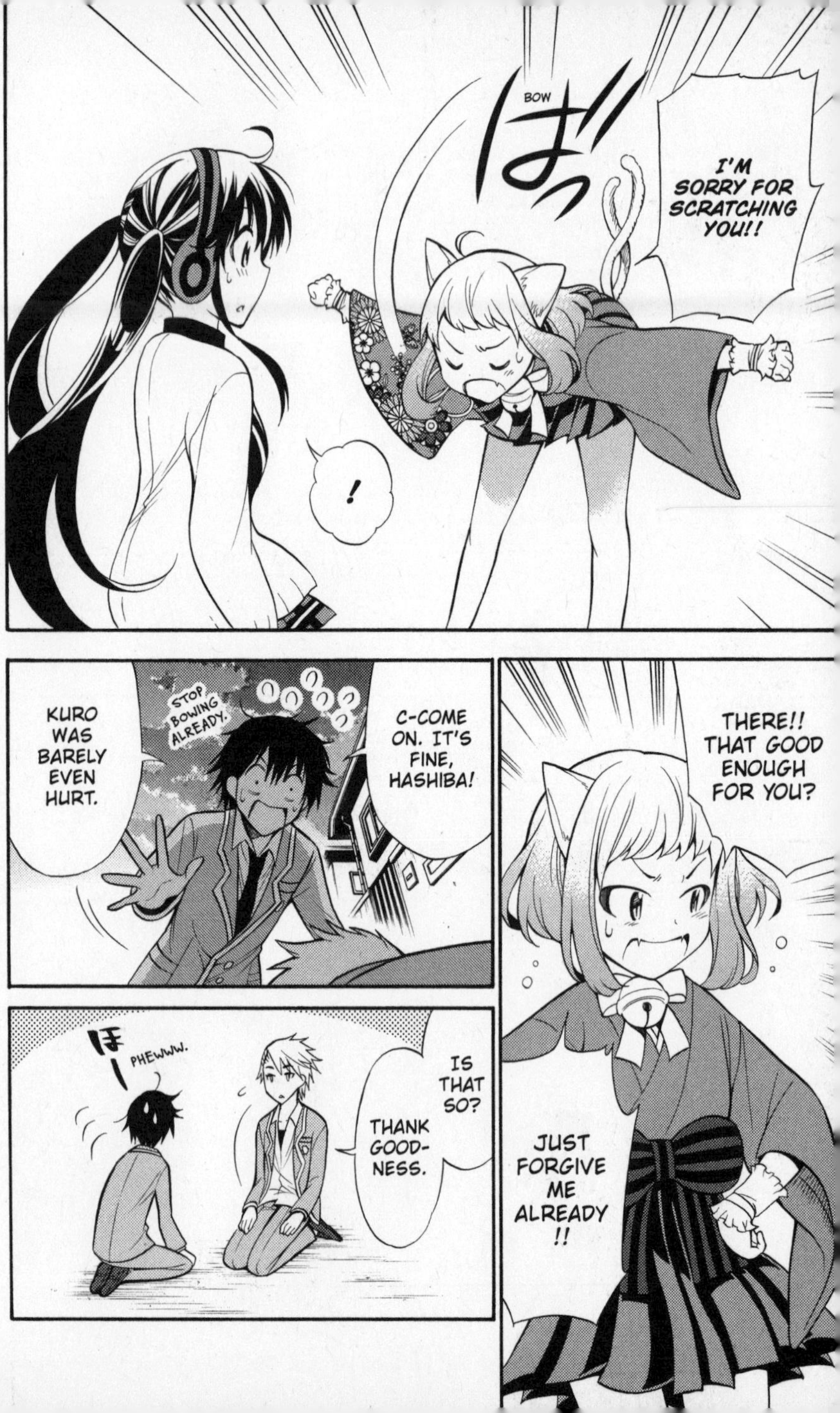
BOW
ばっ
I'M SORRY FOR SCRATCHING YOU!!
!
THERE!! THAT GOOD ENOUGH FOR YOU?
JUST FORGIVE ME ALREADY !!
C-COME ON. IT'S FINE, HASHIBA!
STOP BOWING ALREADY.
KURO WAS BARELY EVEN HURT.
IS THAT SO?
THANK GOODNESS.
ほー
PHEWWW.

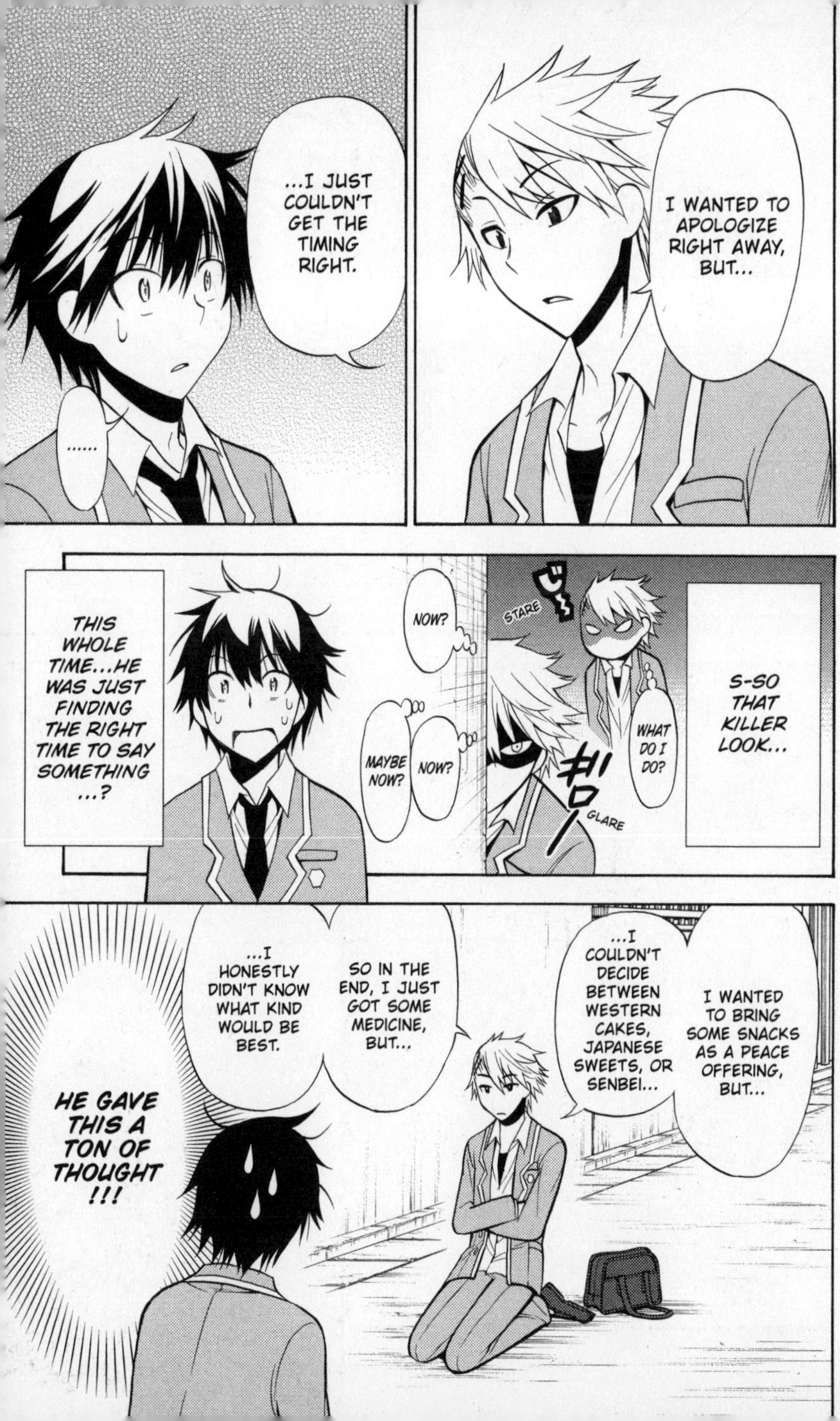
I WANTED TO APOLOGIZE RIGHT AWAY, BUT...
...I JUST COULDN'T GET THE TIMING RIGHT.
......
S-SO THAT KILLER LOOK...
STARE
WHAT DO I DO?
GLARE
NOW?
NOW?
MAYBE NOW?
THIS WHOLE TIME...HE WAS JUST FINDING THE RIGHT TIME TO SAY SOMETHING...?
I WANTED TO BRING SOME SNACKS AS A PEACE OFFERING, BUT...
...I COULDN'T DECIDE BETWEEN WESTERN CAKES, JAPANESE SWEETS, OR SENBEI...
SO IN THE END, I JUST GOT SOME MEDICINE, BUT...
...I HONESTLY DIDN'T KNOW WHAT KIND WOULD BE BEST.
HE GAVE THIS A TON OF THOUGHT!!!

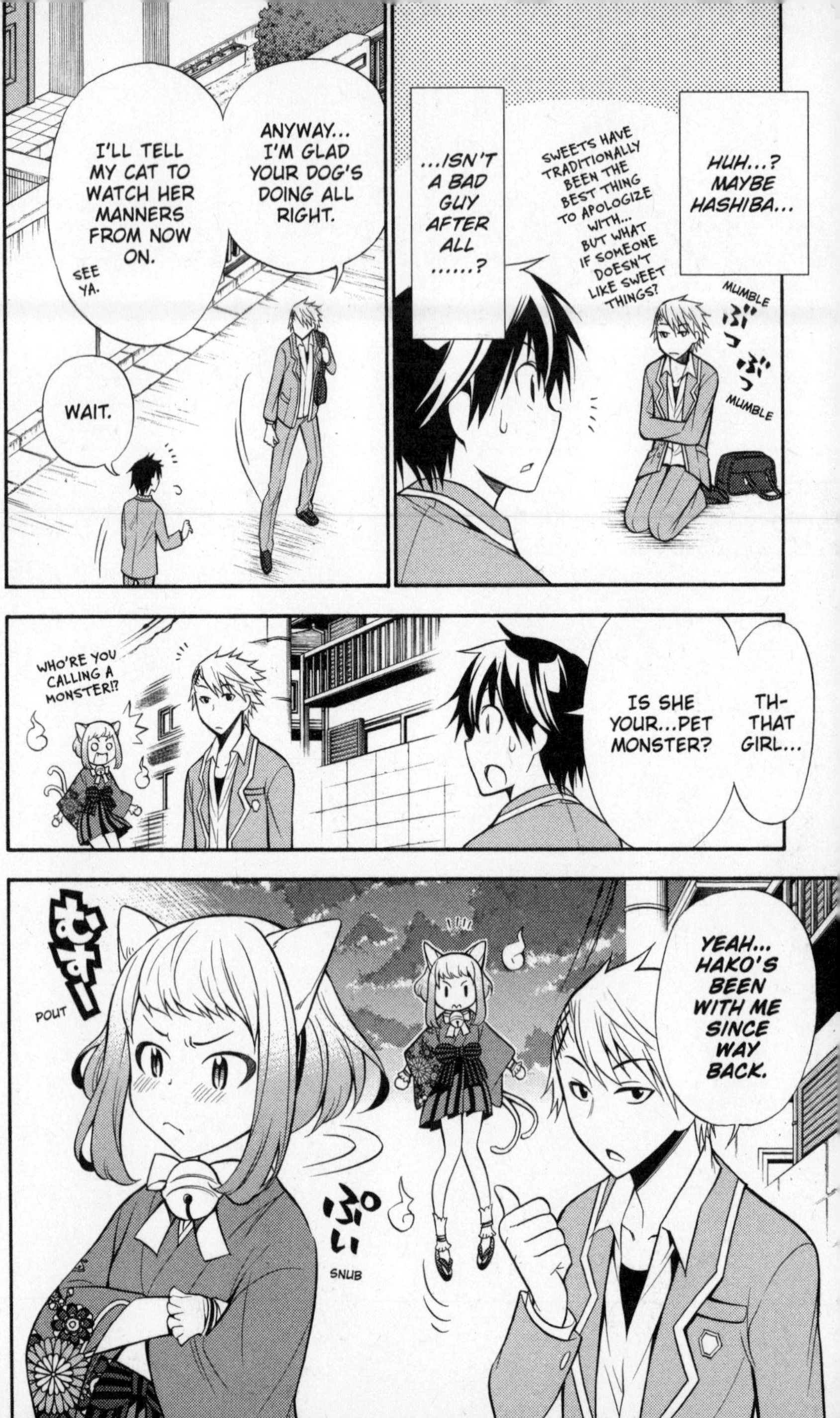
HUH...? MAYBE HASHIBA...
SWEETS HAVE TRADITIONALLY BEEN THE BEST THING TO APOLOGIZE WITH... BUT WHAT IF SOMEONE DOESN'T LIKE SWEET THINGS?
...ISN'T A BAD GUY AFTER ALL ......?
ぶつ MUMBLE
ぶつ MUMBLE
ANYWAY... I'M GLAD YOUR DOG'S DOING ALL RIGHT.
I'LL TELL MY CAT TO WATCH HER MANNERS FROM NOW ON.
SEE YA.
WAIT.
TH- THAT GIRL...
IS SHE YOUR...PET MONSTER?
WHO'RE YOU CALLING A MONSTER!?
YEAH... HAKO'S BEEN WITH ME SINCE WAY BACK.
むすー POUT
ぷい SNUB

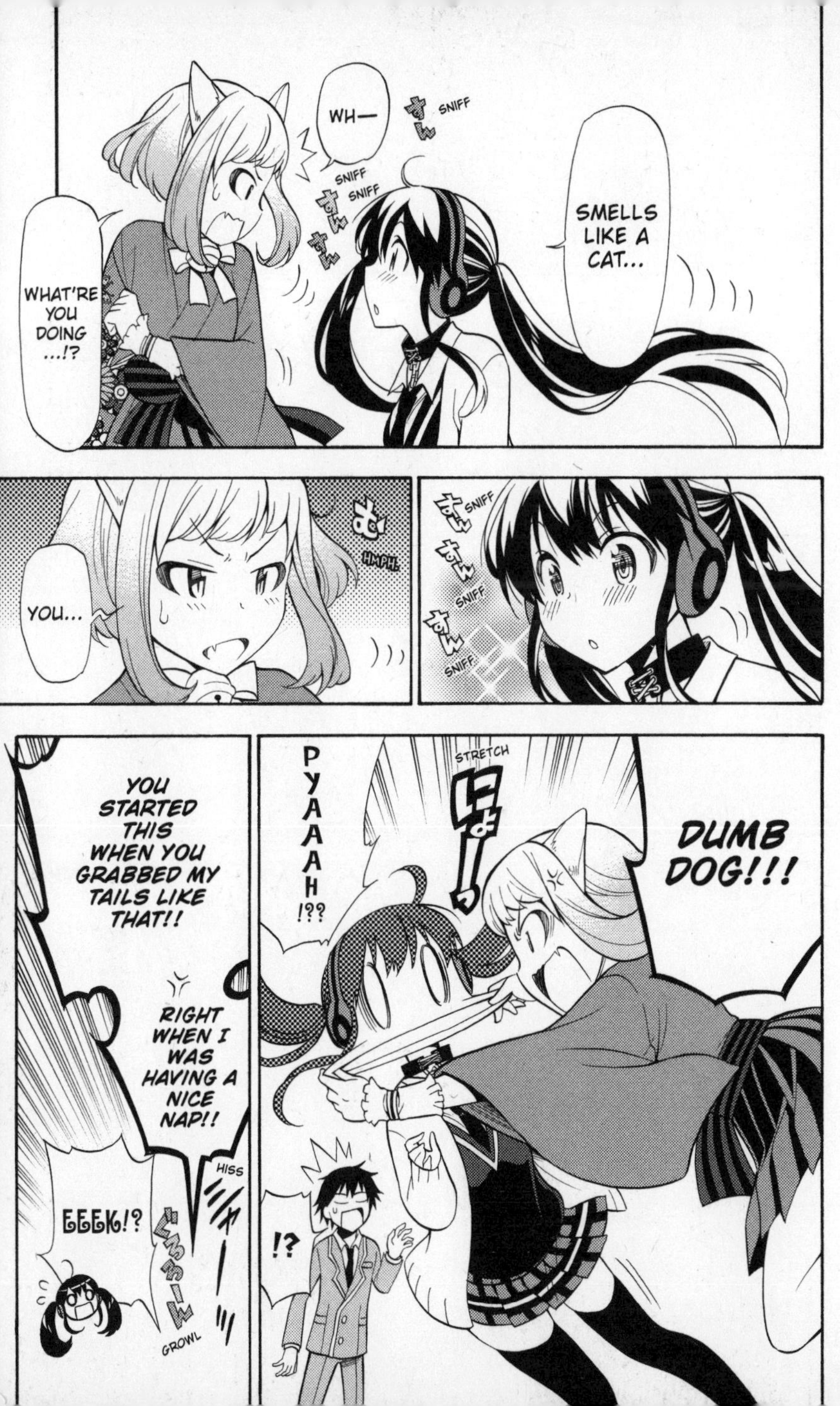
SNIFF
SMELLS LIKE A CAT...
SNIFF
SNIFF
WH—
WHAT'RE YOU DOING ...!?
SNIFF
SNIFF
SNIFF
HMPH.
YOU...
DUMB DOG!!!
STRETCH
PYAAAAH!??
!?
YOU STARTED THIS WHEN YOU GRABBED MY TAILS LIKE THAT!!
RIGHT WHEN I WAS HAVING A NICE NAP!!
HISS
GROWL
EEEK!?

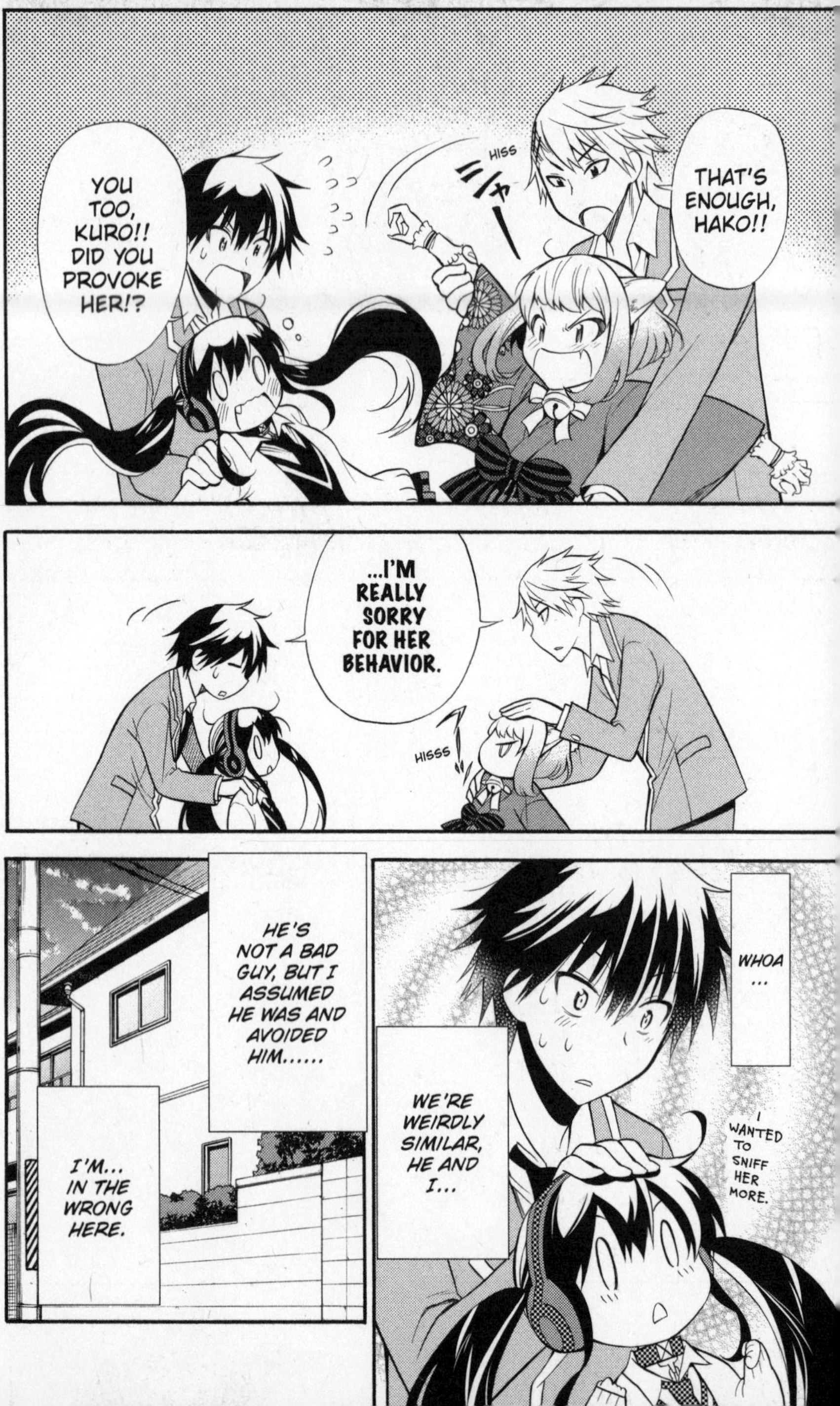
THAT'S ENOUGH, HAKO!!
HISS
YOU TOO, KURO!! DID YOU PROVOKE HER!?
...I'M REALLY SORRY FOR HER BEHAVIOR.
HISSS
WHOA ...
I WANTED TO SNIFF HER MORE.
WE'RE WEIRDLY SIMILAR, HE AND I...
HE'S NOT A BAD GUY, BUT I ASSUMED HE WAS AND AVOIDED HIM......
I'M... IN THE WRONG HERE.

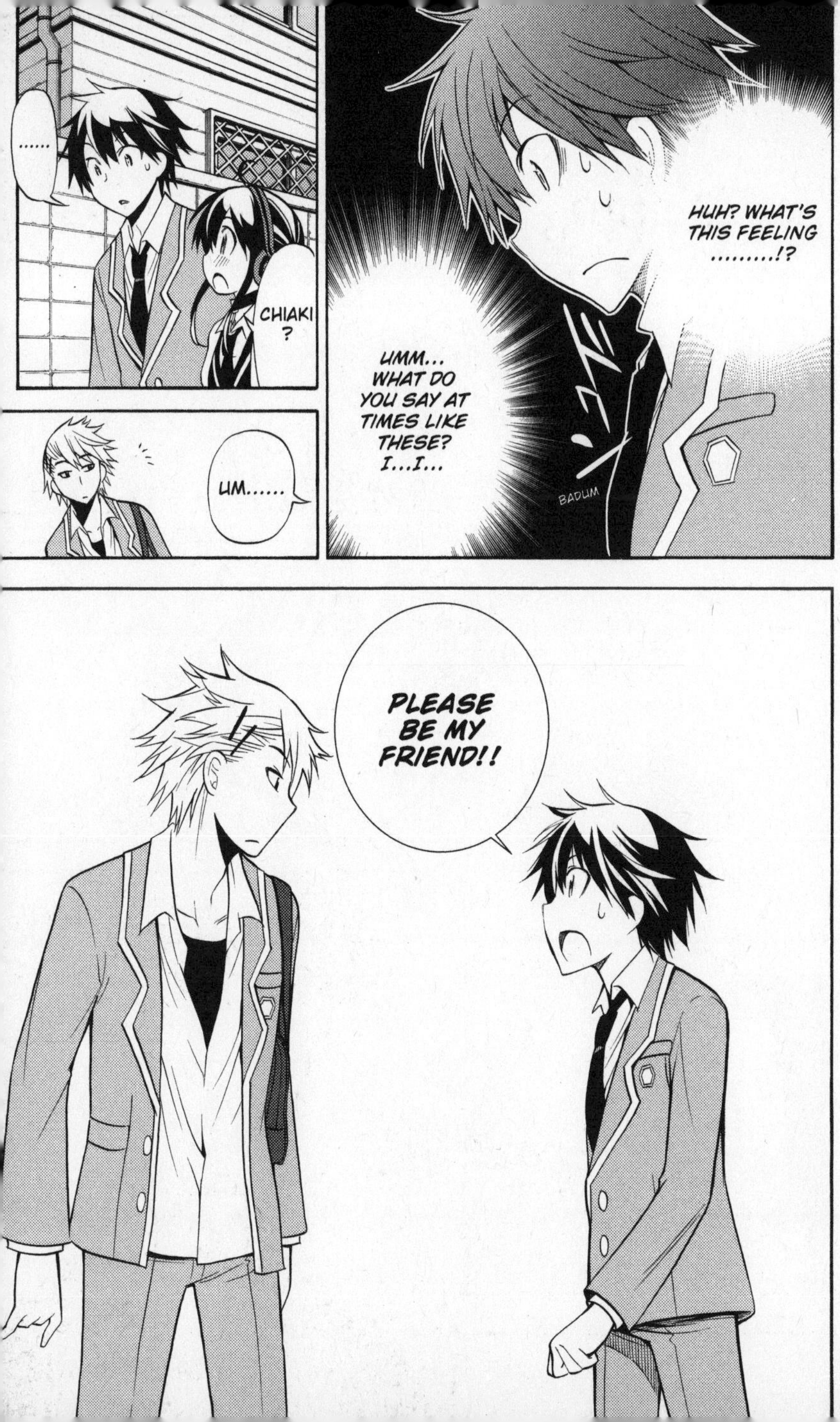
HUH? WHAT'S THIS FEELING ....!?
UMM... WHAT DO YOU SAY AT TIMES LIKE THESE? I...I...
BADUM
......
CHIAKI ?
UM......
PLEASE BE MY FRIEND!!

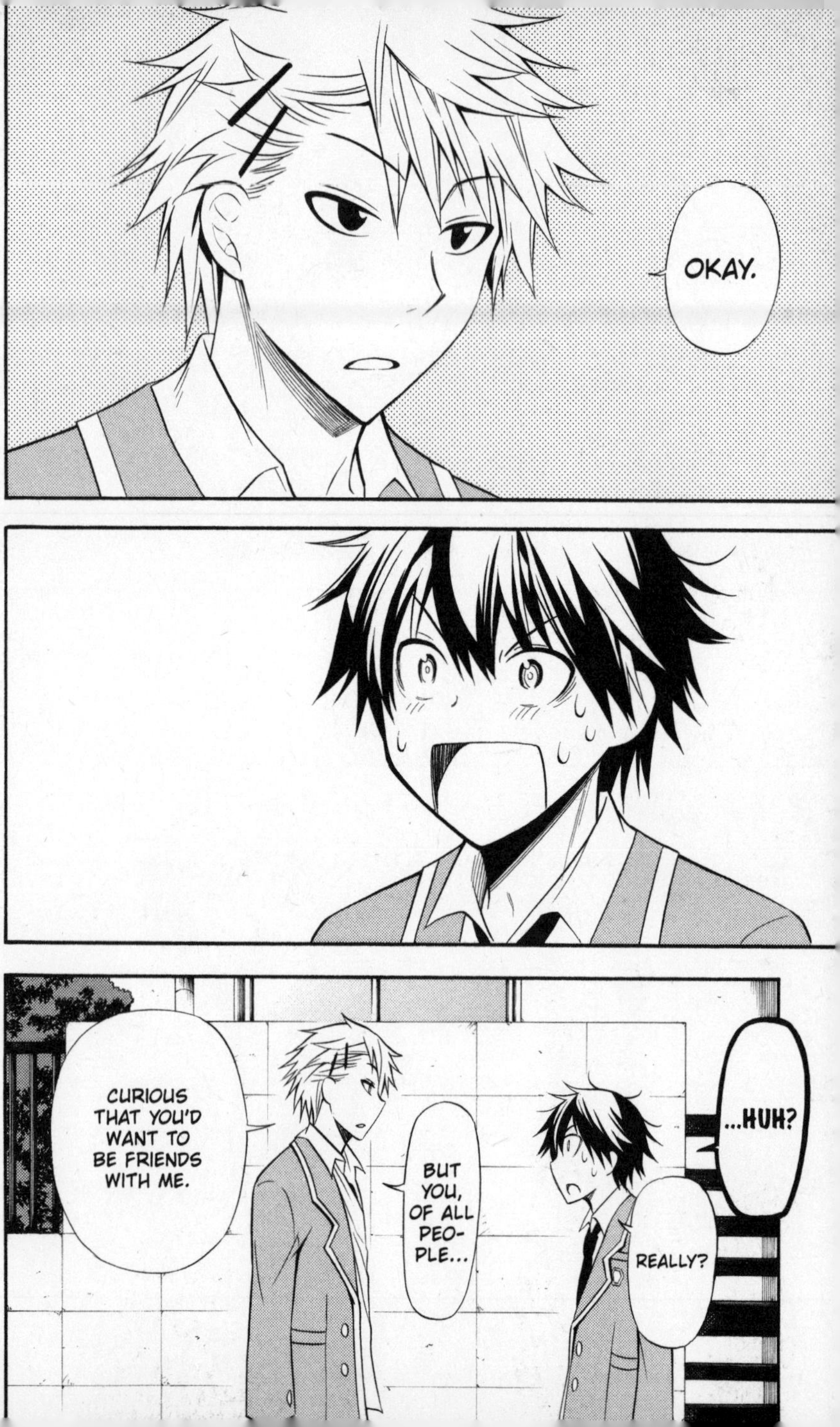
OKAY.
...HUH?
REALLY?
BUT YOU, OF ALL PEO-PLE...
CURIOUS THAT YOU'D WANT TO BE FRIENDS WITH ME.

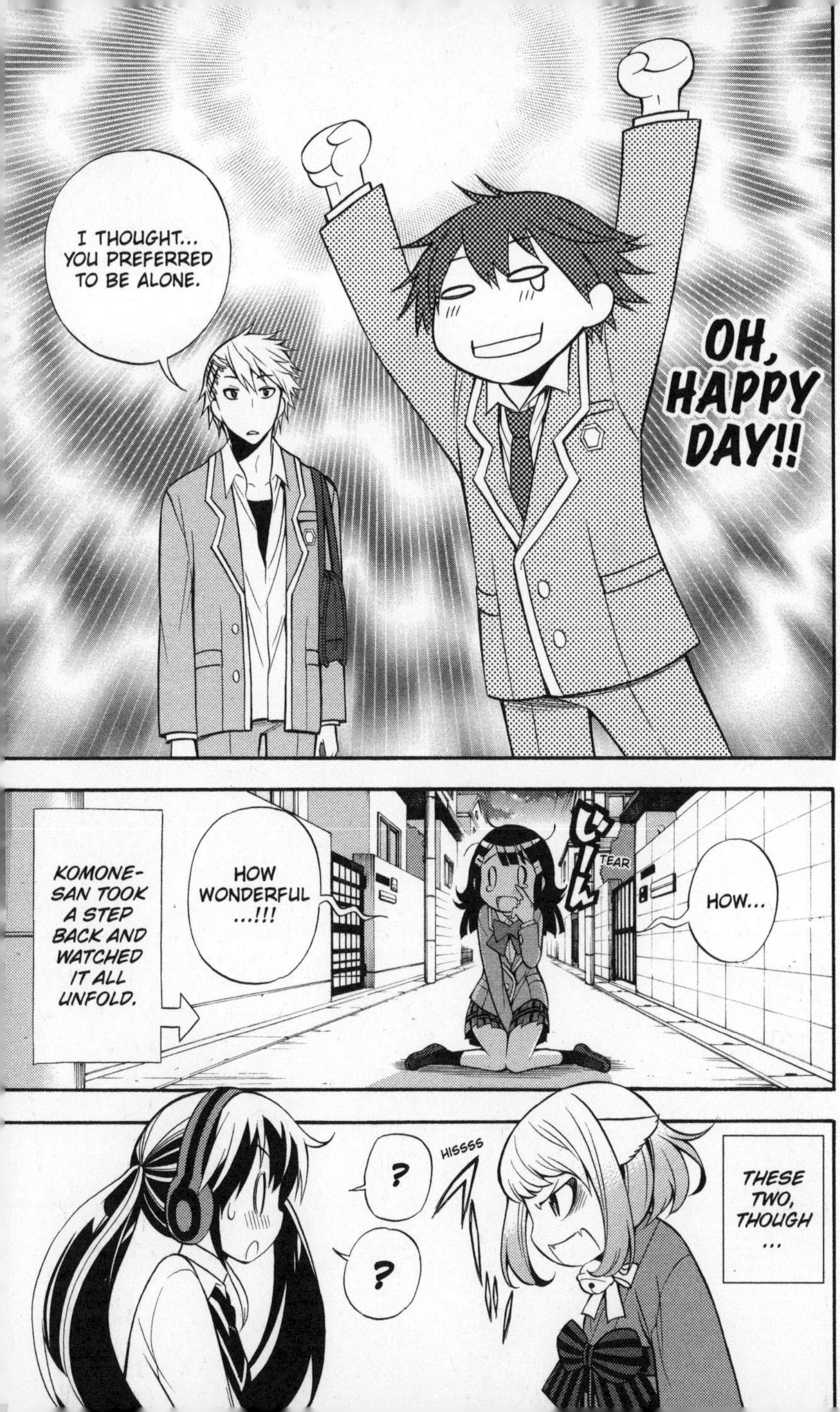
OH, HAPPY DAY!!
I THOUGHT... YOU PREFERRED TO BE ALONE.
HOW...
TEAR
HOW WONDERFUL ...!!!
KOMONE-SAN TOOK A STEP BACK AND WATCHED IT ALL UNFOLD.
THESE TWO, THOUGH ...
HISSSS
?
?

TODAY'S CERBERUS

HOW MANY YEARS SINCE I WROTE IN A DIARY?
TODAY, I MADE A FRIEND...

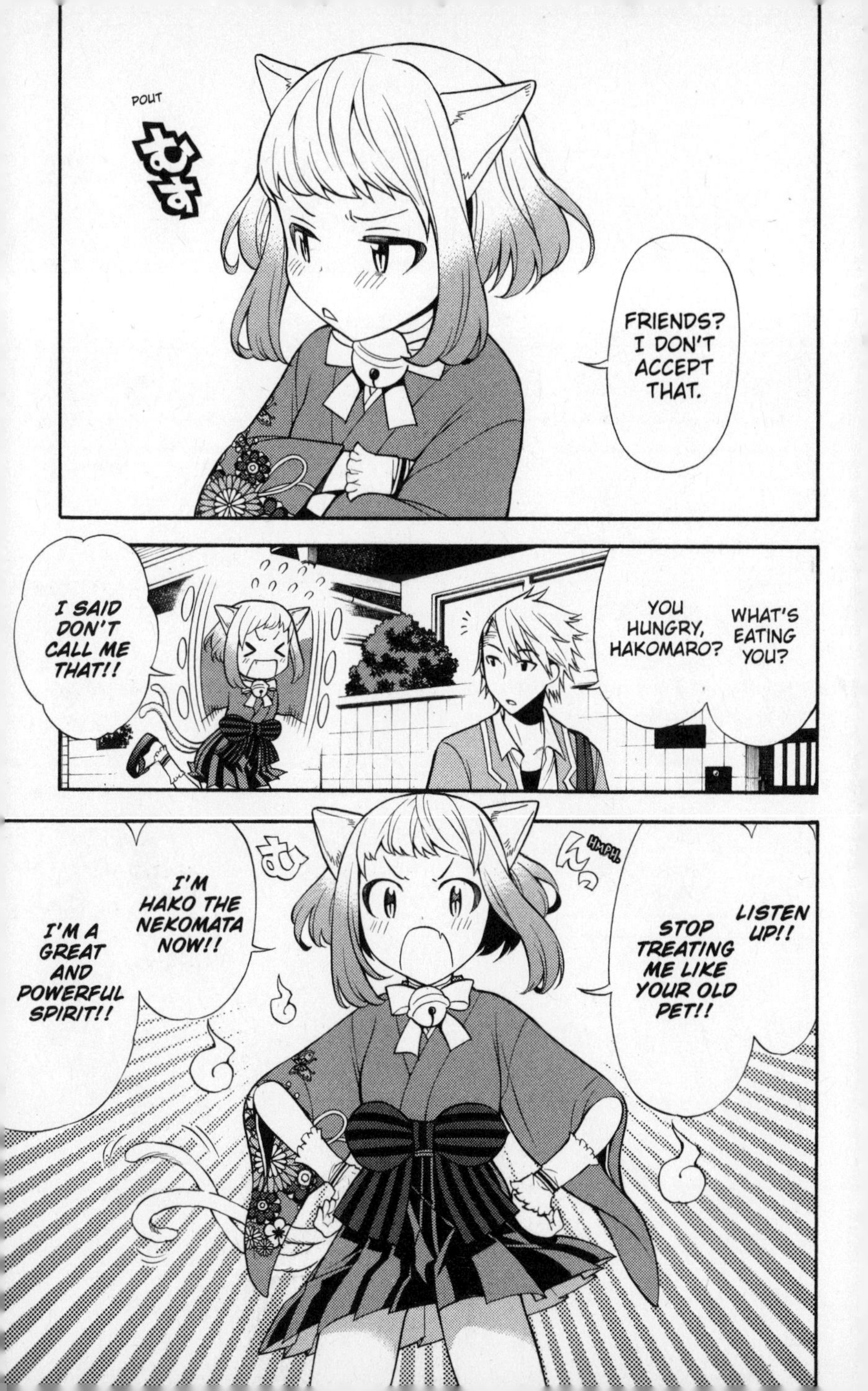

むす
POUT
FRIENDS? I DON'T ACCEPT THAT.
WHAT'S EATING YOU?
YOU HUNGRY, HAKOMARO?
I SAID DON'T CALL ME THAT!!
んっ
HMPH.
LISTEN UP!!
STOP TREATING ME LIKE YOUR OLD PET!!
む
I'M HAKO THE NEKOMATA NOW!!
I'M A GREAT AND POWERFUL SPIRIT!!

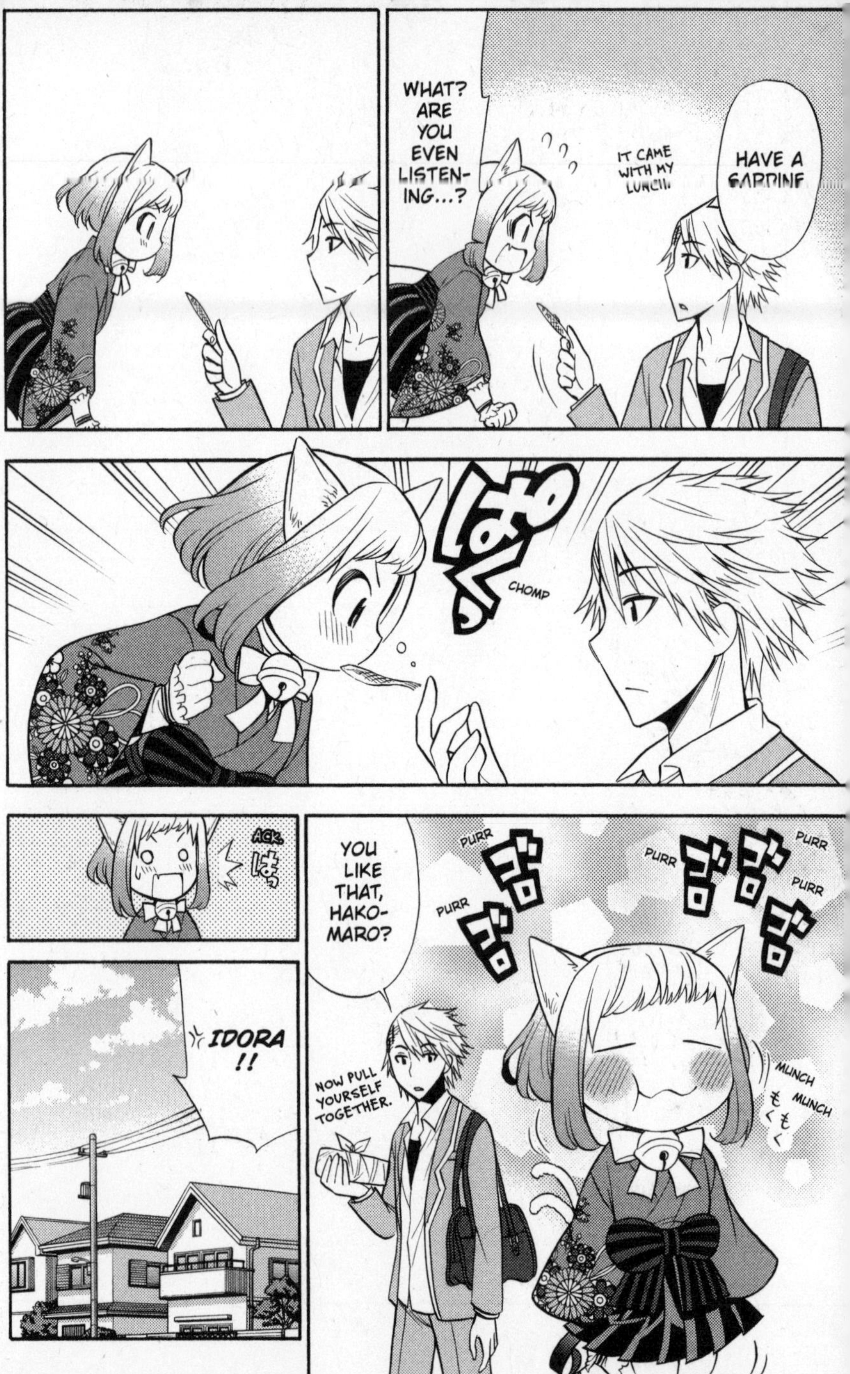
HAVE A SARDINE
IT CAME WITH MY LUNCH
WHAT? ARE YOU EVEN LISTEN-ING...?
ぱくっ
CHOMP
PURR
ゴロ
PURR
ゴロ
PURR
ゴロ
PURR
ゴロ
YOU LIKE THAT, HAKO-MARO?
NOW PULL YOURSELF TOGETHER.
MUNCH MUNCH
もくもく
ACK.
はっ
IDORA !!

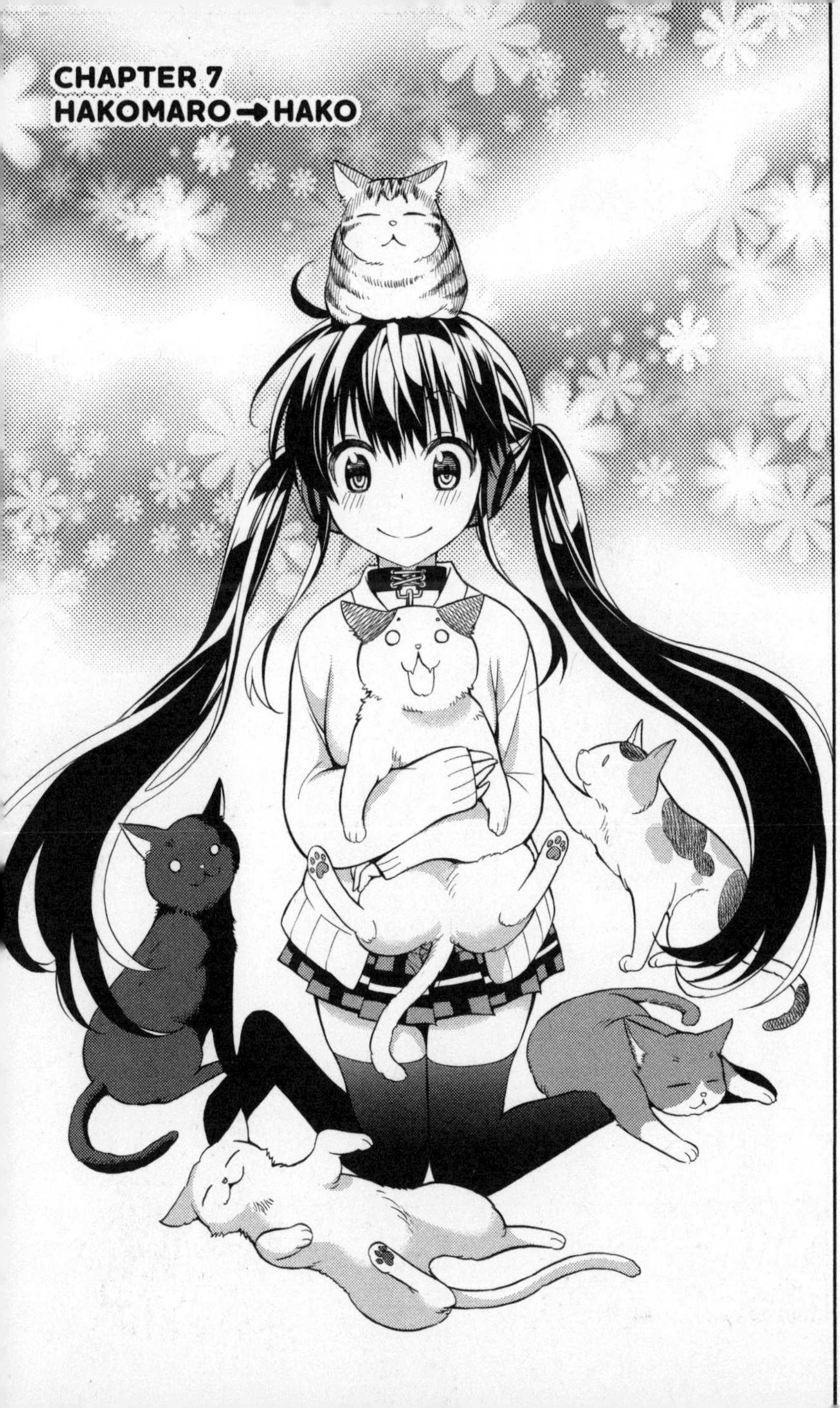
CHAPTER 7
HAKOMARO → HAKO

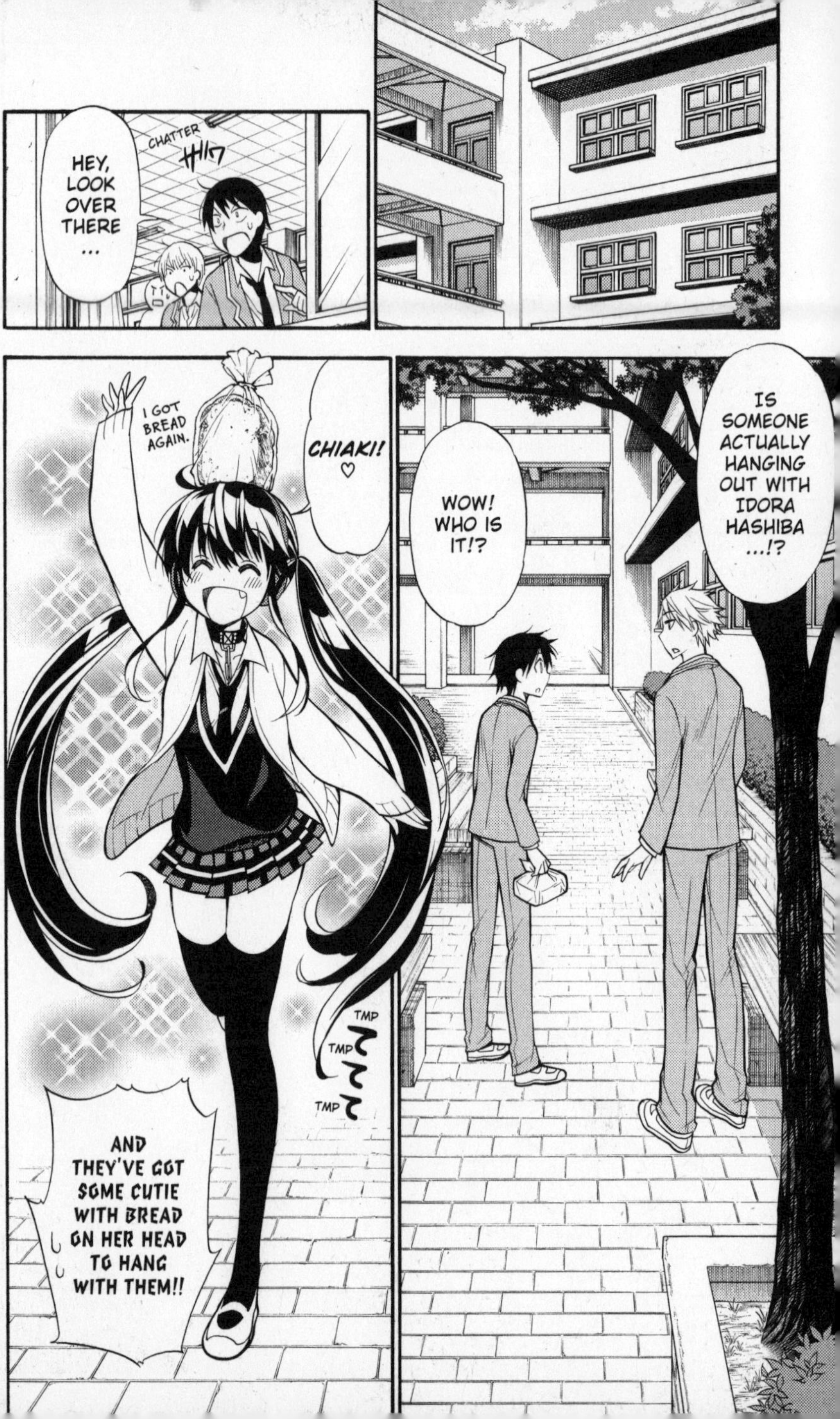
CHATTER
HEY, LOOK OVER THERE ...
IS SOMEONE ACTUALLY HANGING OUT WITH IDORA HASHIBA ...!?
WOW! WHO IS IT!?
CHIAKI! ♡
I GOT BREAD AGAIN.
TMP TMP TMP
AND THEY'VE GOT SOME CUTIE WITH BREAD ON HER HEAD TO HANG WITH THEM!!

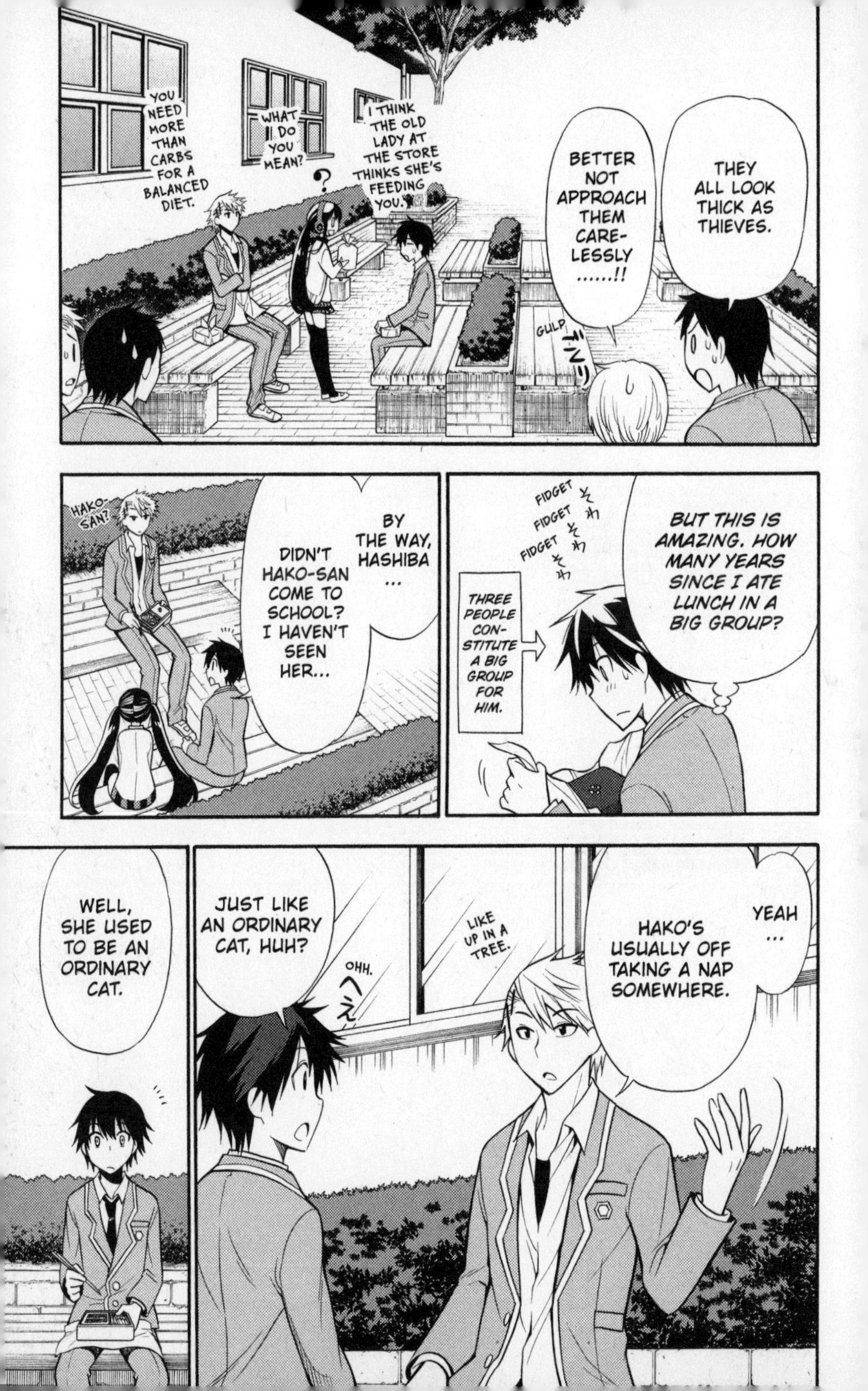
THEY ALL LOOK THICK AS THIEVES.
BETTER NOT APPROACH THEM CARE-LESSLY ......!!
GULP
ゴクリ
I THINK THE OLD LADY AT THE STORE THINKS SHE'S FEEDING YOU.
WHAT DO YOU MEAN?
YOU NEED MORE THAN CARBS FOR A BALANCED DIET.
BUT THIS IS AMAZING. HOW MANY YEARS SINCE I ATE LUNCH IN A BIG GROUP?
FIDGET FIDGET FIDGET
そわ そわ そわ
THREE PEOPLE CON-STITUTE A BIG GROUP FOR HIM.
BY THE WAY, HASHIBA ...
DIDN'T HAKO-SAN COME TO SCHOOL? I HAVEN'T SEEN HER...
HAKO-SAN?
YEAH ...
HAKO'S USUALLY OFF TAKING A NAP SOMEWHERE.
LIKE UP IN A TREE.
OHH.
へえ
JUST LIKE AN ORDINARY CAT, HUH?
WELL, SHE USED TO BE AN ORDINARY CAT.

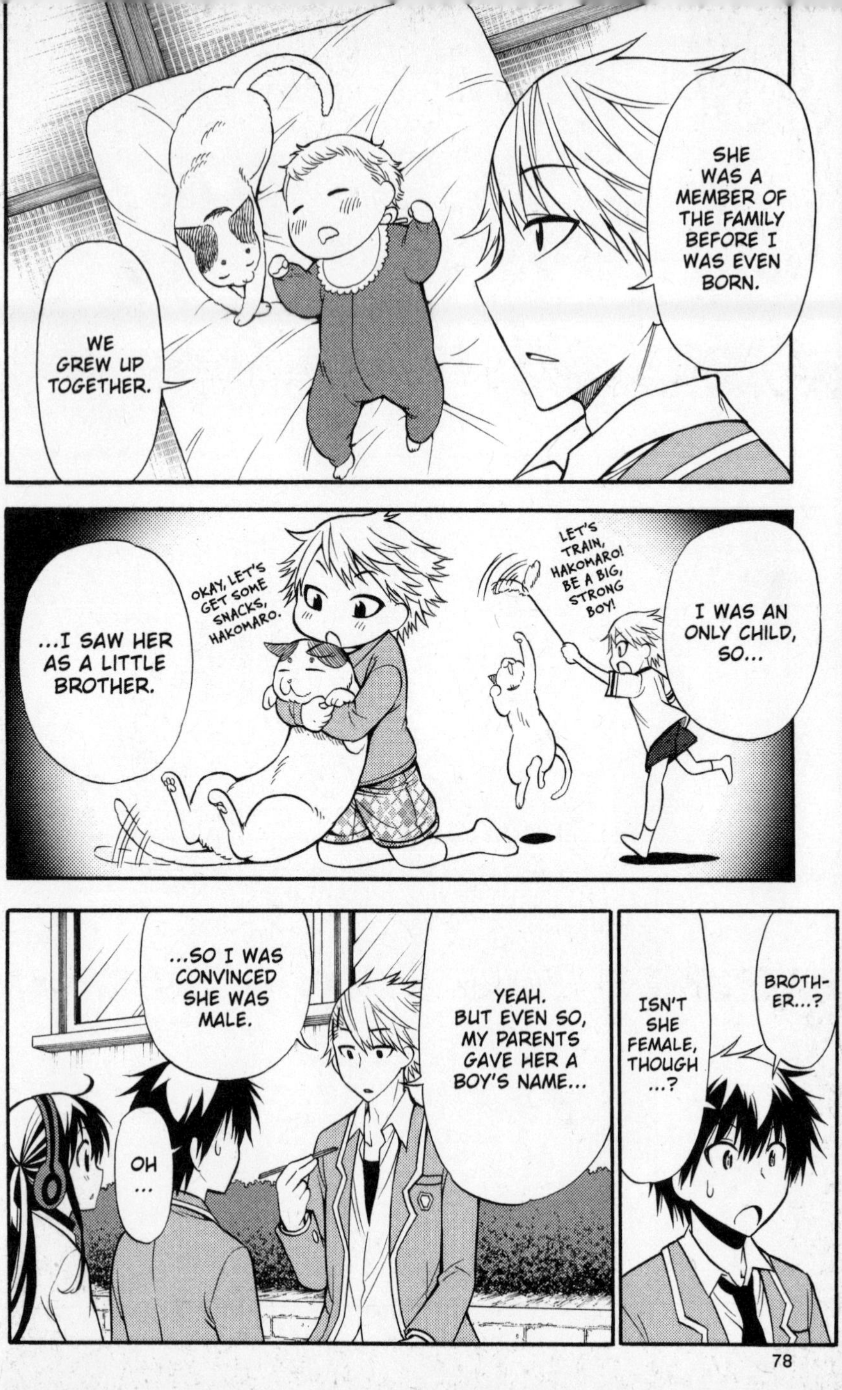

SHE WAS A MEMBER OF THE FAMILY BEFORE I WAS EVEN BORN.
WE GREW UP TOGETHER.
I WAS AN ONLY CHILD, SO...
LET'S TRAIN, HAKOMARO! BE A BIG, STRONG BOY!
OKAY, LET'S GET SOME SNACKS, HAKOMARO.
...I SAW HER AS A LITTLE BROTHER.
BROTH-ER...?
ISN'T SHE FEMALE, THOUGH ...?
YEAH. BUT EVEN SO, MY PARENTS GAVE HER A BOY'S NAME...
...SO I WAS CONVINCED SHE WAS MALE.
OH ...

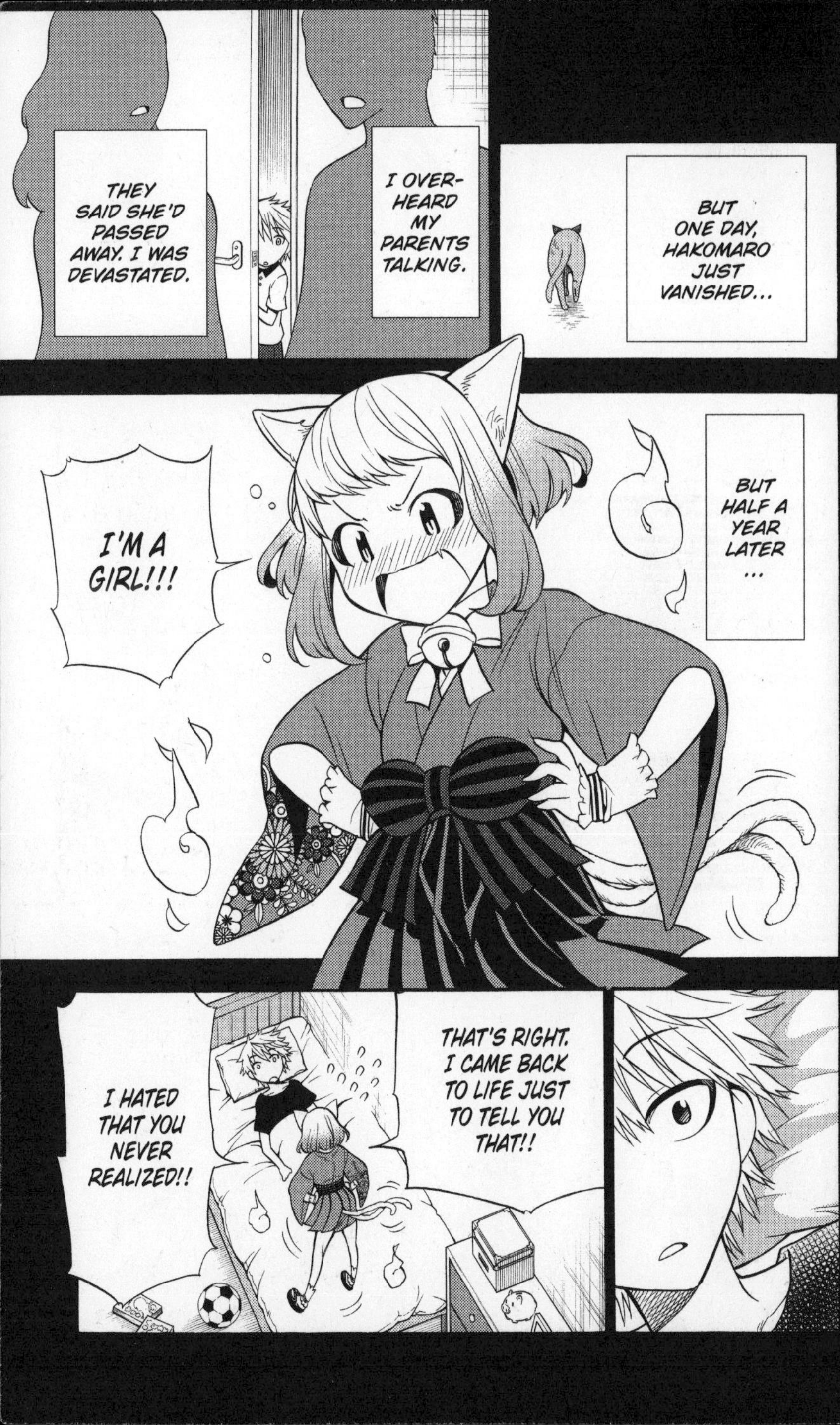
BUT ONE DAY, HAKOMARO JUST VANISHED...
I OVER-HEARD MY PARENTS TALKING.
THEY SAID SHE'D PASSED AWAY. I WAS DEVASTATED.
BUT HALF A YEAR LATER...
I'M A GIRL!!!
THAT'S RIGHT. I CAME BACK TO LIFE JUST TO TELL YOU THAT!!
I HATED THAT YOU NEVER REALIZED!!

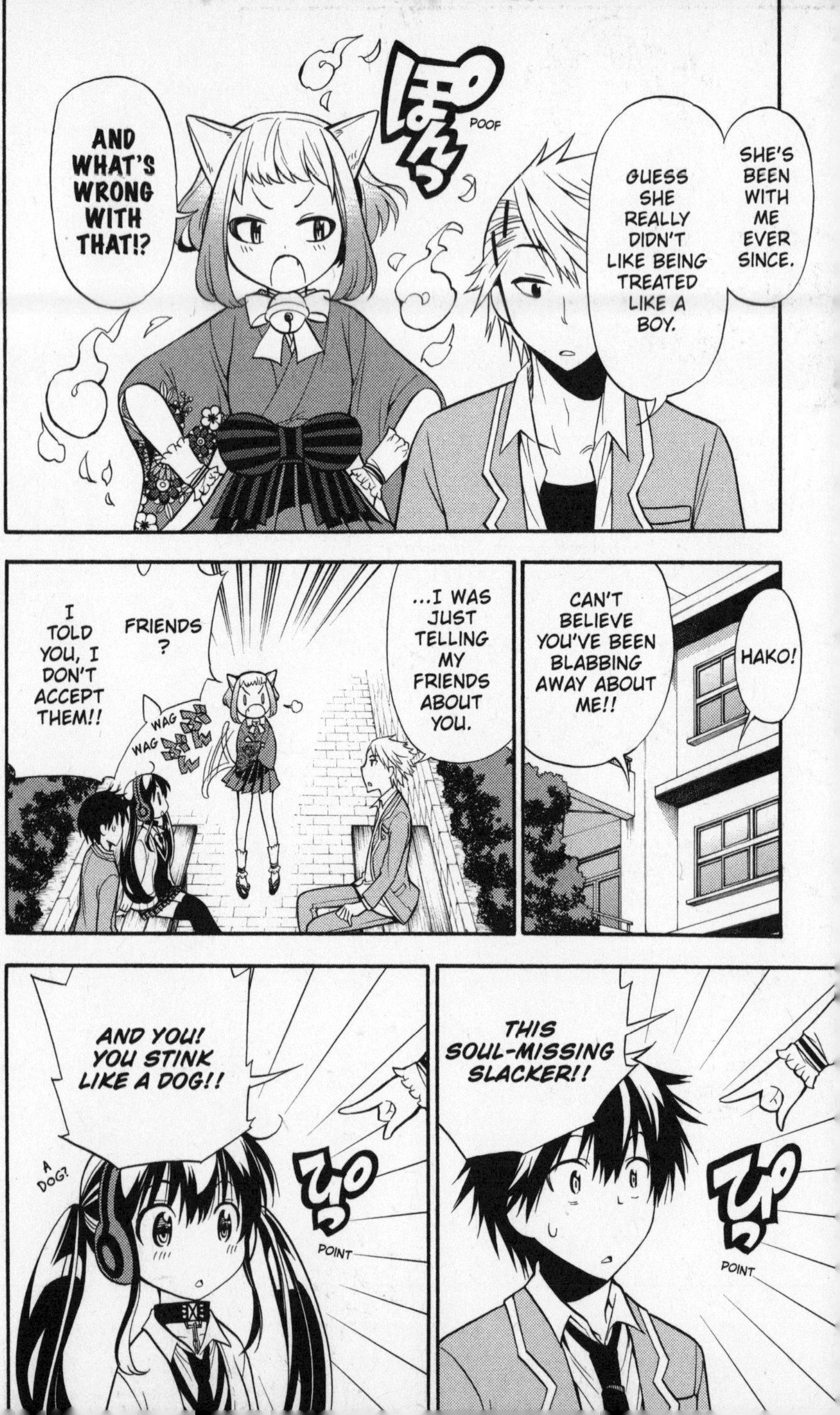
SHE'S BEEN WITH ME EVER SINCE.
GUESS SHE REALLY DIDN'T LIKE BEING TREATED LIKE A BOY.
POOF
AND WHAT'S WRONG WITH THAT!?
HAKO!
CAN'T BELIEVE YOU'VE BEEN BLABBING AWAY ABOUT ME!!
...I WAS JUST TELLING MY FRIENDS ABOUT YOU.
FRIENDS?
I TOLD YOU, I DON'T ACCEPT THEM!!
WAG WAG
THIS SOUL-MISSING SLACKER!!
POINT
AND YOU! YOU STINK LIKE A DOG!!
POINT
A DOG?

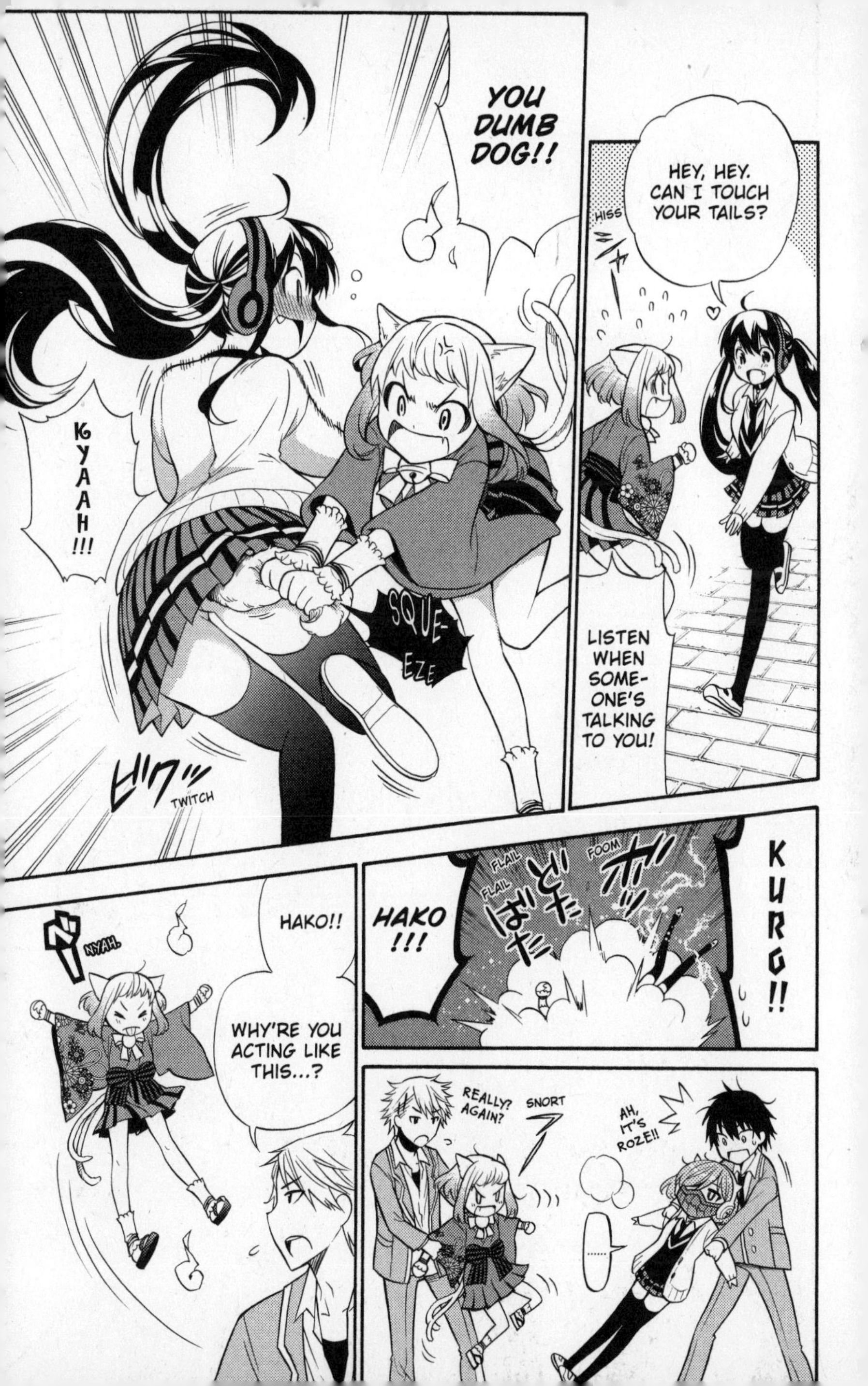
HEY, HEY. CAN I TOUCH YOUR TAILS?
HISS
LISTEN WHEN SOME-ONE'S TALKING TO YOU!
YOU DUMB DOG!!
KYAAAH!!!
SQUE-EZE
TWITCH
KURG!!
FOOM
FLAIL FLAIL
HAKO!!!
AH, IT'S ROZE!!
SNORT
REALLY? AGAIN?
......
HAKO!!
WHY'RE YOU ACTING LIKE THIS...?
NYAH.

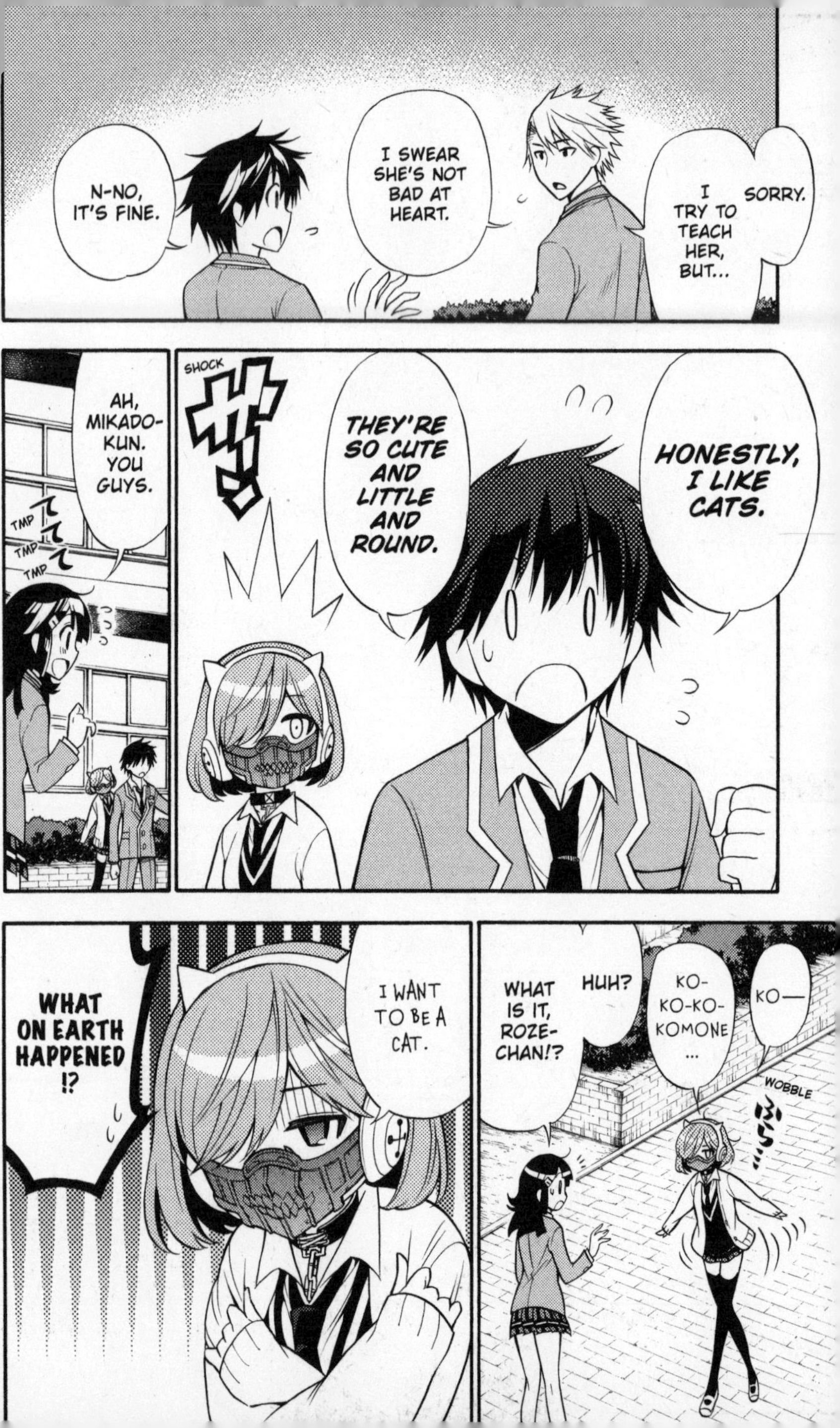
SORRY. I TRY TO TEACH HER, BUT...
I SWEAR SHE'S NOT BAD AT HEART.
N-NO, IT'S FINE.
HONESTLY, I LIKE CATS.
THEY'RE SO CUTE AND LITTLE AND ROUND.
SHOCK
AH, MIKADO-KUN. YOU GUYS.
TMP
TMP
TMP
KO—
KO-KO-KO-KOMONE...
WOBBLE
HUH?
WHAT IS IT, ROZE-CHAN!?
I WANT TO BE A CAT.
WHAT ON EARTH HAPPENED!?

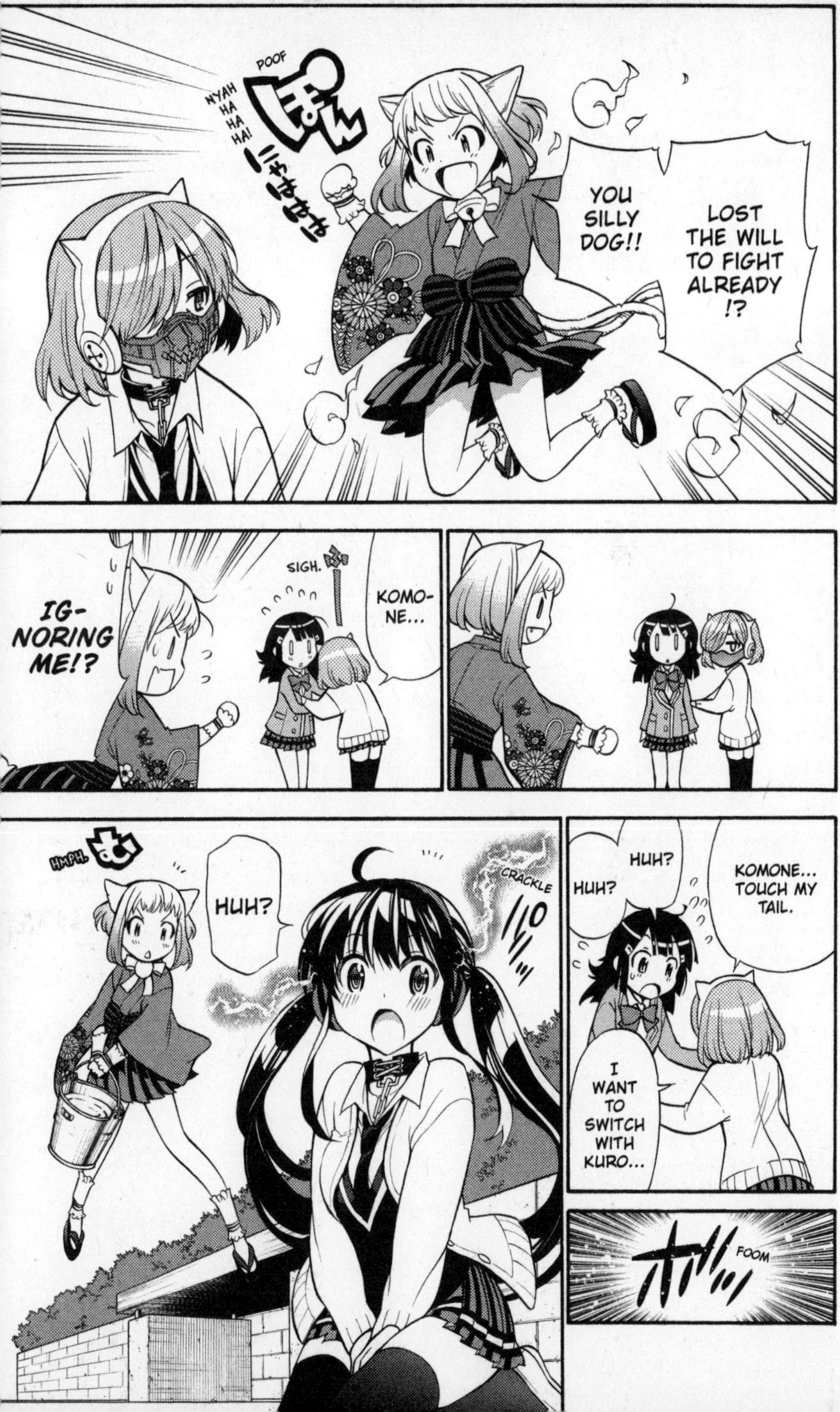

LOST THE WILL TO FIGHT ALREADY !?
YOU SILLY DOG!!
POOF
ぽん
NYAH HA HA HA!
にゃははは
KOMONE...
SIGH.
IG-NORING ME!?
KOMONE... TOUCH MY TAIL.
HUH?
HUH?
I WANT TO SWITCH WITH KURO...
FOOM
CRACKLE
HUH?
HMPH.

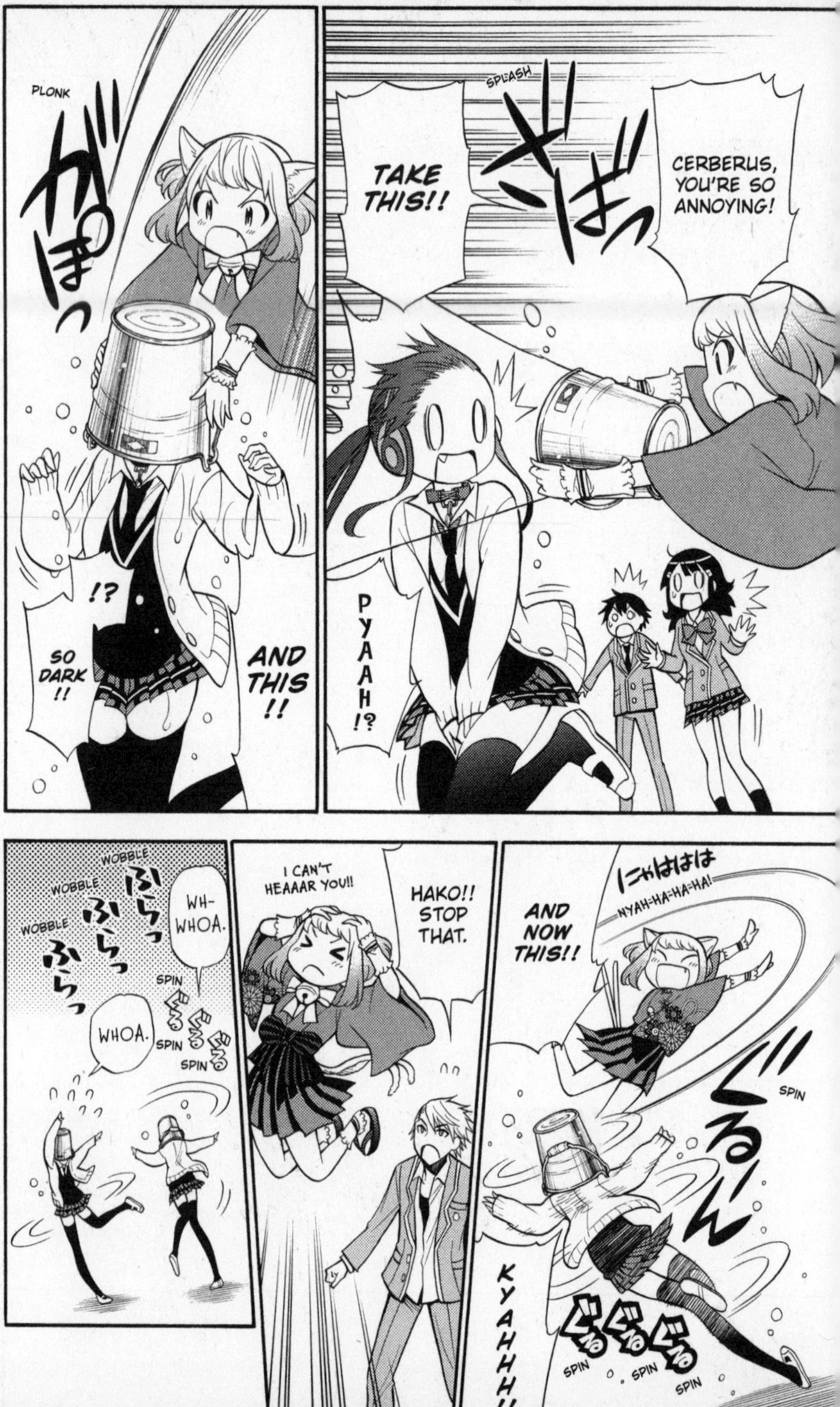
CERBERUS, YOU'RE SO ANNOYING!
SPLASH
ざばっ
TAKE THIS!!
PYAAAH!?
PLONK
かぽっ
AND THIS!!
!?
SO DARK!!
にゃははは
NYAH-HA-HA-HA!
AND NOW THIS!!
SPIN
ぐるーん
KYAHHH!!
ぐるぐるぐる
SPIN SPIN SPIN
HAKO!! STOP THAT.
I CAN'T HEAAAR YOU!!
WH-WHOA.
WOBBLE
ふらっ
WOBBLE
ふらっ
WOBBLE
ふらっ
SPIN
ぐるぐる
SPIN
SPIN
WHOA.

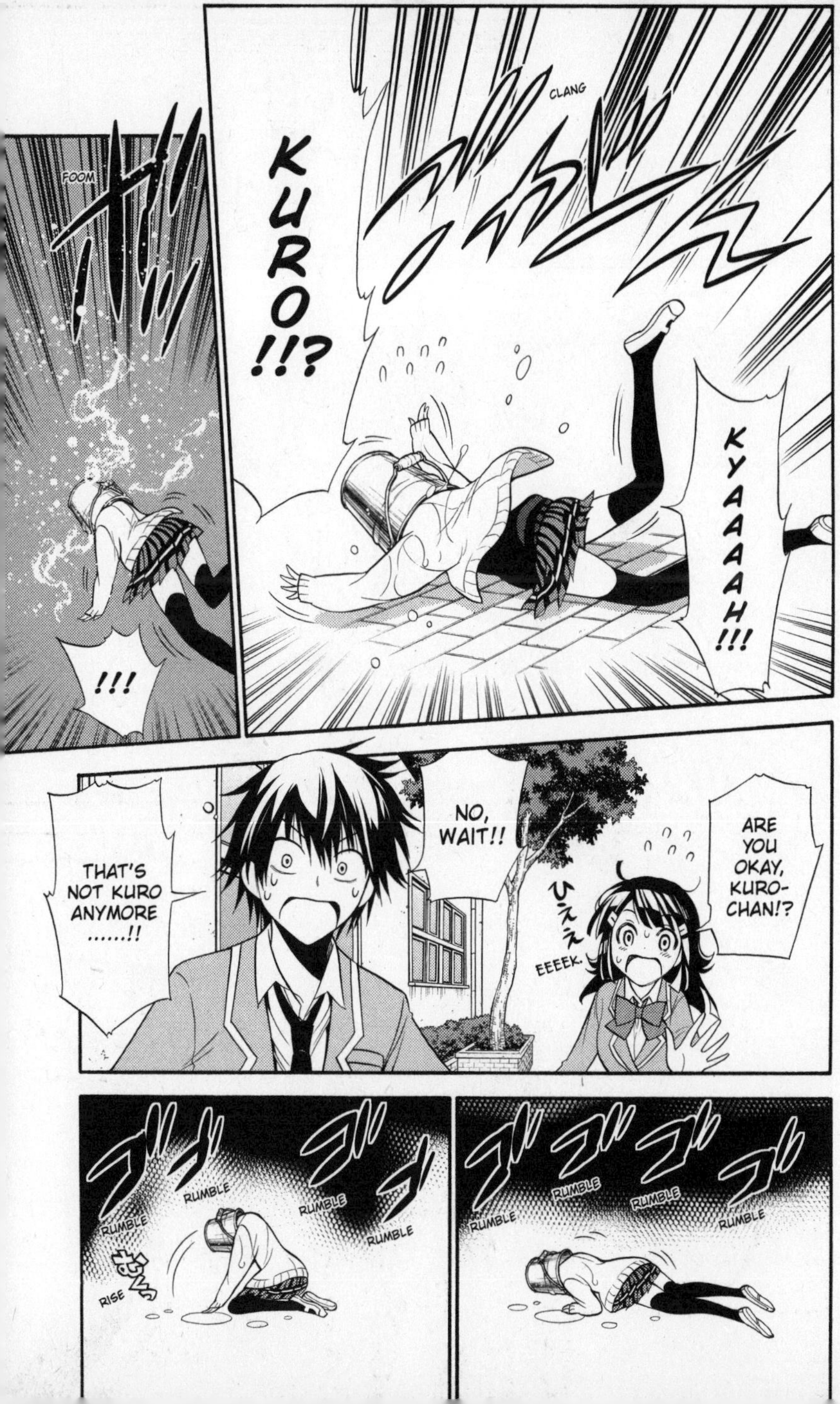
CLANG
KURO!!?
KYAAAAAH!!!
FOOM
!!!
ARE YOU OKAY, KURO-CHAN!?
ひえぇ
EEEEK.
NO, WAIT!!
THAT'S NOT KURO ANYMORE ......!!
RUMBLE
RUMBLE
RUMBLE
RUMBLE
RUMBLE
RUMBLE
RUMBLE
RUMBLE
RISE

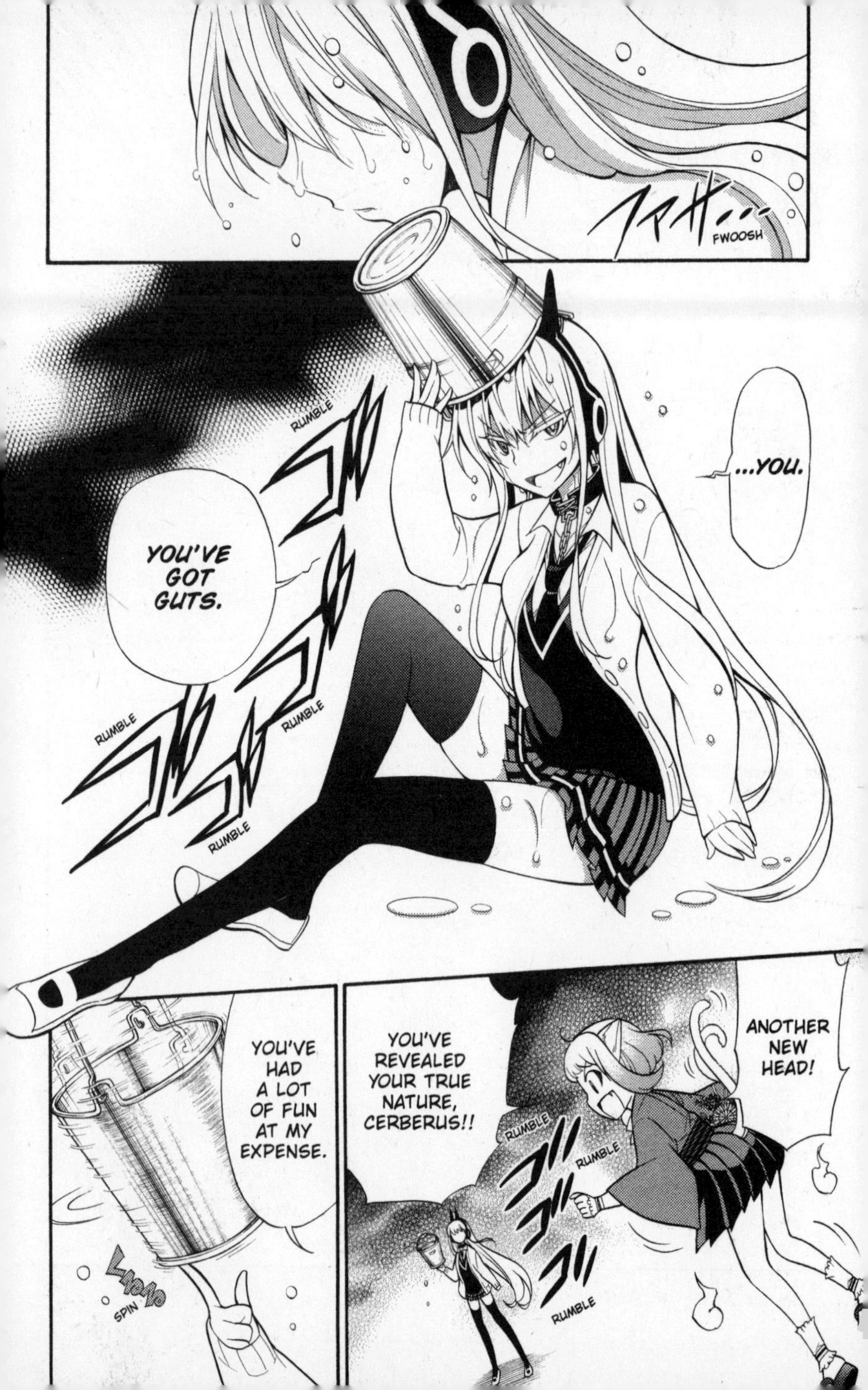
ファサ…
FWOOSH
...YOU.
YOU'VE GOT GUTS.
RUMBLE
RUMBLE
RUMBLE
RUMBLE
ANOTHER NEW HEAD!
YOU'VE REVEALED YOUR TRUE NATURE, CERBERUS!!
RUMBLE
RUMBLE
RUMBLE
YOU'VE HAD A LOT OF FUN AT MY EXPENSE.
SPIN

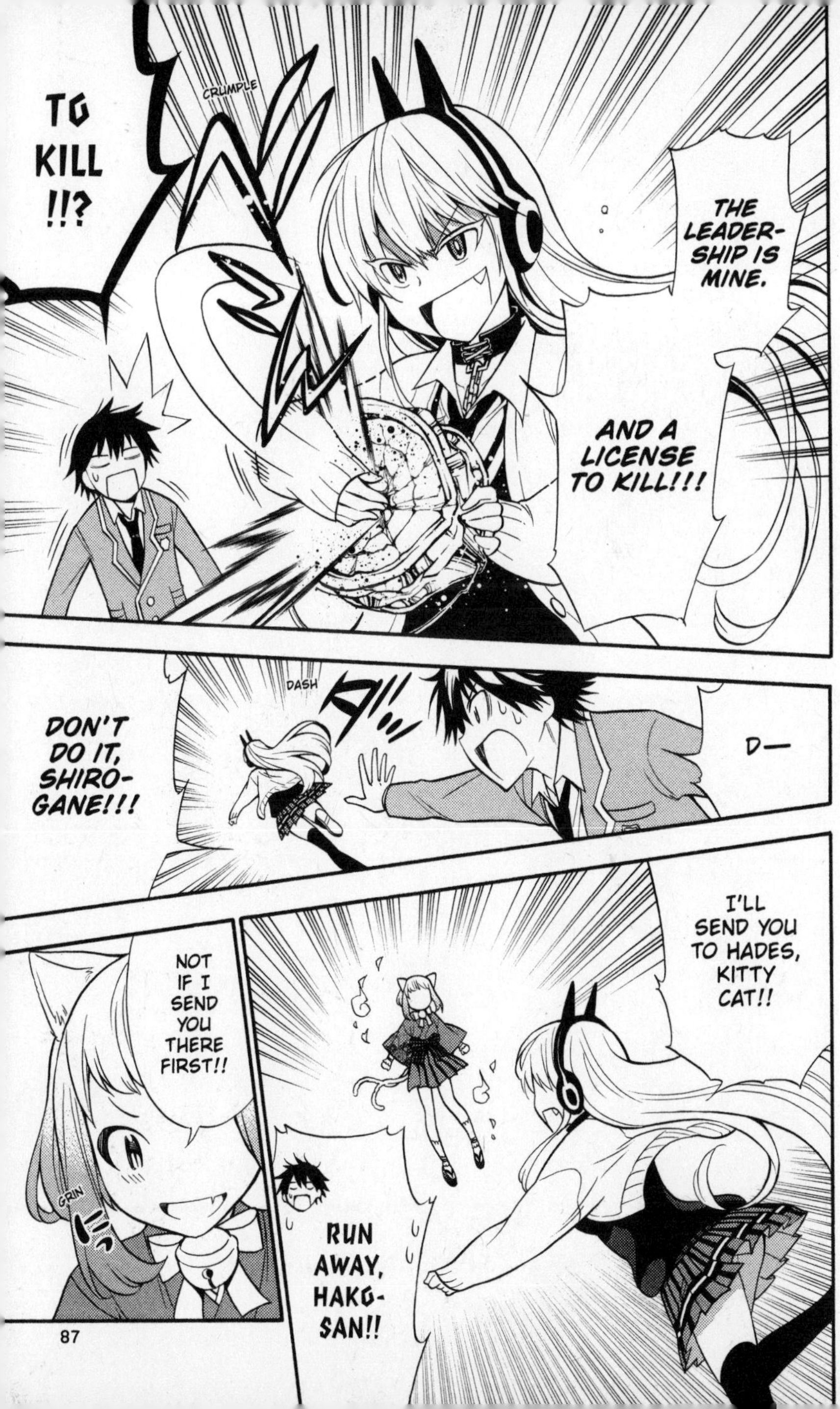
THE LEADER-SHIP IS MINE.
AND A LICENSE TO KILL!!!
CRUMPLE
TO KILL!!?
D—
DASH
DON'T DO IT, SHIRO-GANE!!!
I'LL SEND YOU TO HADES, KITTY CAT!!
RUN AWAY, HAKO-SAN!!
NOT IF I SEND YOU THERE FIRST!!
GRIN

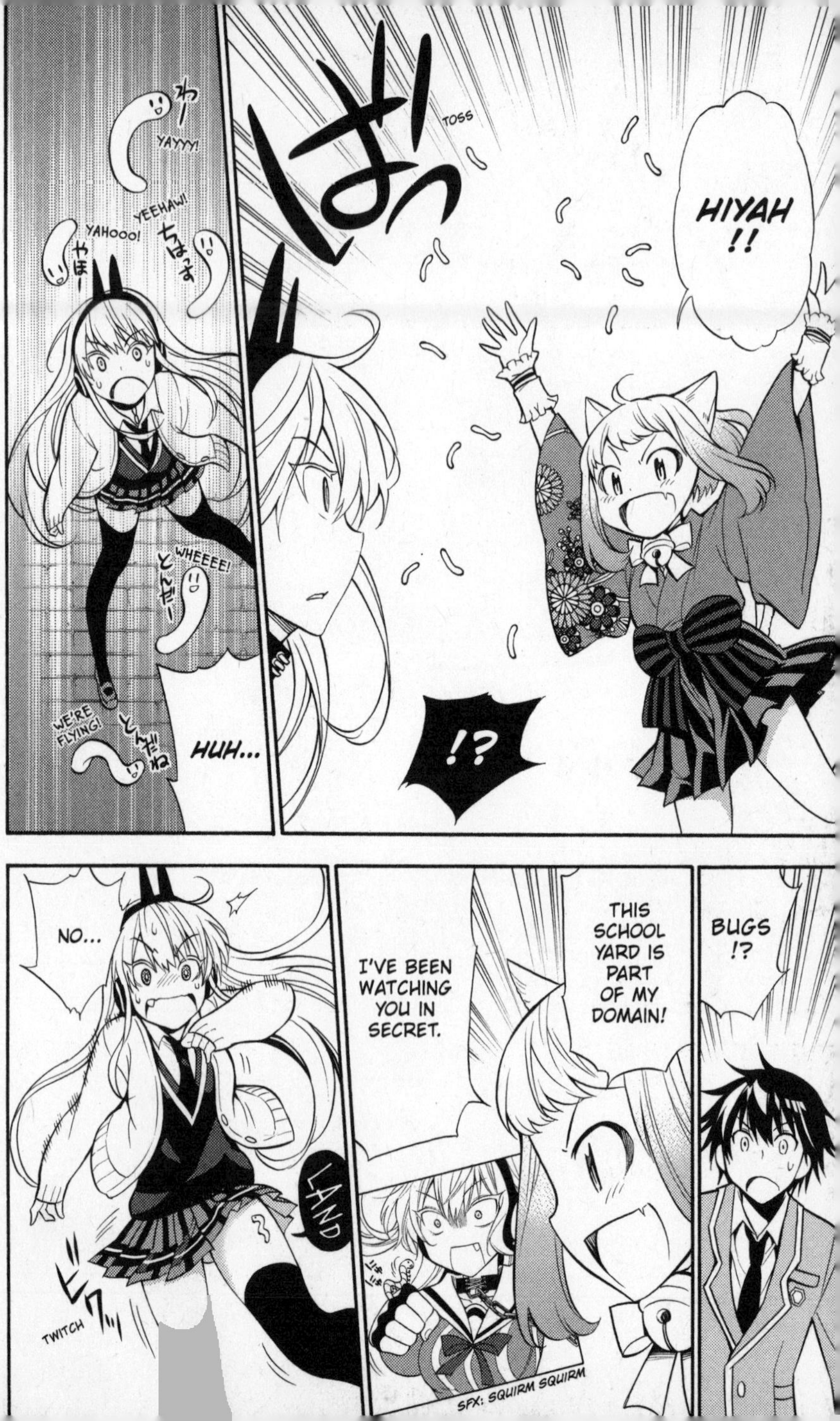
HIYAH!!
ぱっ
TOSS
!?
わー
YAYYY!
ちはっす
YEEHAW!
やほー
YAHOOO!
とんだー
WHEEEE!
とんだね
WE'RE FLYING!
HUH...
BUGS!?
THIS SCHOOL YARD IS PART OF MY DOMAIN!
I'VE BEEN WATCHING YOU IN SECRET.
SFX: SQUIRM SQUIRM
NO...
LAND
ビクッ
TWITCH

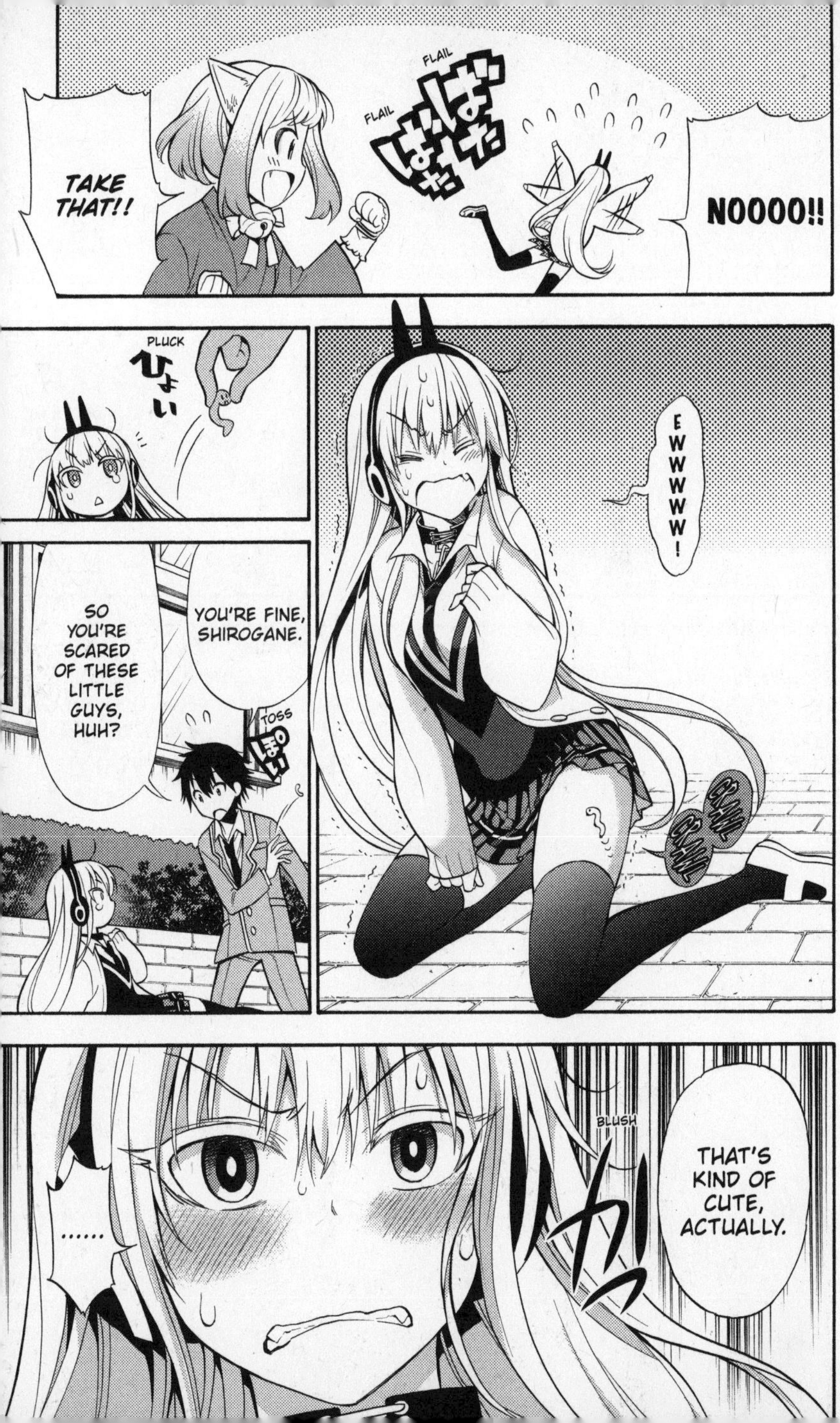
NOOOO!!
FLAIL
FLAIL
TAKE THAT!!
EWWWWWW!
CRAWL
CRAWL
PLUCK
ひょい
YOU'RE FINE, SHIROGANE.
TOSS
SO YOU'RE SCARED OF THESE LITTLE GUYS, HUH?
THAT'S KIND OF CUTE, ACTUALLY.
BLUSH
......

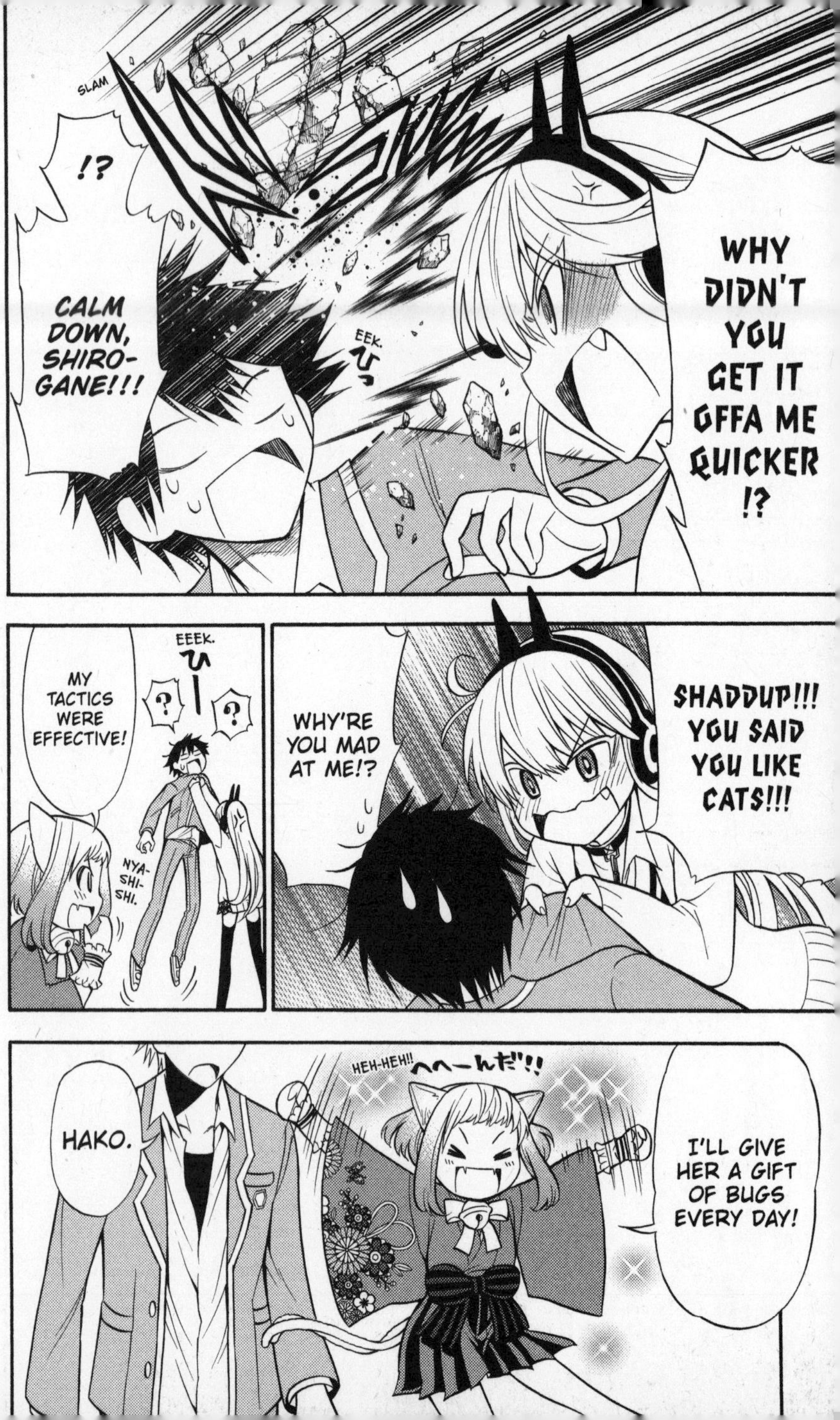
WHY DIDN'T YOU GET IT OFFA ME QUICKER!?
SLAM
EEK. ひっ
!?
CALM DOWN, SHIRO-GANE!!!
SHADDUP!!! YOU SAID YOU LIKE CATS!!!
WHY'RE YOU MAD AT ME!?
EEEK. ひー
MY TACTICS WERE EFFECTIVE!
NYA-SHI-SHI.
I'LL GIVE HER A GIFT OF BUGS EVERY DAY!
HEH-HEH!! へへーんだ!!
HAKO.

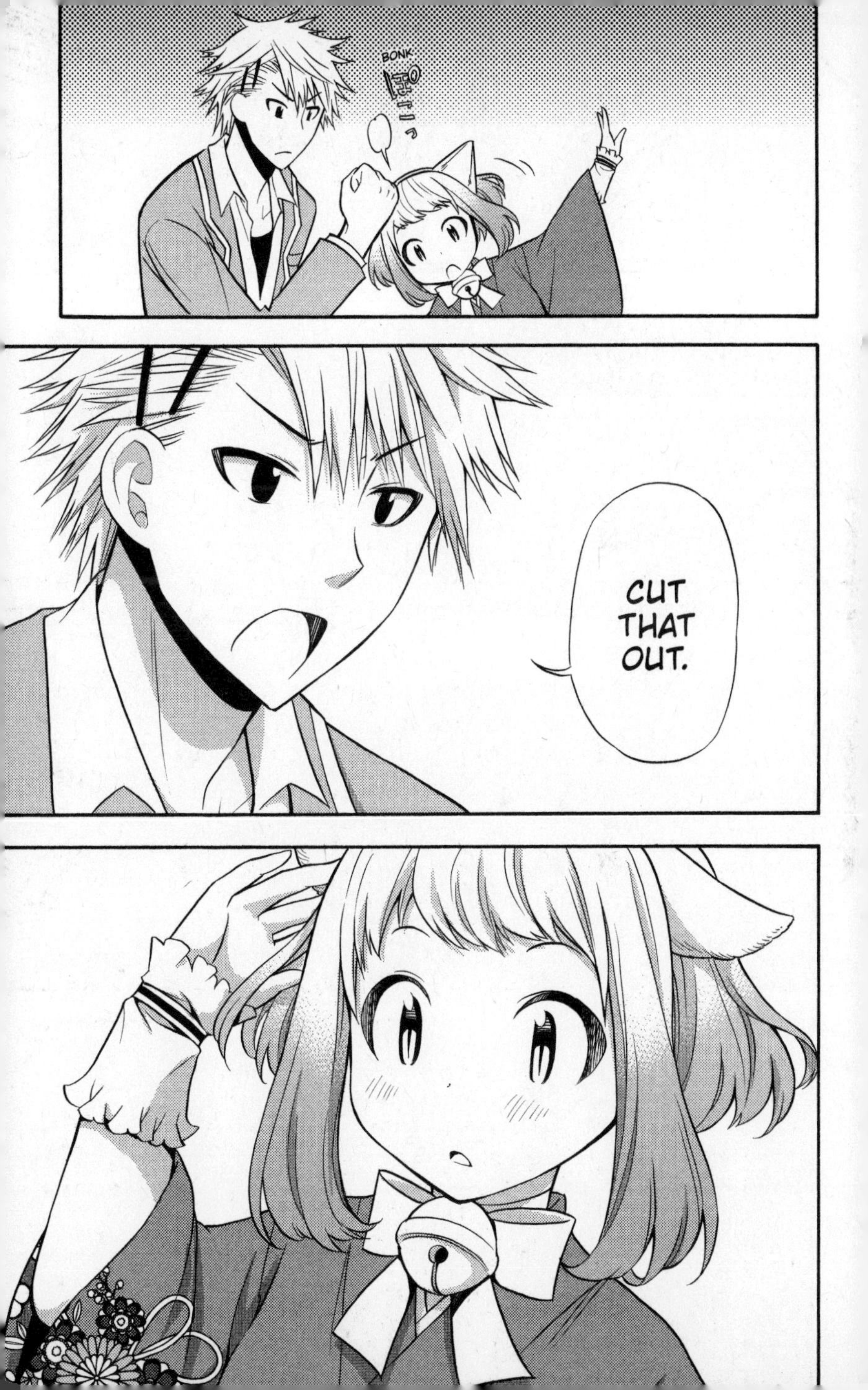
BONK
CUT THAT OUT.

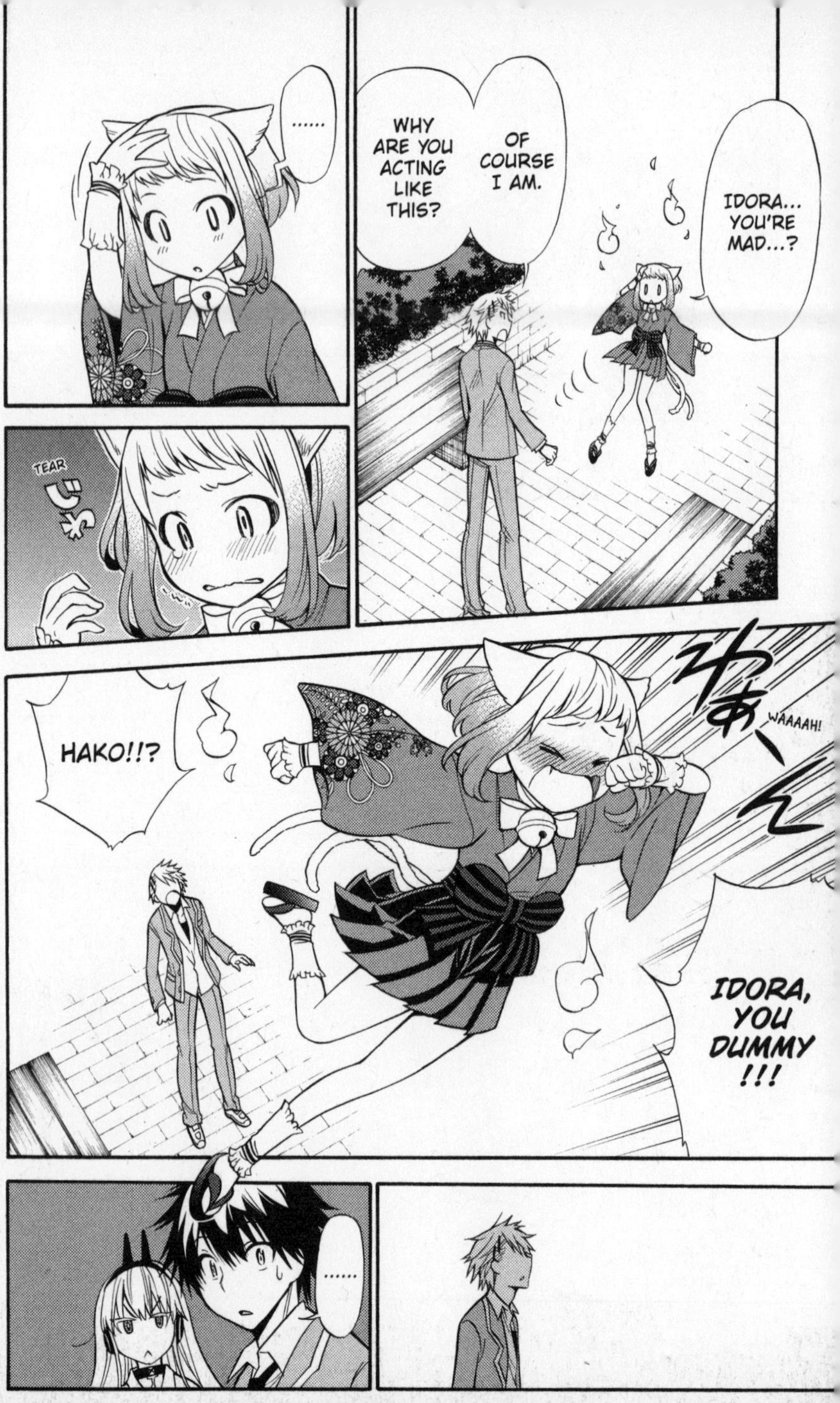
IDORA... YOU'RE MAD...?
OF COURSE I AM.
WHY ARE YOU ACTING LIKE THIS?
......
TEAR
WAAAAH!
IDORA, YOU DUMMY!!!
HAKO!!?
......

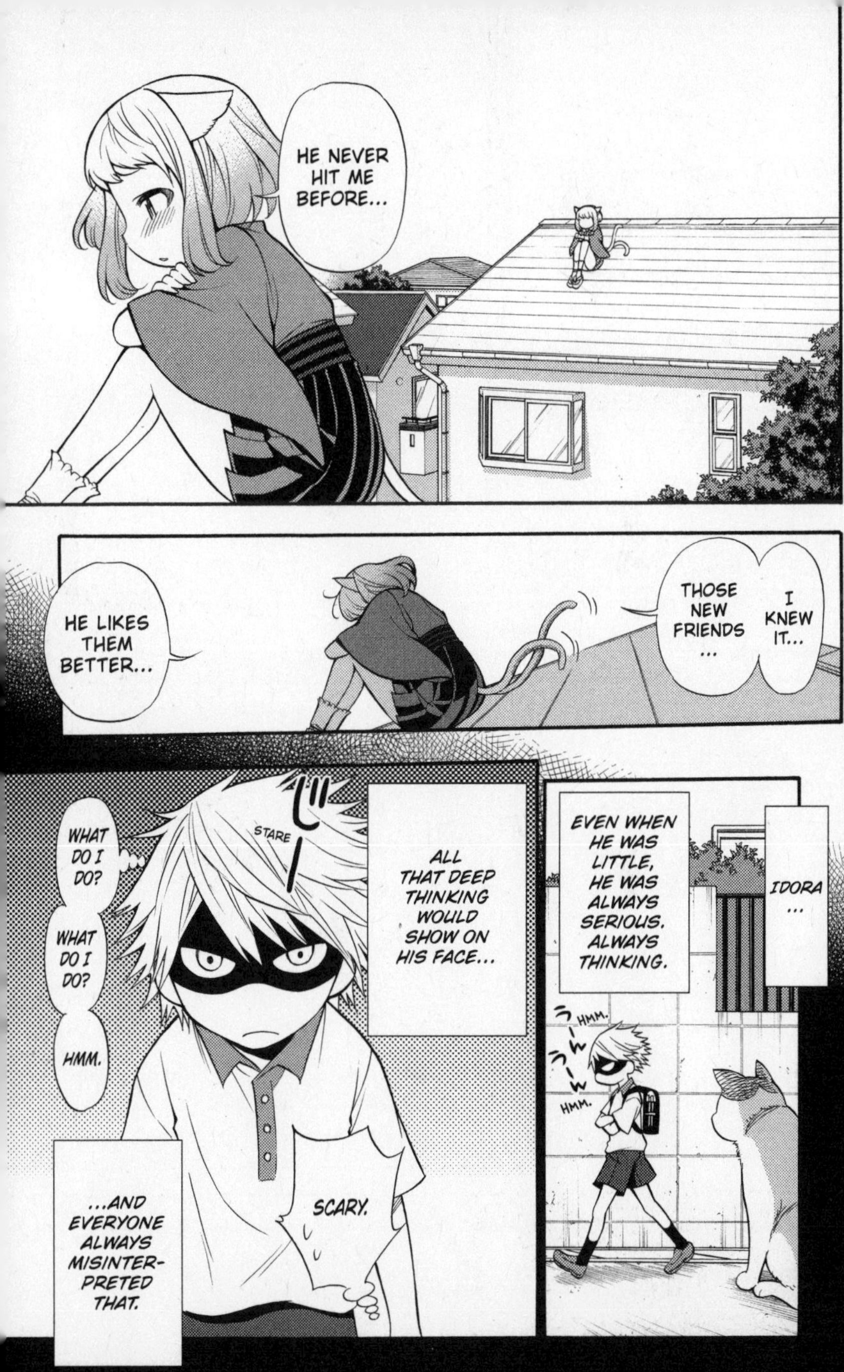
HE NEVER HIT ME BEFORE...
I KNEW IT...
THOSE NEW FRIENDS ...
HE LIKES THEM BETTER...
IDORA ...
EVEN WHEN HE WAS LITTLE, HE WAS ALWAYS SERIOUS. ALWAYS THINKING.
HMM.
HMM.
ALL THAT DEEP THINKING WOULD SHOW ON HIS FACE...
STARE
WHAT DO I DO?
WHAT DO I DO?
HMM.
SCARY.
...AND EVERYONE ALWAYS MISINTERPRETED THAT.

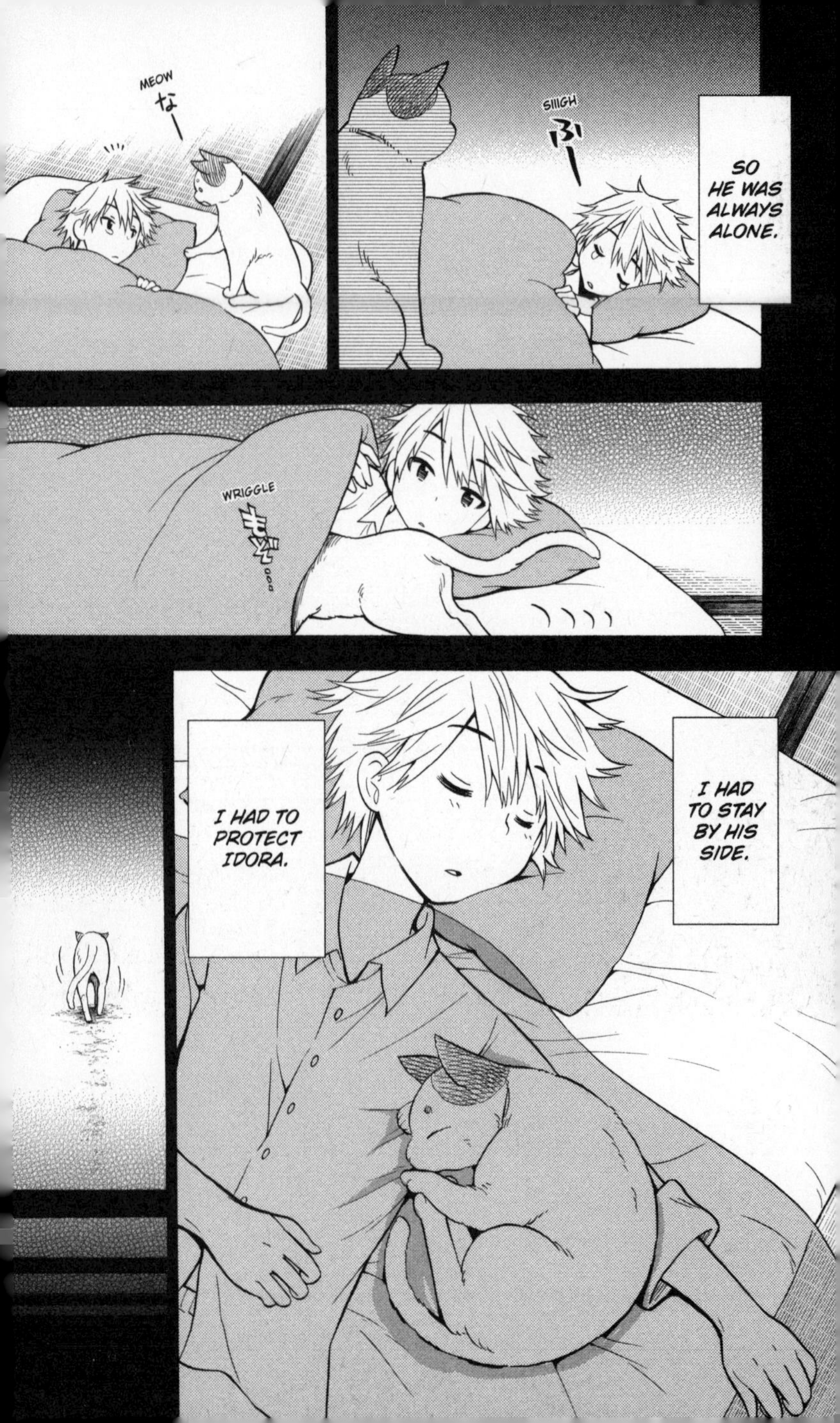
SO HE WAS ALWAYS ALONE.
SIIIGH
ふー
MEOW
なー
WRIGGLE
もぞ
I HAD TO STAY BY HIS SIDE.
I HAD TO PROTECT IDORA.

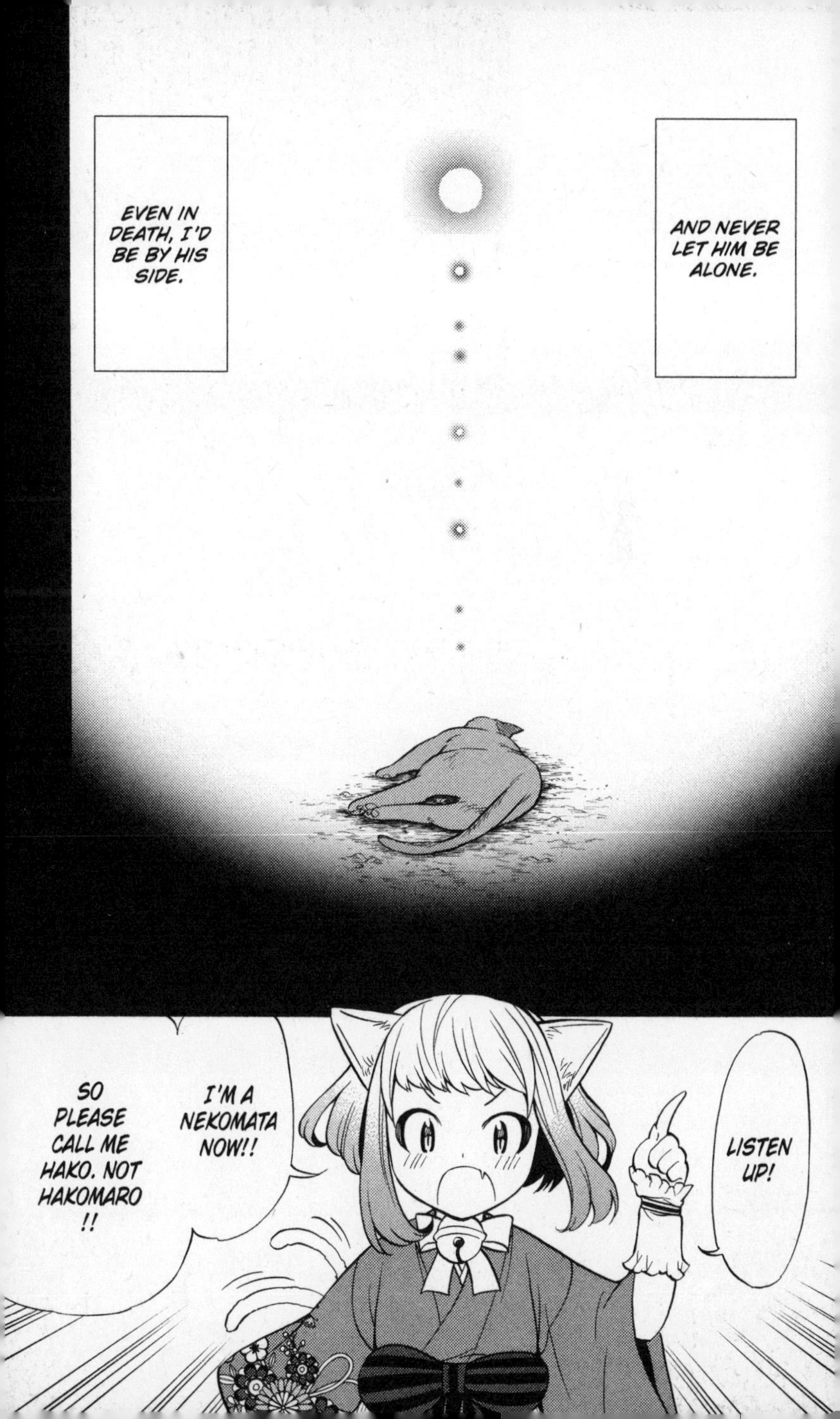
AND NEVER LET HIM BE ALONE.
EVEN IN DEATH, I'D BE BY HIS SIDE.
LISTEN UP!
I'M A NEKOMATA NOW!!
SO PLEASE CALL ME HAKO. NOT HAKOMARO!!

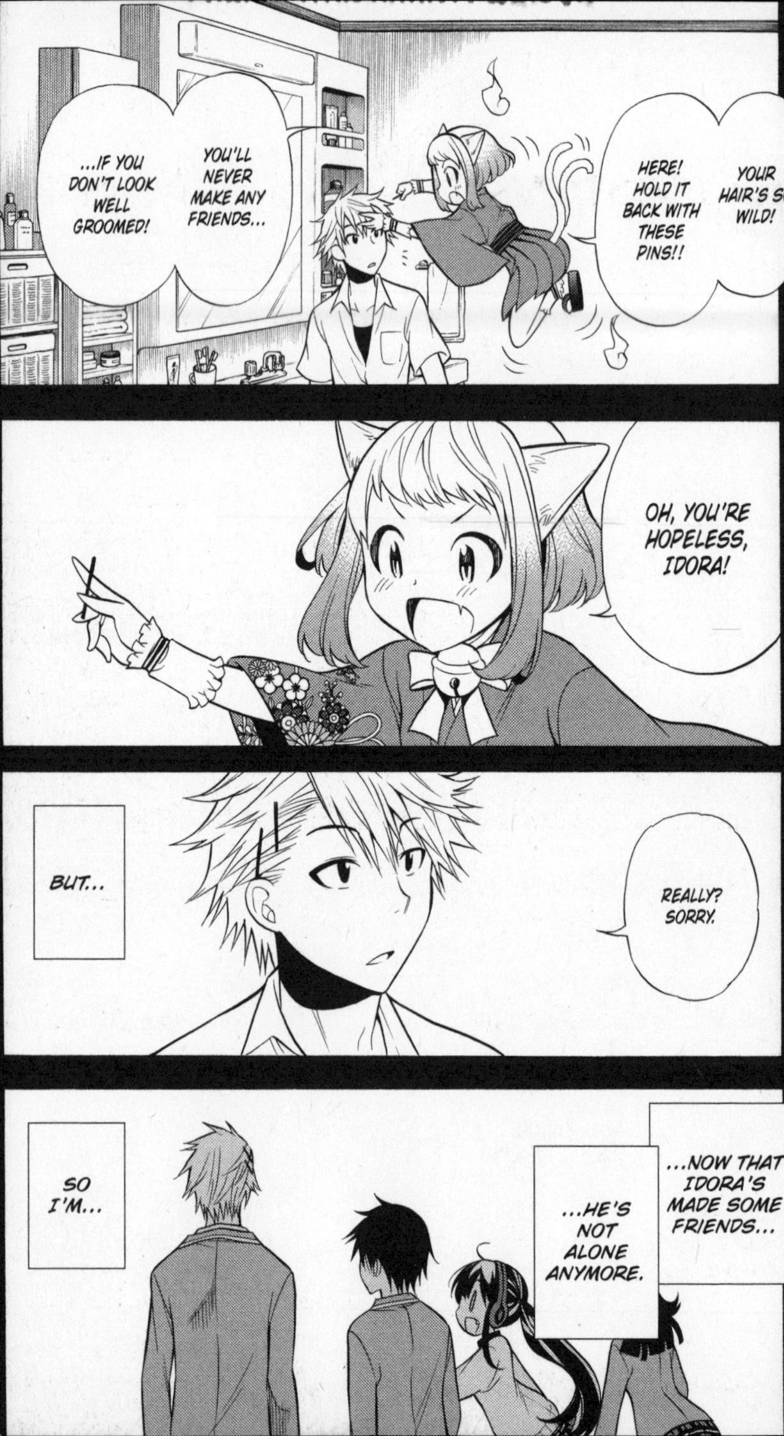
YOUR HAIR'S SO WILD!
HERE! HOLD IT BACK WITH THESE PINS!!
YOU'LL NEVER MAKE ANY FRIENDS...
...IF YOU DON'T LOOK WELL GROOMED!
OH, YOU'RE HOPELESS, IDORA!
REALLY? SORRY.
BUT...
...NOW THAT IDORA'S MADE SOME FRIENDS...
...HE'S NOT ALONE ANYMORE.
SO I'M...

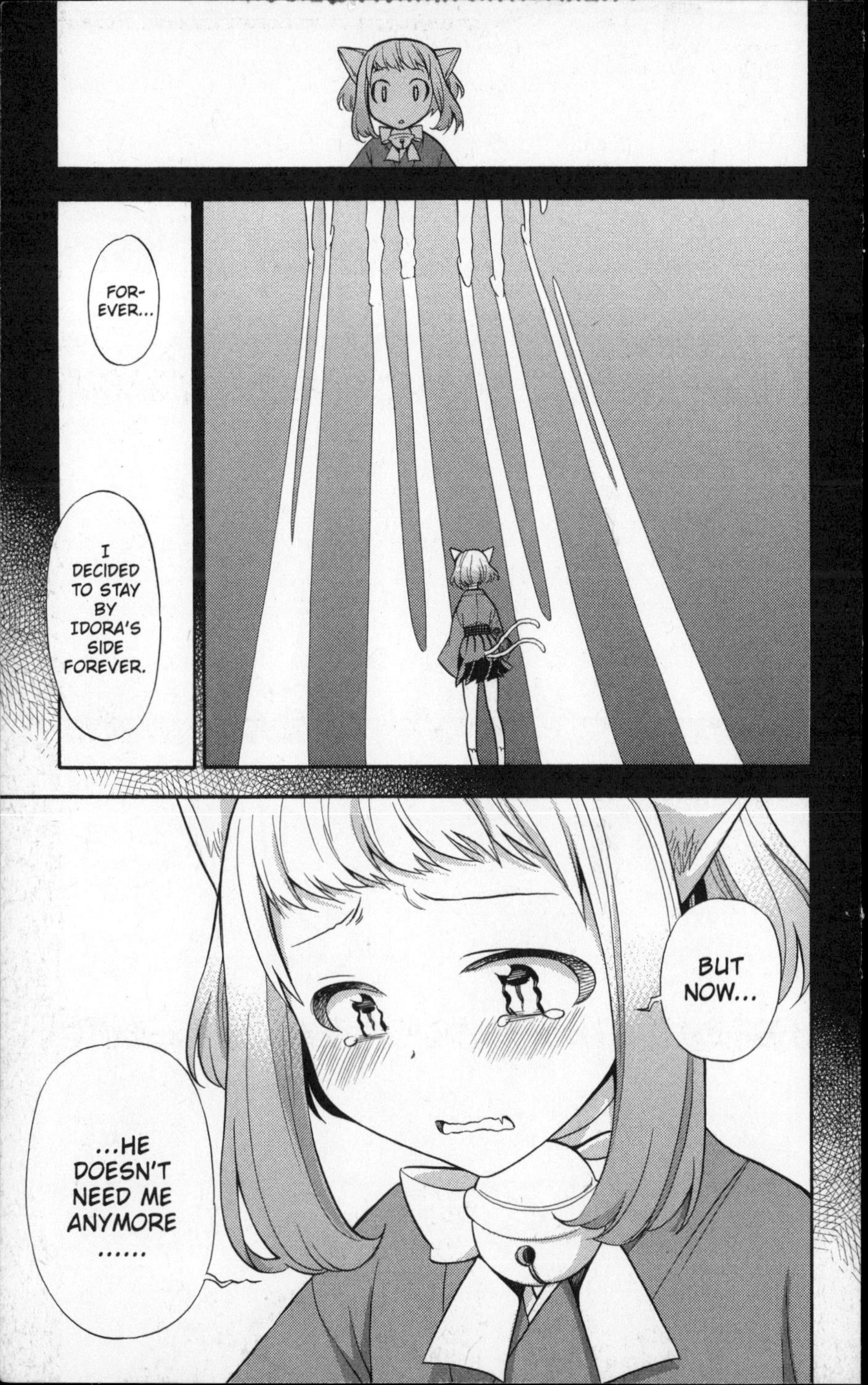
FOR-EVER...
I DECIDED TO STAY BY IDORA'S SIDE FOREVER.
BUT NOW...
...HE DOESN'T NEED ME ANYMORE ......

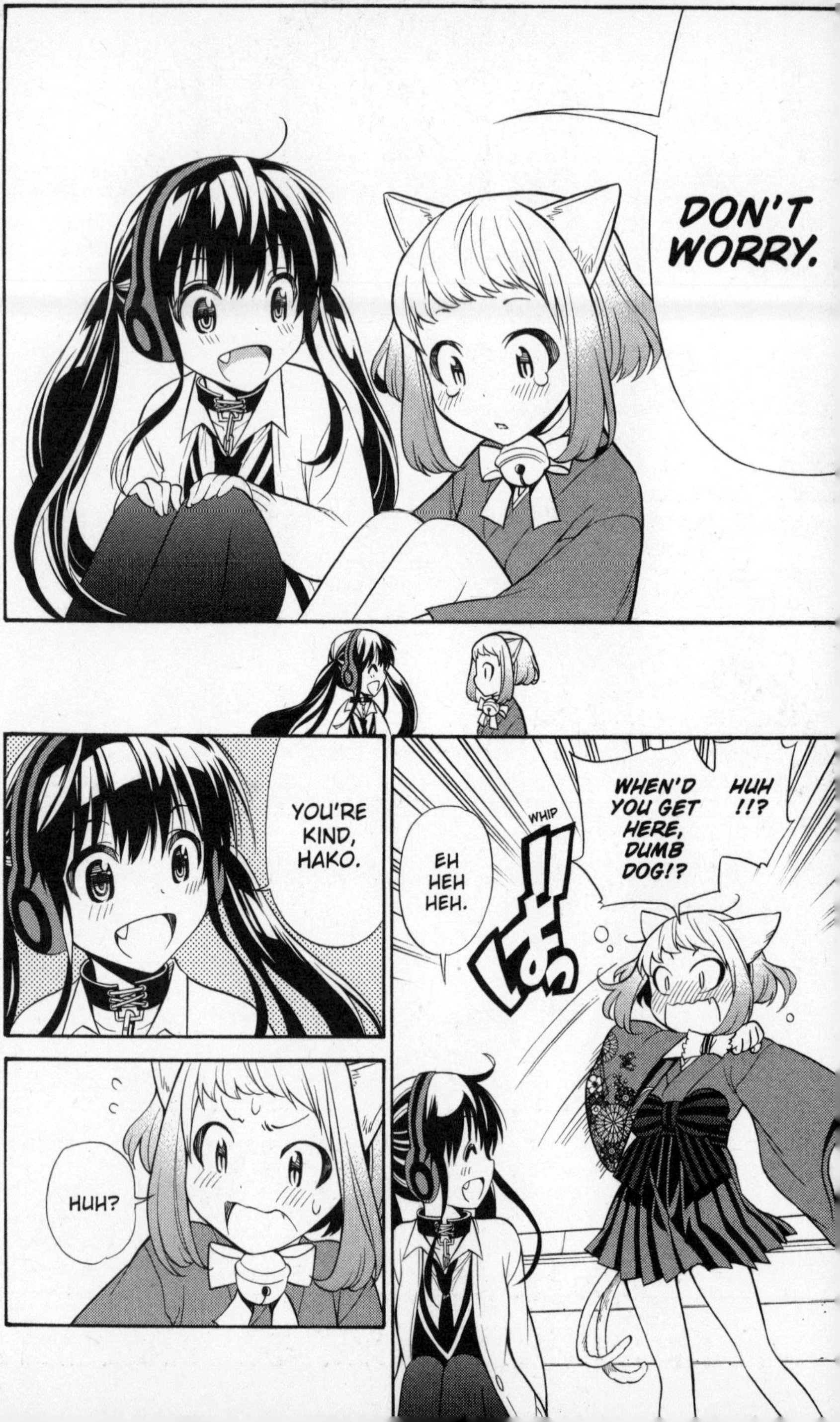
DON'T WORRY.
HUH !!?
WHEN'D YOU GET HERE, DUMB DOG!?
WHIP
ぱっ
EH HEH HEH.
YOU'RE KIND, HAKO.
HUH?

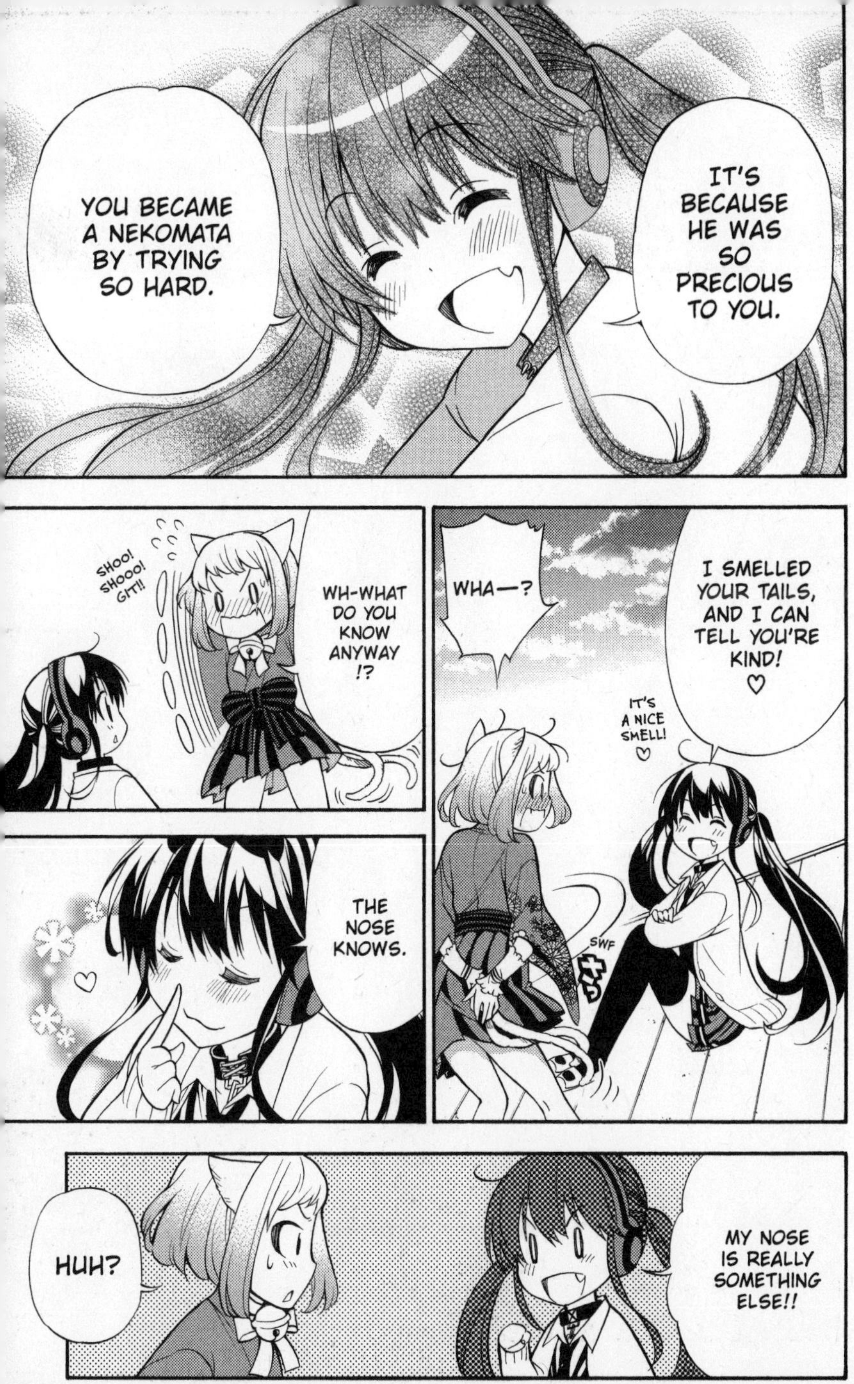
IT'S BECAUSE HE WAS SO PRECIOUS TO YOU.
YOU BECAME A NEKOMATA BY TRYING SO HARD.
I SMELLED YOUR TAILS, AND I CAN TELL YOU'RE KIND! ♡
IT'S A NICE SMELL! ♡
WHA—?
SWF
WH-WHAT DO YOU KNOW ANYWAY!?
SHOO! SHOOO! GIT!!
THE NOSE KNOWS.
MY NOSE IS REALLY SOMETHING ELSE!!
HUH?

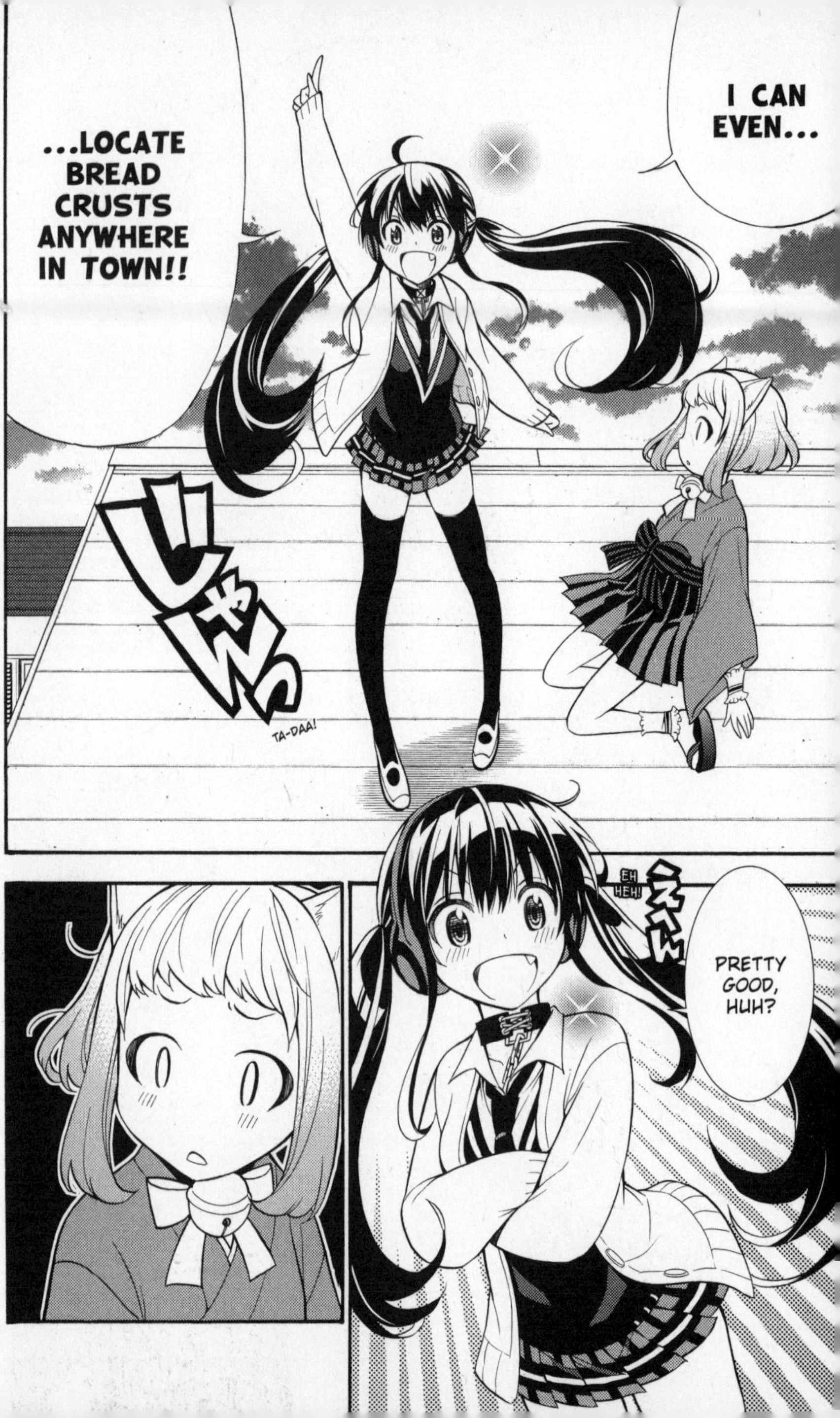
I CAN EVEN...
...LOCATE BREAD CRUSTS ANYWHERE IN TOWN!!
TA-DAA!
EH HEH!
PRETTY GOOD, HUH?

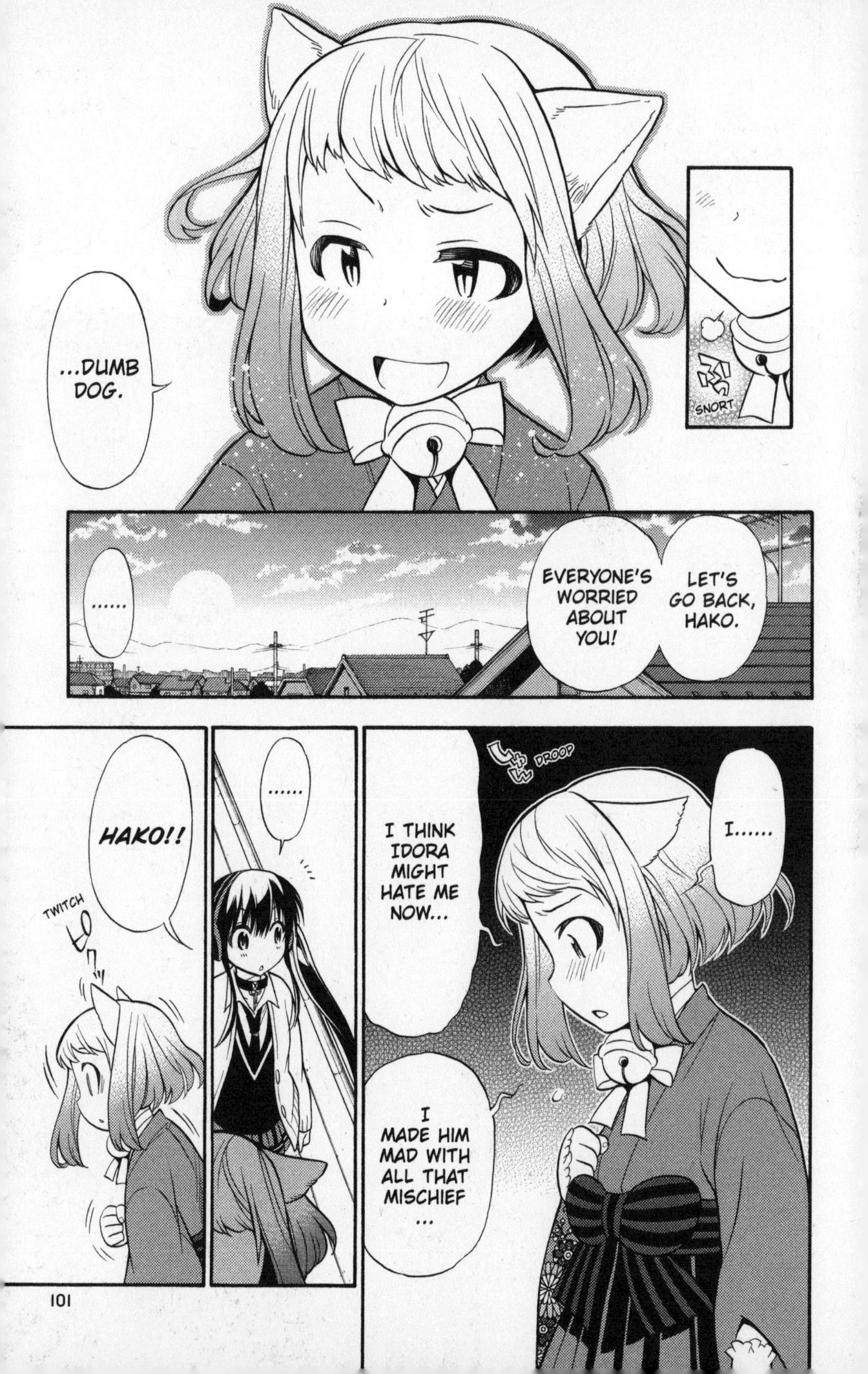
SNORT
...DUMB DOG.
LET'S GO BACK, HAKO.
EVERYONE'S WORRIED ABOUT YOU!
......
DROOP
I......
I THINK IDORA MIGHT HATE ME NOW...
I MADE HIM MAD WITH ALL THAT MISCHIEF ...
......
HAKO!!
TWITCH

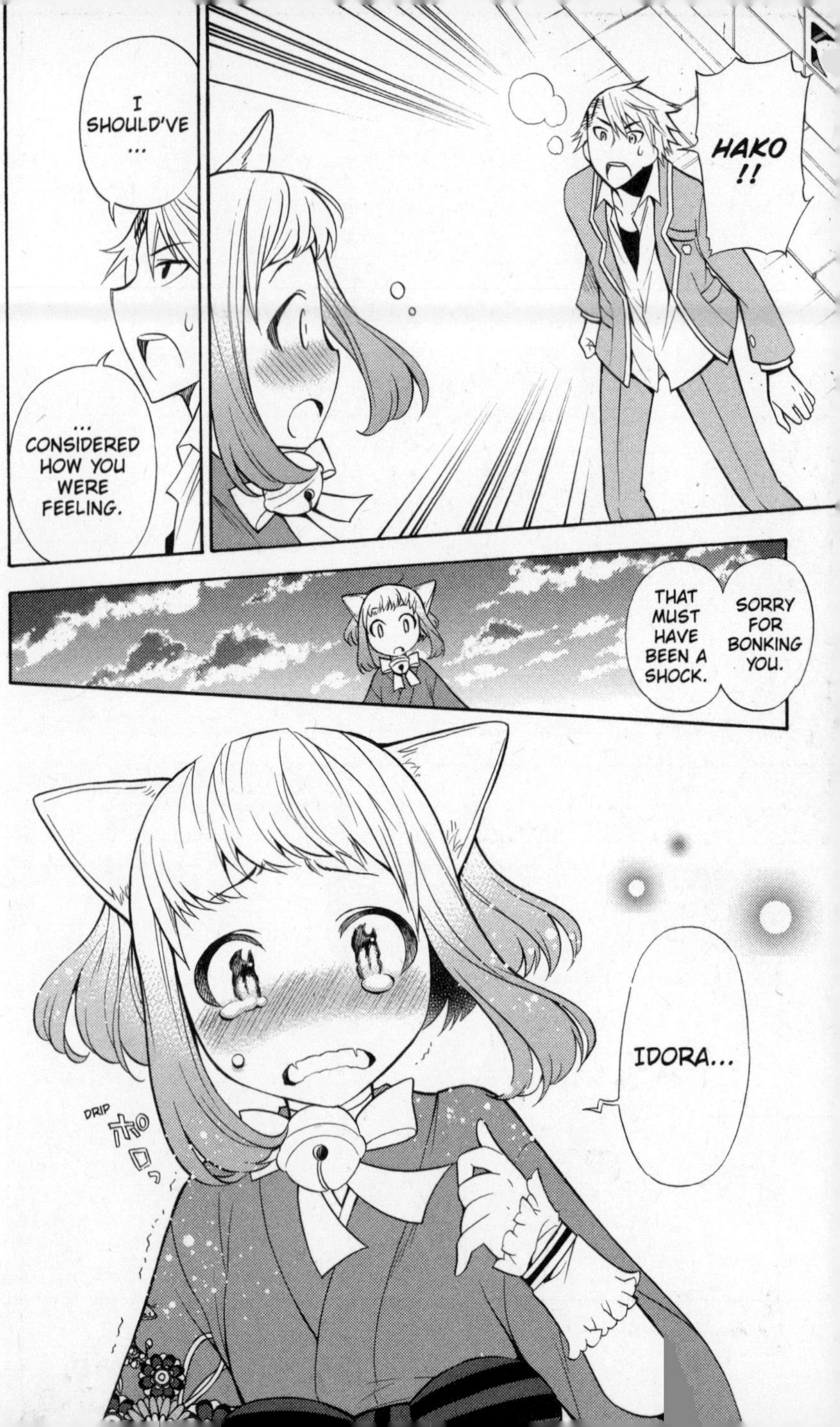
HAKO !!
I SHOULD'VE ...
... CONSIDERED HOW YOU WERE FEELING.
SORRY FOR BONKING YOU.
THAT MUST HAVE BEEN A SHOCK.
IDORA...
DRIP
ポロッ

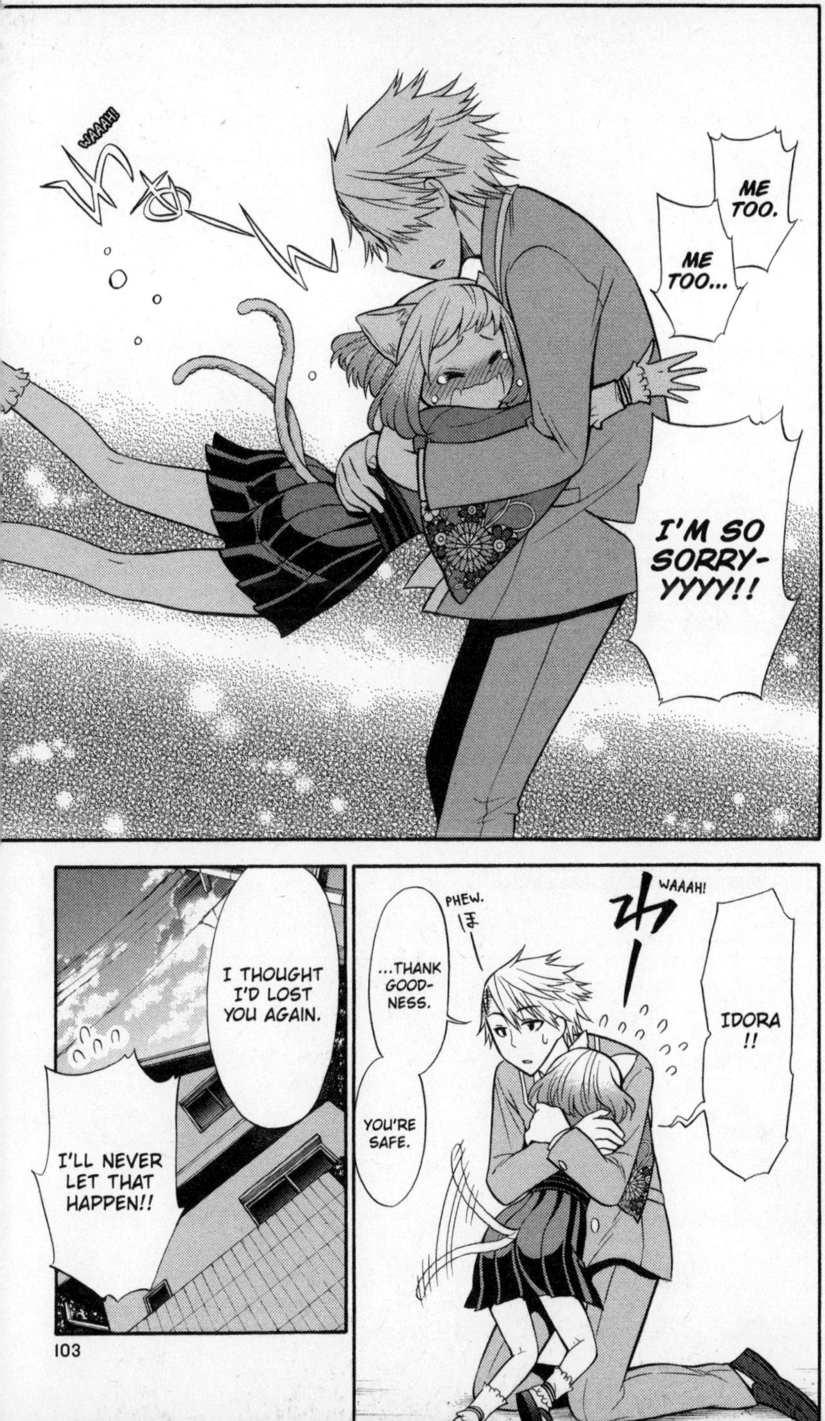
ME TOO.
ME TOO...
I'M SO SORRY-YYYY!!
WAAAH!
IDORA!!
WAAAH!
PHEW.
ほ
...THANK GOOD-NESS.
YOU'RE SAFE.
I THOUGHT I'D LOST YOU AGAIN.
I'LL NEVER LET THAT HAPPEN!!

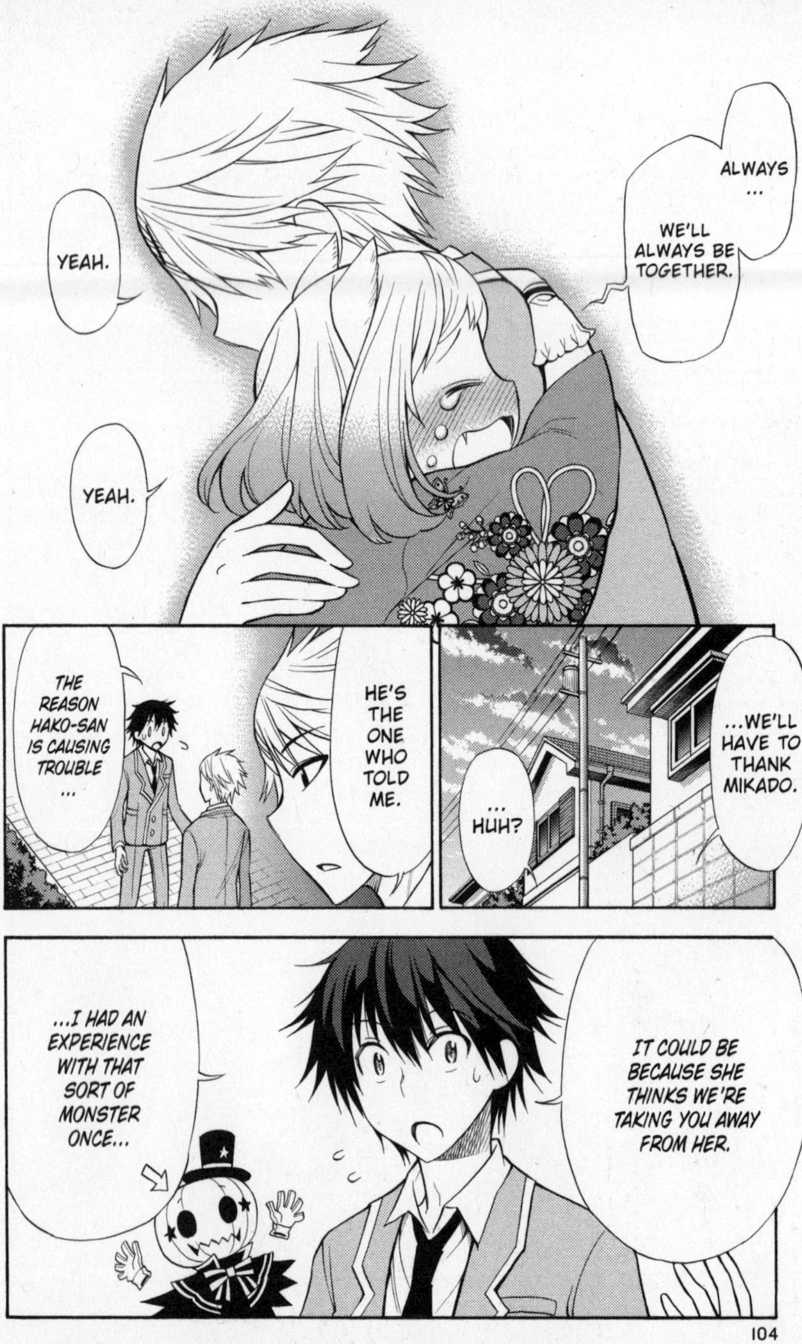
ALWAYS... WE'LL ALWAYS BE TOGETHER.
YEAH.
YEAH.
...WE'LL HAVE TO THANK MIKADO.
...HUH?
HE'S THE ONE WHO TOLD ME.
THE REASON HAKO-SAN IS CAUSING TROUBLE...
IT COULD BE BECAUSE SHE THINKS WE'RE TAKING YOU AWAY FROM HER.
...I HAD AN EXPERIENCE WITH THAT SORT OF MONSTER ONCE...

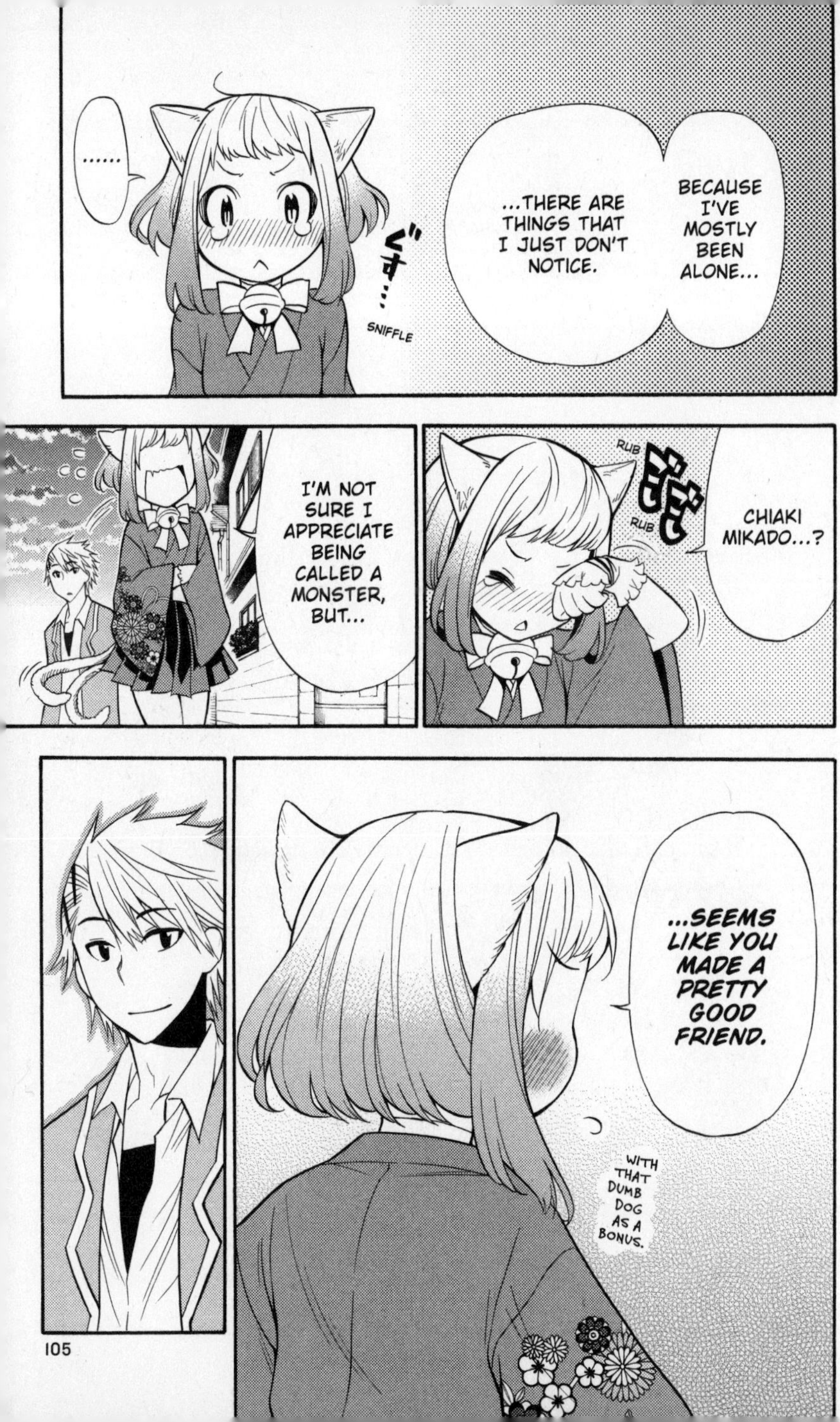
BECAUSE I'VE MOSTLY BEEN ALONE...
...THERE ARE THINGS THAT I JUST DON'T NOTICE.
ぐす...
SNIFFLE
......
CHIAKI MIKADO...?
RUB
RUB
I'M NOT SURE I APPRECIATE BEING CALLED A MONSTER, BUT...
...SEEMS LIKE YOU MADE A PRETTY GOOD FRIEND.
WITH THAT DUMB DOG AS A BONUS.

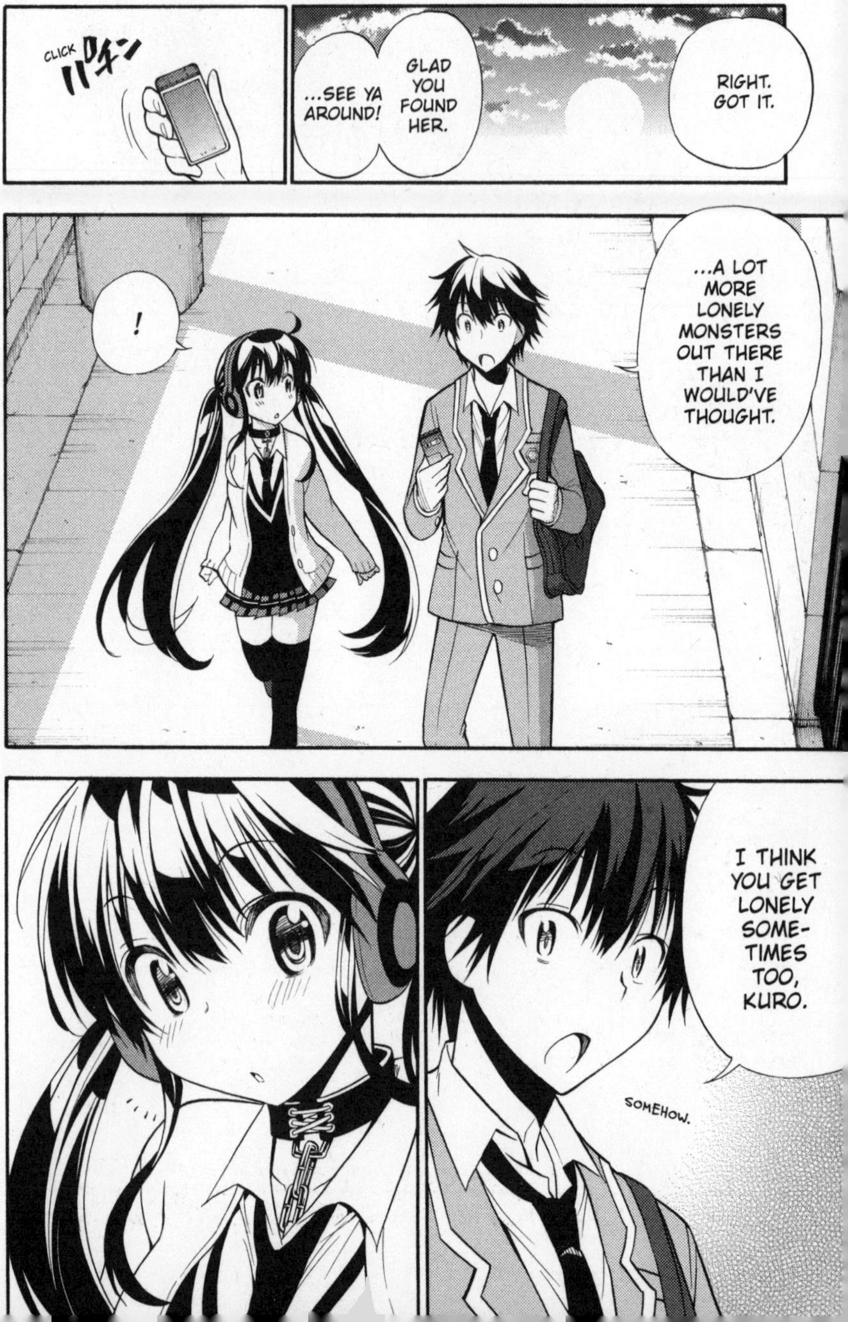
RIGHT. GOT IT.
GLAD YOU FOUND HER.
...SEE YA AROUND!
CLICK
パチン
...A LOT MORE LONELY MONSTERS OUT THERE THAN I WOULD'VE THOUGHT.
!
I THINK YOU GET LONELY SOME-TIMES TOO, KURO.
SOMEHOW.

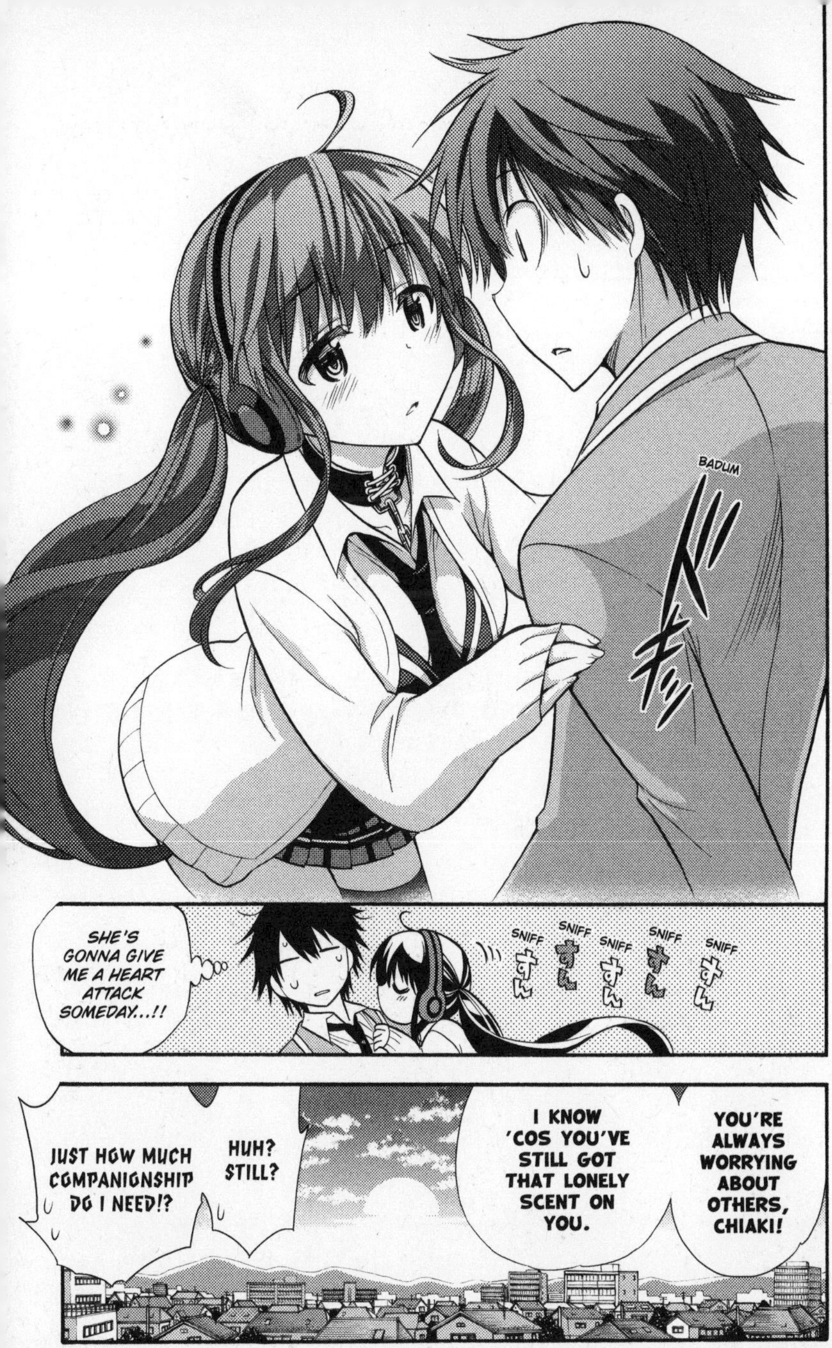
BADUM
ドキッ
SHE'S GONNA GIVE ME A HEART ATTACK SOMEDAY...!!
SNIFF すん
SNIFF すん
SNIFF すん
SNIFF すん
SNIFF すん
YOU'RE ALWAYS WORRYING ABOUT OTHERS, CHIAKI!
I KNOW 'COS YOU'VE STILL GOT THAT LONELY SCENT ON YOU.
HUH? STILL?
JUST HOW MUCH COMPANIONSHIP DO I NEED!?

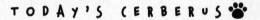

TODAY'S CERBERUS

GETTING
FED IS THE
BEST!

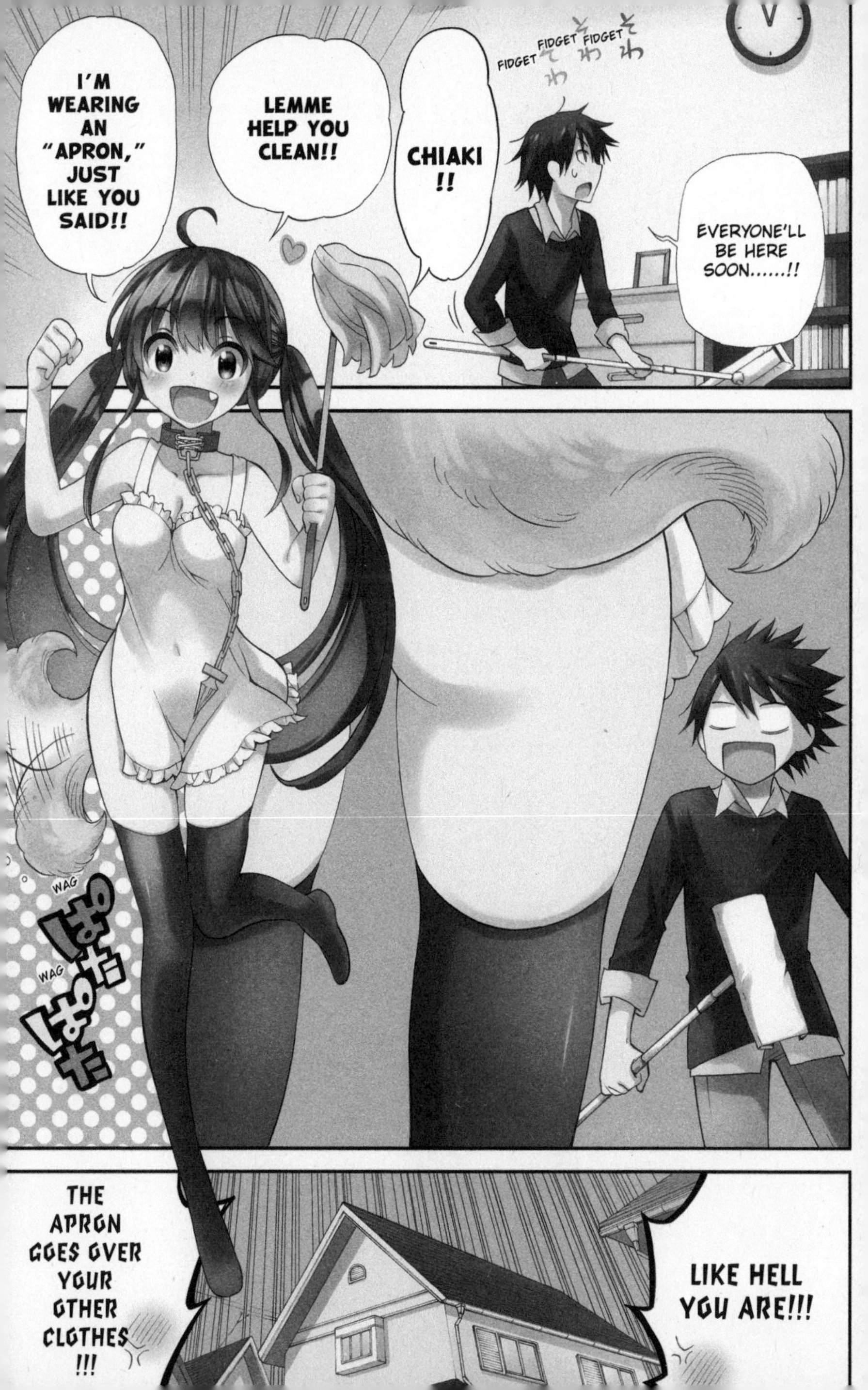
FIDGET FIDGET FIDGET
EVERYONE'LL BE HERE SOON......!!
CHIAKI!!
LEMME HELP YOU CLEAN!!
I'M WEARING AN "APRON," JUST LIKE YOU SAID!!
WAG WAG
LIKE HELL YOU ARE!!!
THE APRON GOES OVER YOUR OTHER CLOTHES!!!

CHAPTER 8
A STUDY PARTY WITH EVERYONE!

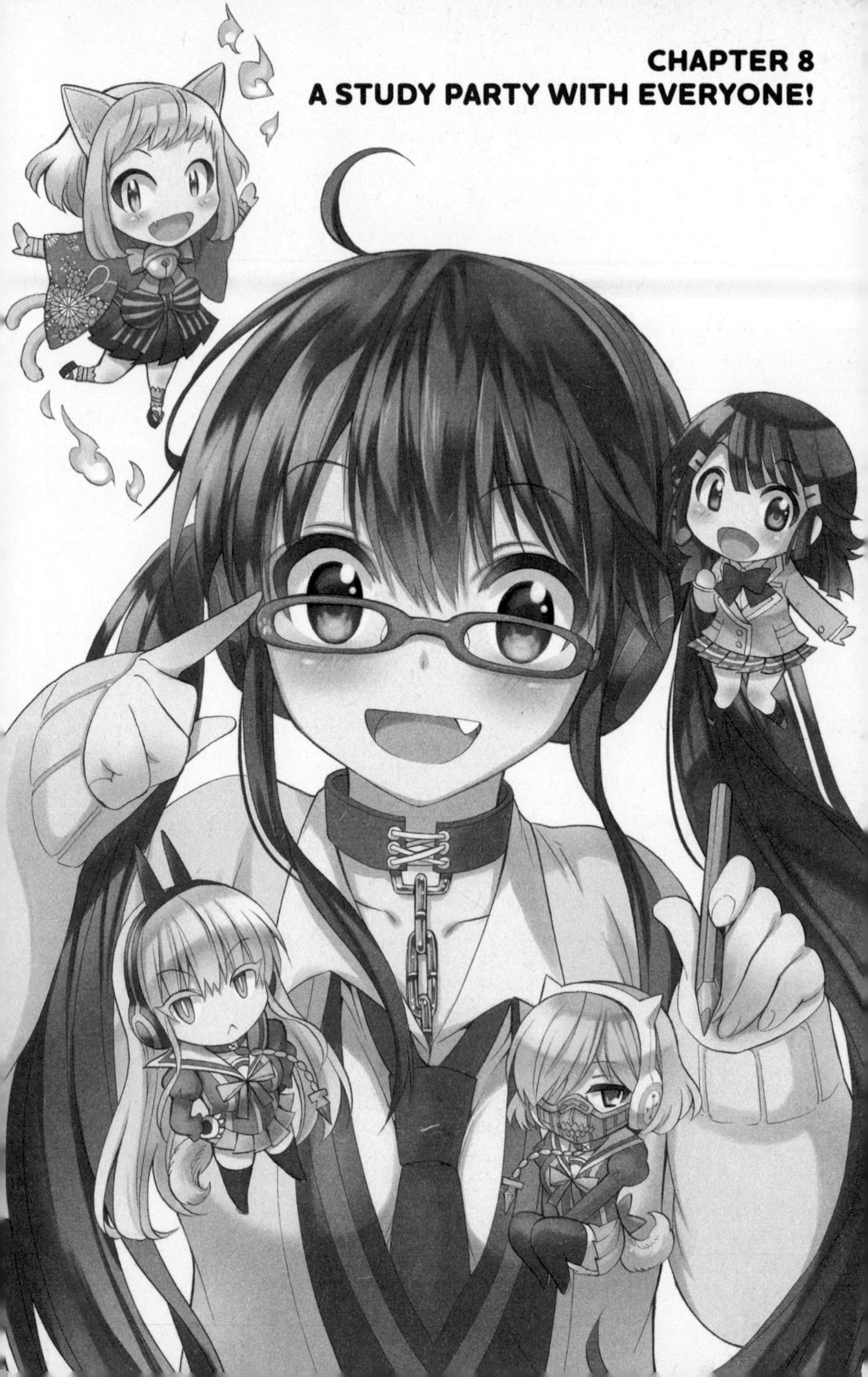

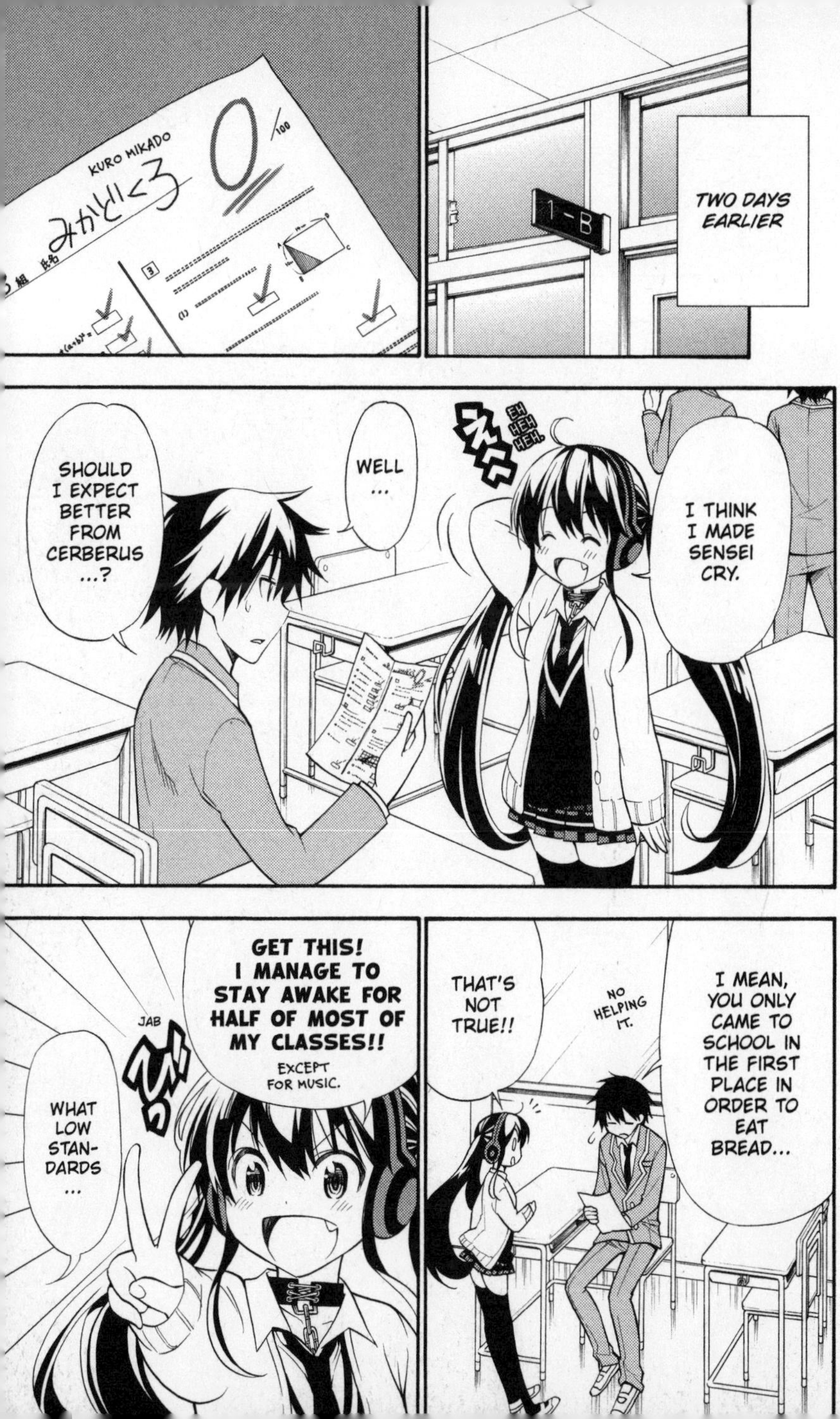

TWO DAYS EARLIER
1-B
KURO MIKADO
みかどくろ
0/100
EH HEH HEH.
I THINK I MADE SENSEI CRY.
WELL...
SHOULD I EXPECT BETTER FROM CERBERUS...?
I MEAN, YOU ONLY CAME TO SCHOOL IN THE FIRST PLACE IN ORDER TO EAT BREAD...
NO HELPING IT.
THAT'S NOT TRUE!!
GET THIS! I MANAGE TO STAY AWAKE FOR HALF OF MOST OF MY CLASSES!!
EXCEPT FOR MUSIC.
JAB
WHAT LOW STANDARDS...

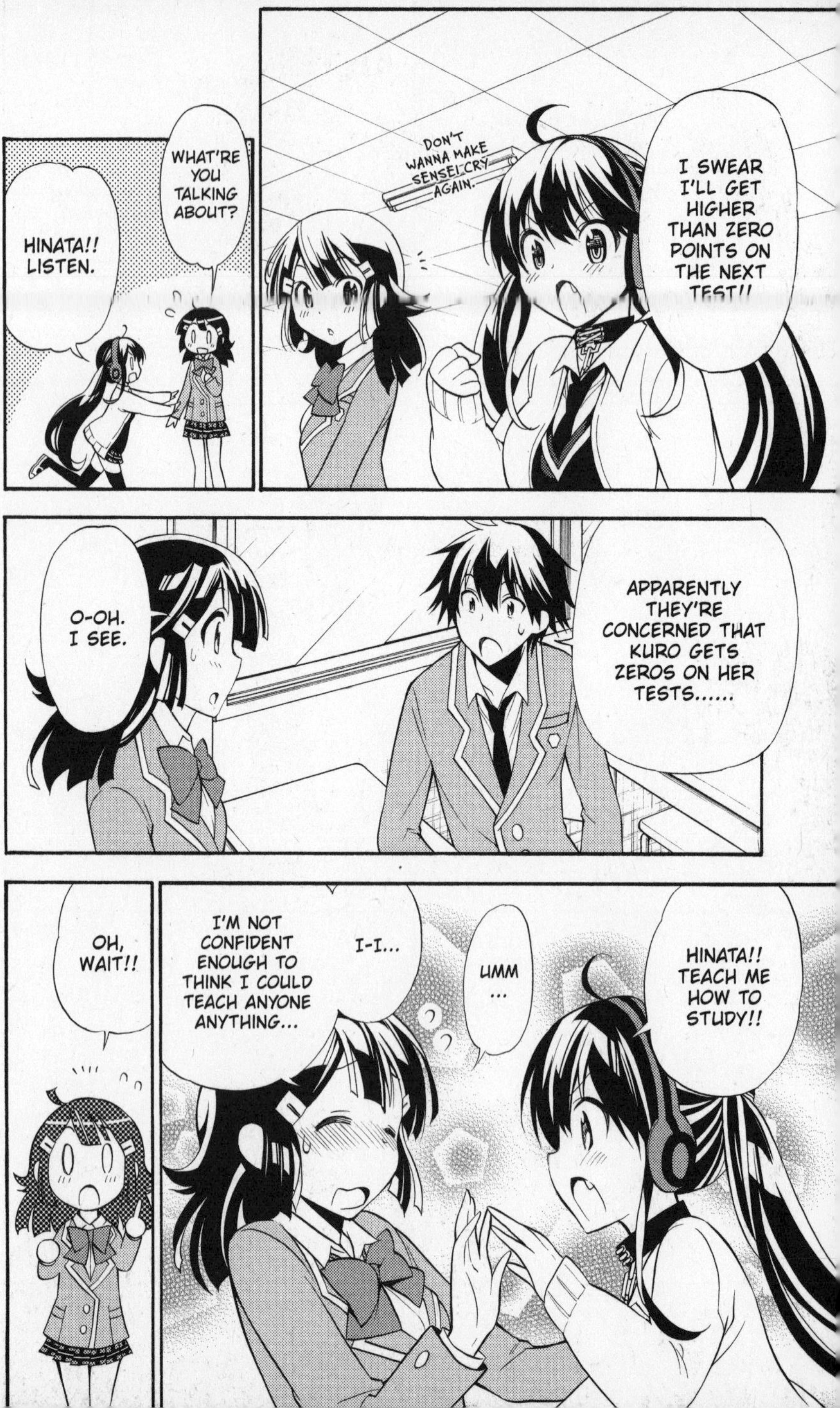
I SWEAR I'LL GET HIGHER THAN ZERO POINTS ON THE NEXT TEST!!
DON'T WANNA MAKE SENSEI CRY AGAIN.
WHAT'RE YOU TALKING ABOUT?
HINATA!! LISTEN.
APPARENTLY THEY'RE CONCERNED THAT KURO GETS ZEROS ON HER TESTS......
O-OH. I SEE.
HINATA!! TEACH ME HOW TO STUDY!!
UMM...
I-I...
I'M NOT CONFIDENT ENOUGH TO THINK I COULD TEACH ANYONE ANYTHING...
OH, WAIT!!

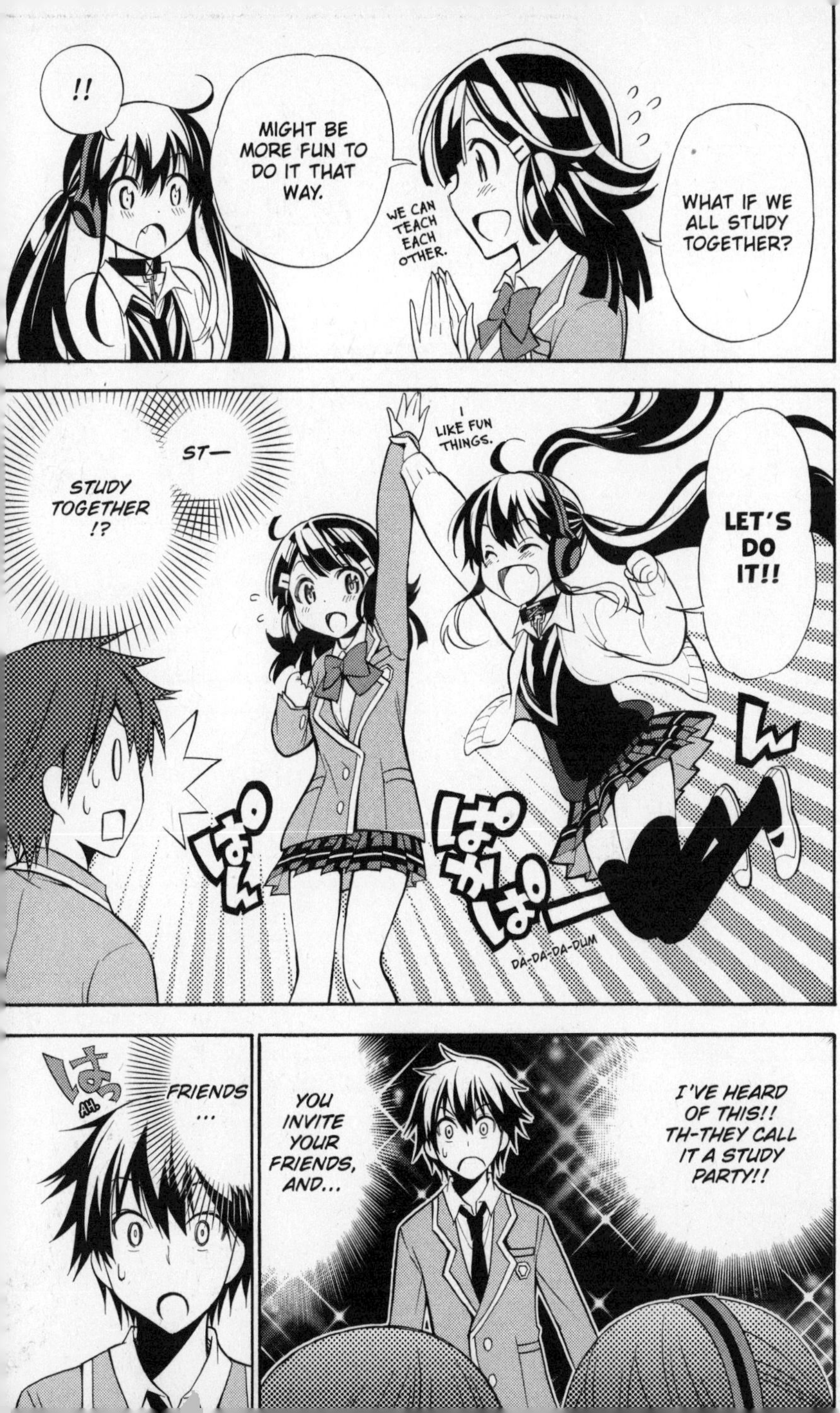
WHAT IF WE ALL STUDY TOGETHER?
WE CAN TEACH EACH OTHER.
MIGHT BE MORE FUN TO DO IT THAT WAY.
!!
LET'S DO IT!!
I LIKE FUN THINGS.
DA-DA-DA-DUM
ST—
STUDY TOGETHER !?
I'VE HEARD OF THIS!! TH-THEY CALL IT A STUDY PARTY!!
YOU INVITE YOUR FRIENDS, AND...
FRIENDS ...
はっ
AH.

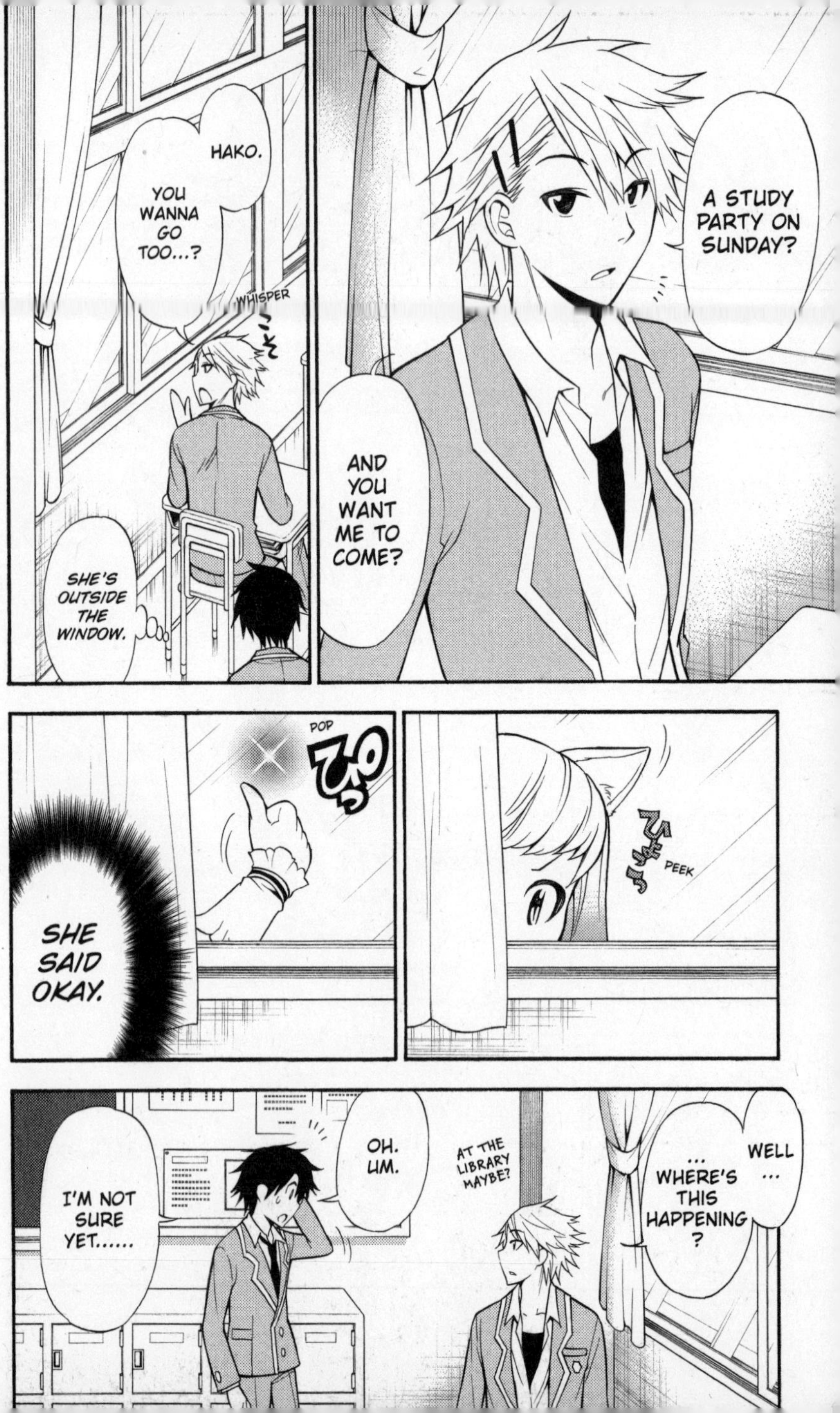
A STUDY PARTY ON SUNDAY?
AND YOU WANT ME TO COME?
HAKO.
YOU WANNA GO TOO...?
WHISPER
SHE'S OUTSIDE THE WINDOW.
PEEK
POP
SHE SAID OKAY.
WELL ...
... WHERE'S THIS HAPPENING ?
AT THE LIBRARY MAYBE?
OH. UM.
I'M NOT SURE YET......

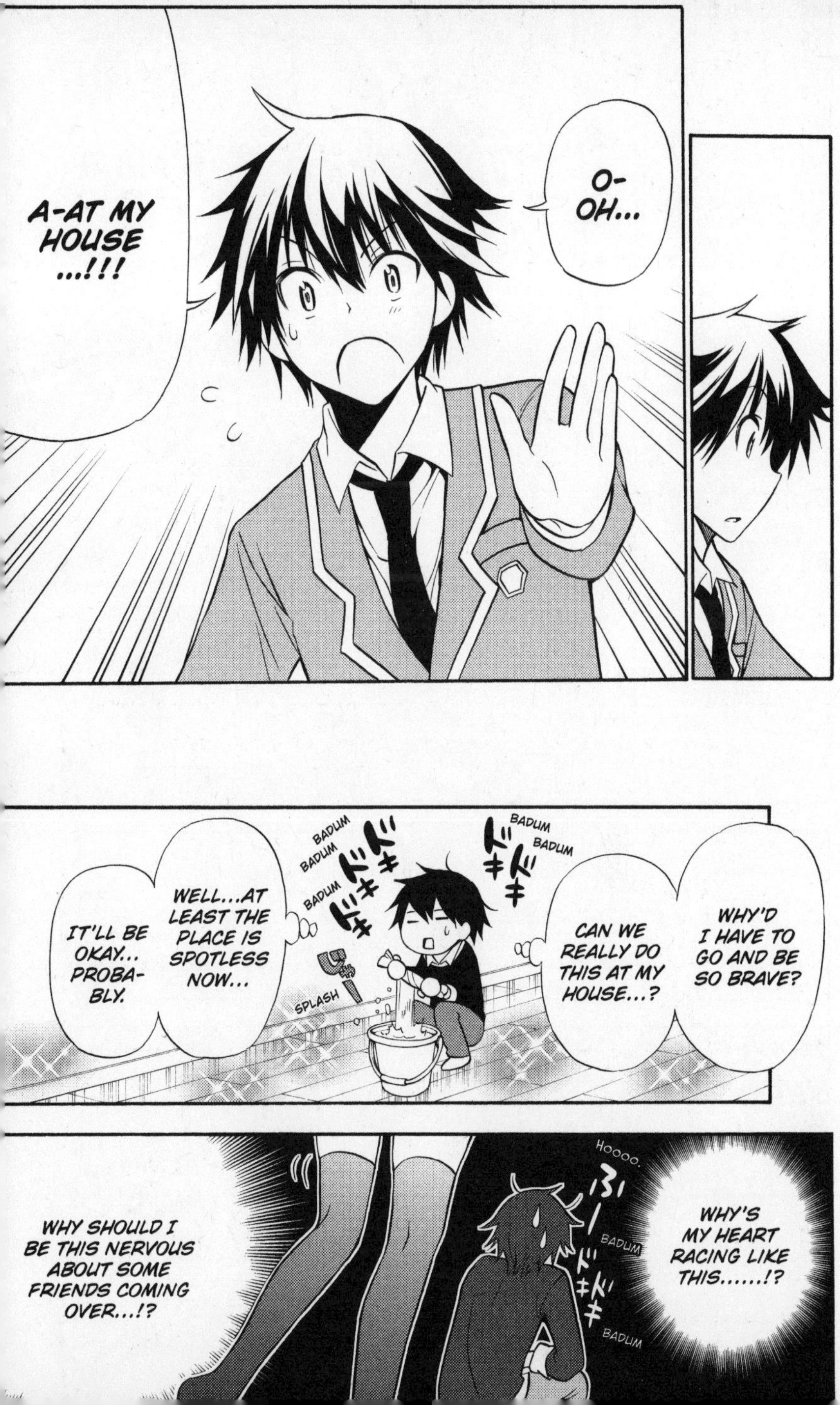
O-
OH...
A-AT MY HOUSE ...!!!
BADUM
BADUM
WHY'D I HAVE TO GO AND BE SO BRAVE?
CAN WE REALLY DO THIS AT MY HOUSE...?
BADUM
BADUM
BADUM
WELL...AT LEAST THE PLACE IS SPOTLESS NOW...
IT'LL BE OKAY... PROBA-BLY.
SPLASH
HOOOO.
WHY'S MY HEART RACING LIKE THIS......!?
BADUM
BADUM
WHY SHOULD I BE THIS NERVOUS ABOUT SOME FRIENDS COMING OVER...!?

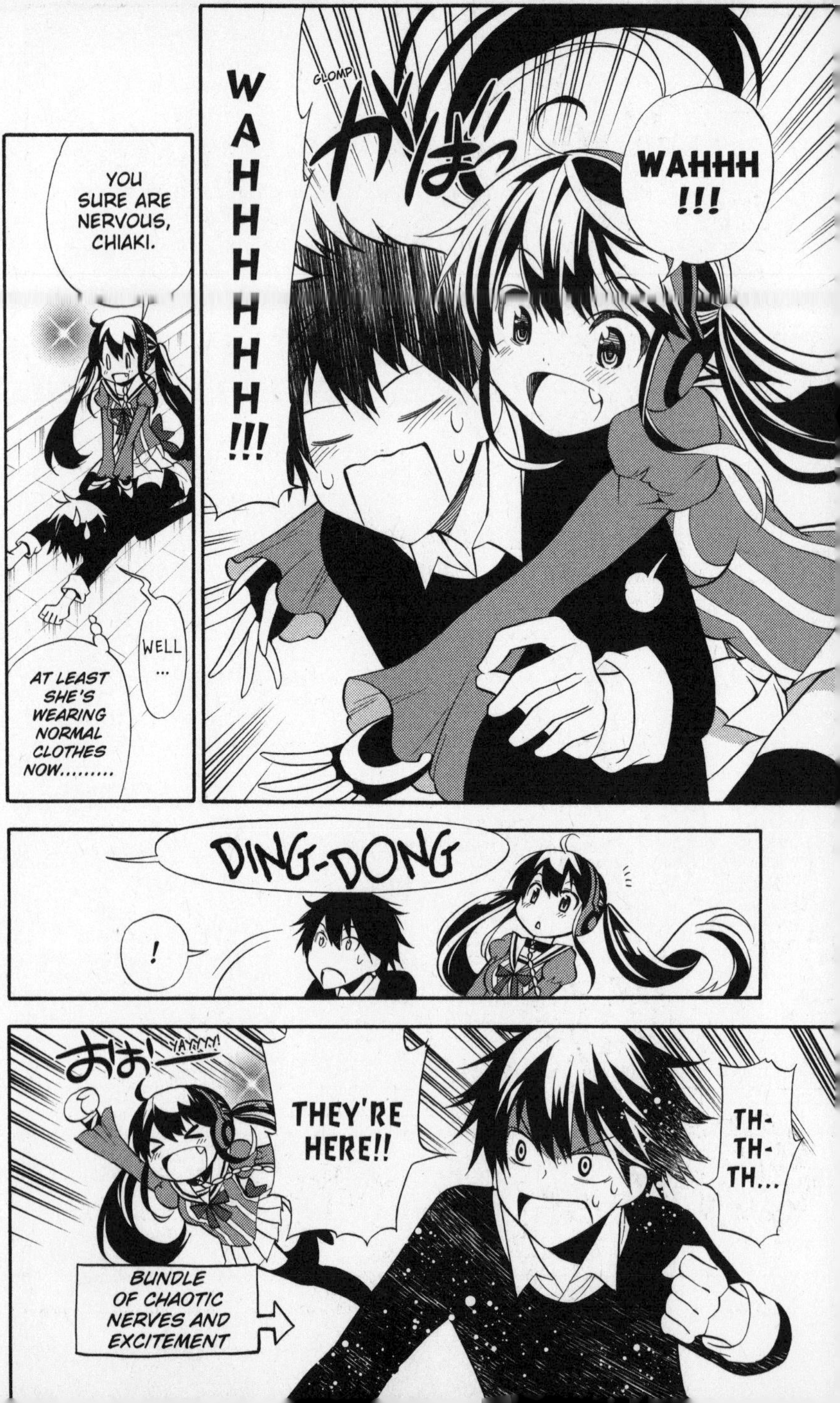
WAHHH!!!
GLOMP
WAHHHHHHHH!!!
YOU SURE ARE NERVOUS, CHIAKI.
WELL...
AT LEAST SHE'S WEARING NORMAL CLOTHES NOW.........
DING-DONG
!
TH-TH-TH...
THEY'RE HERE!!
おお!
YAYYYY!
BUNDLE OF CHAOTIC NERVES AND EXCITEMENT

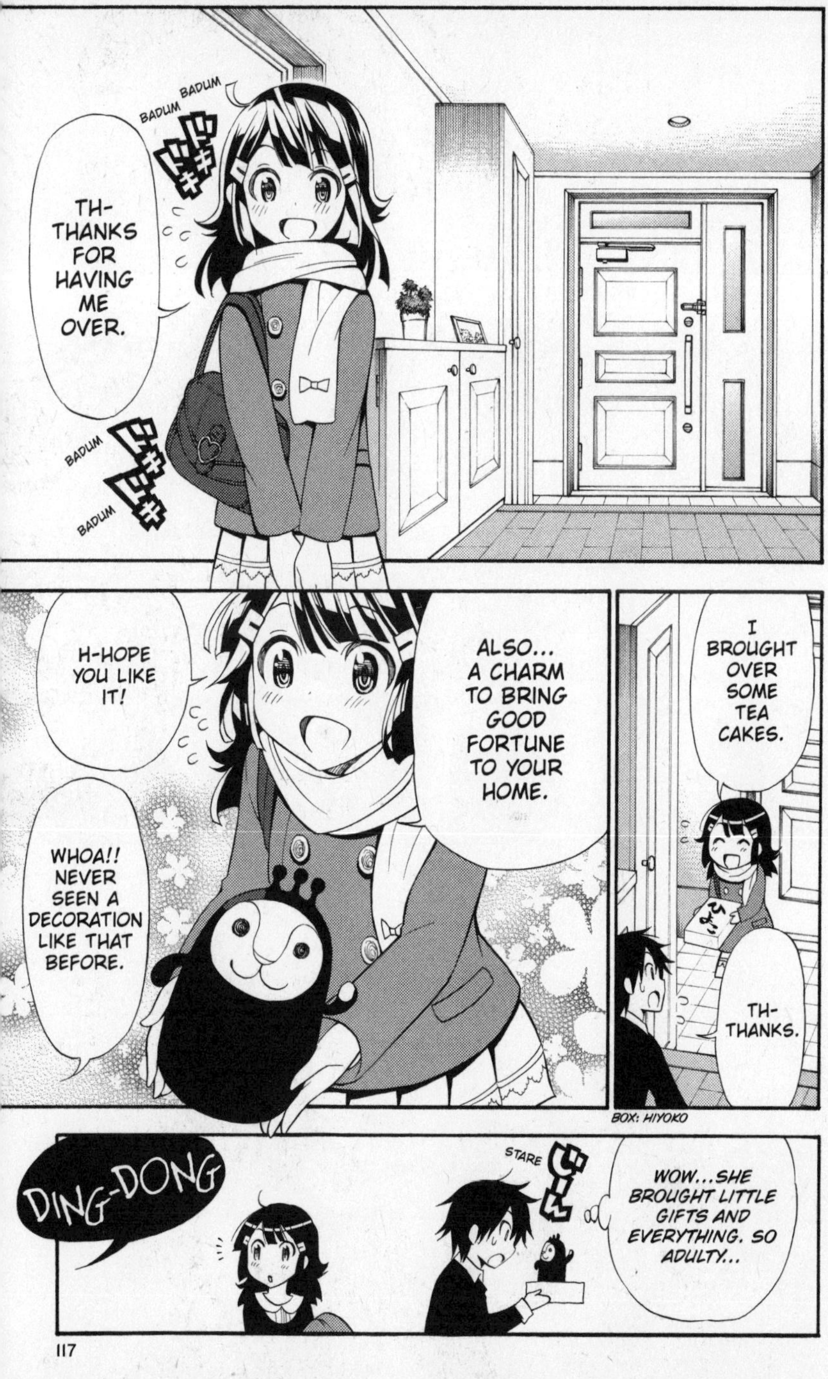
BADUM BADUM
TH-THANKS FOR HAVING ME OVER.
BADUM BADUM
I BROUGHT OVER SOME TEA CAKES.
TH-THANKS.
BOX: HIYOKO
ALSO... A CHARM TO BRING GOOD FORTUNE TO YOUR HOME.
H-HOPE YOU LIKE IT!
WHOA!! NEVER SEEN A DECORATION LIKE THAT BEFORE.
WOW...SHE BROUGHT LITTLE GIFTS AND EVERYTHING. SO ADULTY...
STARE
DING-DONG

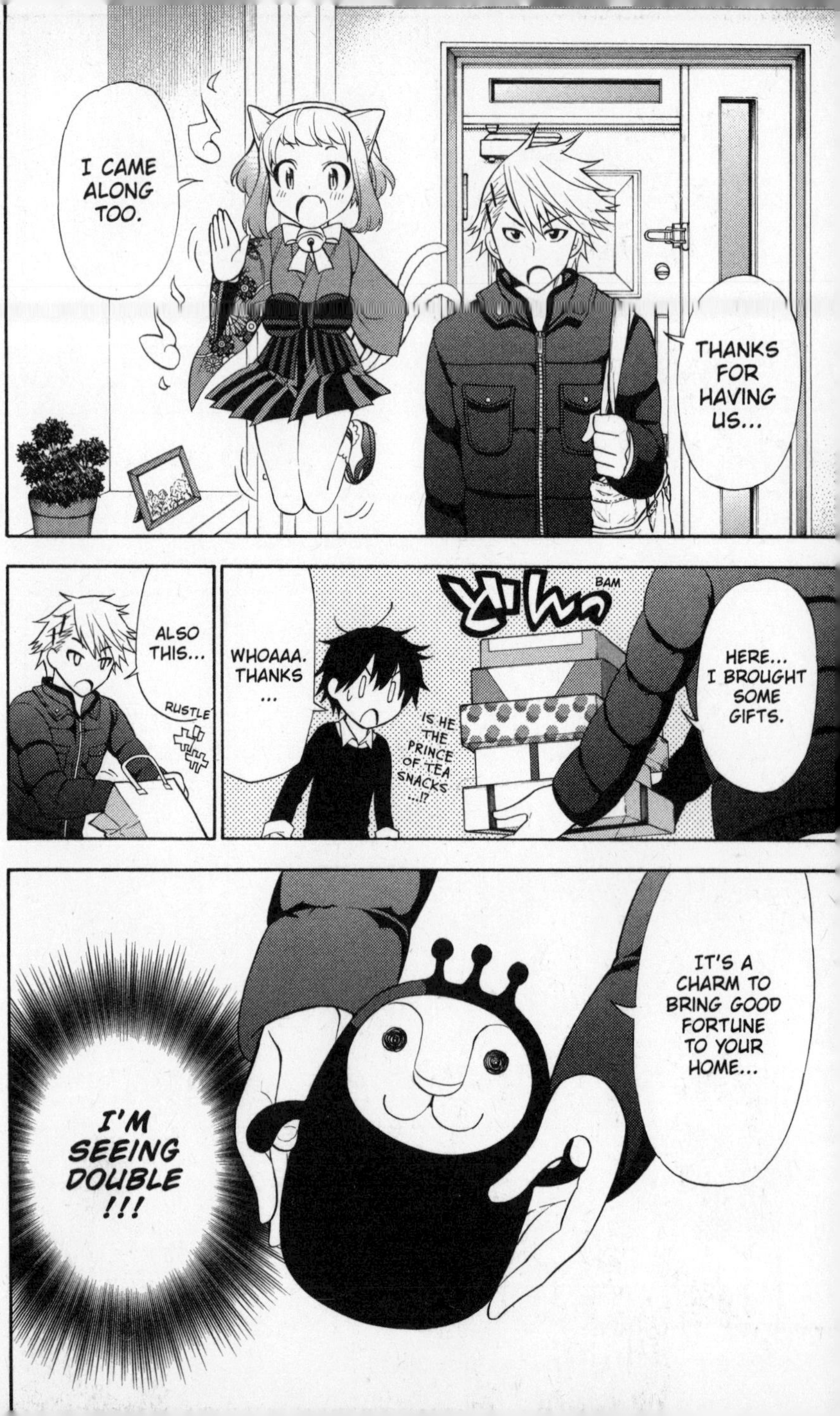
THANKS FOR HAVING US...
I CAME ALONG TOO.
BAM
HERE... I BROUGHT SOME GIFTS.
WHOAAA. THANKS ...
IS HE THE PRINCE OF TEA SNACKS ...!?
ALSO THIS...
RUSTLE
IT'S A CHARM TO BRING GOOD FORTUNE TO YOUR HOME...
I'M SEEING DOUBLE !!!

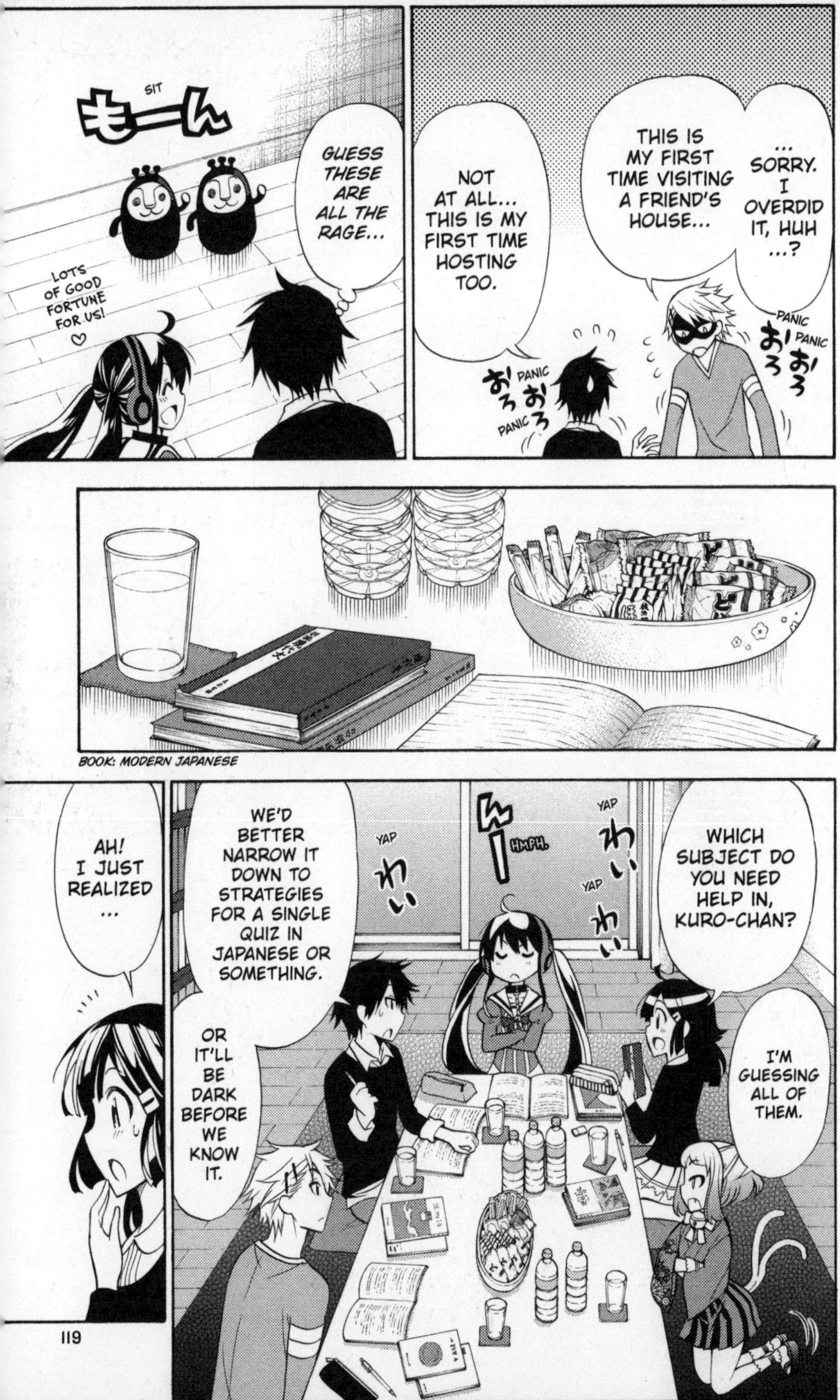
... SORRY. I OVERDID IT, HUH ...?
THIS IS MY FIRST TIME VISITING A FRIEND'S HOUSE...
PANIC おろ PANIC おろ
NOT AT ALL... THIS IS MY FIRST TIME HOSTING TOO.
PANIC おろ PANIC おろ
GUESS THESE ARE ALL THE RAGE...
SIT
もーん
LOTS OF GOOD FORTUNE FOR US! ♡
BOOK: MODERN JAPANESE
WHICH SUBJECT DO YOU NEED HELP IN, KURO-CHAN?
YAP わい
YAP わい
HMPH. ん—
YAP わい
I'M GUESSING ALL OF THEM.
WE'D BETTER NARROW IT DOWN TO STRATEGIES FOR A SINGLE QUIZ IN JAPANESE OR SOMETHING.
OR IT'LL BE DARK BEFORE WE KNOW IT.
AH! I JUST REALIZED ...

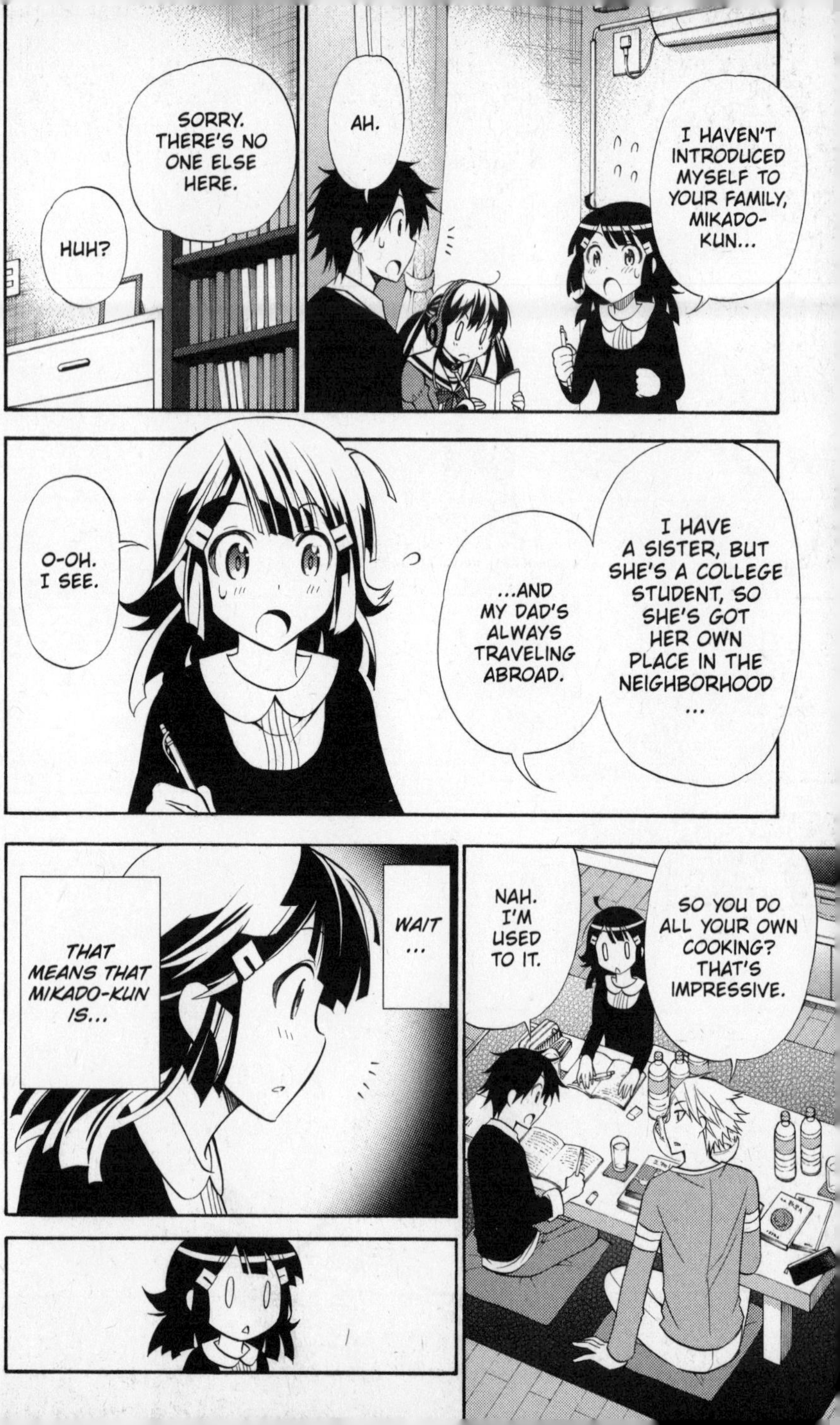
I HAVEN'T INTRODUCED MYSELF TO YOUR FAMILY, MIKADO-KUN...
AH.
SORRY. THERE'S NO ONE ELSE HERE.
HUH?
I HAVE A SISTER, BUT SHE'S A COLLEGE STUDENT, SO SHE'S GOT HER OWN PLACE IN THE NEIGHBORHOOD...
...AND MY DAD'S ALWAYS TRAVELING ABROAD.
O-OH. I SEE.
SO YOU DO ALL YOUR OWN COOKING? THAT'S IMPRESSIVE.
NAH. I'M USED TO IT.
WAIT...
THAT MEANS THAT MIKADO-KUN IS...

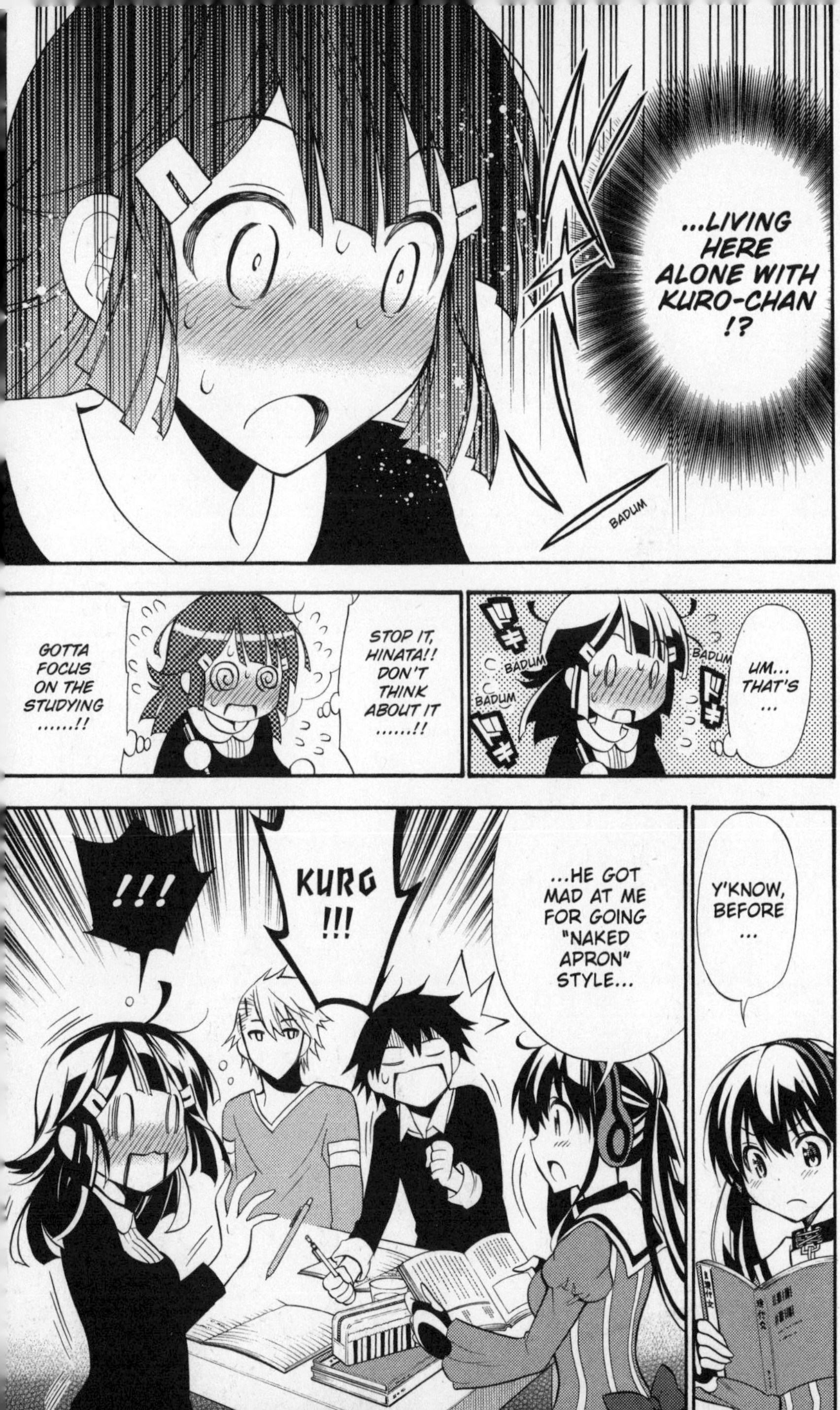
...LIVING HERE ALONE WITH KURO-CHAN !?
BADUM
UM... THAT'S ...
BADUM
BADUM
BADUM
STOP IT, HINATA!! DON'T THINK ABOUT IT ......!!
GOTTA FOCUS ON THE STUDYING ......!!
Y'KNOW, BEFORE ...
...HE GOT MAD AT ME FOR GOING "NAKED APRON" STYLE...
KURO !!!
!!!

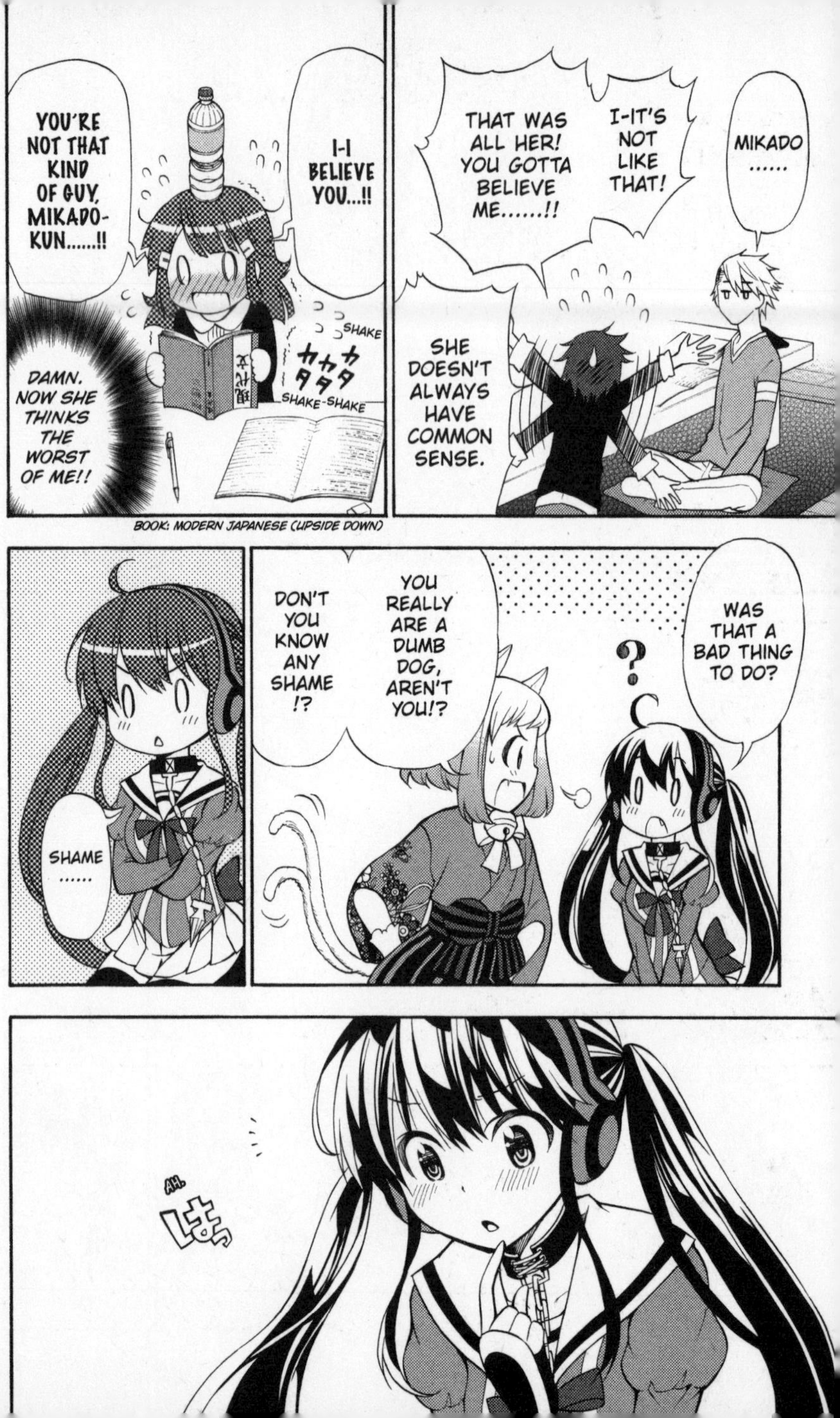
MIKADO ......
I-IT'S NOT LIKE THAT!
THAT WAS ALL HER! YOU GOTTA BELIEVE ME......!!
SHE DOESN'T ALWAYS HAVE COMMON SENSE.
I-I BELIEVE YOU...!!
SHAKE
カタカタ
SHAKE-SHAKE
YOU'RE NOT THAT KIND OF GUY, MIKADO-KUN......!!
DAMN. NOW SHE THINKS THE WORST OF ME!!
BOOK: MODERN JAPANESE (UPSIDE DOWN)
WAS THAT A BAD THING TO DO?
?
YOU REALLY ARE A DUMB DOG, AREN'T YOU!?
DON'T YOU KNOW ANY SHAME !?
SHAME ......
AH.
はっ

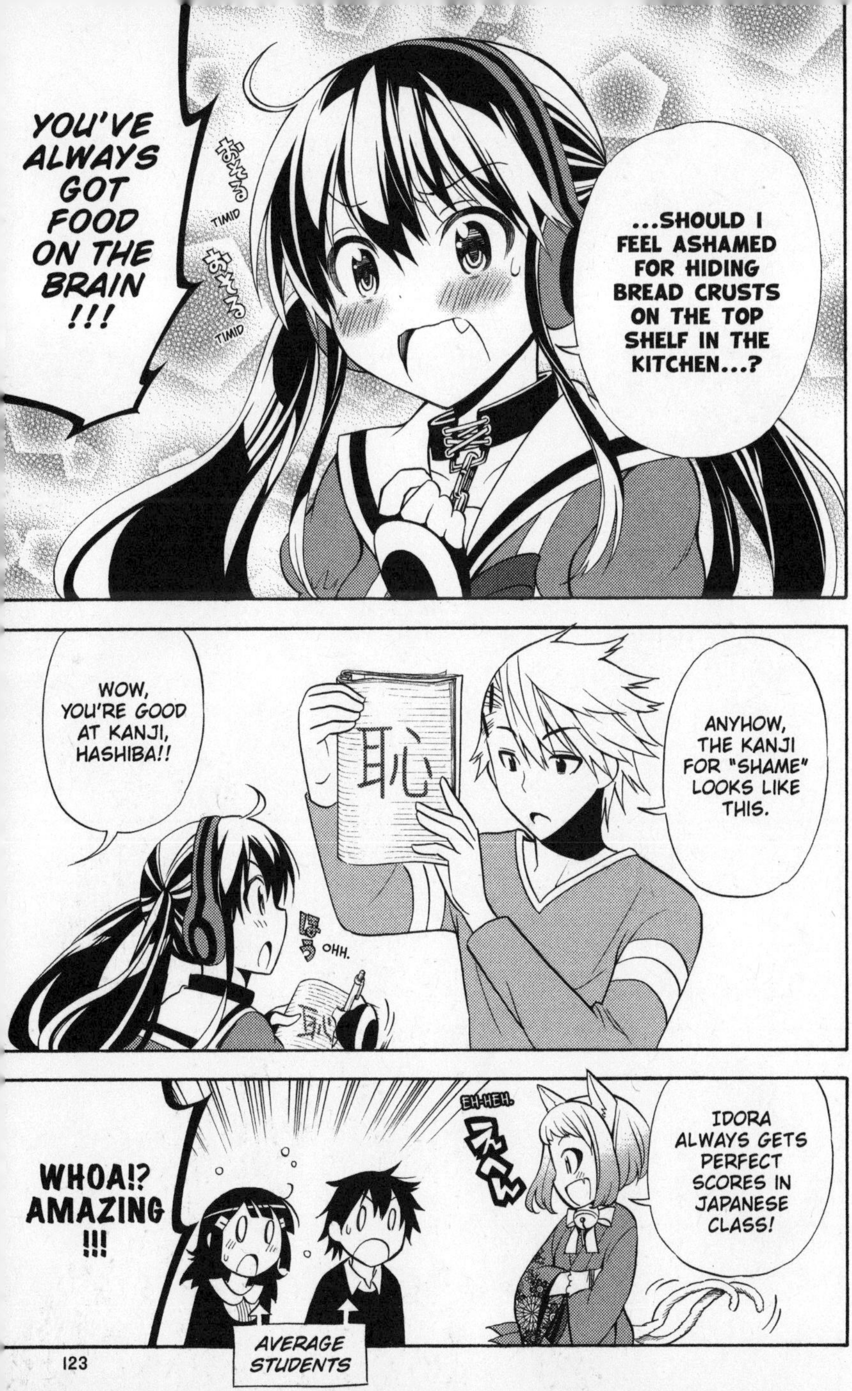
...SHOULD I FEEL ASHAMED FOR HIDING BREAD CRUSTS ON THE TOP SHELF IN THE KITCHEN...?
おそる TIMID
おそる TIMID
YOU'VE ALWAYS GOT FOOD ON THE BRAIN !!!
ANYHOW, THE KANJI FOR "SHAME" LOOKS LIKE THIS.
恥
OHH.
WOW, YOU'RE GOOD AT KANJI, HASHIBA!!
IDORA ALWAYS GETS PERFECT SCORES IN JAPANESE CLASS!
EH-HEH.
WHOA!? AMAZING !!!
AVERAGE STUDENTS

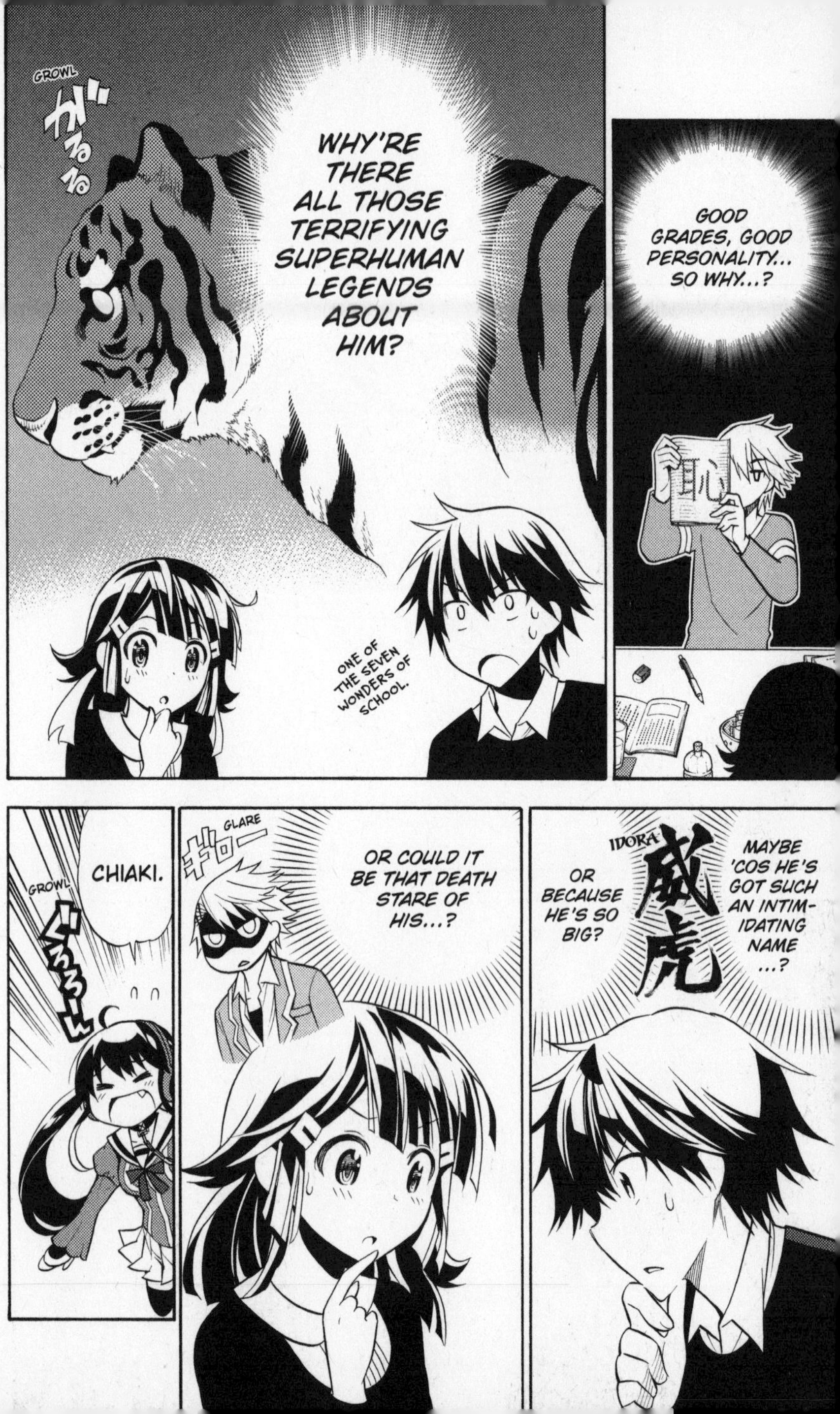
GOOD GRADES, GOOD PERSONALITY... SO WHY...?
GROWL
WHY'RE THERE ALL THOSE TERRIFYING SUPERHUMAN LEGENDS ABOUT HIM?
ONE OF THE SEVEN WONDERS OF SCHOOL.
MAYBE 'COS HE'S GOT SUCH AN INTIM-IDATING NAME ...?
IDORA
威虎
OR BECAUSE HE'S SO BIG?
GLARE
OR COULD IT BE THAT DEATH STARE OF HIS...?
CHIAKI.
GROWL

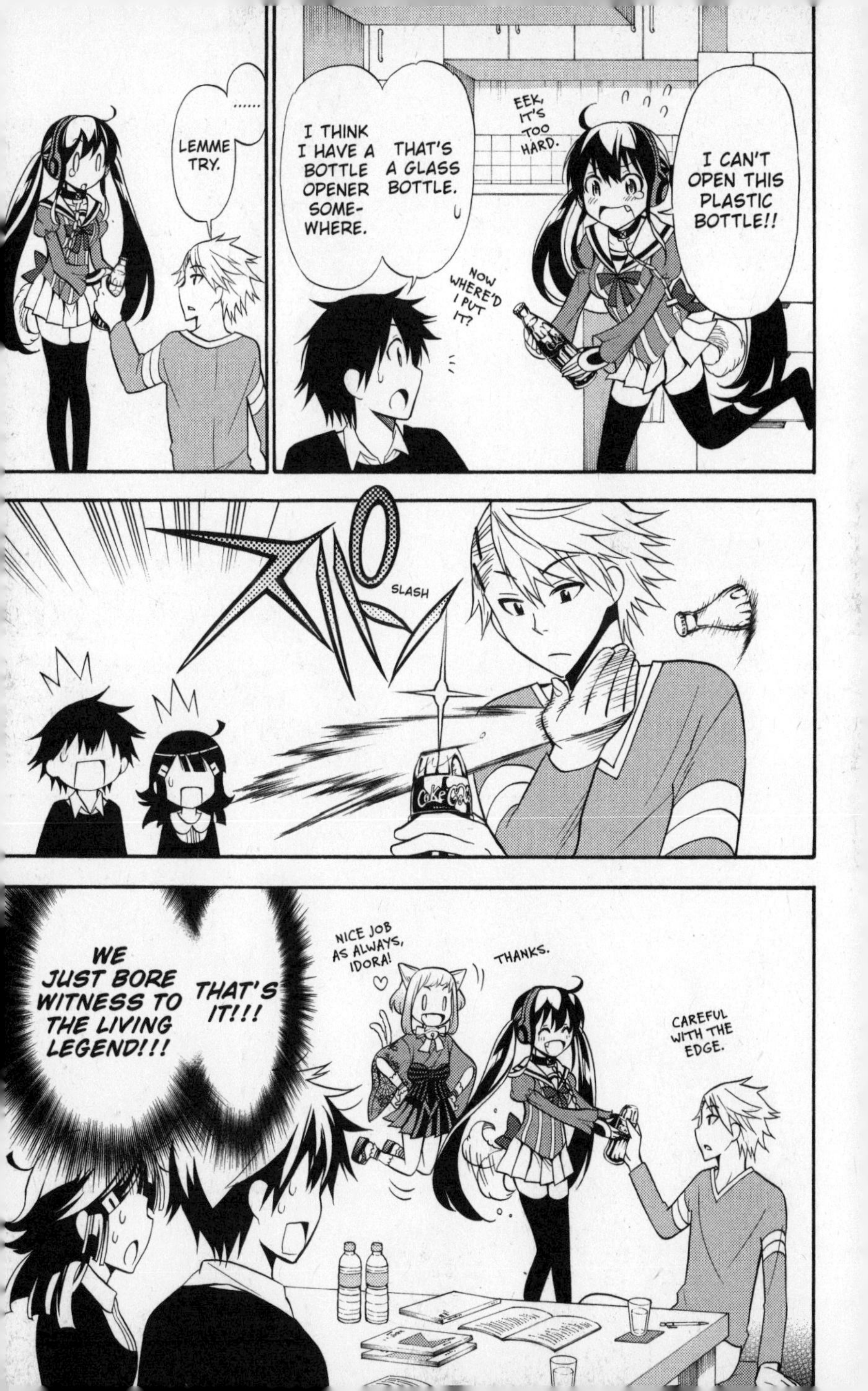
I CAN'T OPEN THIS PLASTIC BOTTLE!!
EEK, IT'S TOO HARD.
THAT'S A GLASS BOTTLE.
I THINK I HAVE A BOTTLE OPENER SOME-WHERE.
NOW WHERE'D I PUT IT?
......
LEMME TRY.
SLASH
CAREFUL WITH THE EDGE.
THANKS.
NICE JOB AS ALWAYS, IDORA!
THAT'S IT!!!
WE JUST BORE WITNESS TO THE LIVING LEGEND!!!

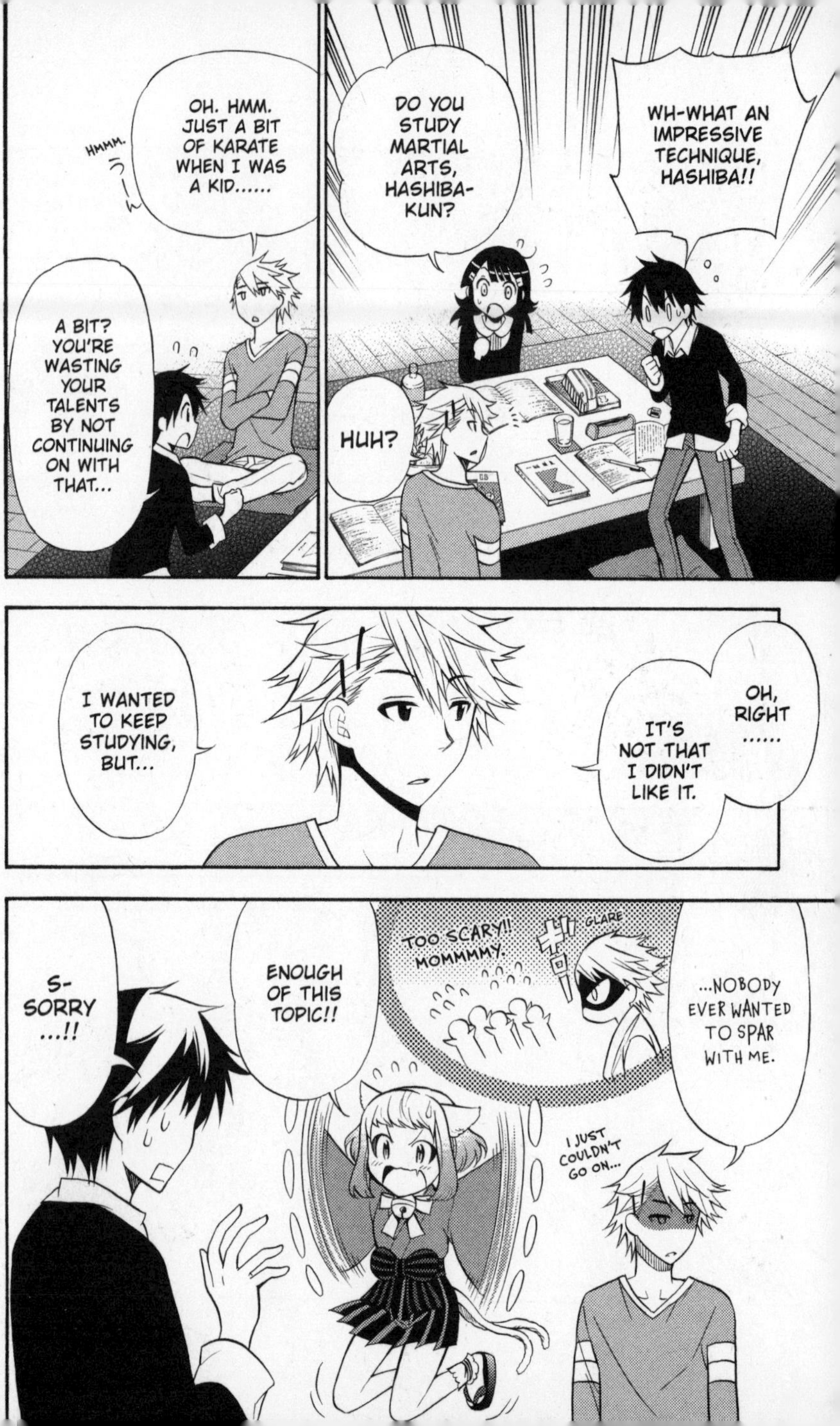
WH-WHAT AN IMPRESSIVE TECHNIQUE, HASHIBA!!
DO YOU STUDY MARTIAL ARTS, HASHIBA-KUN?
HUH?
OH. HMM. JUST A BIT OF KARATE WHEN I WAS A KID......
HMMM.
A BIT? YOU'RE WASTING YOUR TALENTS BY NOT CONTINUING ON WITH THAT...
OH, RIGHT ......
IT'S NOT THAT I DIDN'T LIKE IT.
I WANTED TO KEEP STUDYING, BUT...
...NOBODY EVER WANTED TO SPAR WITH ME.
GLARE
TOO SCARY!! MOMMMMY.
I JUST COULDN'T GO ON...
ENOUGH OF THIS TOPIC!!
S-SORRY ...!!

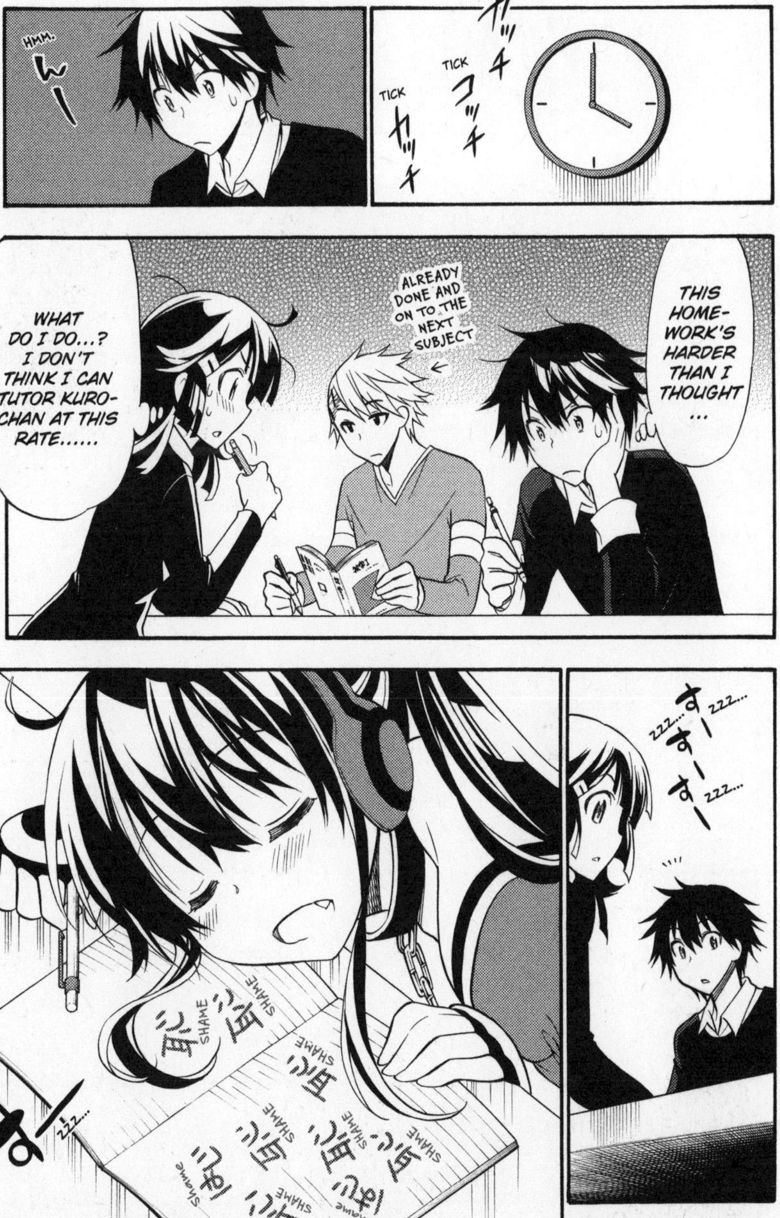
TICK
TICK
TICK
HMM.
THIS HOMEWORK'S HARDER THAN I THOUGHT...
ALREADY DONE AND ON TO THE NEXT SUBJECT
WHAT DO I DO...? I DON'T THINK I CAN TUTOR KURO-CHAN AT THIS RATE......
ZZZ...
ZZZ...
ZZZ...
SHAME
ZZZ...

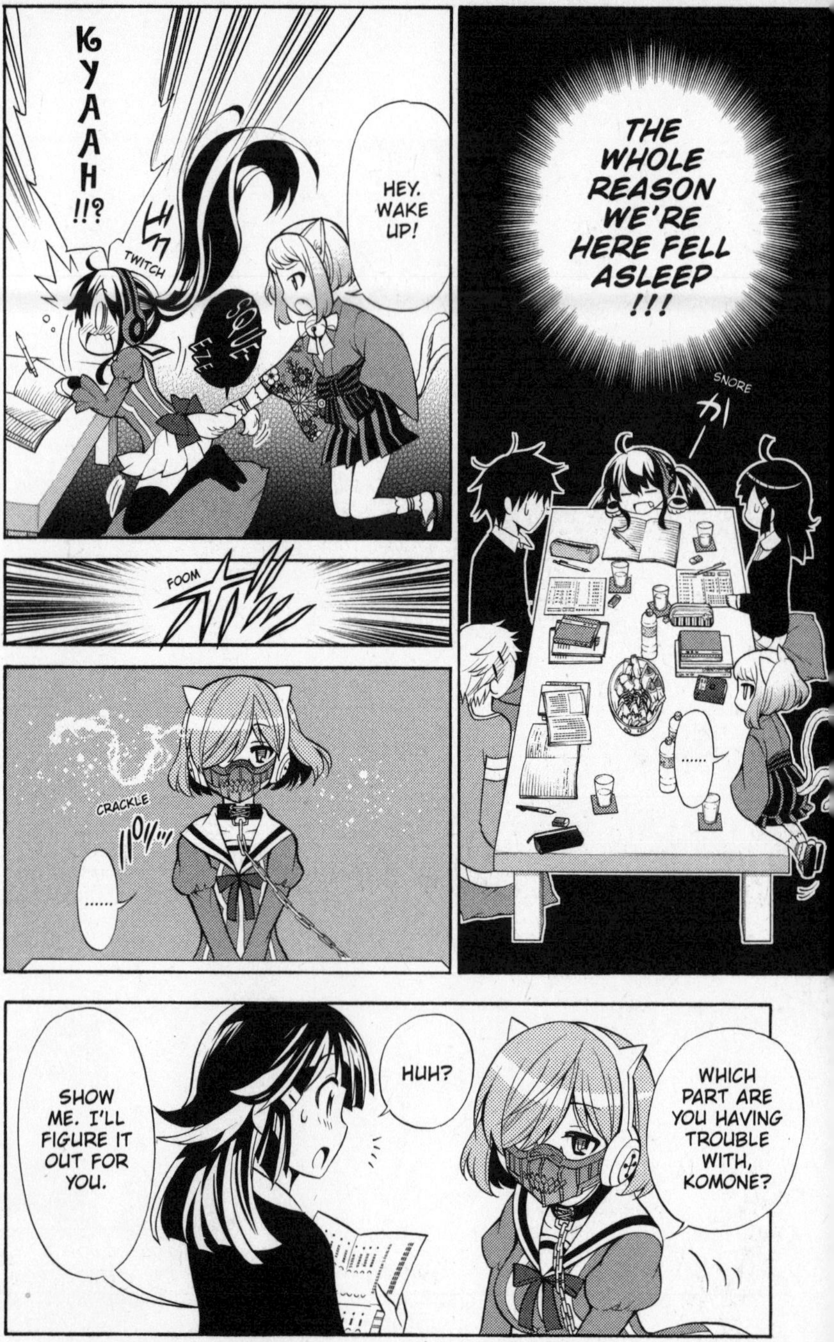
THE WHOLE REASON WE'RE HERE FELL ASLEEP!!!
SNORE
......
HEY. WAKE UP!
KYAAH!!?
TWITCH
SQUEEZE
FOOM
CRACKLE
......
WHICH PART ARE YOU HAVING TROUBLE WITH, KOMONE?
HUH?
SHOW ME. I'LL FIGURE IT OUT FOR YOU.

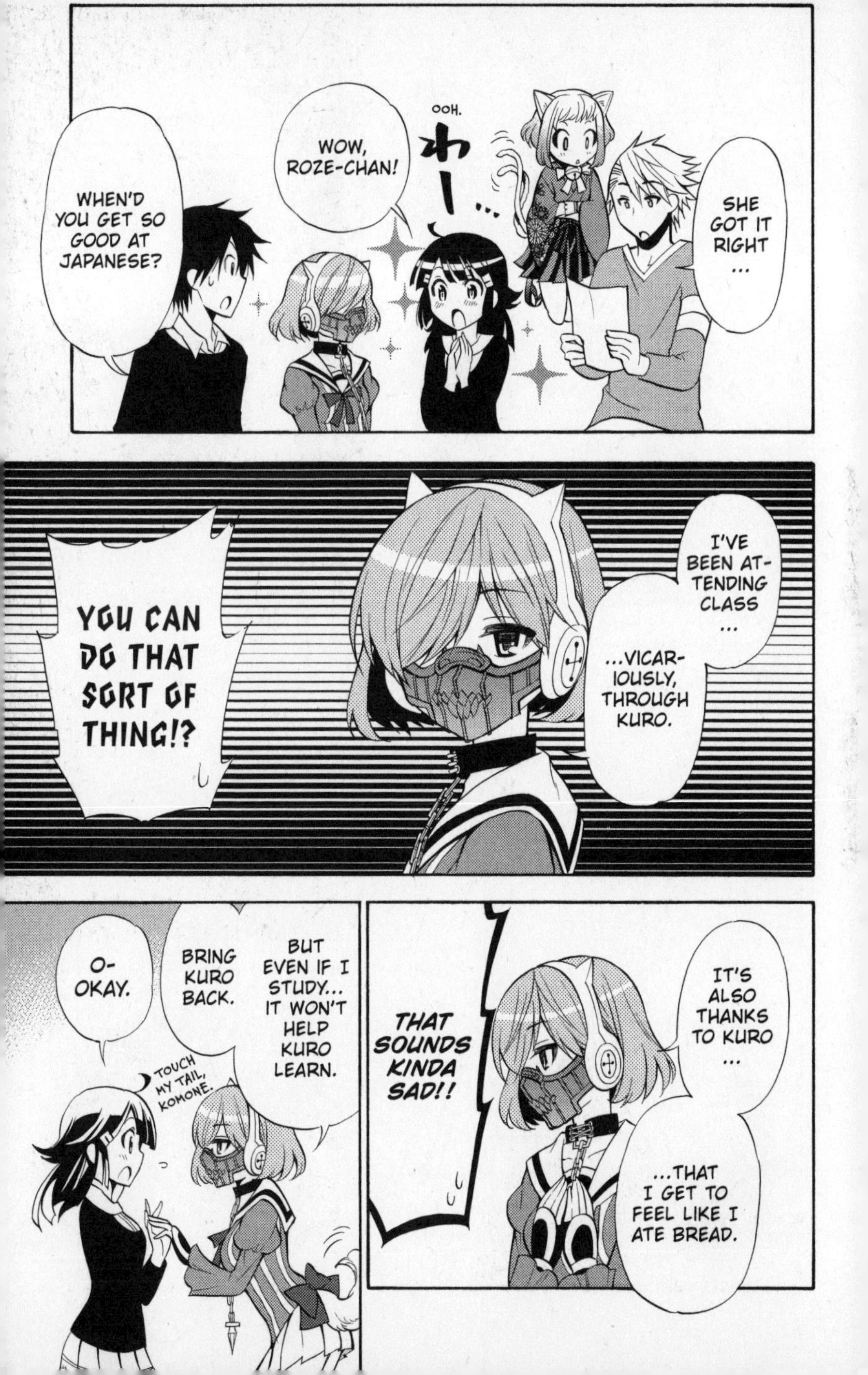
SHE GOT IT RIGHT ...
OOH.
わー…
WOW, ROZE-CHAN!
WHEN'D YOU GET SO GOOD AT JAPANESE?
I'VE BEEN AT-TENDING CLASS ...
...VICAR-IOUSLY, THROUGH KURO.
YOU CAN DO THAT SORT OF THING!?
IT'S ALSO THANKS TO KURO ...
...THAT I GET TO FEEL LIKE I ATE BREAD.
THAT SOUNDS KINDA SAD!!
BUT EVEN IF I STUDY... IT WON'T HELP KURO LEARN.
BRING KURO BACK.
O-OKAY.
TOUCH MY TAIL, KOMONE.

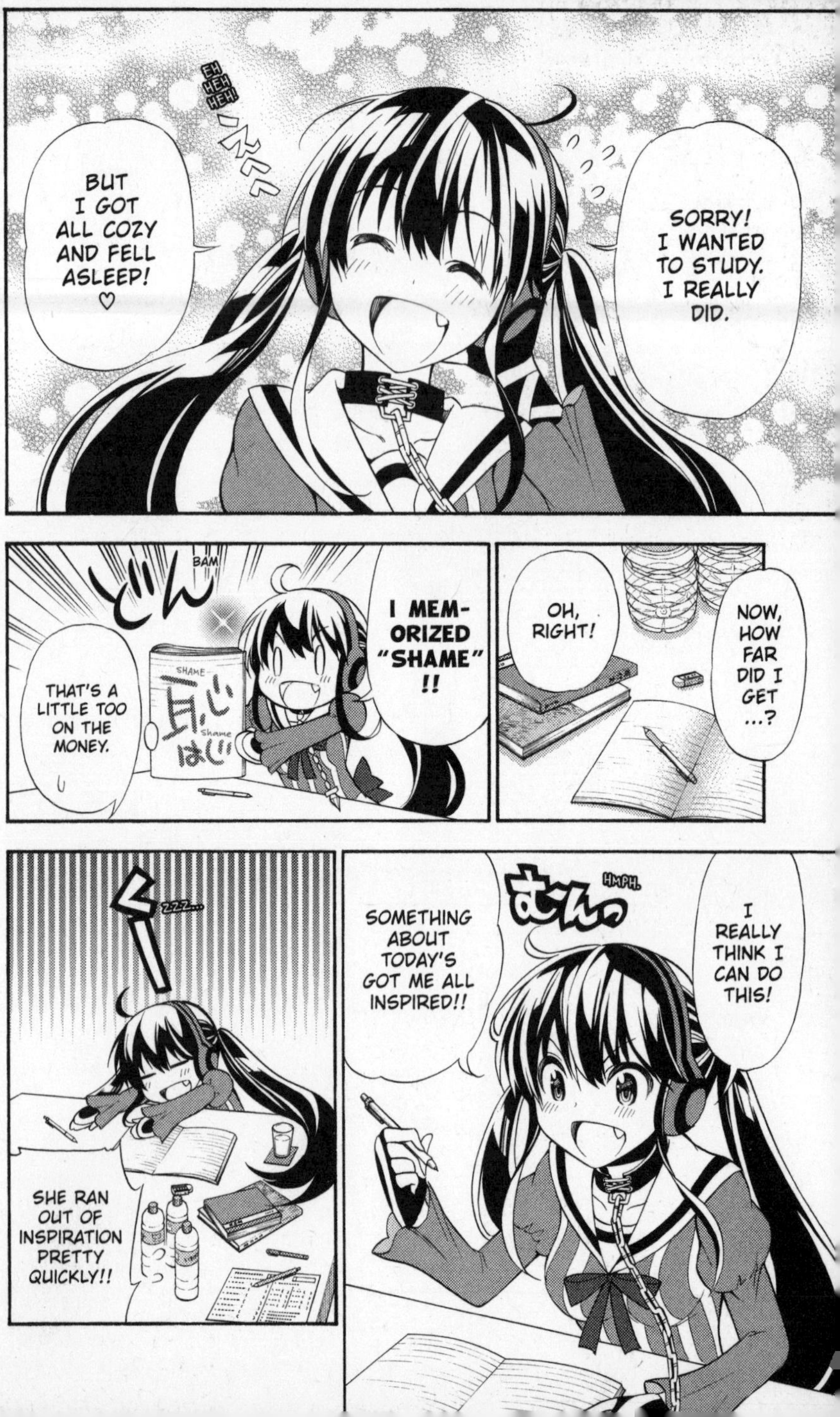
SORRY! I WANTED TO STUDY. I REALLY DID.
EH HEH HEH!
BUT I GOT ALL COZY AND FELL ASLEEP! ♡
NOW, HOW FAR DID I GET ...?
OH, RIGHT!
I MEM-ORIZED "SHAME" !!
BAM
SHAME
Shame
THAT'S A LITTLE TOO ON THE MONEY.
I REALLY THINK I CAN DO THIS!
HMPH.
SOMETHING ABOUT TODAY'S GOT ME ALL INSPIRED!!
zzz...
SHE RAN OUT OF INSPIRATION PRETTY QUICKLY!!

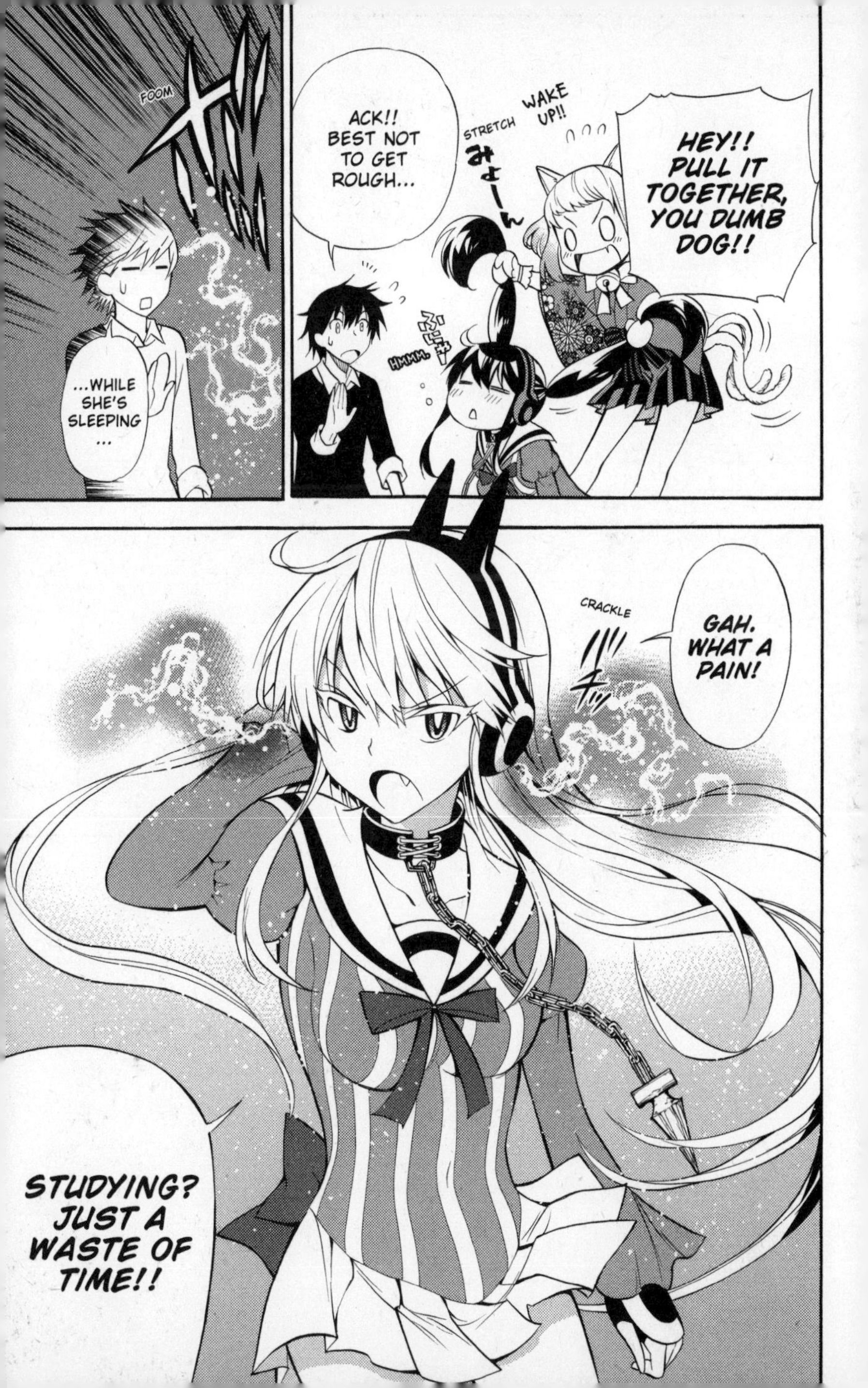
HEY!! PULL IT TOGETHER, YOU DUMB DOG!!
WAKE UP!!
STRETCH
みょーん
ACK!! BEST NOT TO GET ROUGH...
HMMM.
FOOM
...WHILE SHE'S SLEEPING ...
GAH. WHAT A PAIN!
CRACKLE
STUDYING? JUST A WASTE OF TIME!!

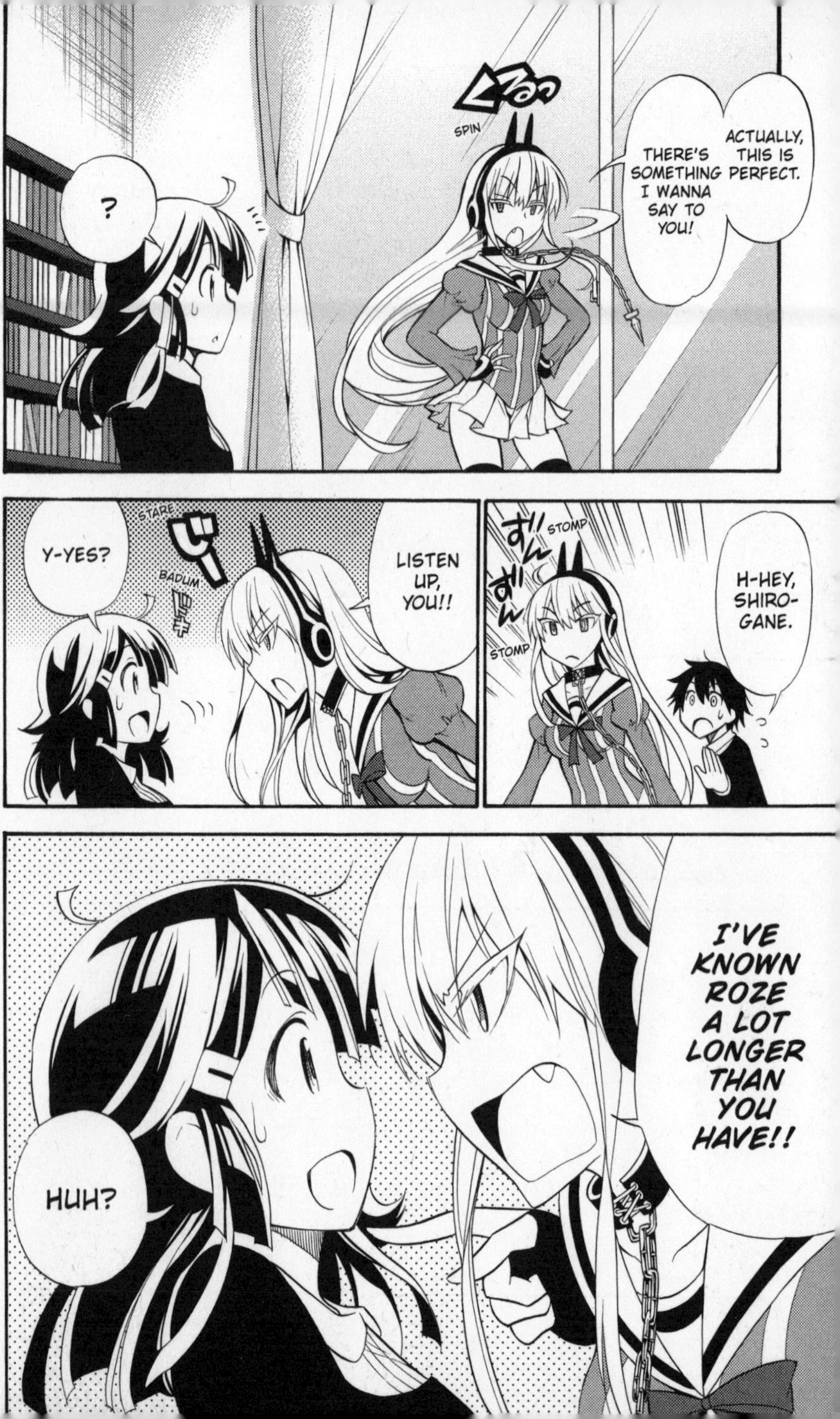
SPIN
ACTUALLY, THIS IS PERFECT.
THERE'S SOMETHING I WANNA SAY TO YOU!
?
STOMP
STOMP
H-HEY, SHIRO-GANE.
LISTEN UP, YOU!!
STARE
BADUM
Y-YES?
I'VE KNOWN ROZE A LOT LONGER THAN YOU HAVE!!
HUH?

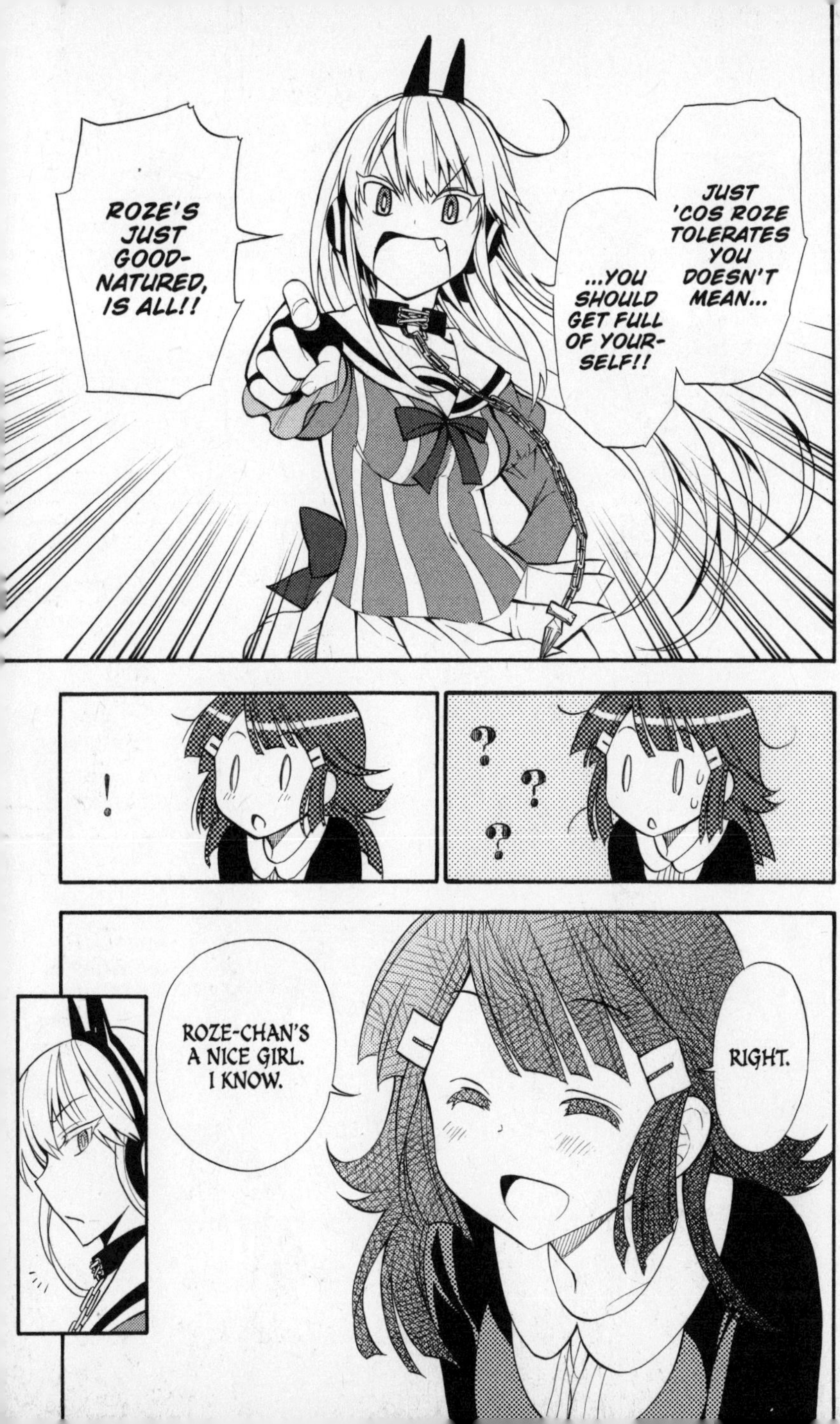
JUST 'COS ROZE TOLERATES YOU DOESN'T MEAN...
...YOU SHOULD GET FULL OF YOUR-SELF!!
ROZE'S JUST GOOD-NATURED, IS ALL!!
? ? ?
!
RIGHT.
ROZE-CHAN'S A NICE GIRL. I KNOW.

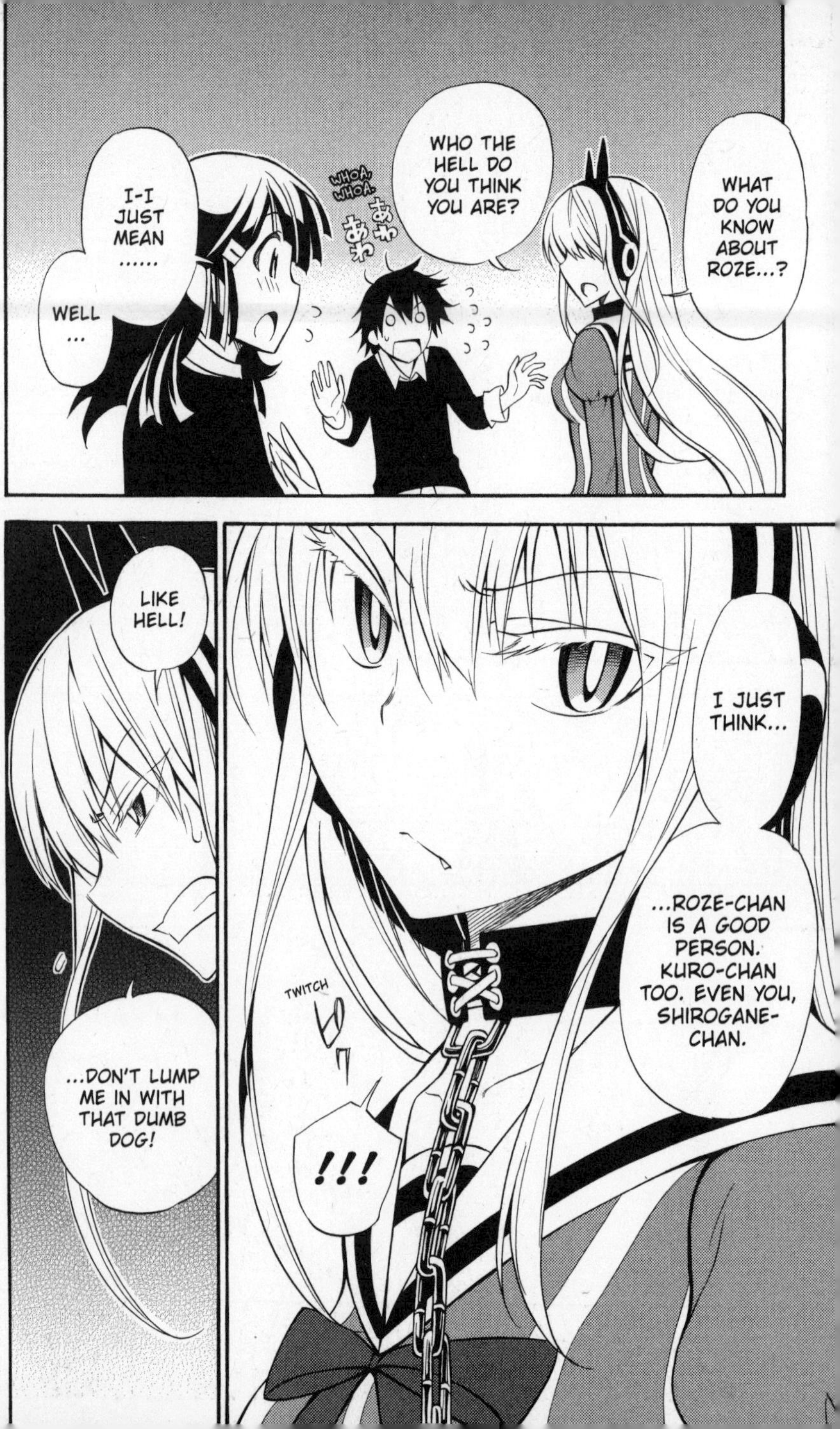
WHAT DO YOU KNOW ABOUT ROZE...?
WHO THE HELL DO YOU THINK YOU ARE?
WHOA, WHOA.
あわあわ
I-I JUST MEAN ......
WELL ...
I JUST THINK...
...ROZE-CHAN IS A GOOD PERSON. KURO-CHAN TOO. EVEN YOU, SHIROGANE-CHAN.
TWITCH
!!!
LIKE HELL!
...DON'T LUMP ME IN WITH THAT DUMB DOG!

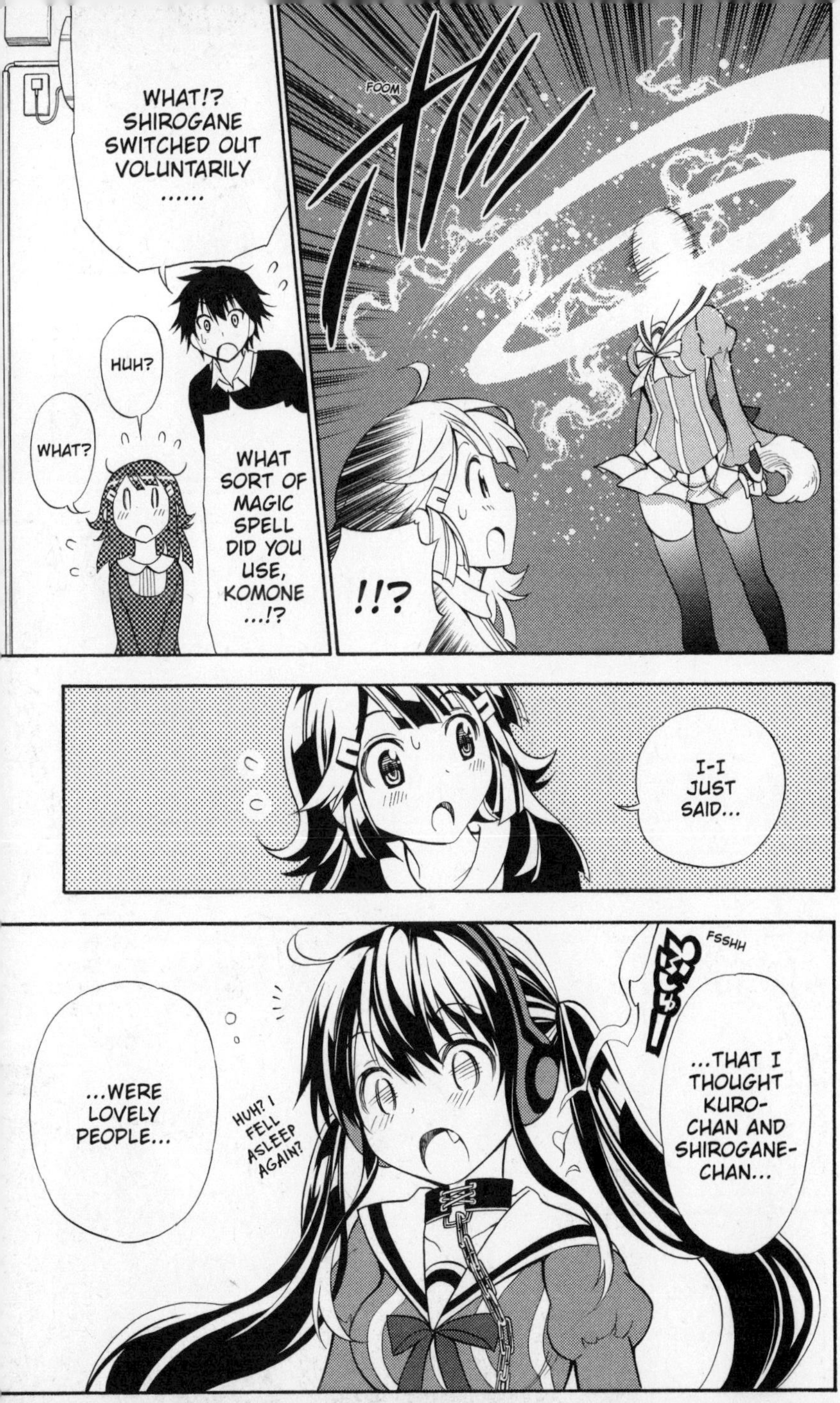
FOOM
!!?
WHAT!? SHIROGANE SWITCHED OUT VOLUNTARILY ......
WHAT SORT OF MAGIC SPELL DID YOU USE, KOMONE ...!?
HUH?
WHAT?
I-I JUST SAID...
FSSHH
...THAT I THOUGHT KURO-CHAN AND SHIROGANE-CHAN...
HUH? I FELL ASLEEP AGAIN?
...WERE LOVELY PEOPLE...

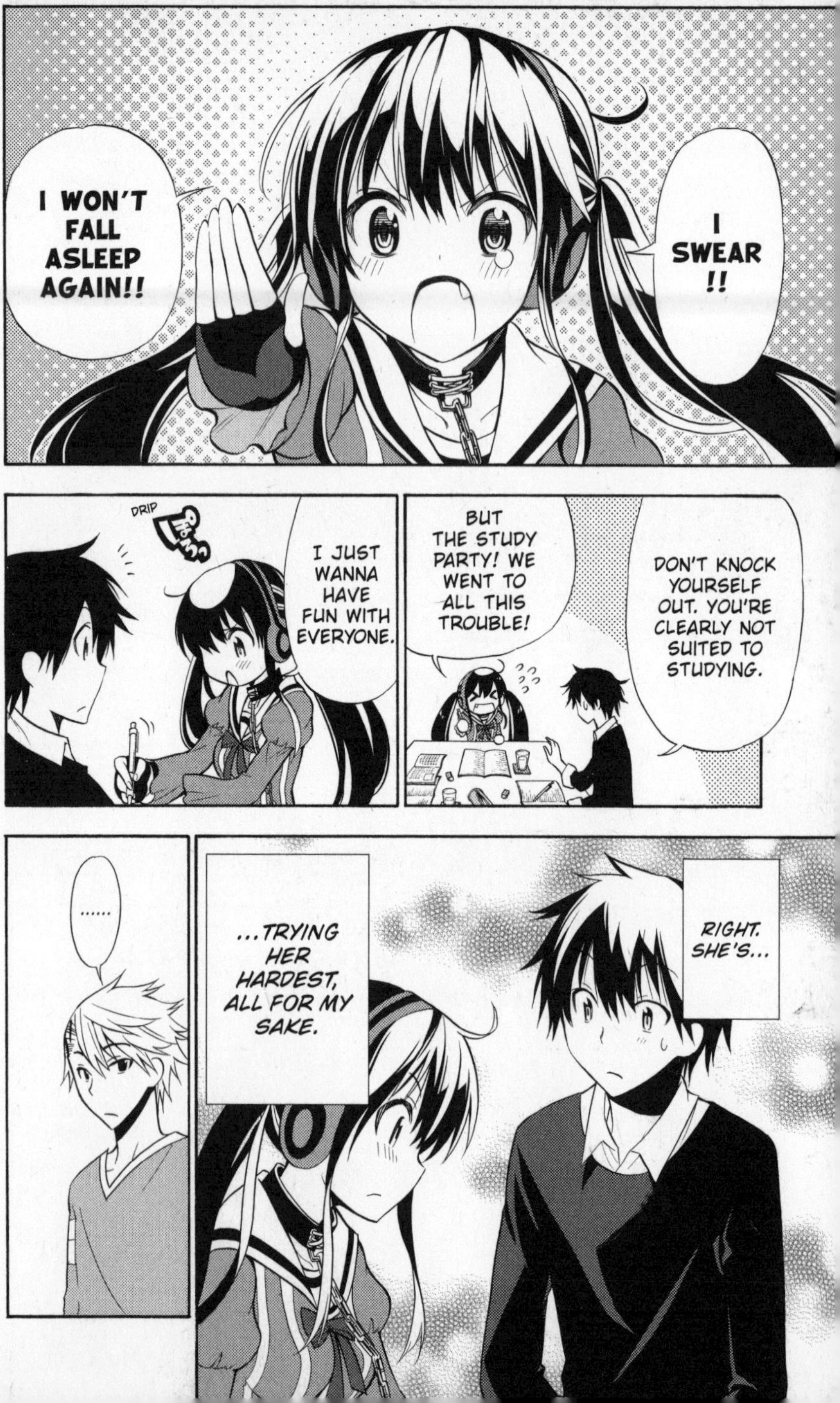
I SWEAR!!
I WON'T FALL ASLEEP AGAIN!!
DON'T KNOCK YOURSELF OUT. YOU'RE CLEARLY NOT SUITED TO STUDYING.
BUT THE STUDY PARTY! WE WENT TO ALL THIS TROUBLE!
I JUST WANNA HAVE FUN WITH EVERYONE.
DRIP
RIGHT. SHE'S...
...TRYING HER HARDEST, ALL FOR MY SAKE.
......

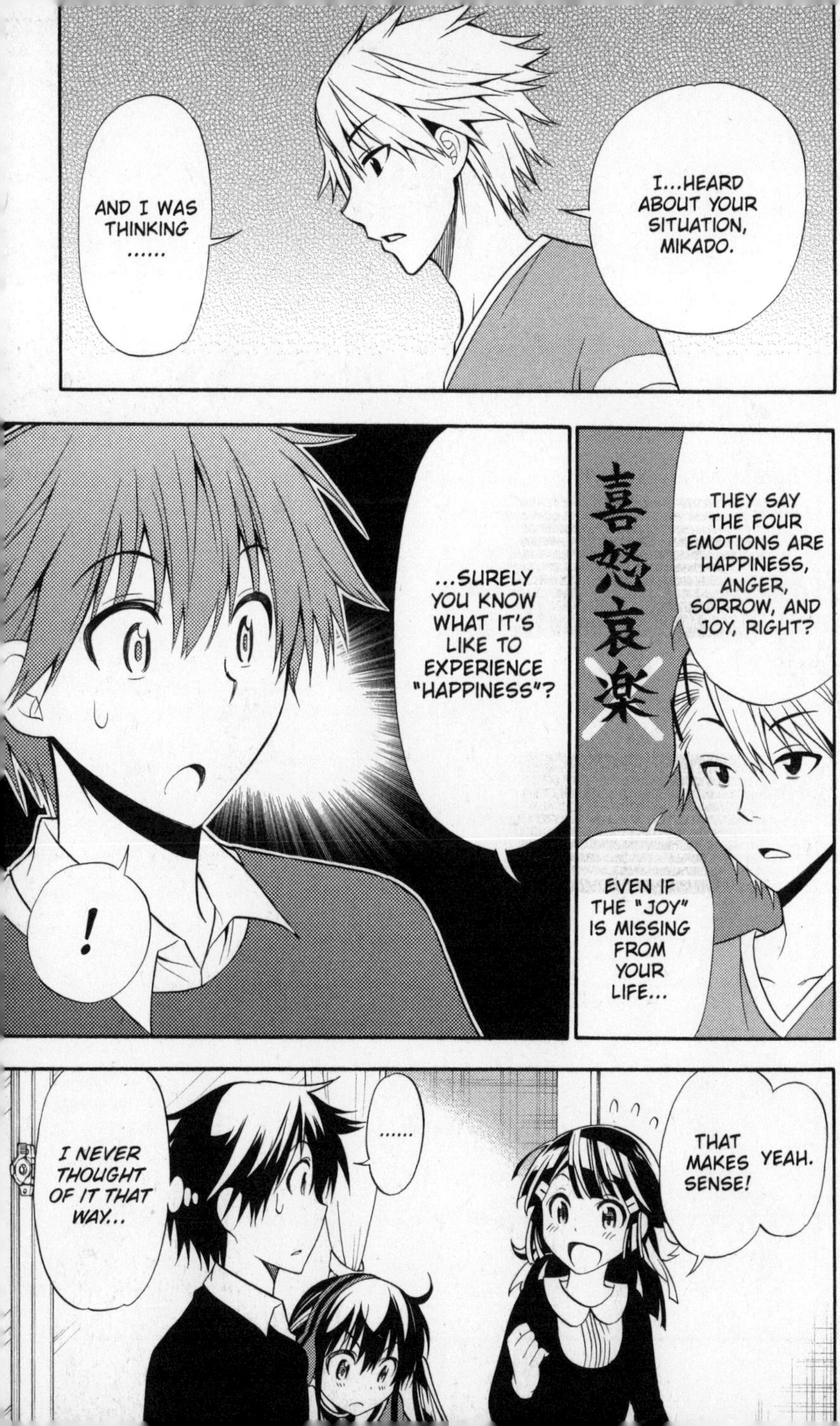
I...HEARD ABOUT YOUR SITUATION, MIKADO.
AND I WAS THINKING ......
喜怒哀楽
THEY SAY THE FOUR EMOTIONS ARE HAPPINESS, ANGER, SORROW, AND JOY, RIGHT?
EVEN IF THE "JOY" IS MISSING FROM YOUR LIFE...
...SURELY YOU KNOW WHAT IT'S LIKE TO EXPERIENCE "HAPPINESS"?
!
YEAH.
THAT MAKES SENSE!
......
I NEVER THOUGHT OF IT THAT WAY...

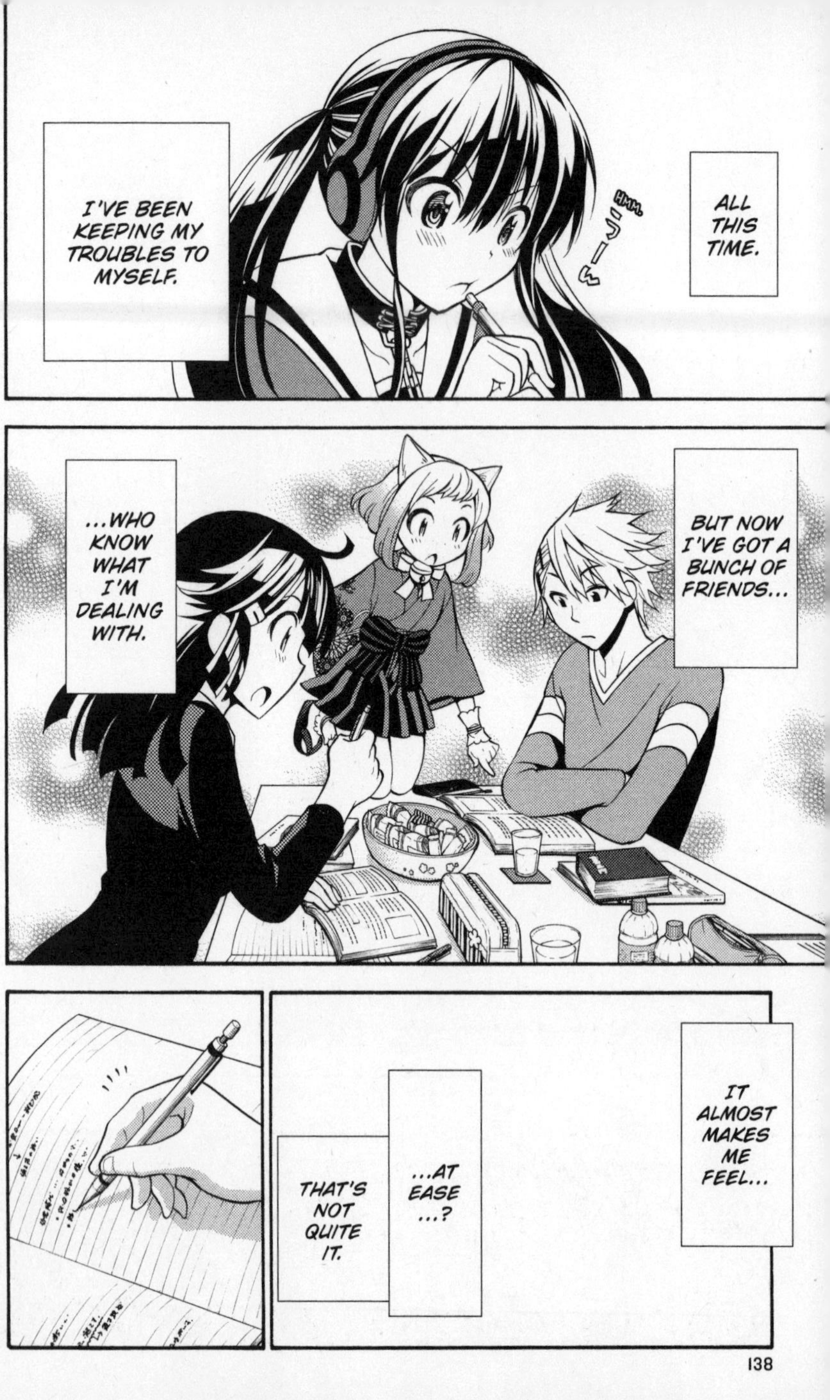
ALL THIS TIME.
HMM.
I'VE BEEN KEEPING MY TROUBLES TO MYSELF.
BUT NOW I'VE GOT A BUNCH OF FRIENDS...
...WHO KNOW WHAT I'M DEALING WITH.
IT ALMOST MAKES ME FEEL...
...AT EASE ...?
THAT'S NOT QUITE IT.

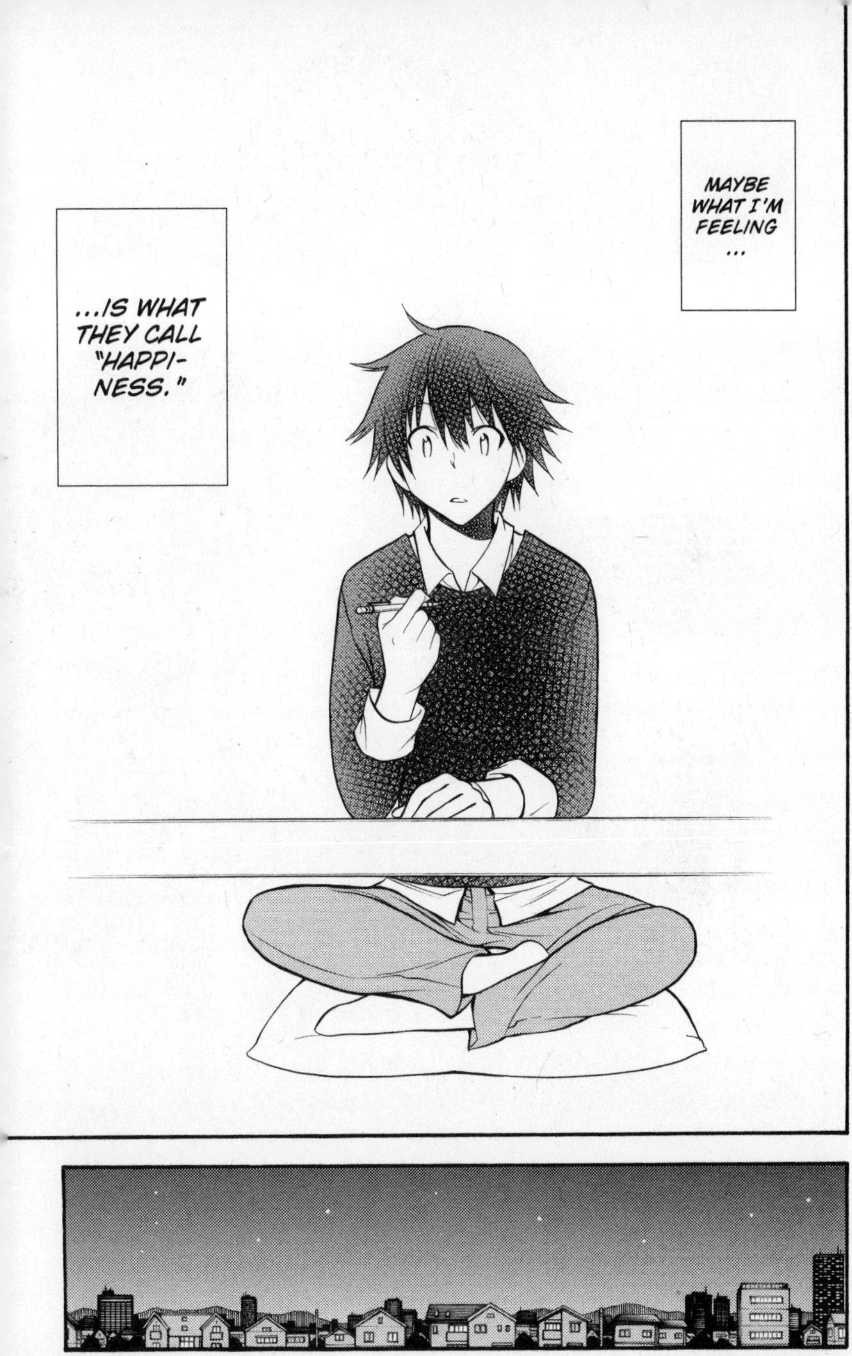
MAYBE WHAT I'M FEELING ...
...IS WHAT THEY CALL "HAPPINESS."

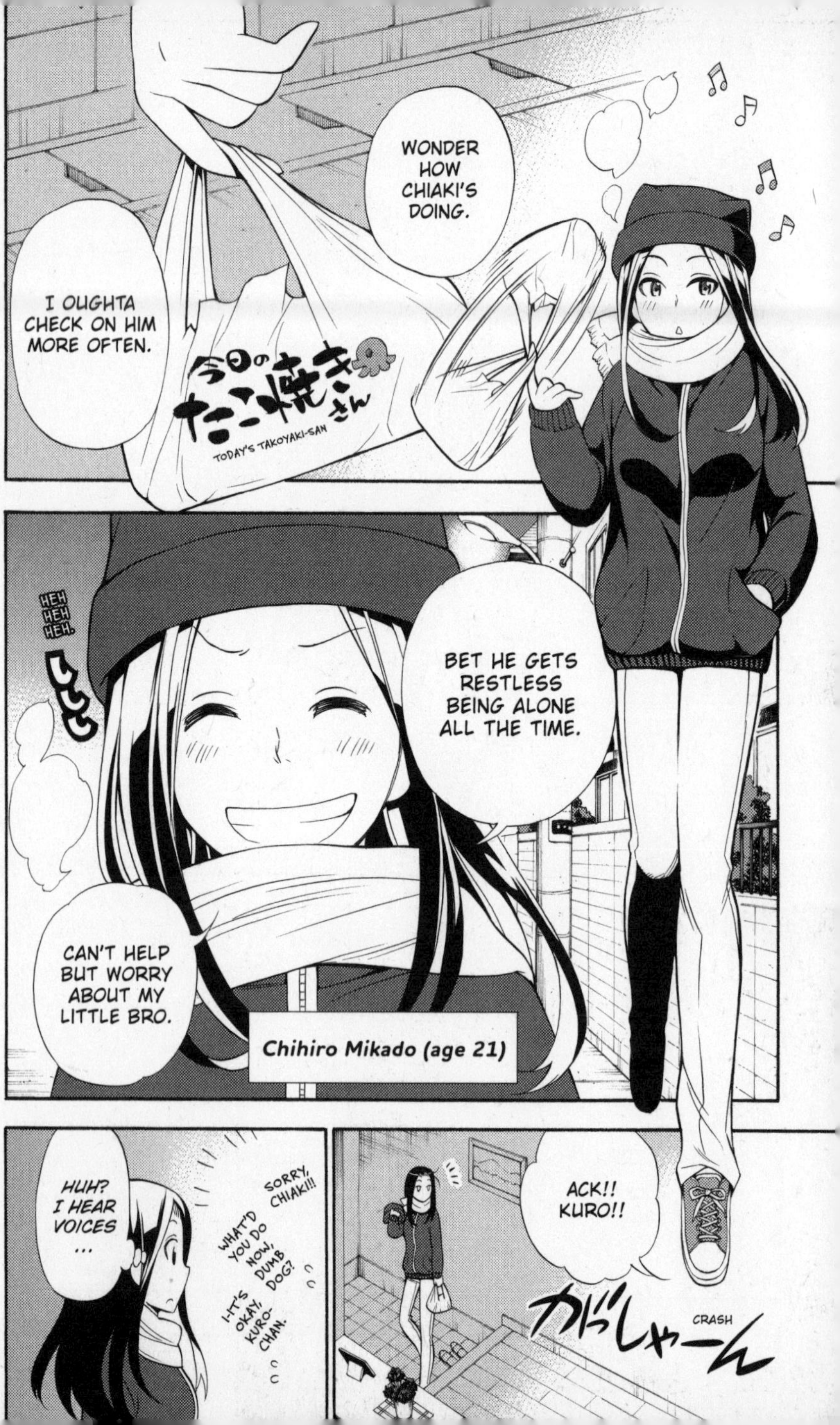
WONDER HOW CHIAKI'S DOING.
I OUGHTA CHECK ON HIM MORE OFTEN.
今日のたこ焼きさん
TODAY'S TAKOYAKI-SAN
BET HE GETS RESTLESS BEING ALONE ALL THE TIME.
HEH HEH HEH.
CAN'T HELP BUT WORRY ABOUT MY LITTLE BRO.
Chihiro Mikado (age 21)
ACK!! KURO!!
CRASH
SORRY, CHIAKI!!!
WHAT'D YOU DO NOW, DUMB DOG?
I-IT'S OKAY, KURO-CHAN.
HUH? I HEAR VOICES ...

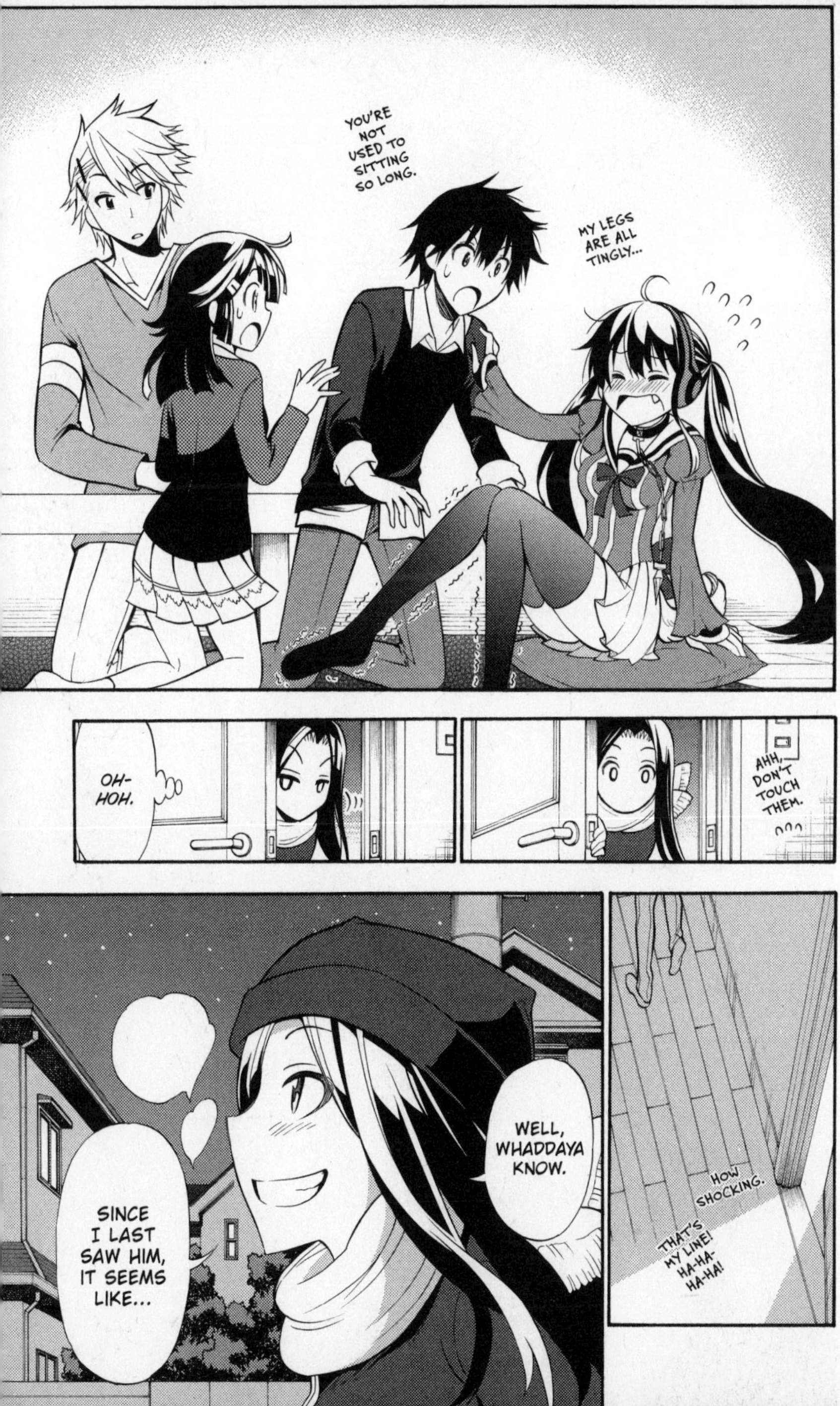
MY LEGS ARE ALL TINGLY...
YOU'RE NOT USED TO SITTING SO LONG.
AHH, DON'T TOUCH THEM.
OH-HOH.
HOW SHOCKING.
THAT'S MY LINE! HA-HA-HA-HA!
WELL, WHADDAYA KNOW.
SINCE I LAST SAW HIM, IT SEEMS LIKE...

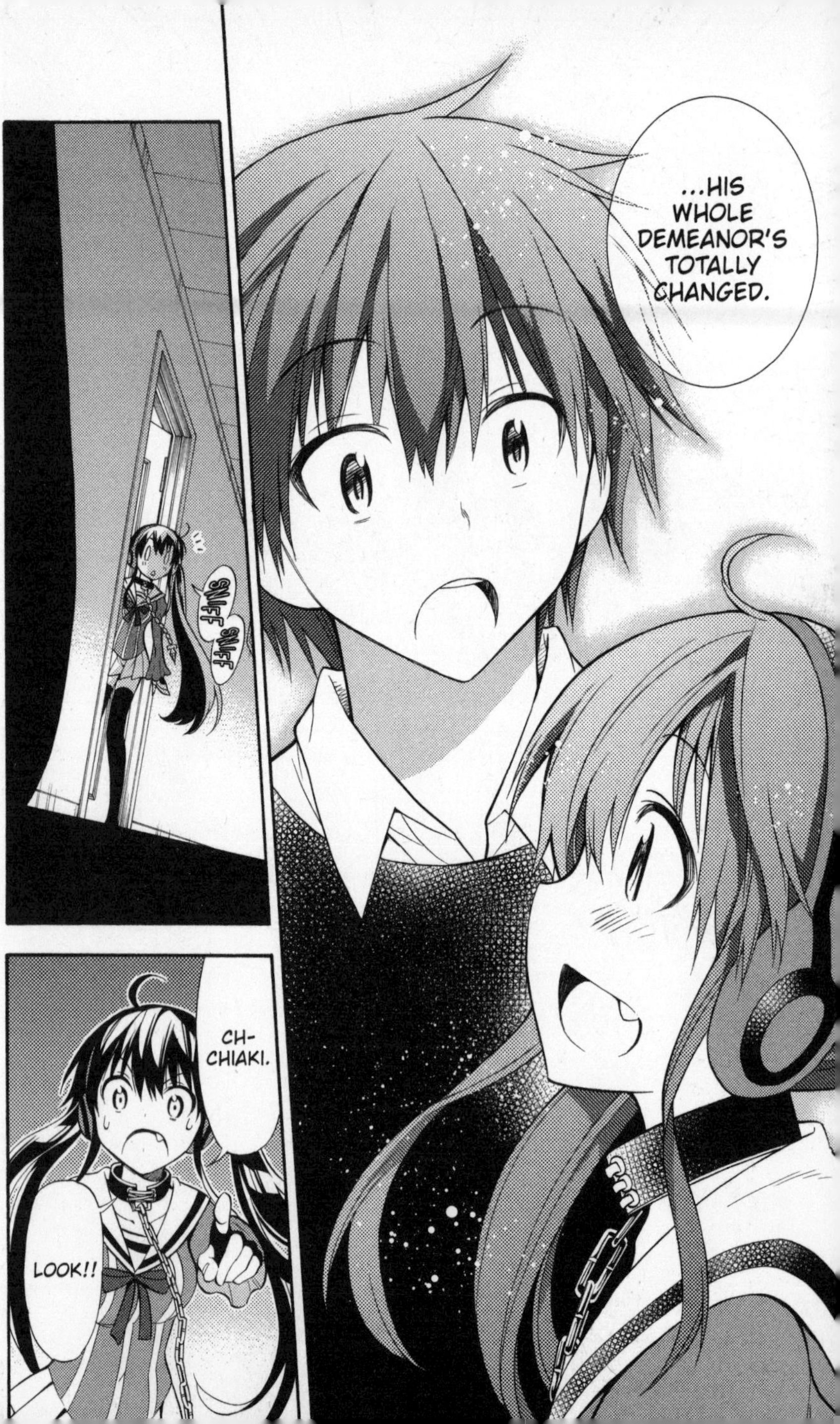
...HIS WHOLE DEMEANOR'S TOTALLY CHANGED.
SNIFF
SNIFF SNIFF
CH-CHIAKI.
LOOK!!

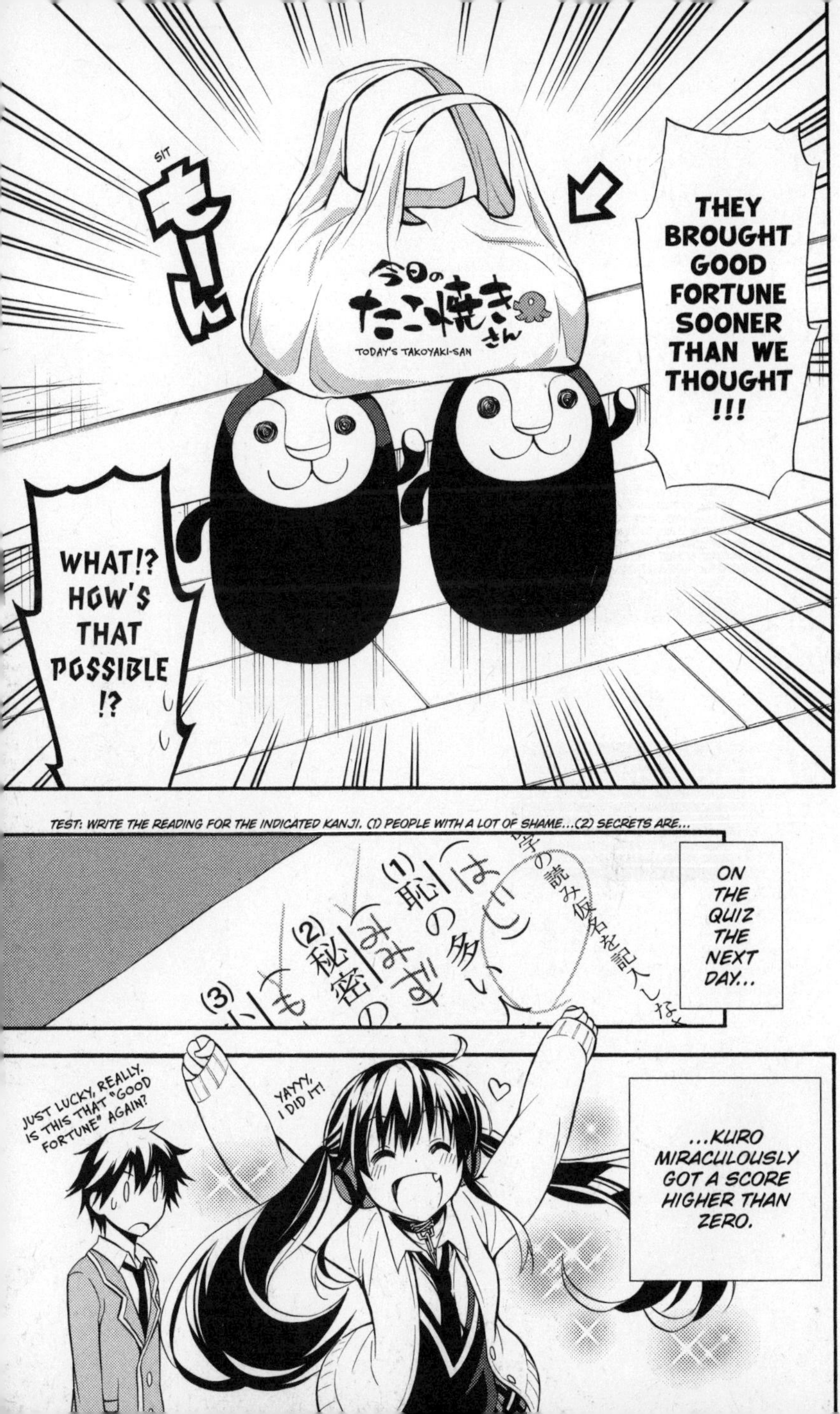
THEY BROUGHT GOOD FORTUNE SOONER THAN WE THOUGHT!!!
今日のたこ焼きさん
TODAY'S TAKOYAKI-SAN
SIT
WHAT!? HOW'S THAT POSSIBLE!?
TEST: WRITE THE READING FOR THE INDICATED KANJI. (1) PEOPLE WITH A LOT OF SHAME...(2) SECRETS ARE...
ON THE QUIZ THE NEXT DAY...
...KURO MIRACULOUSLY GOT A SCORE HIGHER THAN ZERO.
YAYYY, I DID IT!
JUST LUCKY, REALLY. IS THIS THAT "GOOD FORTUNE" AGAIN?

TODAY'S CERBERUS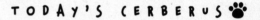

YOU'RE
SAYING IT
TOO NOW.

THAT
DUMB
DOG...!

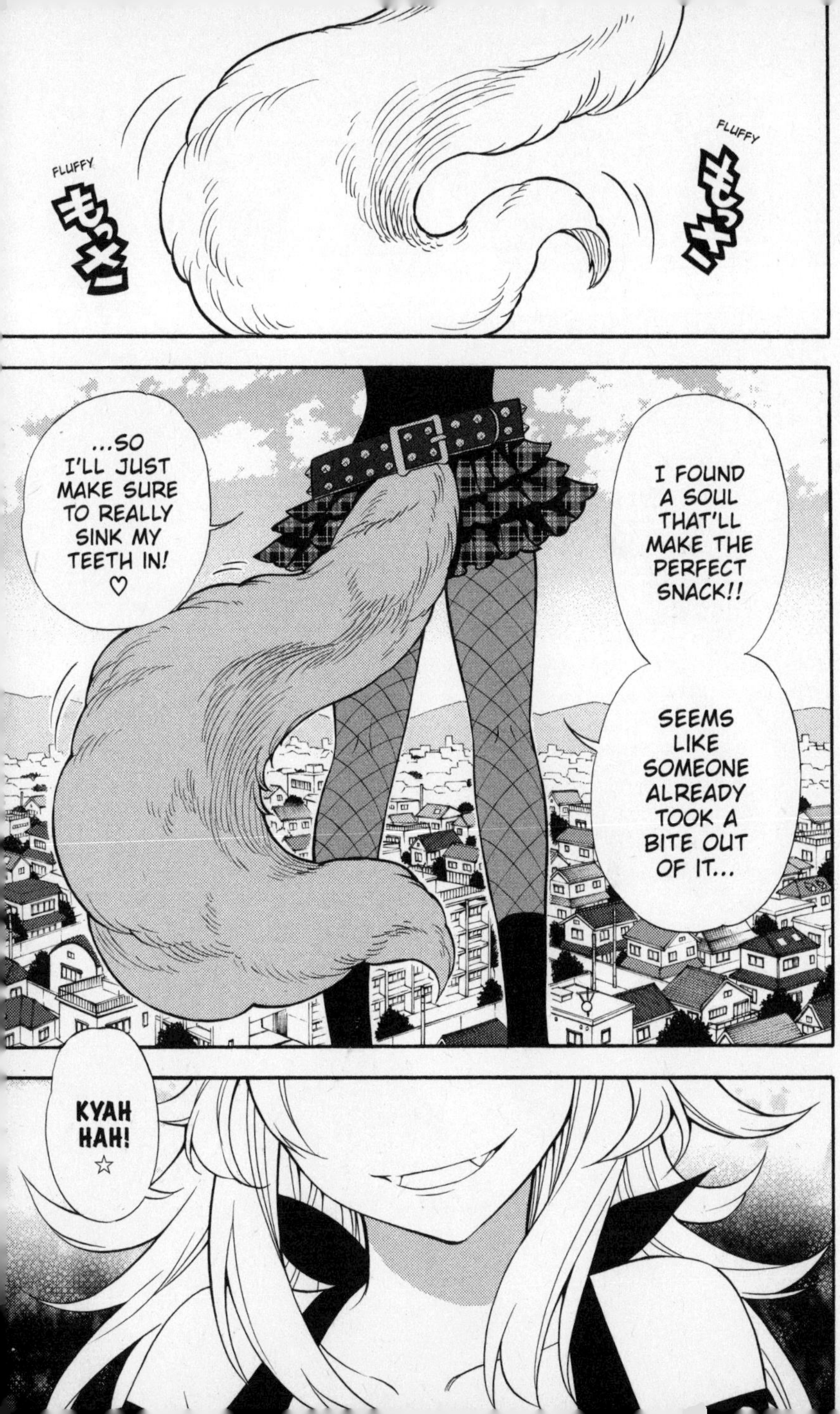
FLUFFY
FLUFFY
I FOUND A SOUL THAT'LL MAKE THE PERFECT SNACK!!
SEEMS LIKE SOMEONE ALREADY TOOK A BITE OUT OF IT...
...SO I'LL JUST MAKE SURE TO REALLY SINK MY TEETH IN! ♡
KYAH HAH! ☆

CHAPTER 9
RIR RIR

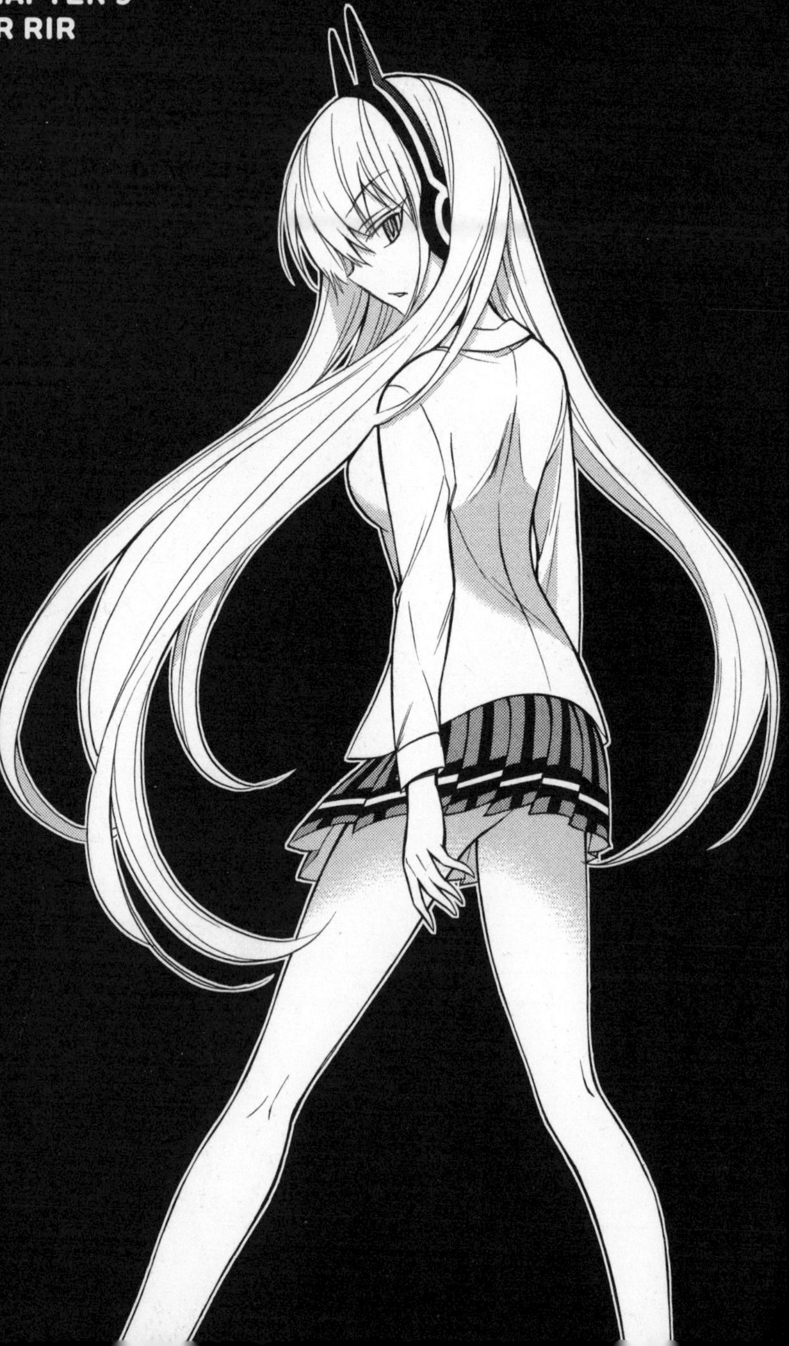

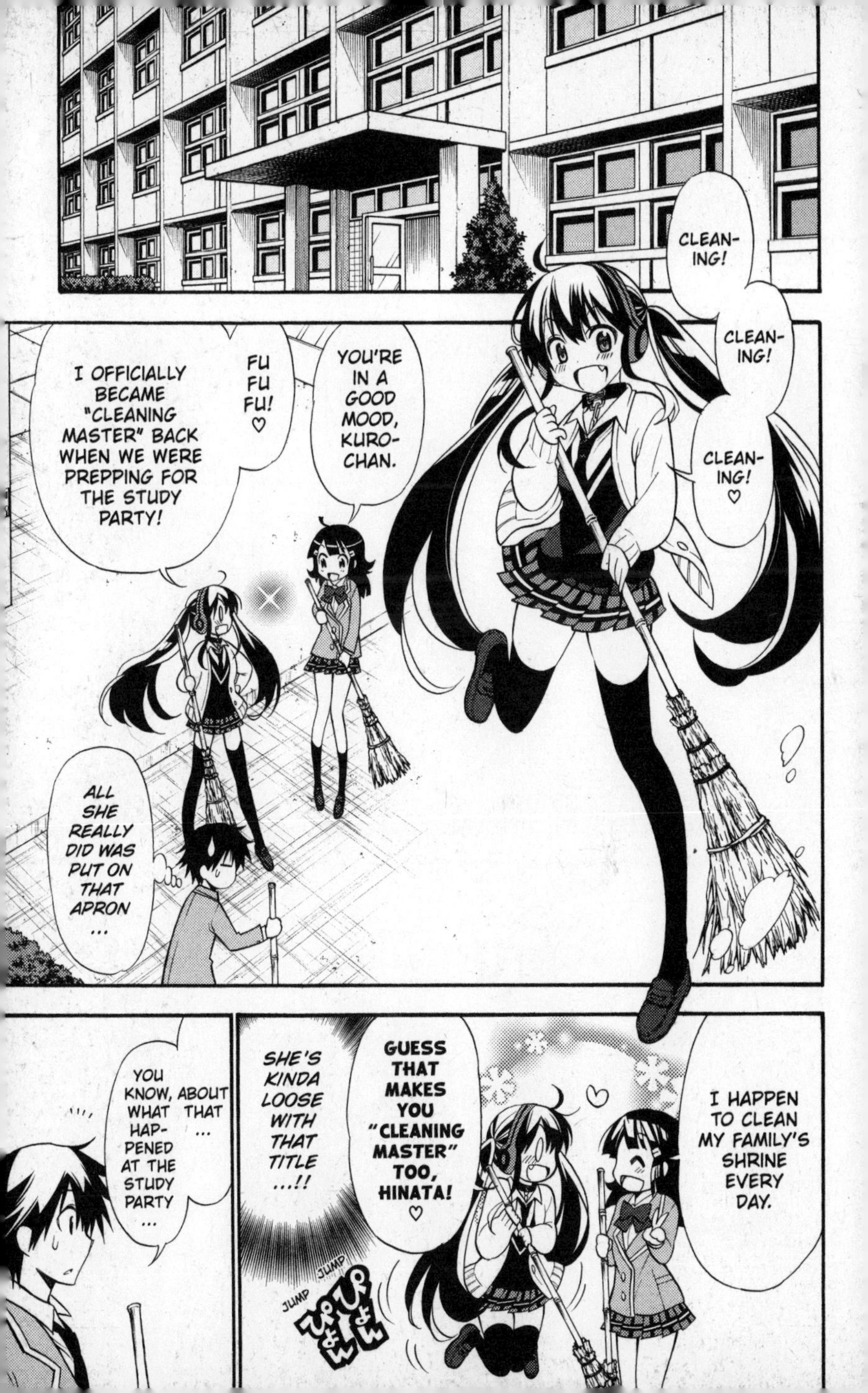
CLEAN-ING!
CLEAN-ING!
CLEAN-ING! ♡
YOU'RE IN A GOOD MOOD, KURO-CHAN.
FU FU FU! ♡
I OFFICIALLY BECAME "CLEANING MASTER" BACK WHEN WE WERE PREPPING FOR THE STUDY PARTY!
ALL SHE REALLY DID WAS PUT ON THAT APRON ...
I HAPPEN TO CLEAN MY FAMILY'S SHRINE EVERY DAY.
GUESS THAT MAKES YOU "CLEANING MASTER" TOO, HINATA! ♡
SHE'S KINDA LOOSE WITH THAT TITLE ...!!
JUMP JUMP
ぴょんぴょん
ABOUT THAT ...
YOU KNOW, WHAT HAP-PENED AT THE STUDY PARTY ...

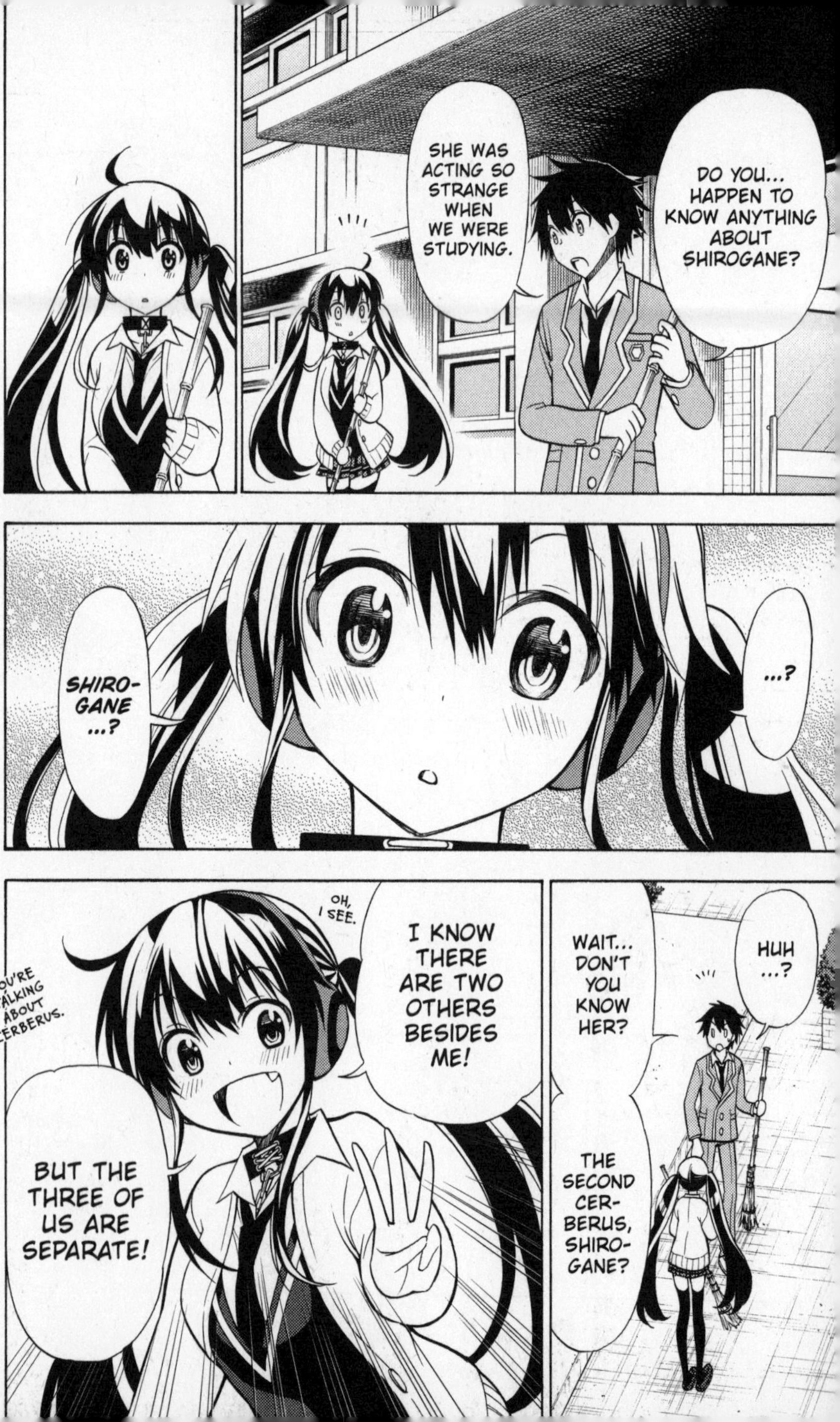
DO YOU... HAPPEN TO KNOW ANYTHING ABOUT SHIROGANE?
SHE WAS ACTING SO STRANGE WHEN WE WERE STUDYING.
...?
SHIRO-GANE ...?
HUH ...?
WAIT... DON'T YOU KNOW HER?
THE SECOND CER-BERUS, SHIRO-GANE?
OH, I SEE.
I KNOW THERE ARE TWO OTHERS BESIDES ME!
YOU'RE TALKING ABOUT CERBERUS.
BUT THE THREE OF US ARE SEPARATE!

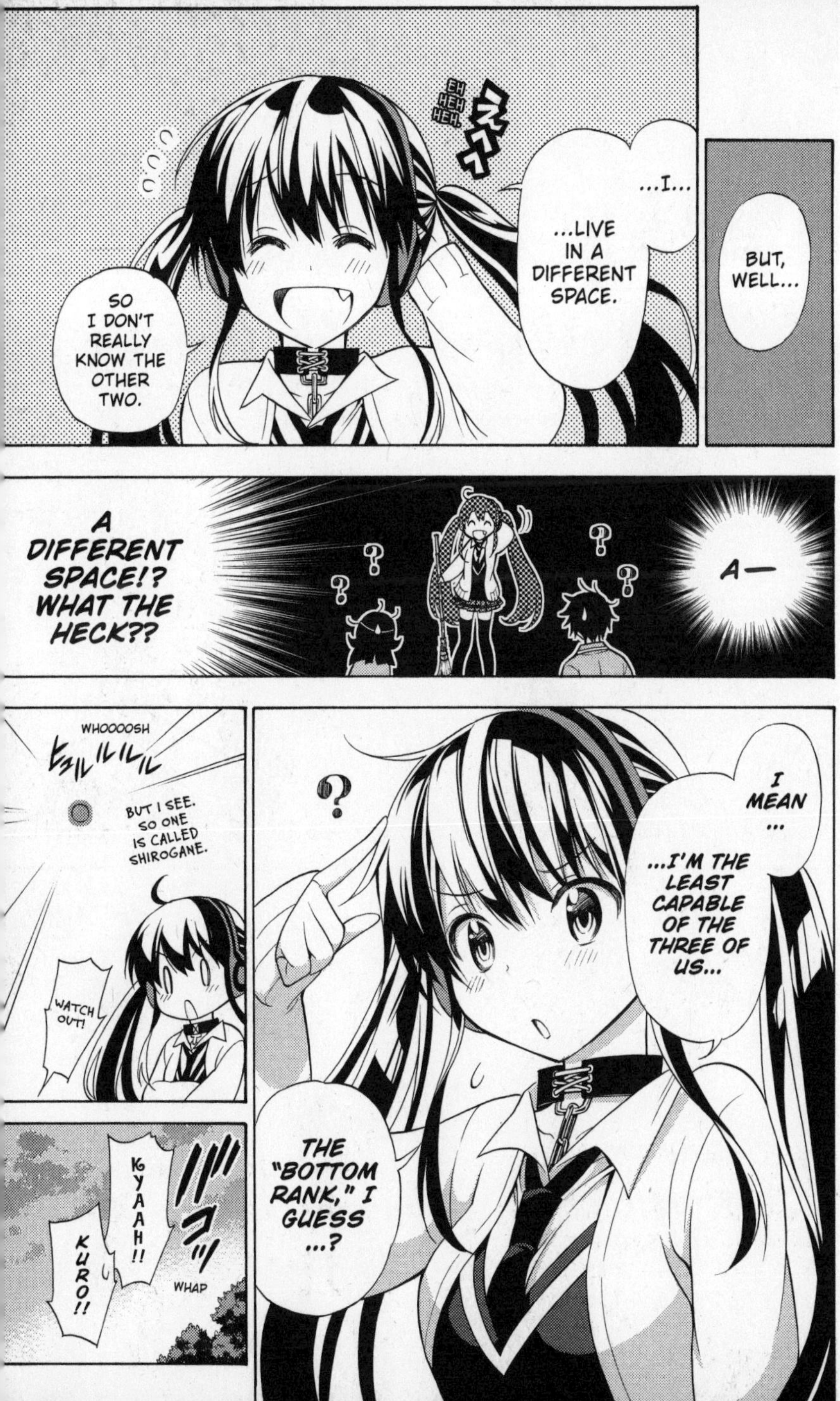
BUT, WELL...
...I...
...LIVE IN A DIFFERENT SPACE.
EH HEH HEH.
SO I DON'T REALLY KNOW THE OTHER TWO.
A—
A DIFFERENT SPACE!? WHAT THE HECK??
I MEAN ...
...I'M THE LEAST CAPABLE OF THE THREE OF US...
THE "BOTTOM RANK," I GUESS ...?
WHOOOOSH
BUT I SEE. SO ONE IS CALLED SHIROGANE.
WATCH OUT!
KYAAAH!!
KURO!!
WHAP

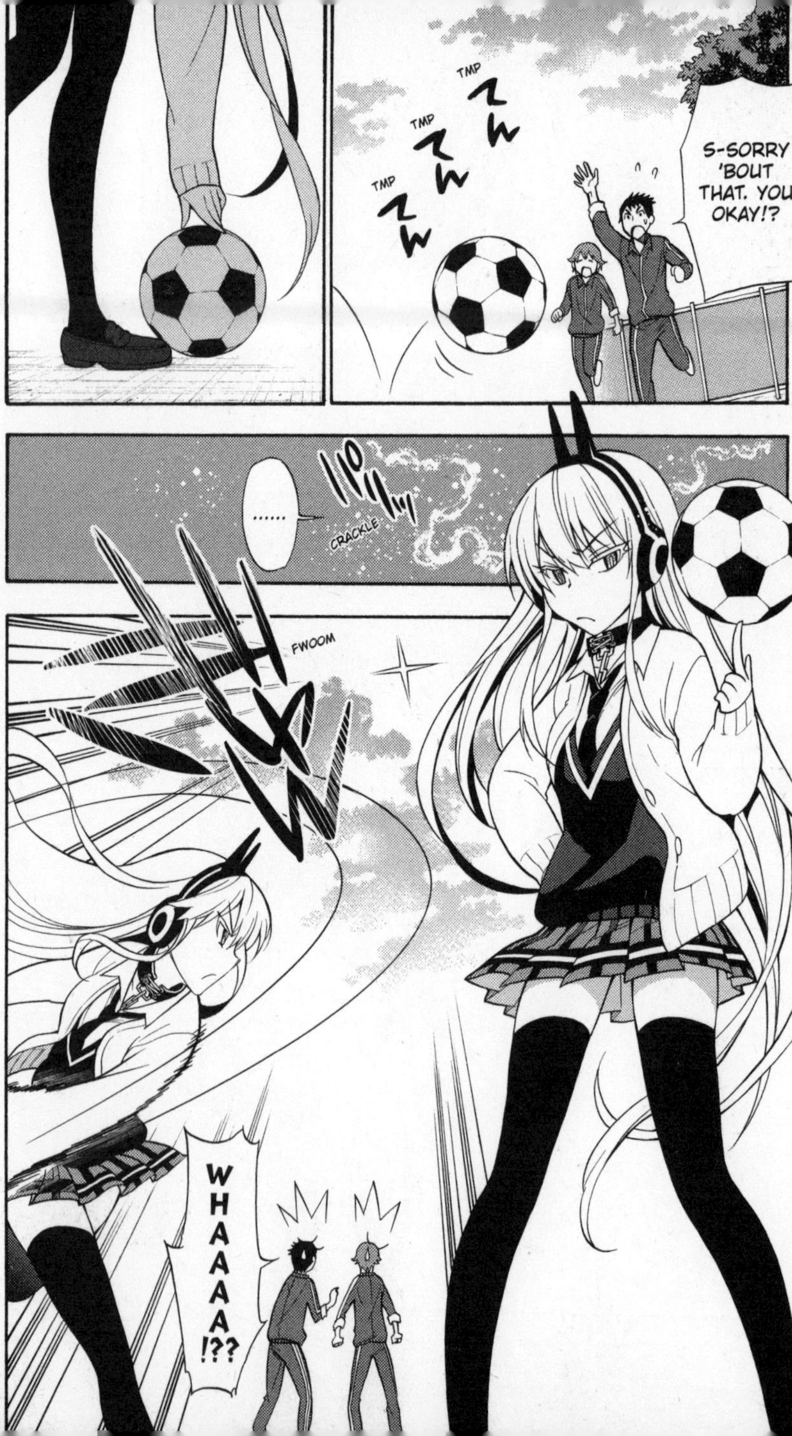
TMP
TMP
TMP
S-SORRY 'BOUT THAT. YOU OKAY!?
......
CRACKLE
FWOOM
WHAAAAA!??

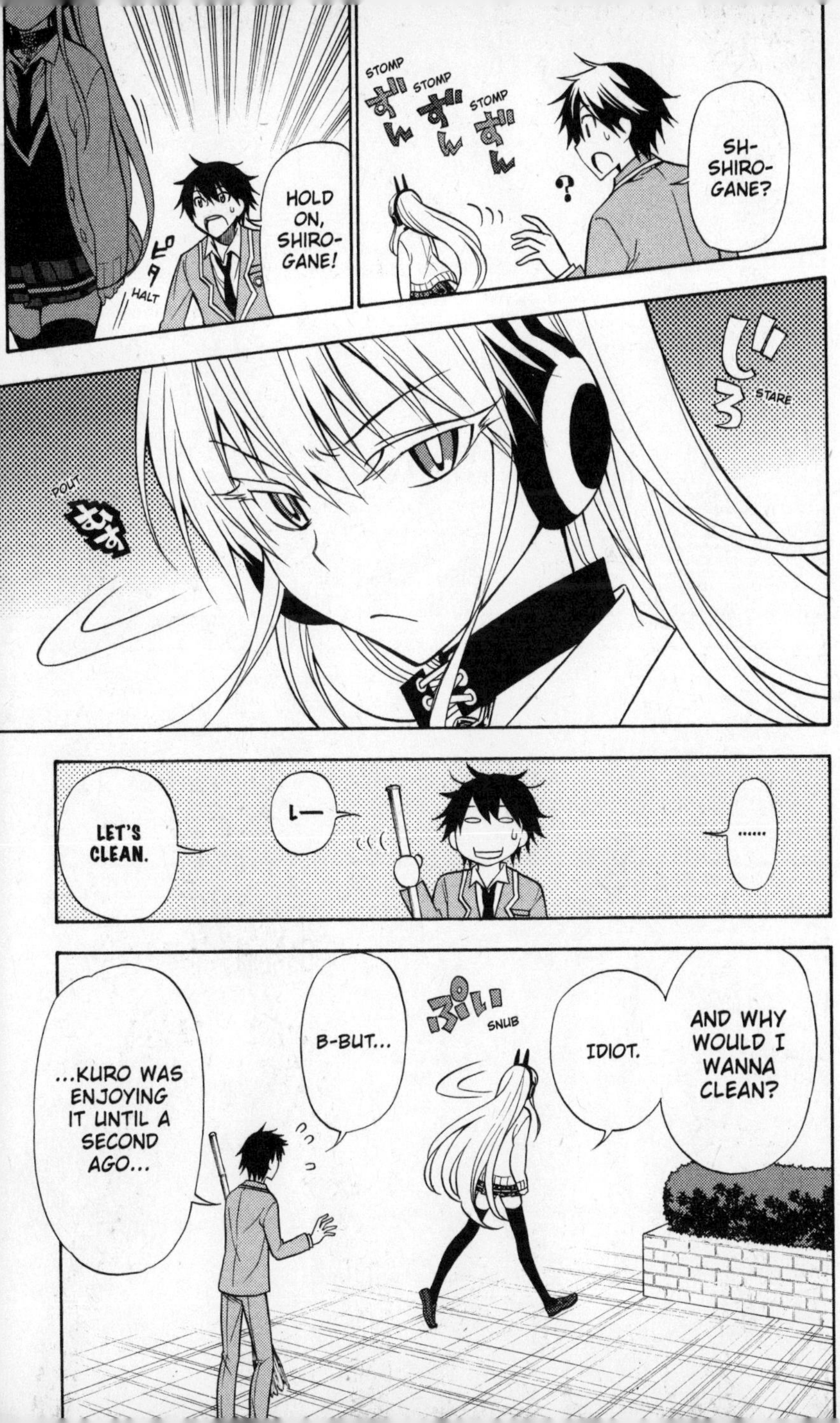
SH-SHIROGANE?
?
STOMP ずん
STOMP ずん
STOMP ずん
HOLD ON, SHIROGANE!
ピタ HALT
じろ STARE
むす POUT
......
I—
LET'S CLEAN.
AND WHY WOULD I WANNA CLEAN?
IDIOT.
ぷい SNUB
B-BUT...
...KURO WAS ENJOYING IT UNTIL A SECOND AGO...

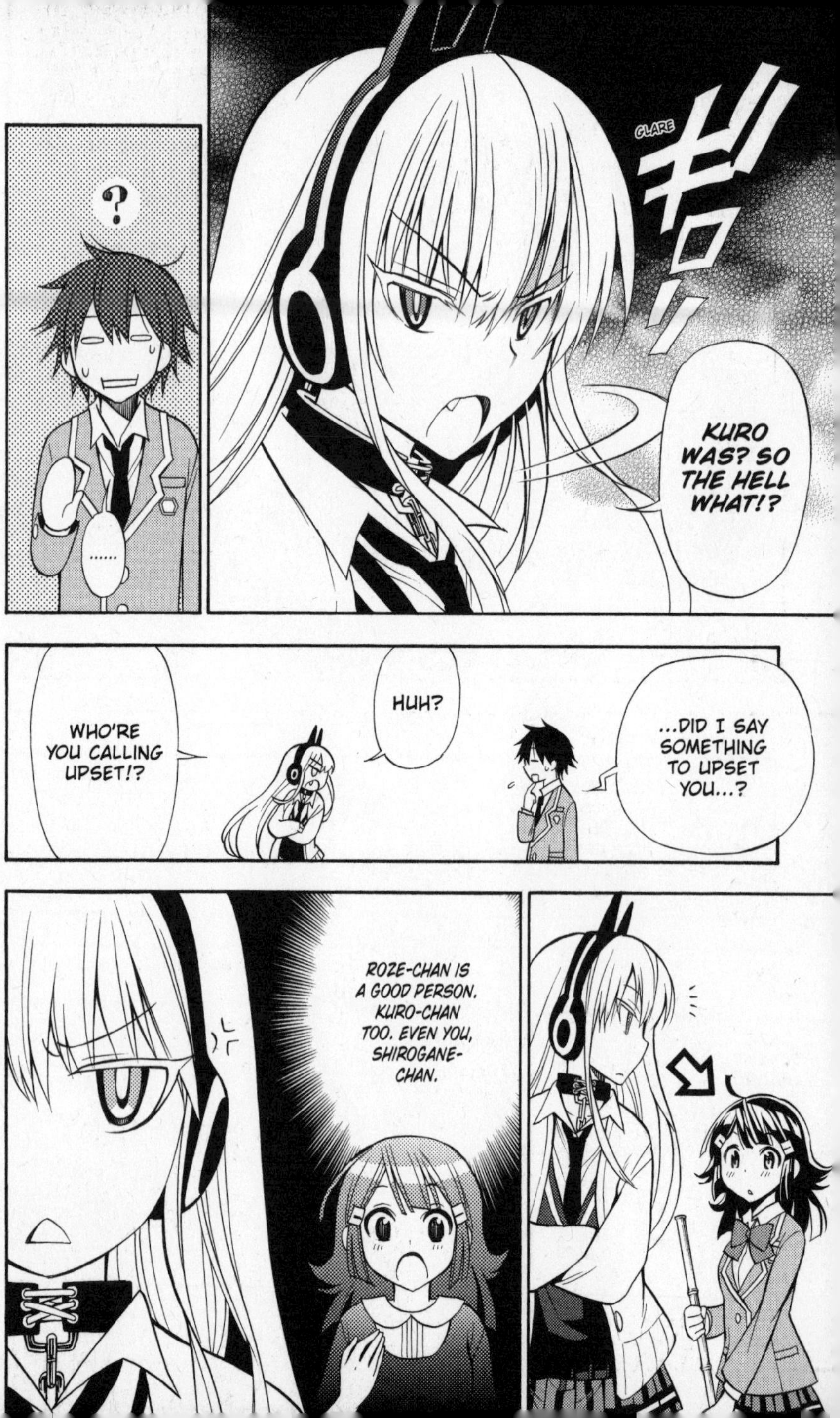
GLARE
KURO WAS? SO THE HELL WHAT!?
?
......
...DID I SAY SOMETHING TO UPSET YOU...?
HUH?
WHO'RE YOU CALLING UPSET!?
ROZE-CHAN IS A GOOD PERSON. KURO-CHAN TOO. EVEN YOU, SHIROGANE-CHAN.

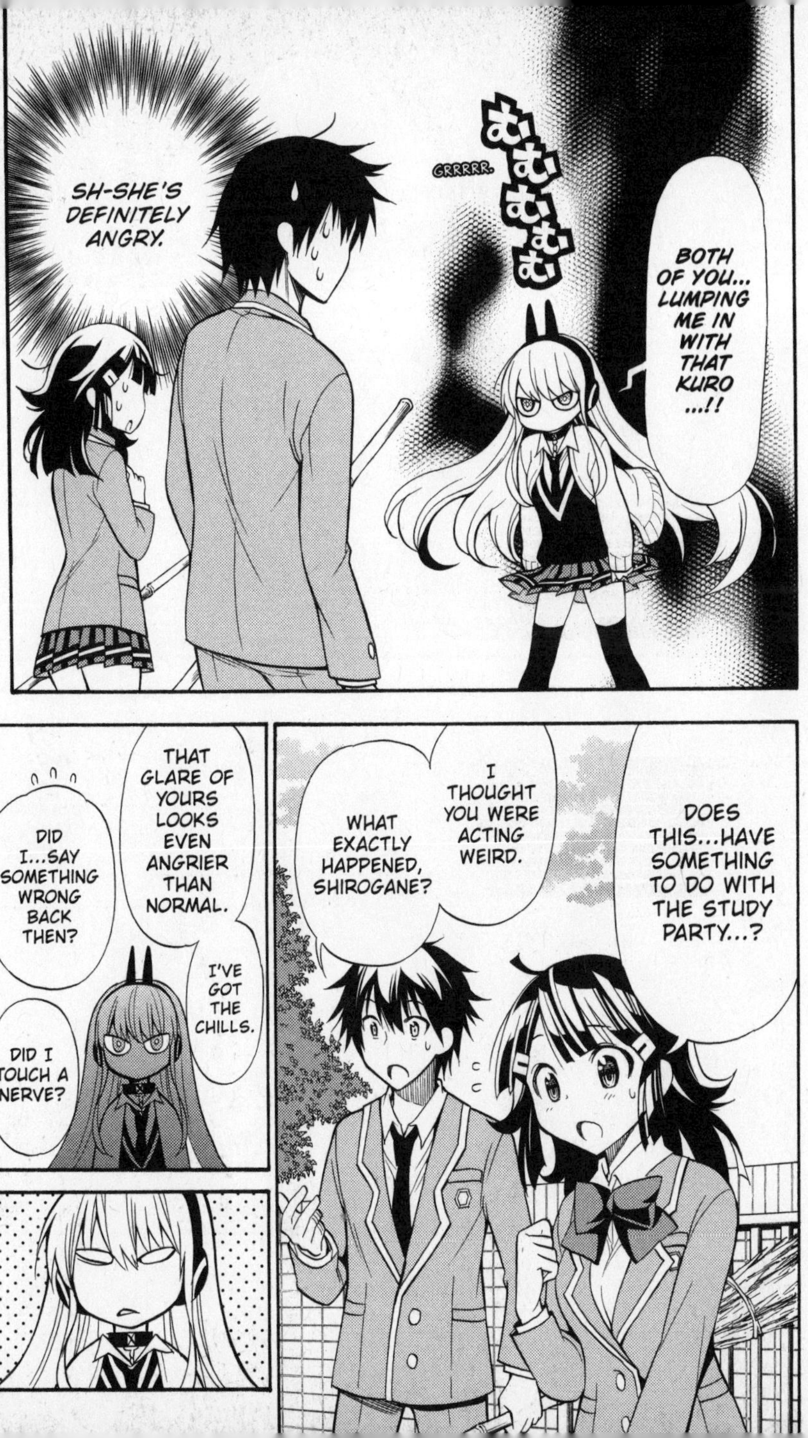
BOTH OF YOU... LUMPING ME IN WITH THAT KURO ...!!
むむむむむ
GRRRRR.
SH-SHE'S DEFINITELY ANGRY.
DOES THIS...HAVE SOMETHING TO DO WITH THE STUDY PARTY...?
I THOUGHT YOU WERE ACTING WEIRD.
WHAT EXACTLY HAPPENED, SHIROGANE?
THAT GLARE OF YOURS LOOKS EVEN ANGRIER THAN NORMAL.
I'VE GOT THE CHILLS.
DID I...SAY SOMETHING WRONG BACK THEN?
DID I TOUCH A NERVE?

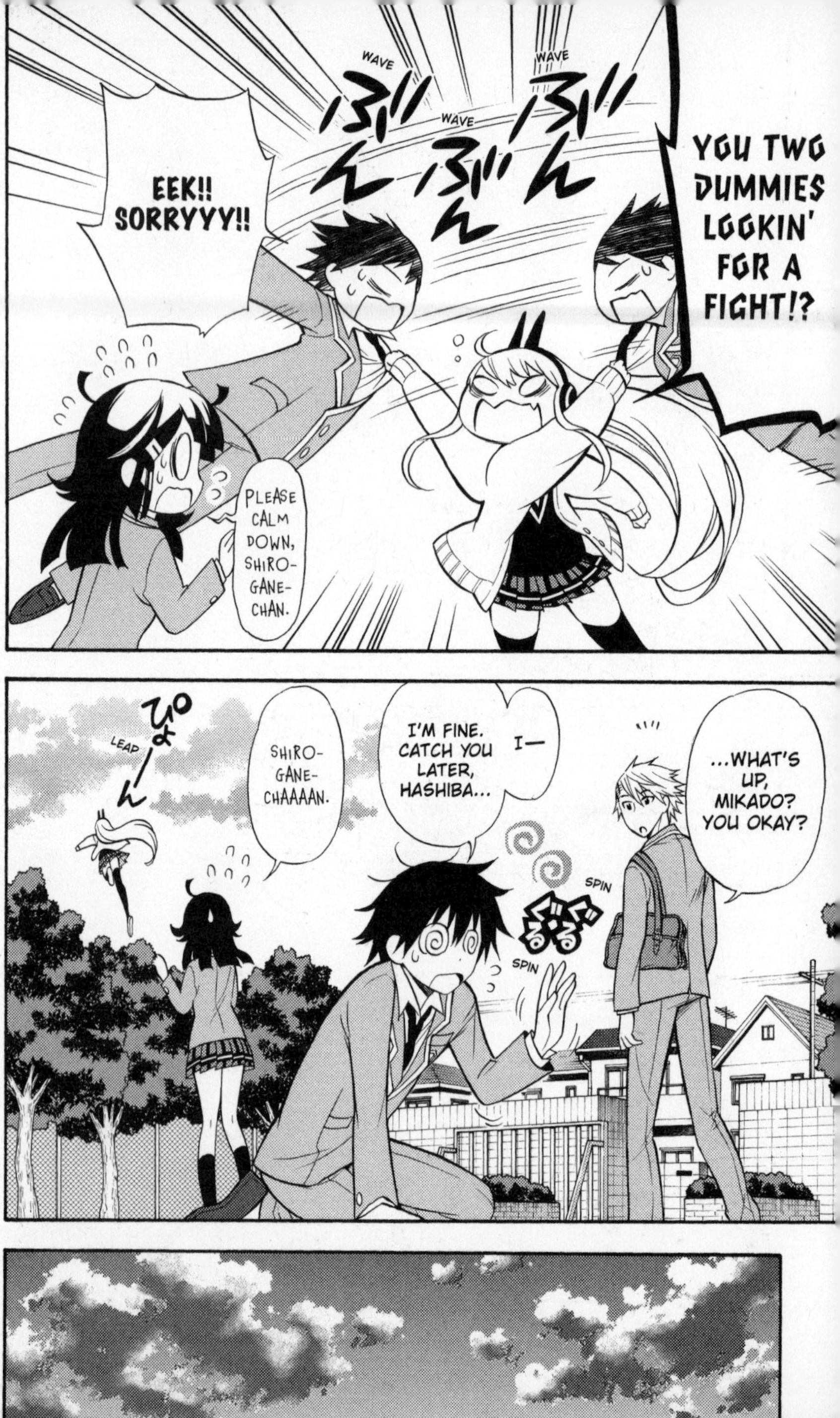
YOU TWO DUMMIES LOOKIN' FOR A FIGHT!?
WAVE
WAVE
WAVE
EEK!! SORRYYY!!
PLEASE CALM DOWN, SHIRO-GANE-CHAN.
...WHAT'S UP, MIKADO? YOU OKAY?
I—
I'M FINE. CATCH YOU LATER, HASHIBA...
SPIN
SPIN
SHIRO-GANE-CHAAAAN.
LEAP

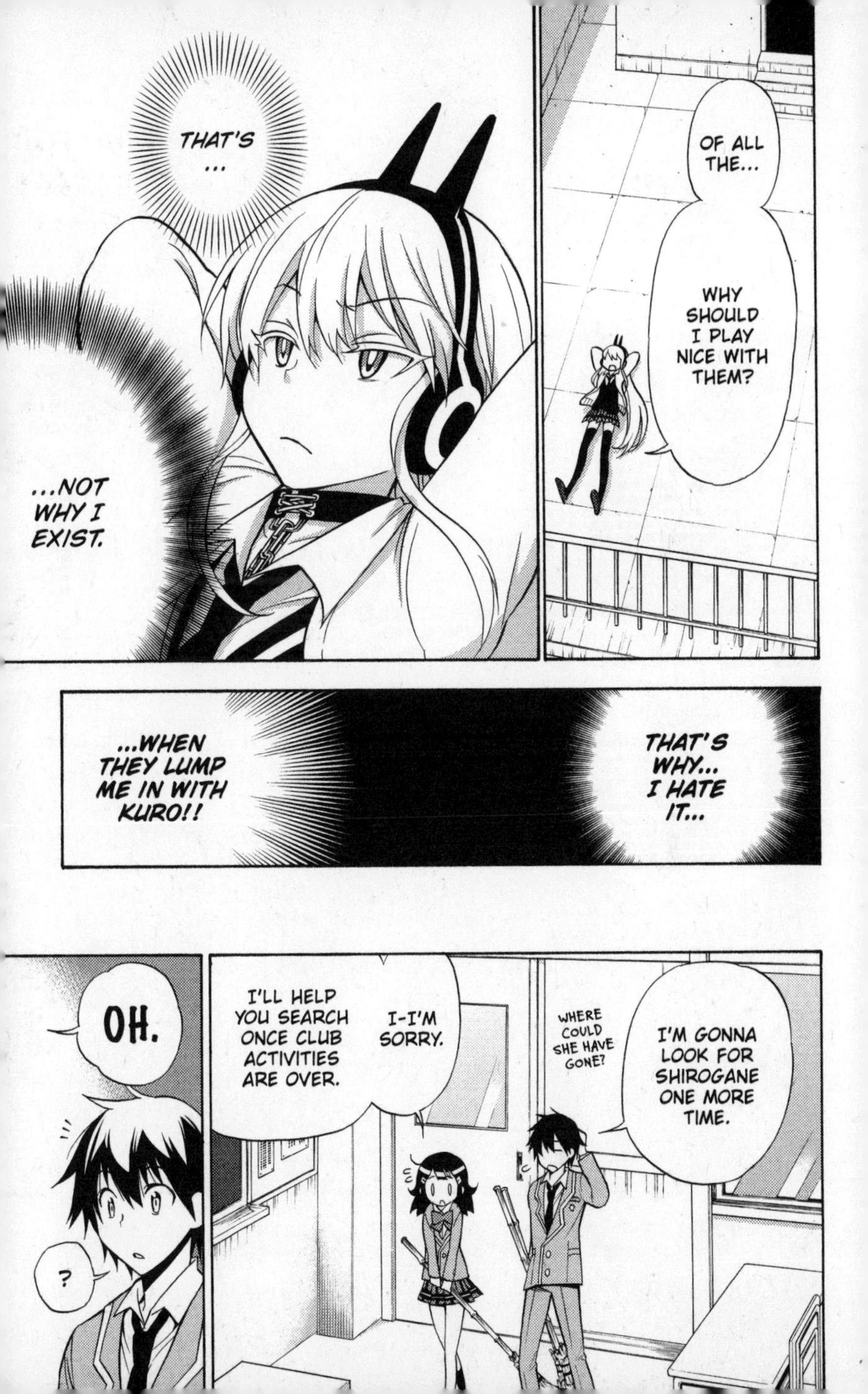
OF ALL THE...
WHY SHOULD I PLAY NICE WITH THEM?
THAT'S ...
...NOT WHY I EXIST.
THAT'S WHY... I HATE IT...
...WHEN THEY LUMP ME IN WITH KURO!!
I'M GONNA LOOK FOR SHIROGANE ONE MORE TIME.
WHERE COULD SHE HAVE GONE?
I-I'M SORRY.
I'LL HELP YOU SEARCH ONCE CLUB ACTIVITIES ARE OVER.
OH.
?

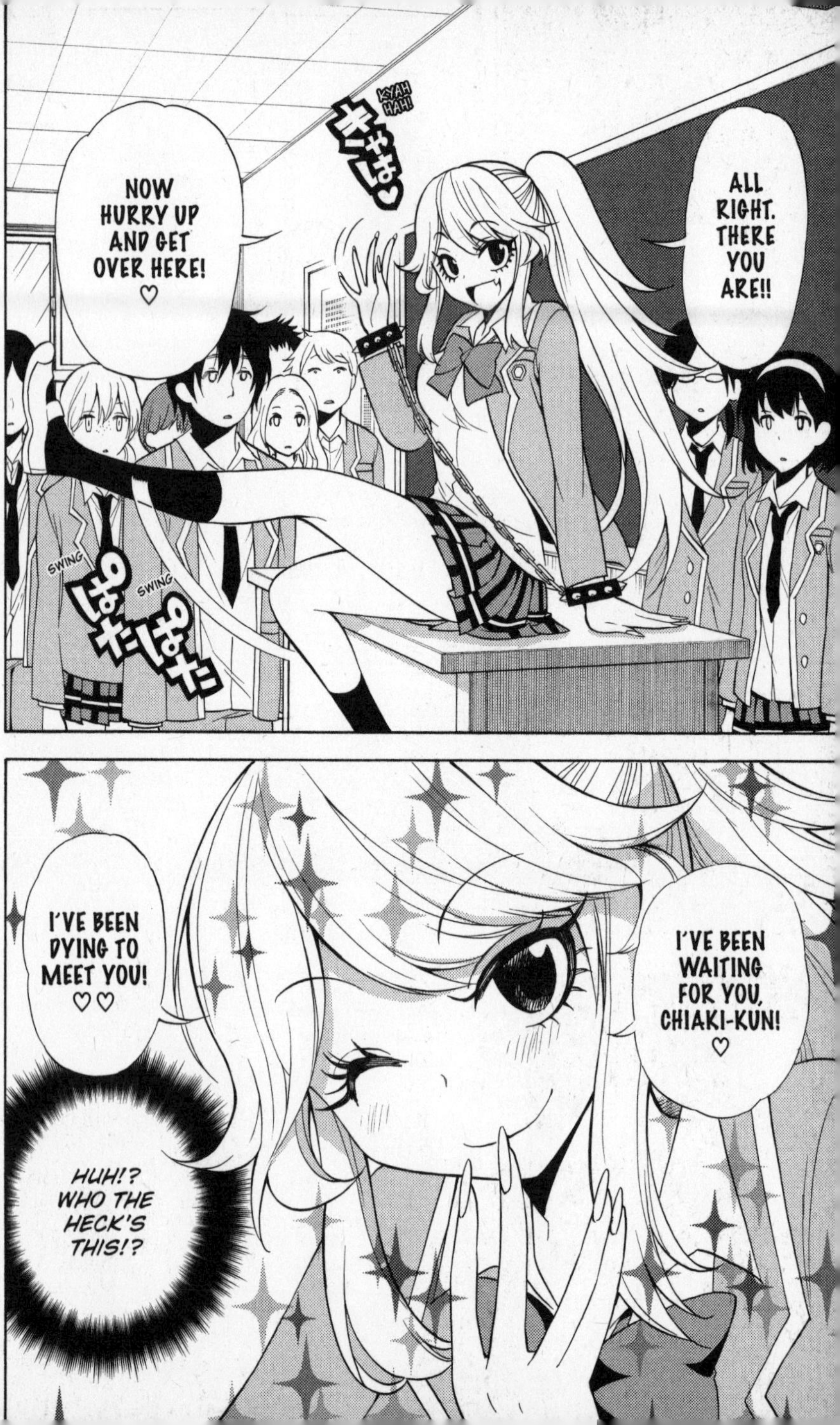
ALL RIGHT. THERE YOU ARE!!
きゃは♡
KYAH HAH!
NOW HURRY UP AND GET OVER HERE! ♡
ぱたぱた
SWING SWING
I'VE BEEN WAITING FOR YOU, CHIAKI-KUN! ♡
I'VE BEEN DYING TO MEET YOU! ♡♡
HUH!? WHO THE HECK'S THIS!?

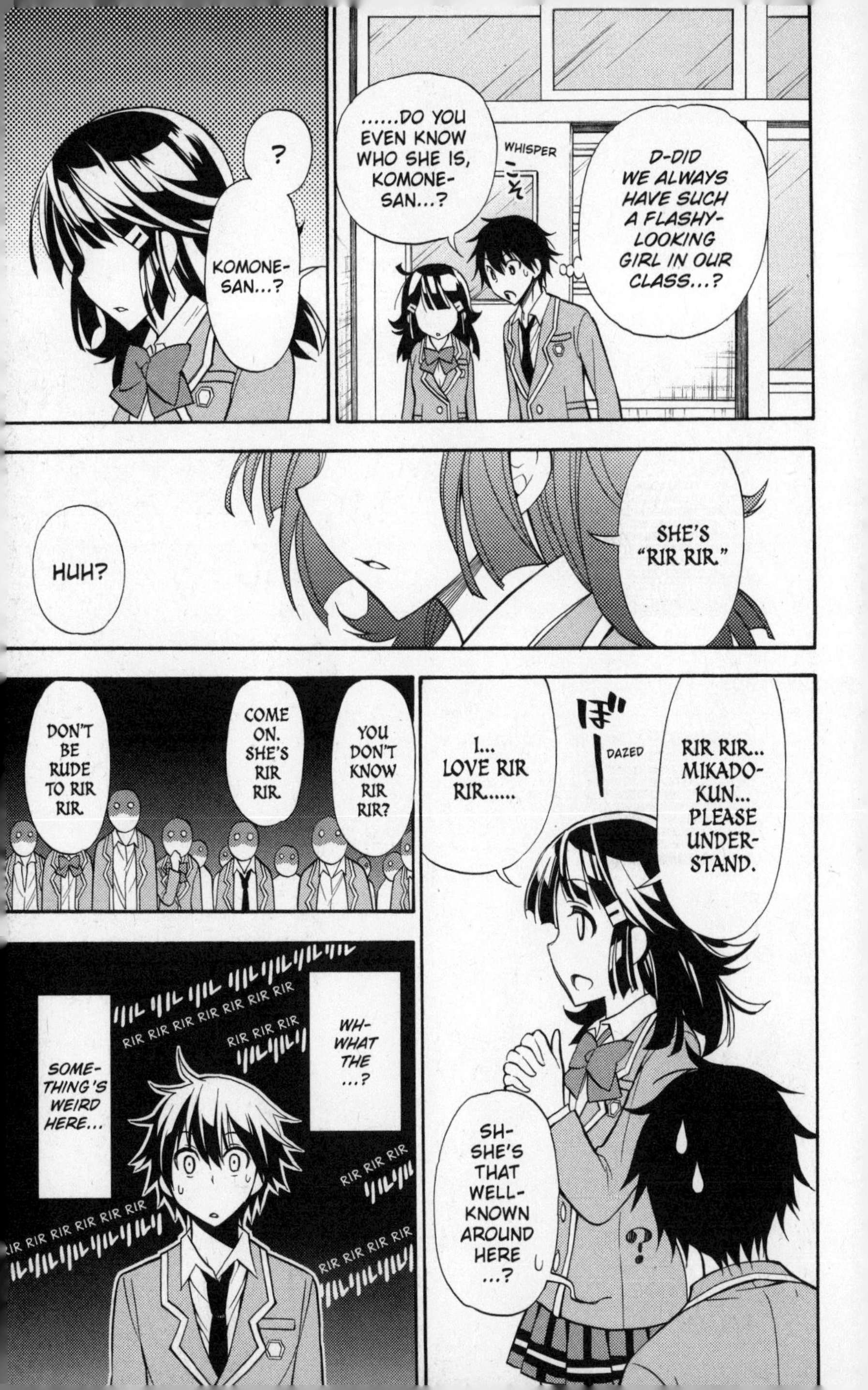
D-DID WE ALWAYS HAVE SUCH A FLASHY-LOOKING GIRL IN OUR CLASS...?
WHISPER
......DO YOU EVEN KNOW WHO SHE IS, KOMONE-SAN...?
?
KOMONE-SAN...?
SHE'S "RIR RIR."
HUH?
RIR RIR... MIKADO-KUN... PLEASE UNDER-STAND.
DAZED
I... LOVE RIR RIR.....
SH-SHE'S THAT WELL-KNOWN AROUND HERE...?
YOU DON'T KNOW RIR RIR?
COME ON. SHE'S RIR RIR.
DON'T BE RUDE TO RIR RIR.
WH-WHAT THE...?
RIR RIR RIR RIR RIR RIR RIR
RIR RIR RIR
SOME-THING'S WEIRD HERE...
RIR RIR RIR
RIR RIR RIR RIR RIR RIR RIR
RIR RIR RIR RIR RIR

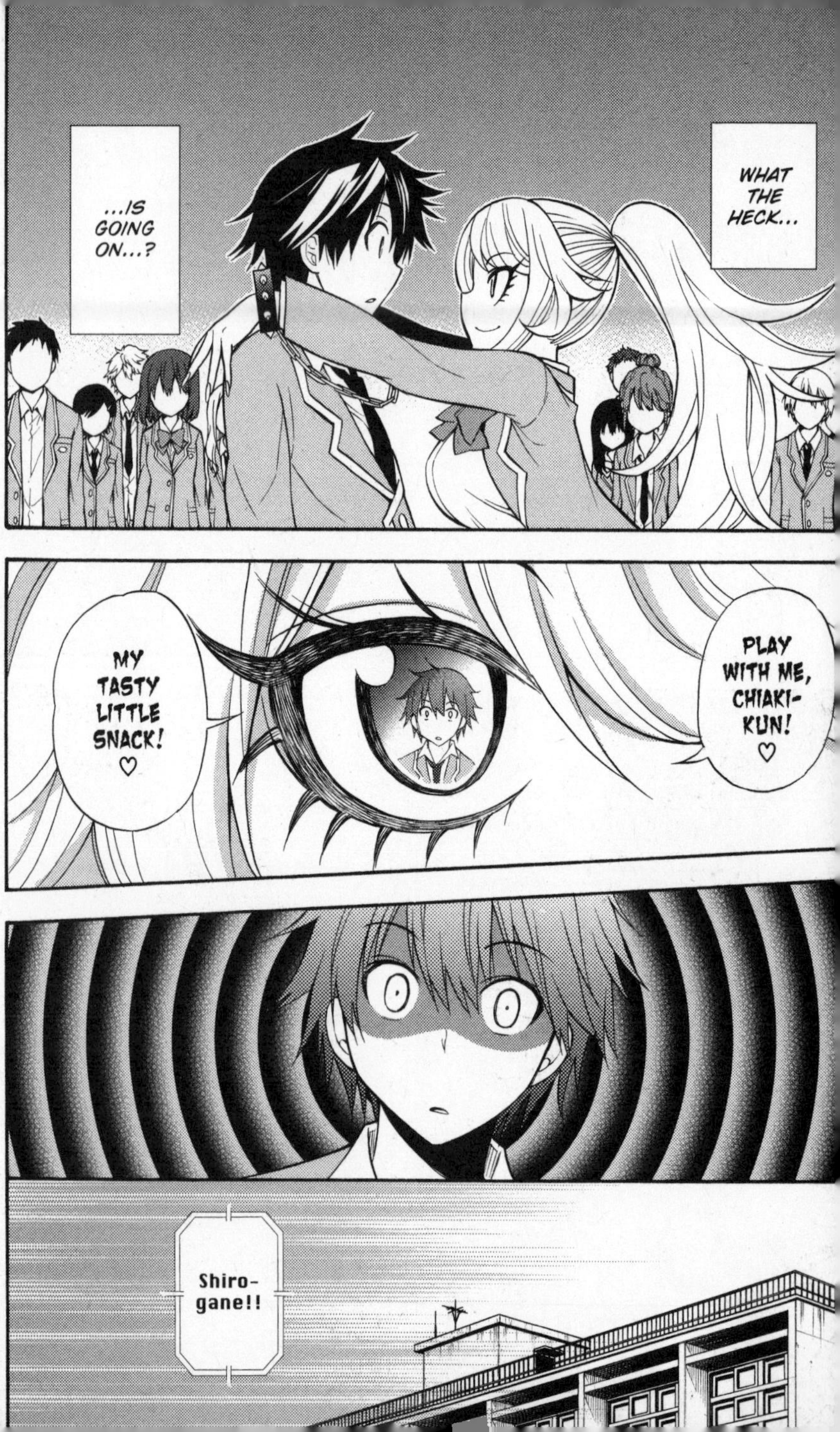
WHAT THE HECK...
...IS GOING ON...?
PLAY WITH ME, CHIAKI-KUN! ♡
MY TASTY LITTLE SNACK! ♡
Shiro-gane!!

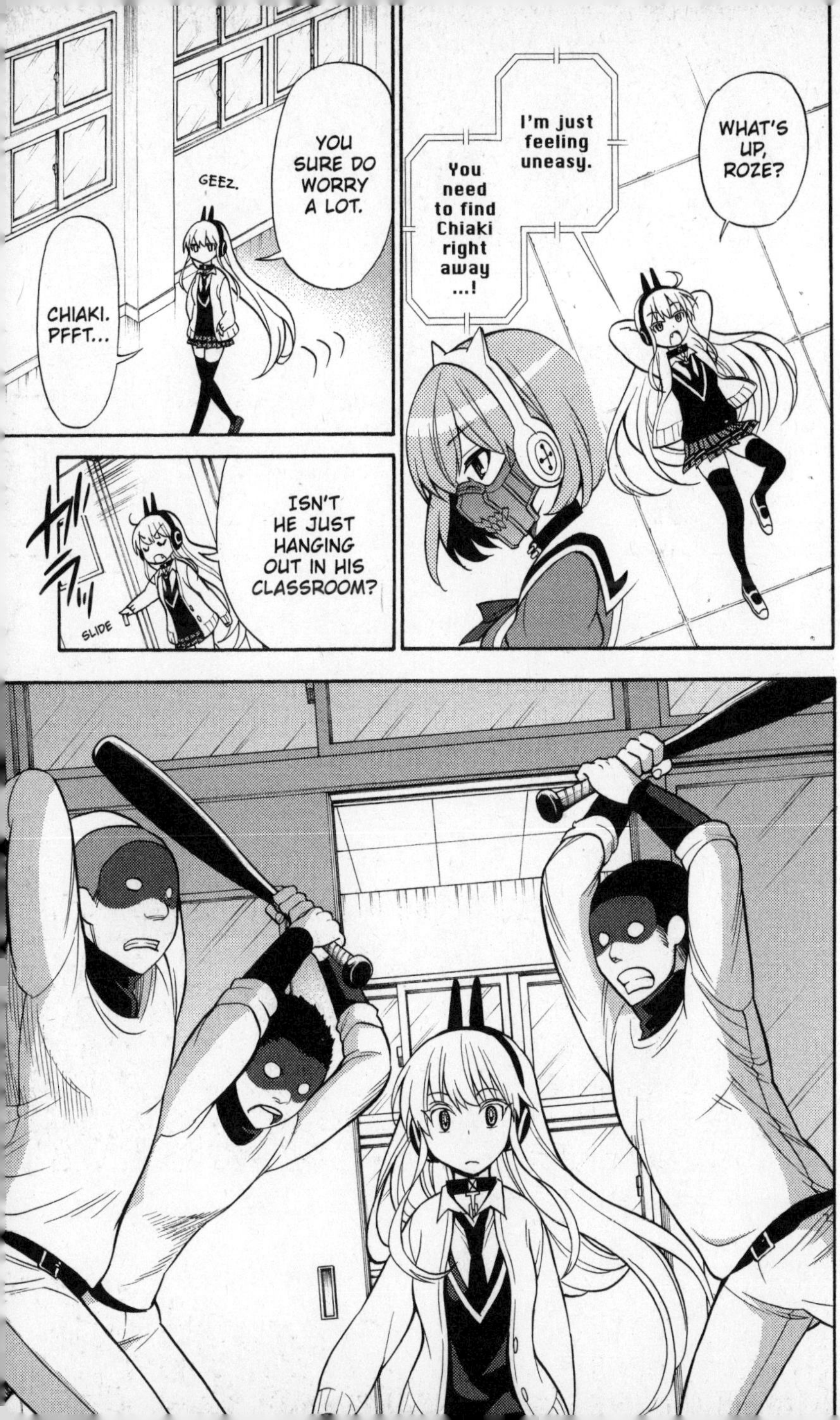
WHAT'S UP, ROZE?
I'm just feeling uneasy.
You need to find Chiaki right away...!
YOU SURE DO WORRY A LOT.
GEEZ.
CHIAKI. PFFT...
ISN'T HE JUST HANGING OUT IN HIS CLASSROOM?
SLIDE

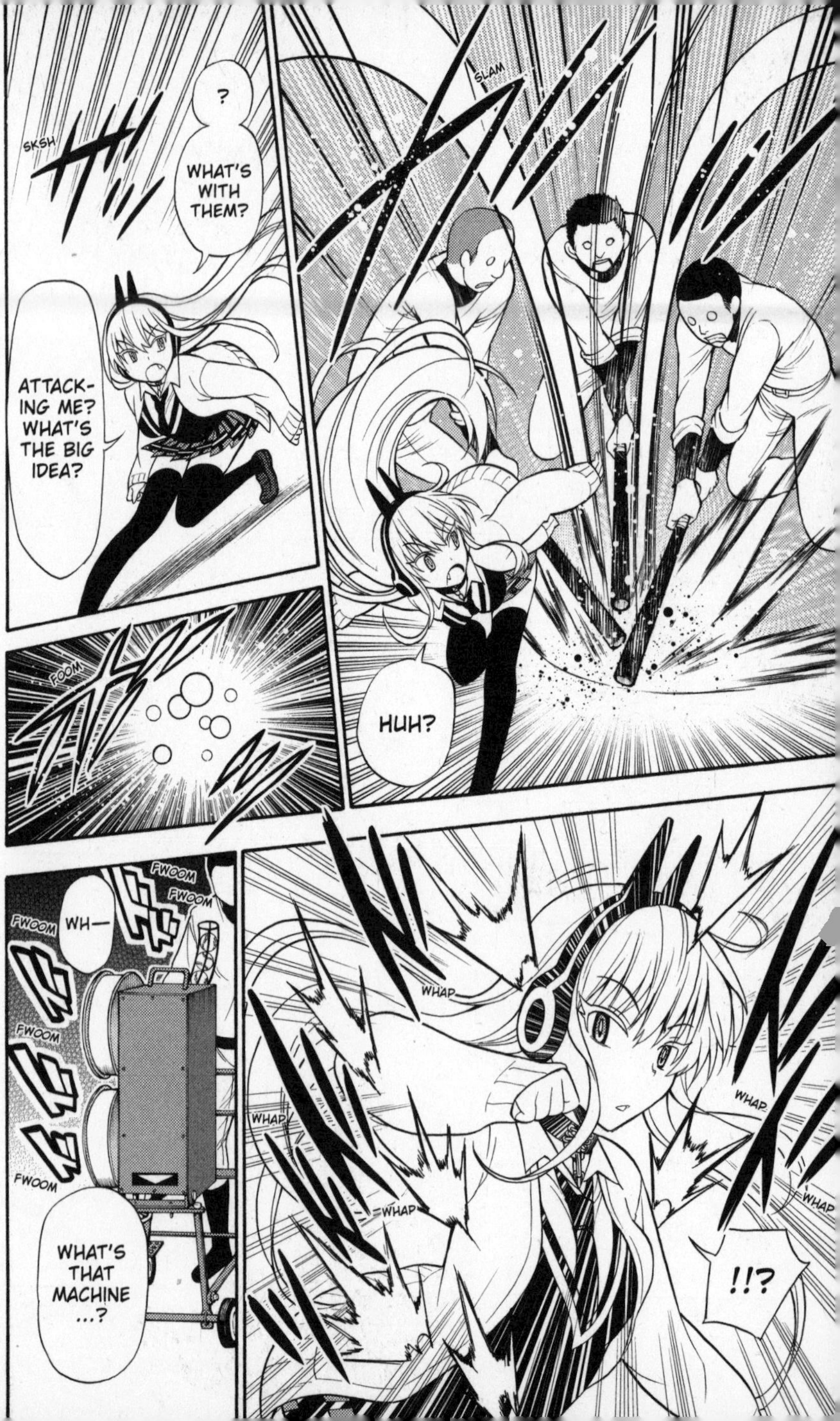
SLAM
HUH?
SKSH
?
WHAT'S WITH THEM?
ATTACKING ME? WHAT'S THE BIG IDEA?
FOOM
WHAP
WHAP
WHAP
WHAP
WHAP
!!?
FWOOM
FWOOM
FWOOM
WH—
FWOOM
FWOOM
WHAT'S THAT MACHINE ...?

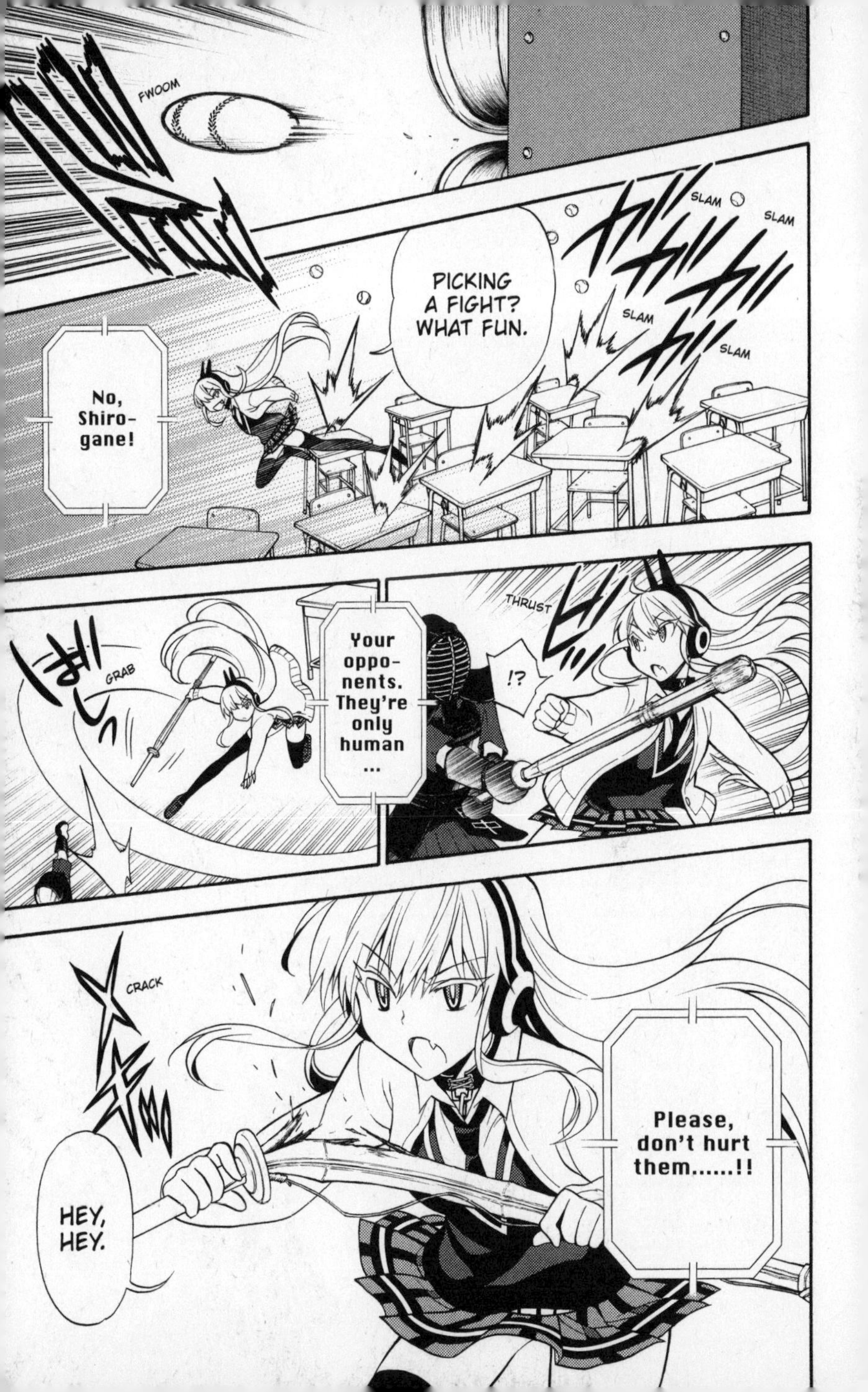
FWOOM
SLAM
SLAM
SLAM
SLAM
PICKING A FIGHT? WHAT FUN.
No, Shiro-gane!
THRUST
!?
Your oppo-nents. They're only human ...
GRAB
CRACK
Please, don't hurt them......!!
HEY, HEY.

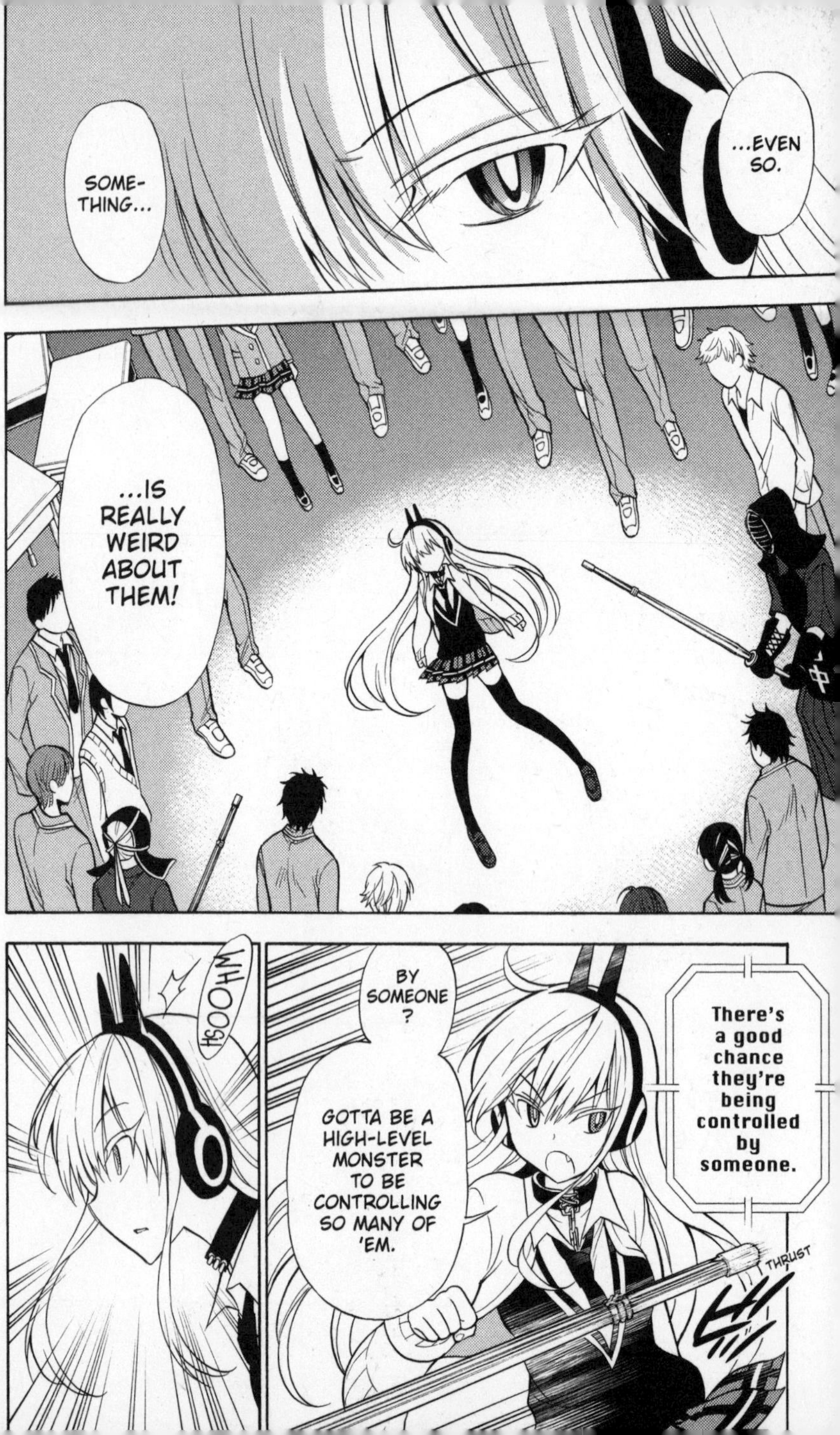
...EVEN SO.
SOME-THING...
...IS REALLY WEIRD ABOUT THEM!
There's a good chance they're being controlled by someone.
BY SOMEONE?
GOTTA BE A HIGH-LEVEL MONSTER TO BE CONTROLLING SO MANY OF 'EM.
THRUST
WHOOSH!

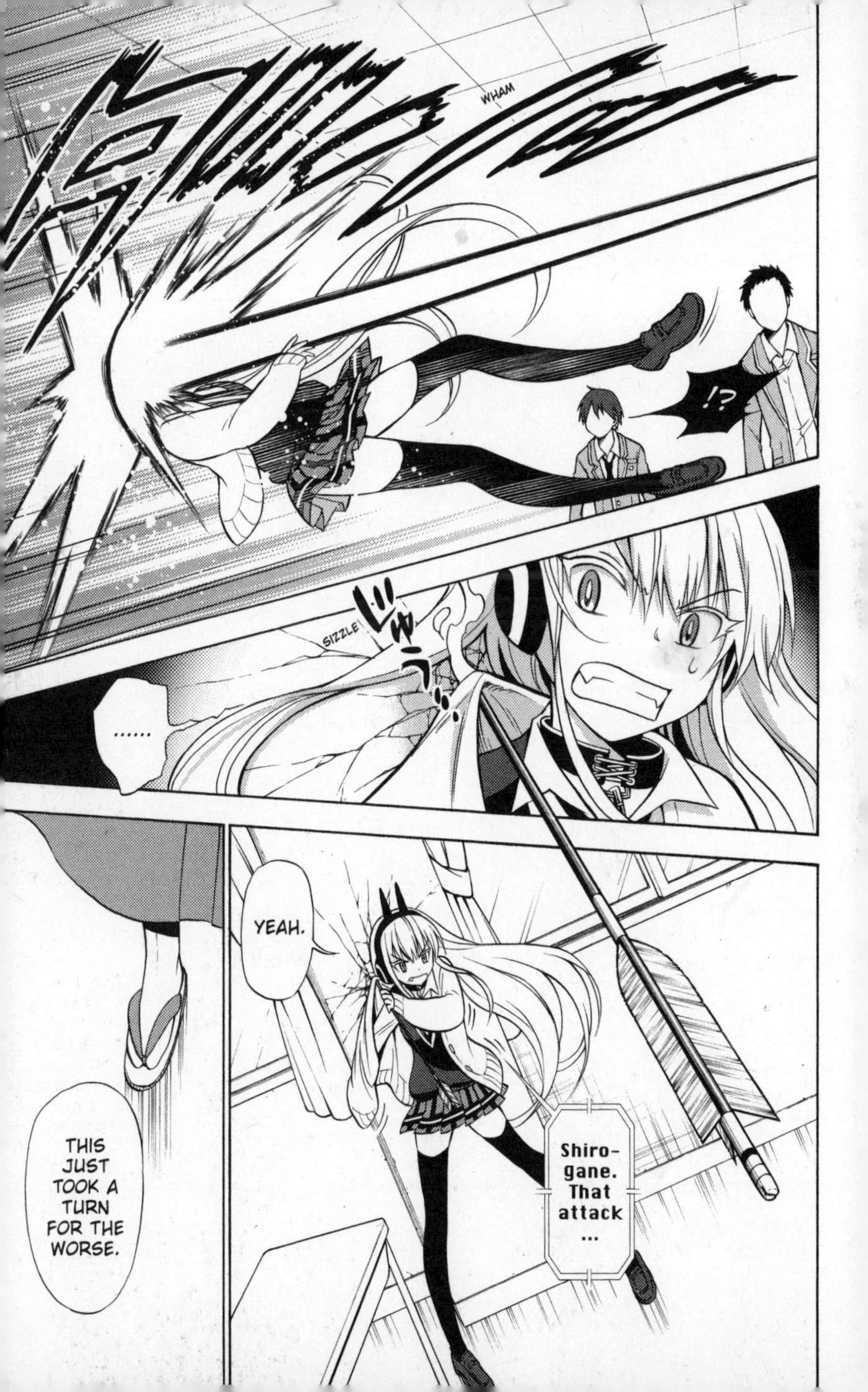
WHAM
!?
SIZZLE
......
Shiro-gane. That attack ...
YEAH.
THIS JUST TOOK A TURN FOR THE WORSE.

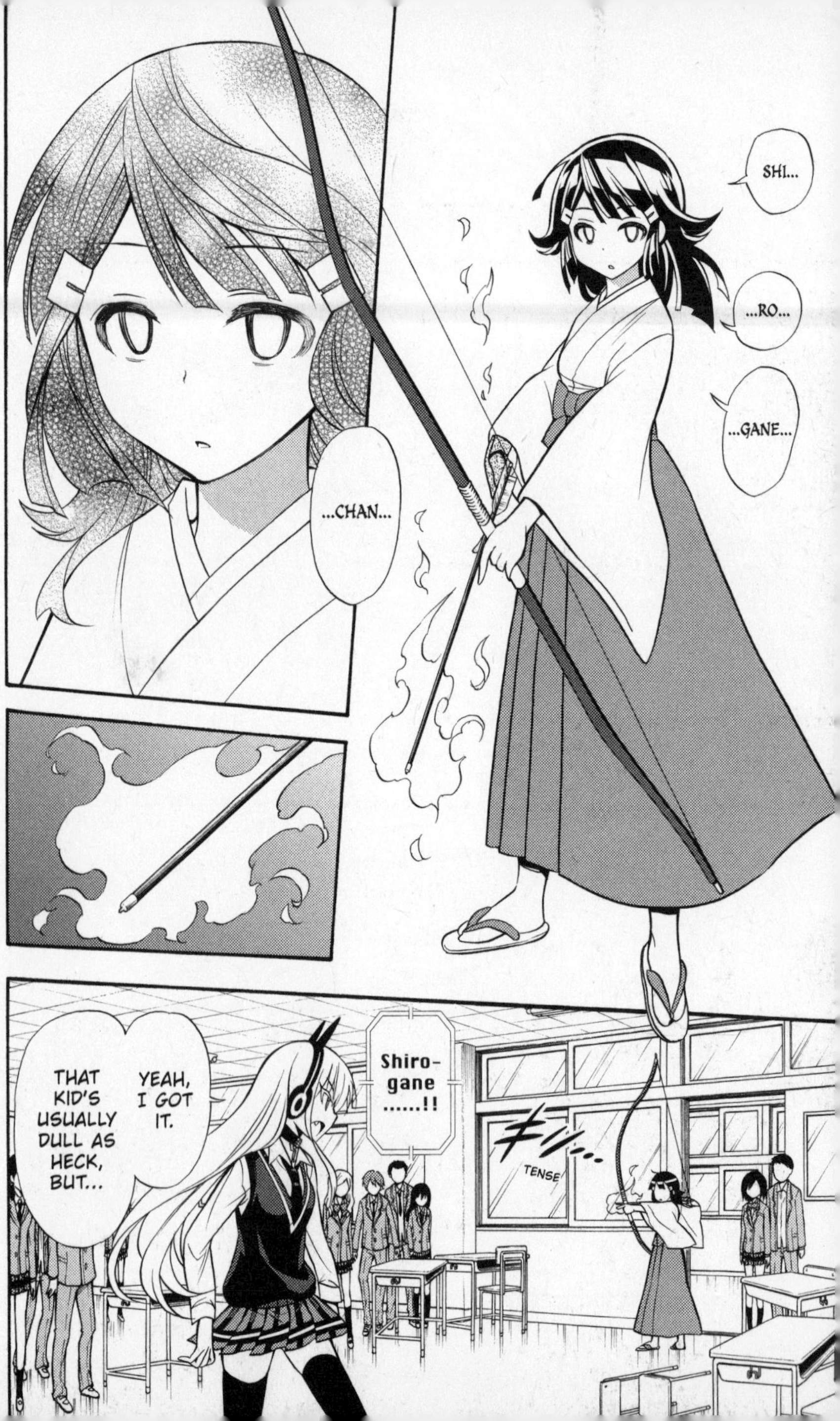
SHI...
...RO...
...GANE...
...CHAN...
Shiro-gane ......!!
TENSE
YEAH, I GOT IT.
THAT KID'S USUALLY DULL AS HECK, BUT...

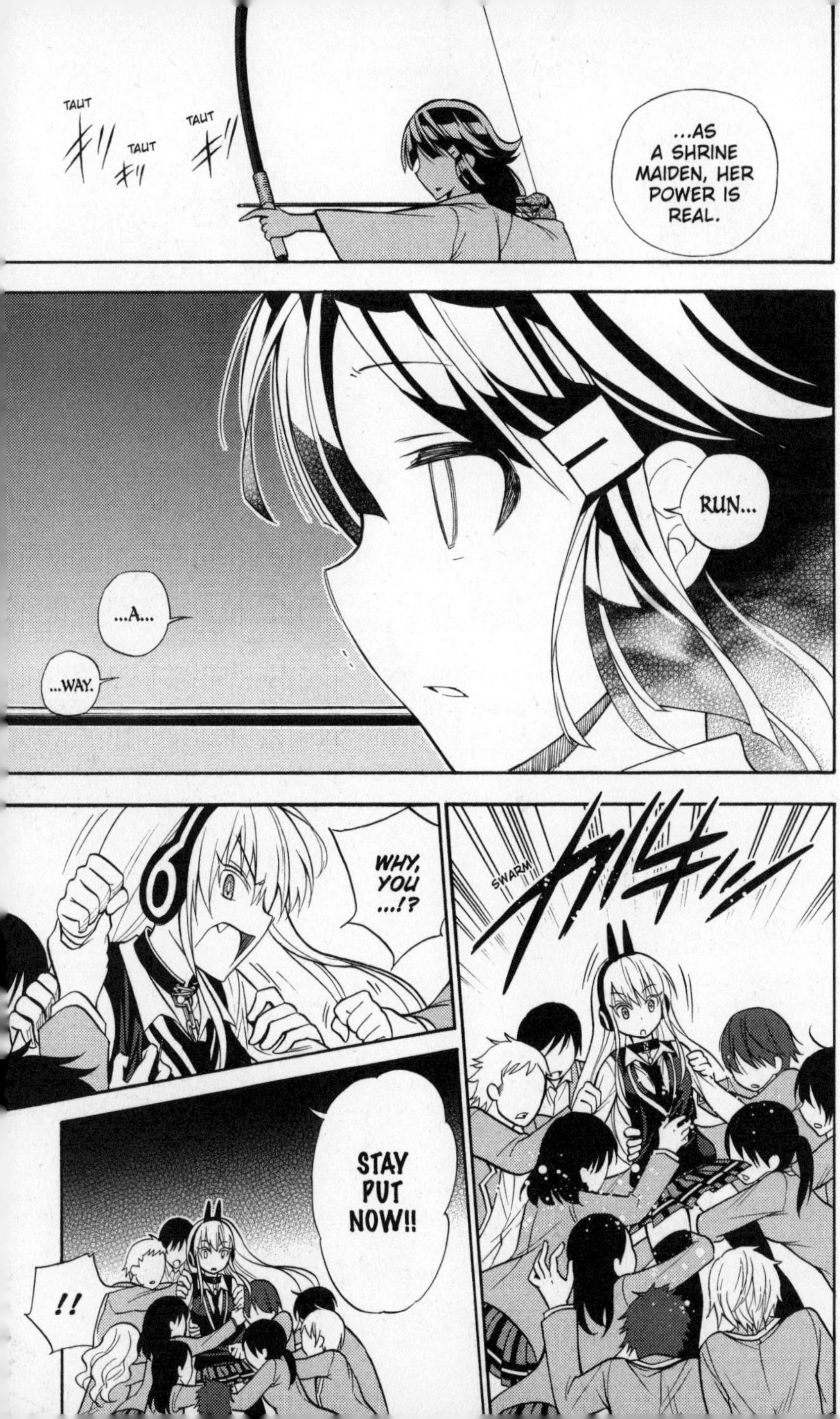
...AS A SHRINE MAIDEN, HER POWER IS REAL.
TAUT
TAUT
TAUT
RUN...
...A...
...WAY.
SWARM
WHY, YOU ...!?
STAY PUT NOW!!
!!

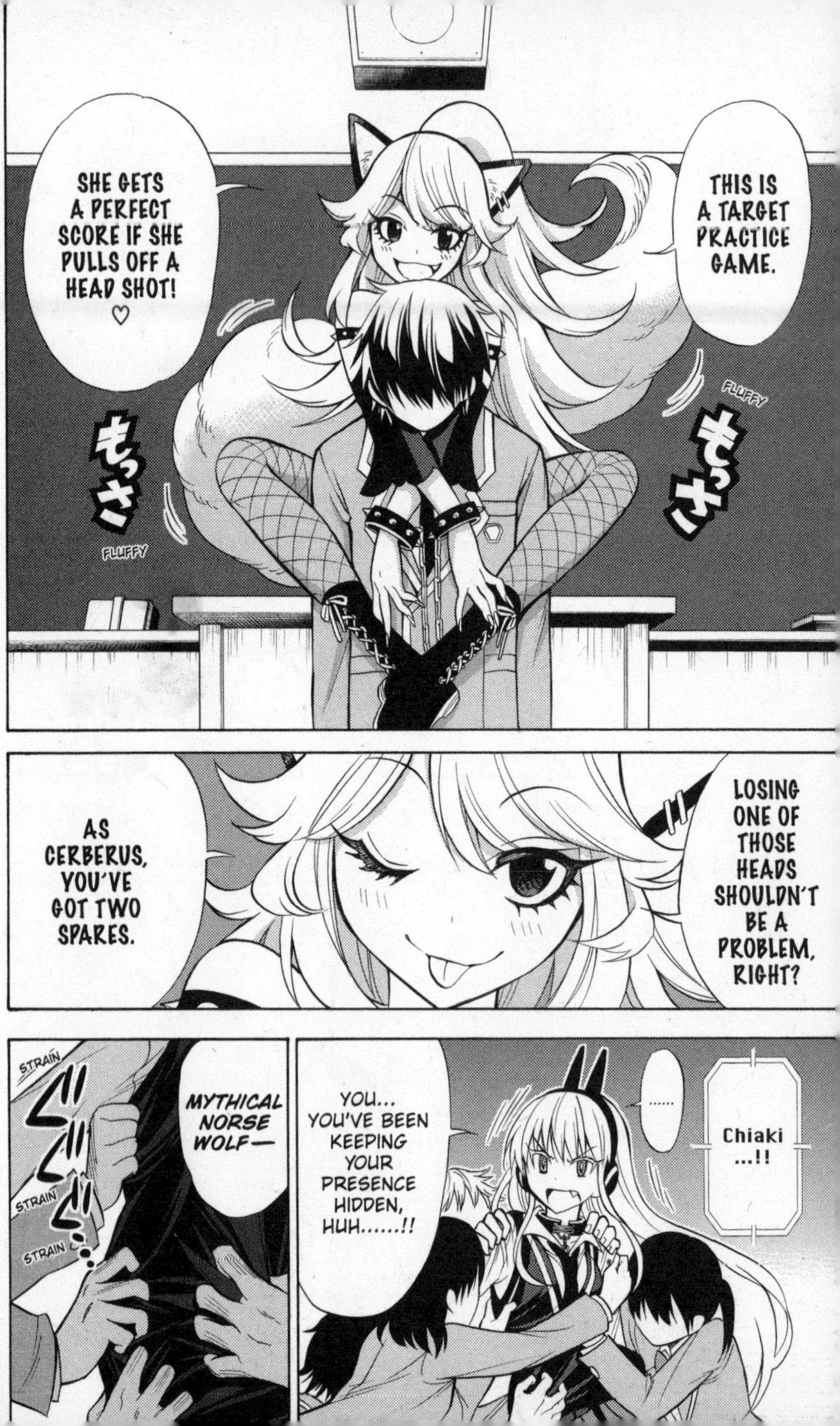
THIS IS A TARGET PRACTICE GAME.
SHE GETS A PERFECT SCORE IF SHE PULLS OFF A HEAD SHOT! ♡
もっさ
FLUFFY
もっさ
FLUFFY
LOSING ONE OF THOSE HEADS SHOULDN'T BE A PROBLEM, RIGHT?
AS CERBERUS, YOU'VE GOT TWO SPARES.
Chiaki ...!!
......
YOU... YOU'VE BEEN KEEPING YOUR PRESENCE HIDDEN, HUH......!!
MYTHICAL NORSE WOLF—
STRAIN
STRAIN
STRAIN

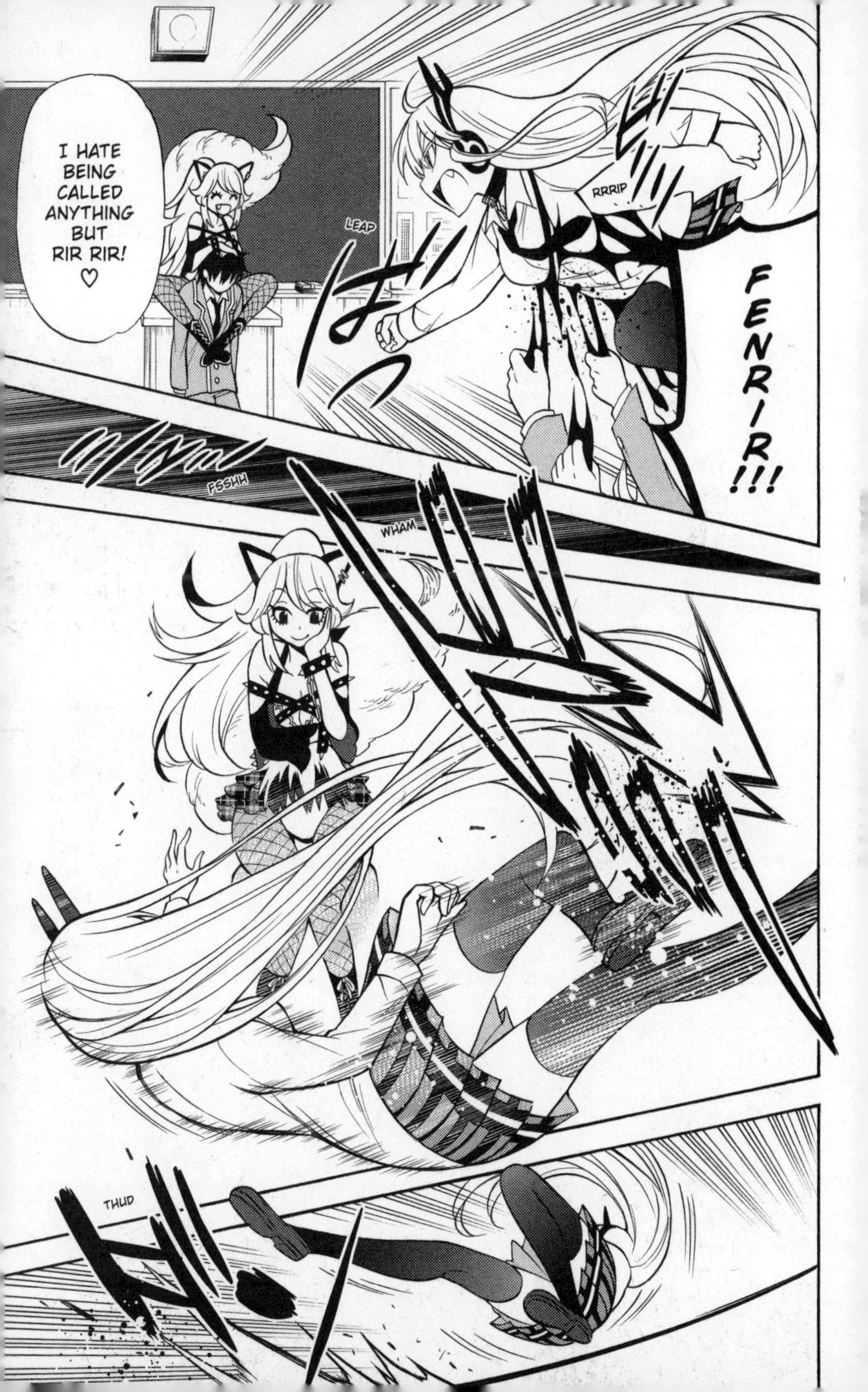
FENRIR!!!
RRRIP
LEAP
I HATE BEING CALLED ANYTHING BUT RIR RIR! ♡
FSSHH
WHAM
THUD

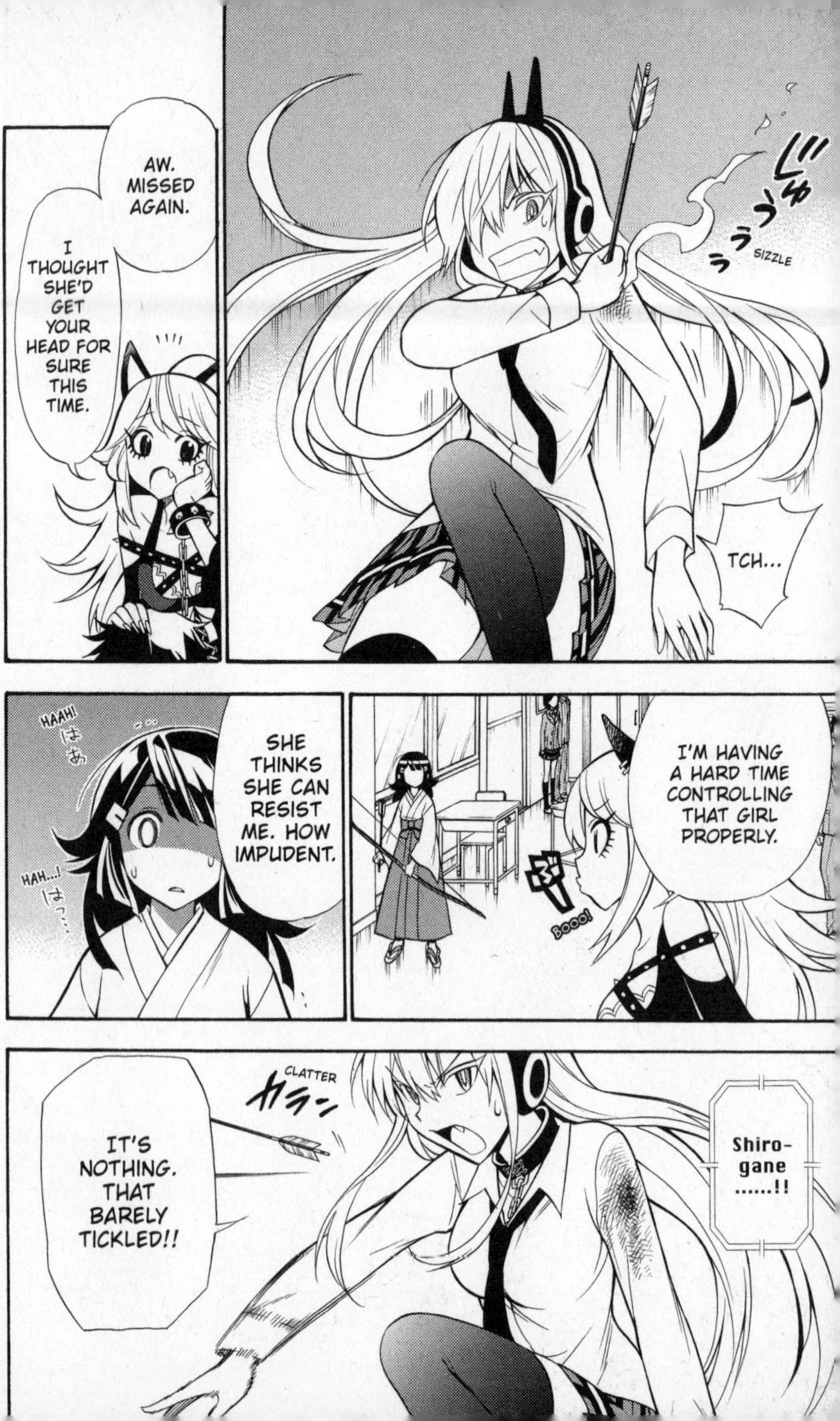
じゅううう
SIZZLE
TCH...
AW. MISSED AGAIN.
I THOUGHT SHE'D GET YOUR HEAD FOR SURE THIS TIME.
I'M HAVING A HARD TIME CONTROLLING THAT GIRL PROPERLY.
BOOO!
SHE THINKS SHE CAN RESIST ME. HOW IMPUDENT.
HAAH! はあ
HAH...! はっ...
Shiro-gane ......!!
カラン
CLATTER
IT'S NOTHING. THAT BARELY TICKLED!!

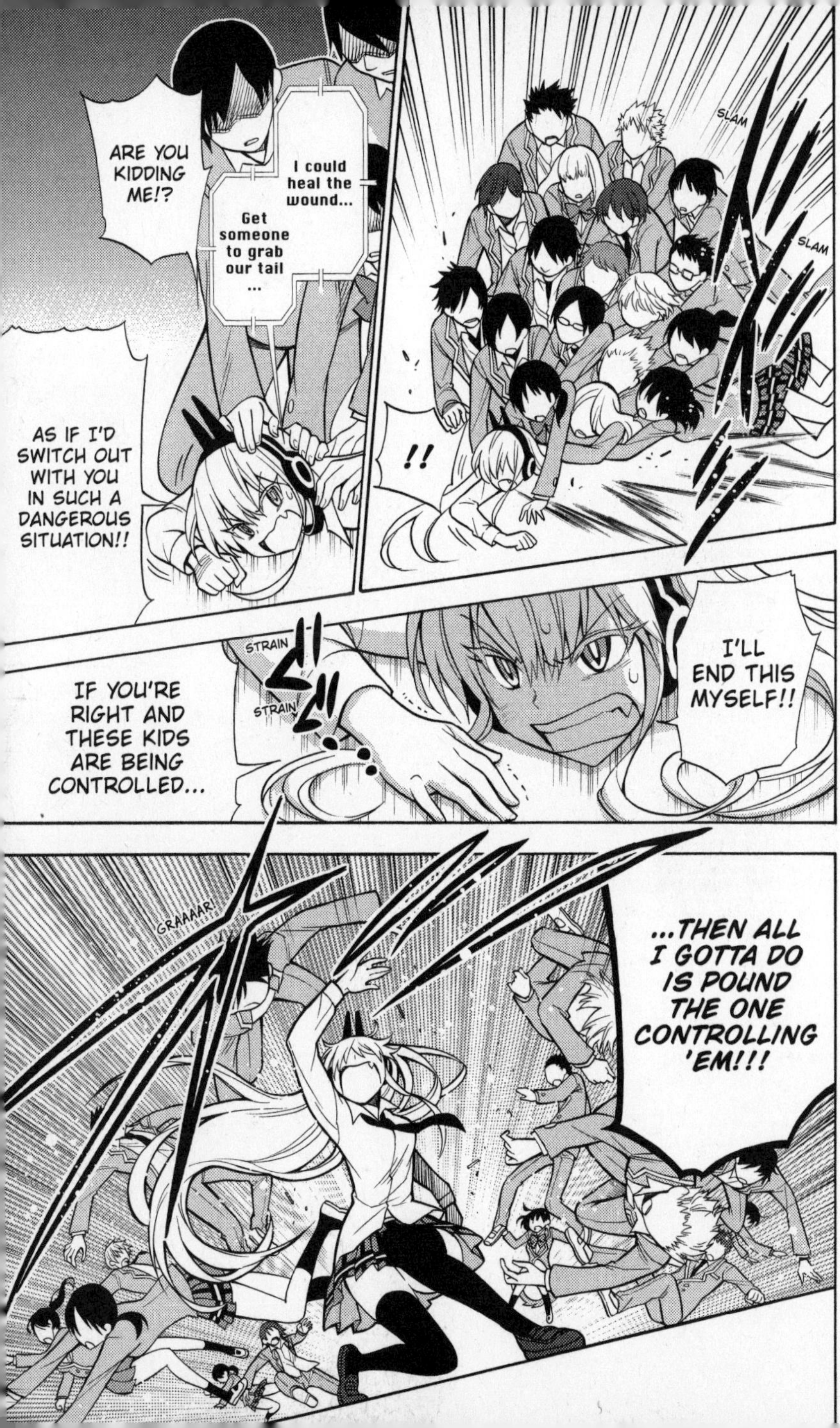
SLAM
SLAM
!!
I could heal the wound...
Get someone to grab our tail ...
ARE YOU KIDDING ME!?
AS IF I'D SWITCH OUT WITH YOU IN SUCH A DANGEROUS SITUATION!!
I'LL END THIS MYSELF!!
STRAIN
STRAIN
IF YOU'RE RIGHT AND THESE KIDS ARE BEING CONTROLLED...
...THEN ALL I GOTTA DO IS POUND THE ONE CONTROLLING 'EM!!!
GRAAAAR!

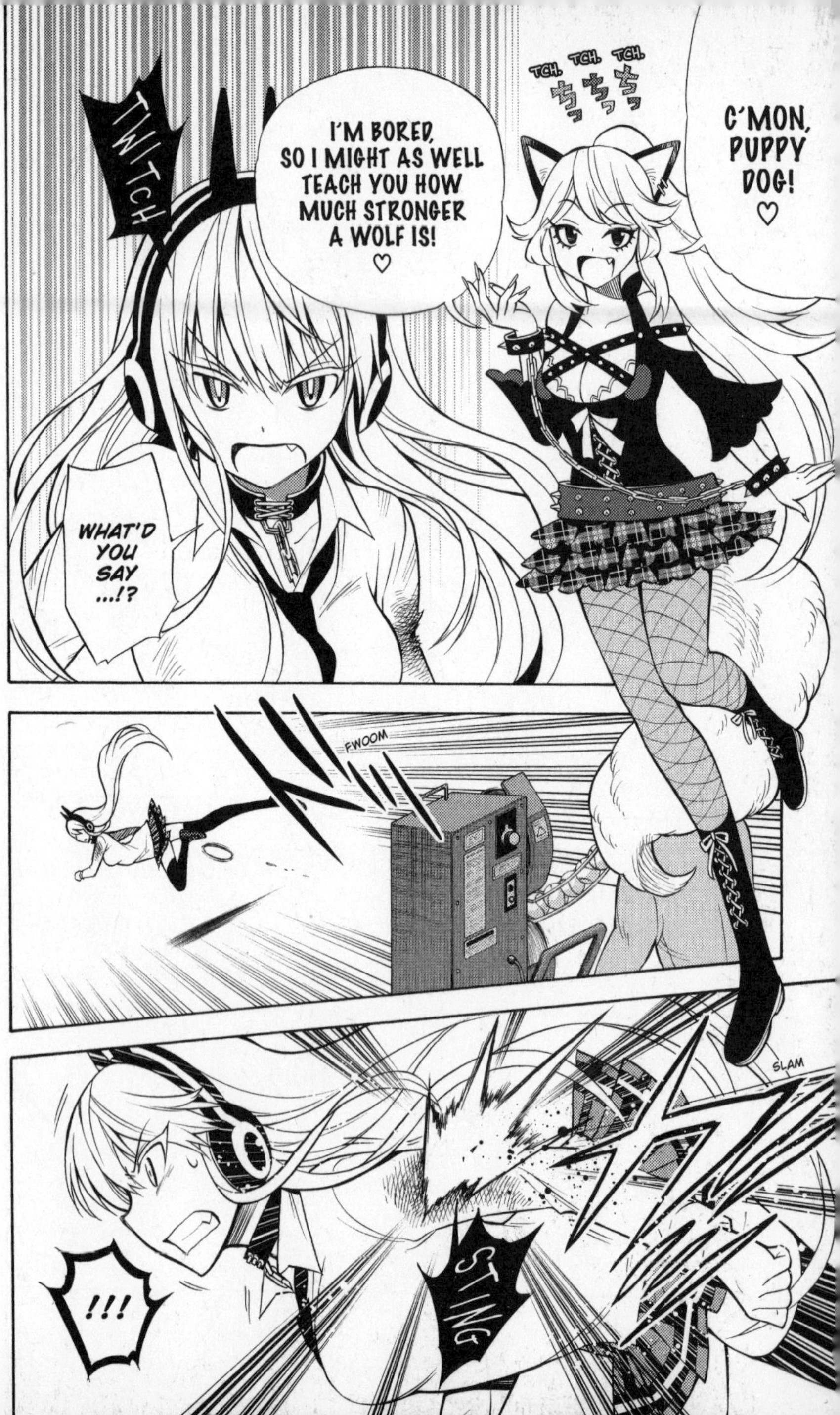

C'MON, PUPPY DOG! ♡
TCH. TCH. TCH.
ちちち
I'M BORED, SO I MIGHT AS WELL TEACH YOU HOW MUCH STRONGER A WOLF IS! ♡
TWITCH
WHAT'D YOU SAY ...!?
FWOOM
SLAM
STING
!!!

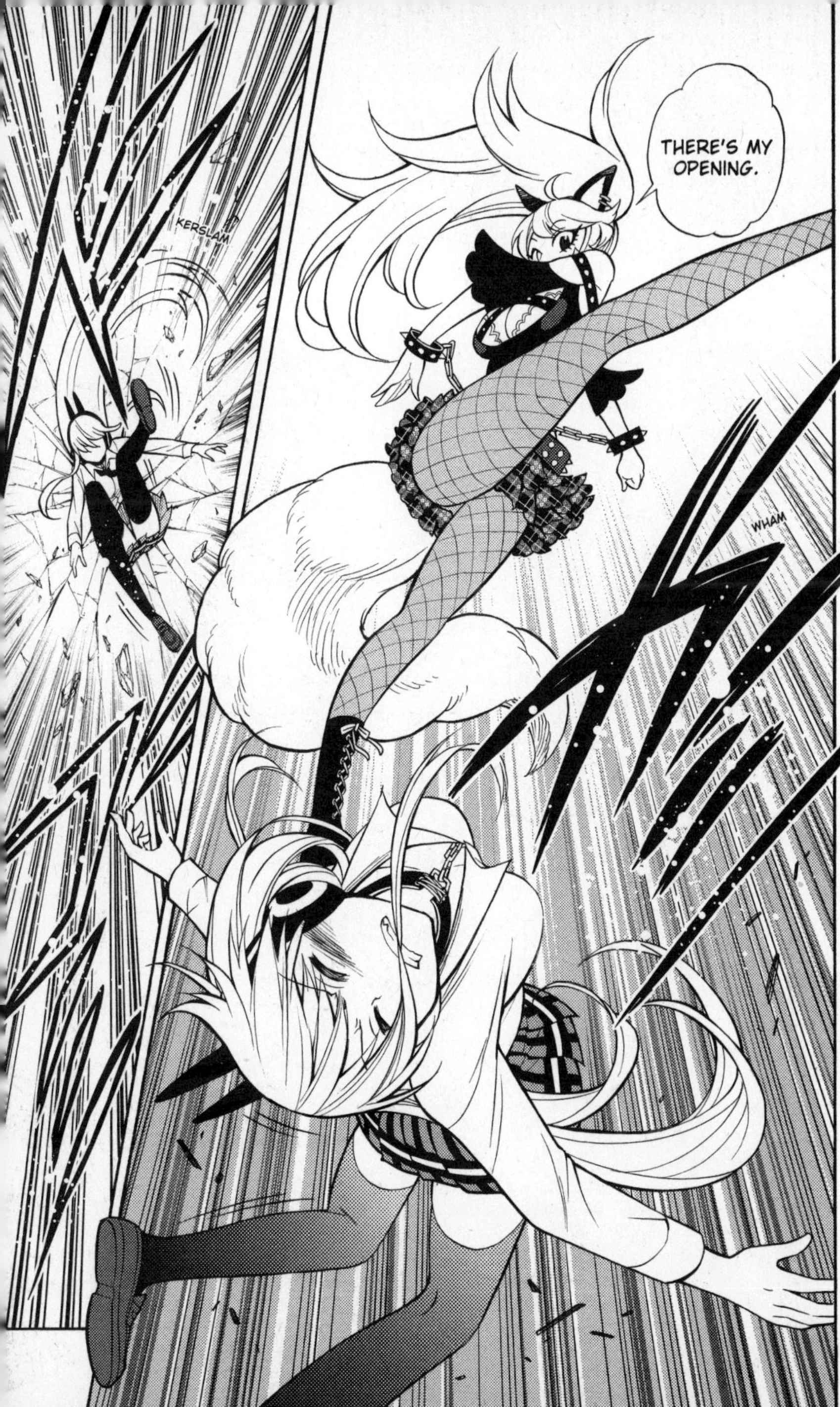
THERE'S MY OPENING.
WHAM
KERSLAM

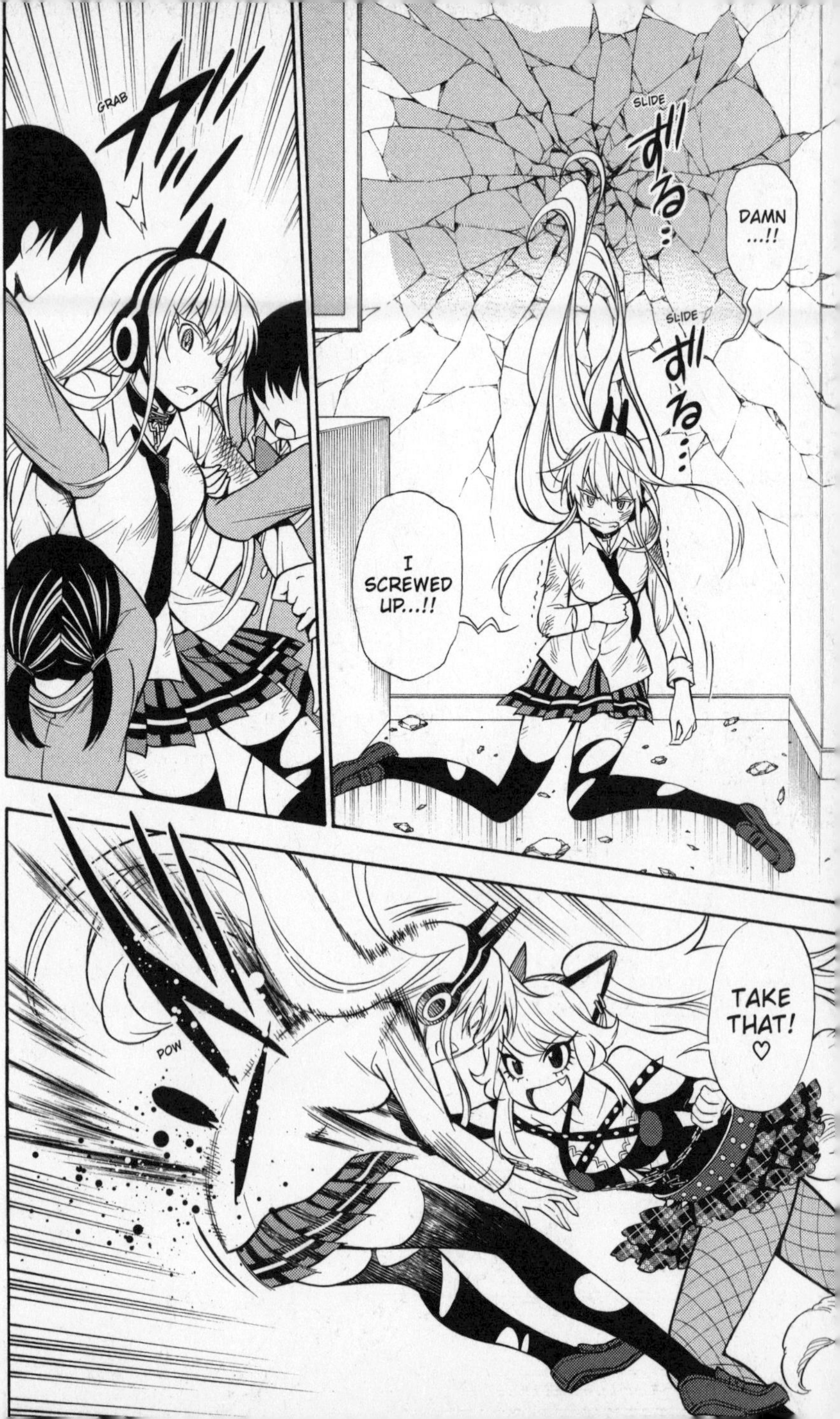
SLIDE
ずる…
DAMN ...!!
SLIDE
ずる…
I SCREWED UP...!!
GRAB
ガッ
TAKE THAT! ♡
POW

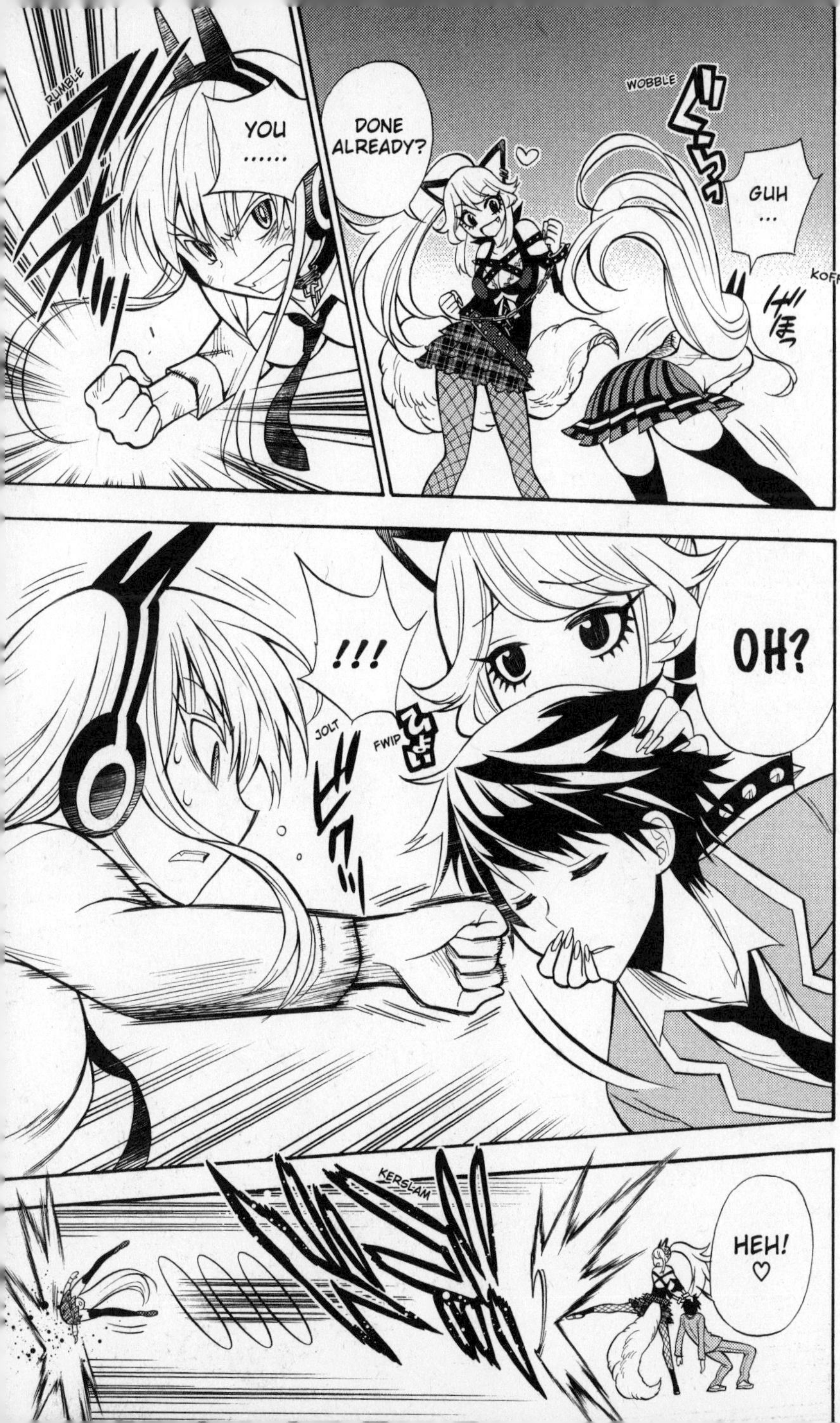
WOBBLE
ぐらっ
GUH ...
KOFF!
げほっ
DONE ALREADY?
RUMBLE
YOU ......
OH?
!!!
FWIP
ひょい
JOLT
HEH! ♡
KERSLAM

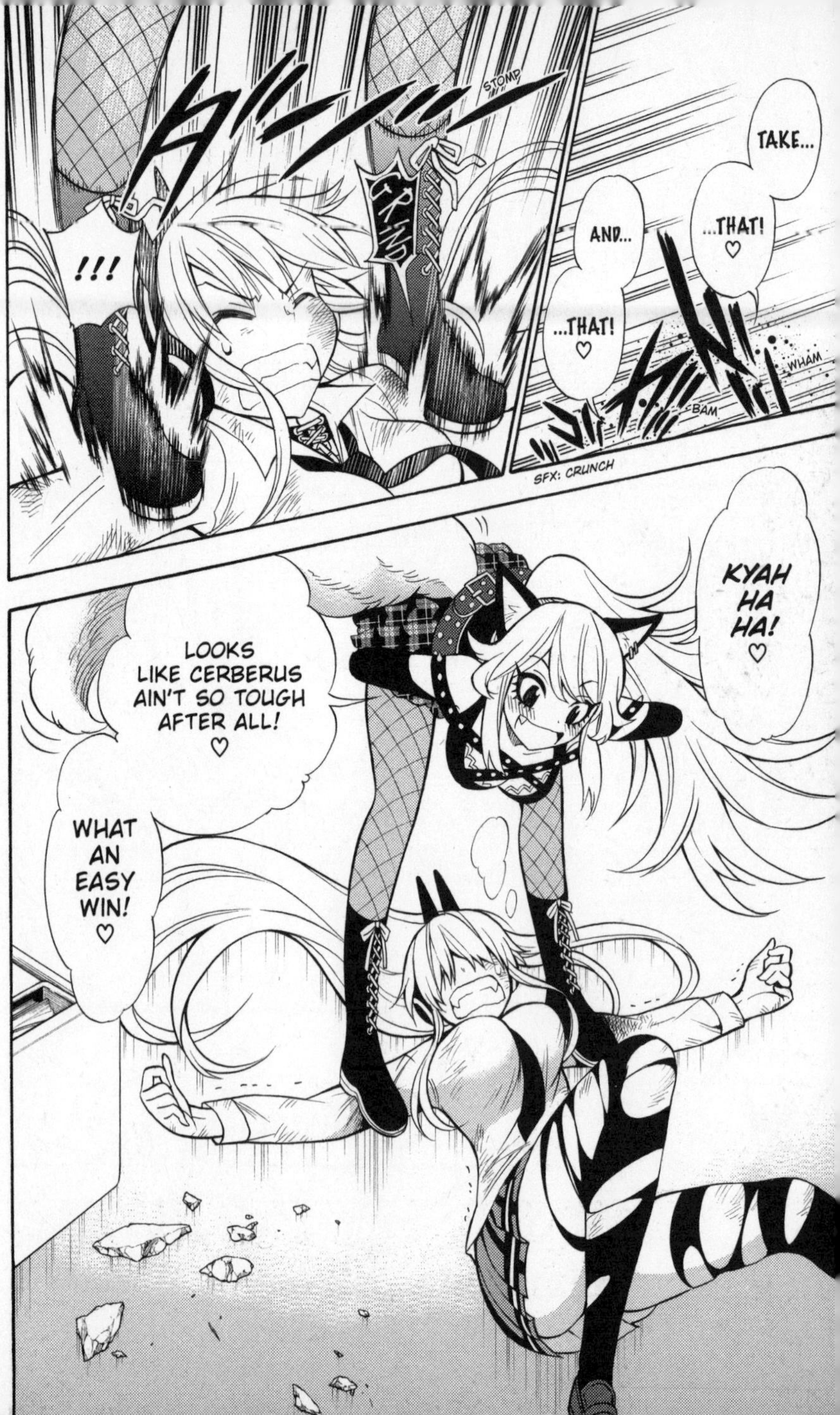
TAKE...
...THAT! ♡
AND...
...THAT! ♡
WHAM
BAM
SFX: CRUNCH
STOMP
GRIND
!!!
KYAH HA HA! ♡
LOOKS LIKE CERBERUS AIN'T SO TOUGH AFTER ALL! ♡
WHAT AN EASY WIN! ♡

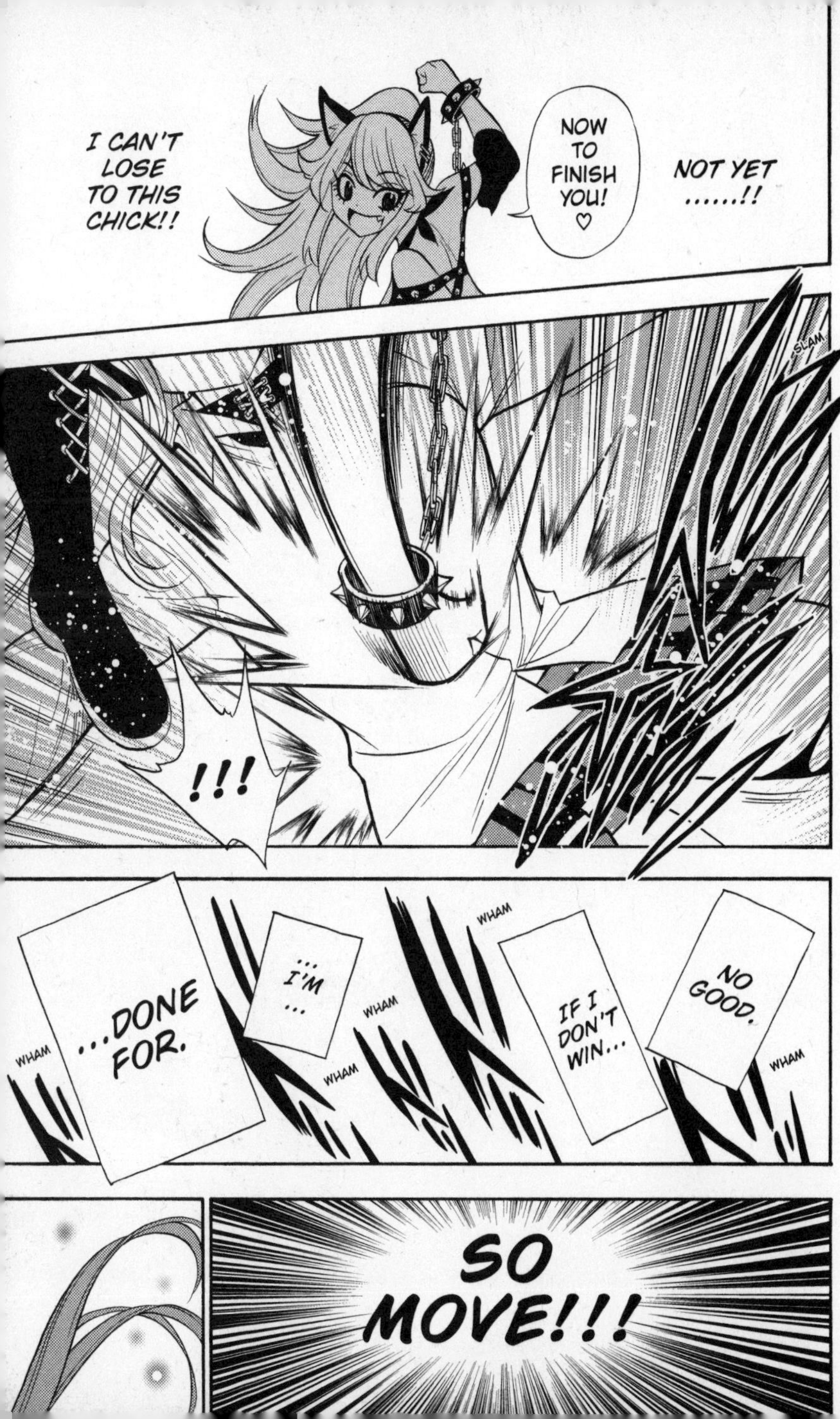
NOT YET ......!!
NOW TO FINISH YOU! ♡
I CAN'T LOSE TO THIS CHICK!!
SLAM
!!!
WHAM
NO GOOD.
IF I DON'T WIN...
WHAM
... I'M ...
WHAM
WHAM
...DONE FOR.
WHAM
SO MOVE!!!

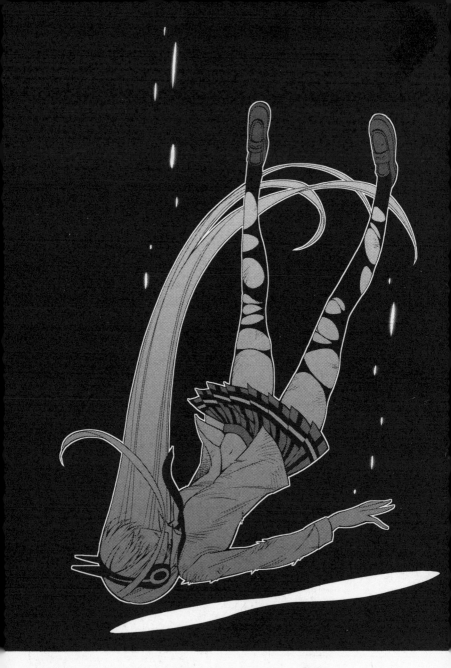

YOU'RE KIDDING ME.

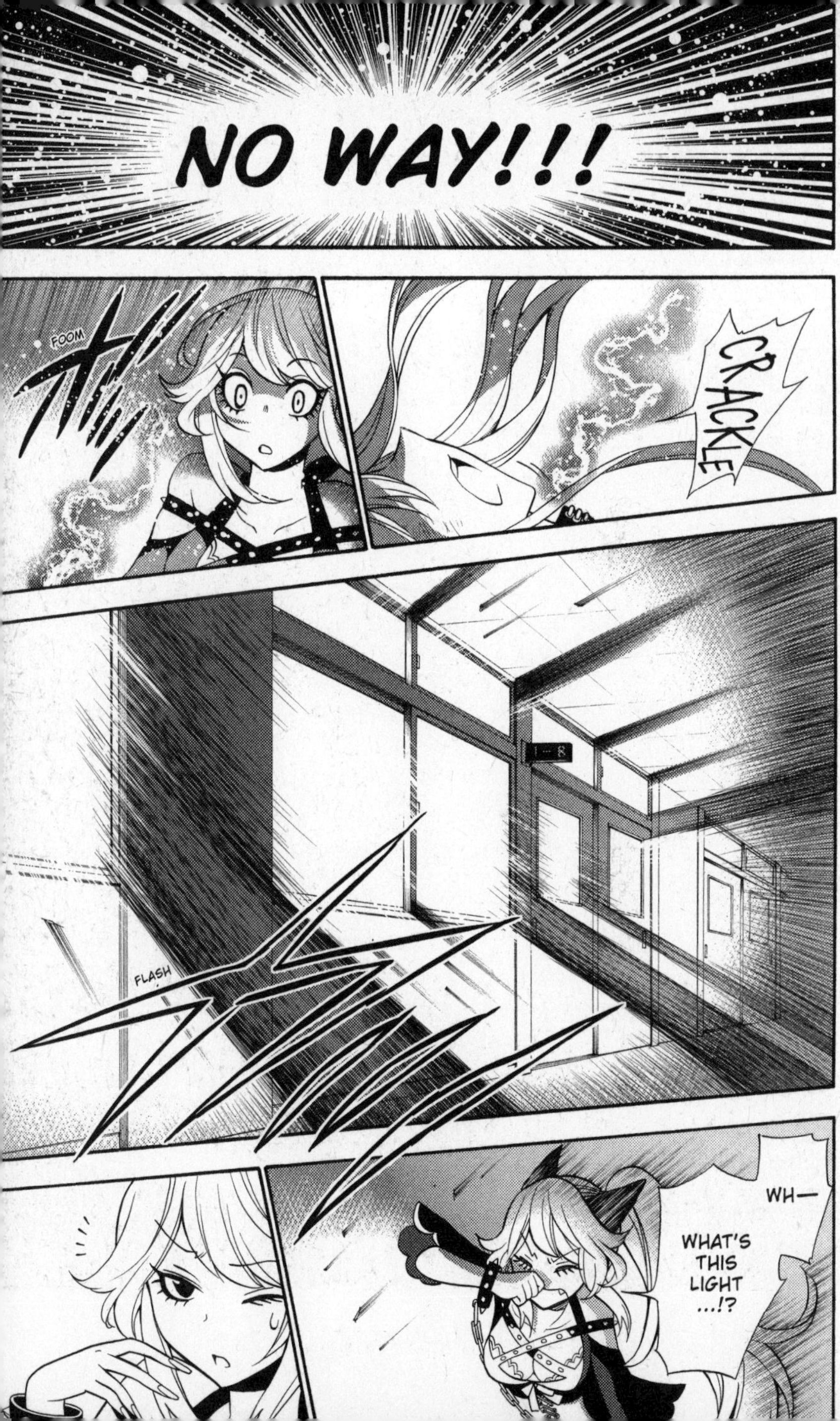
NO WAY!!!
CRACKLE
FOOM
FLASH
WH—
WHAT'S THIS LIGHT ...!?

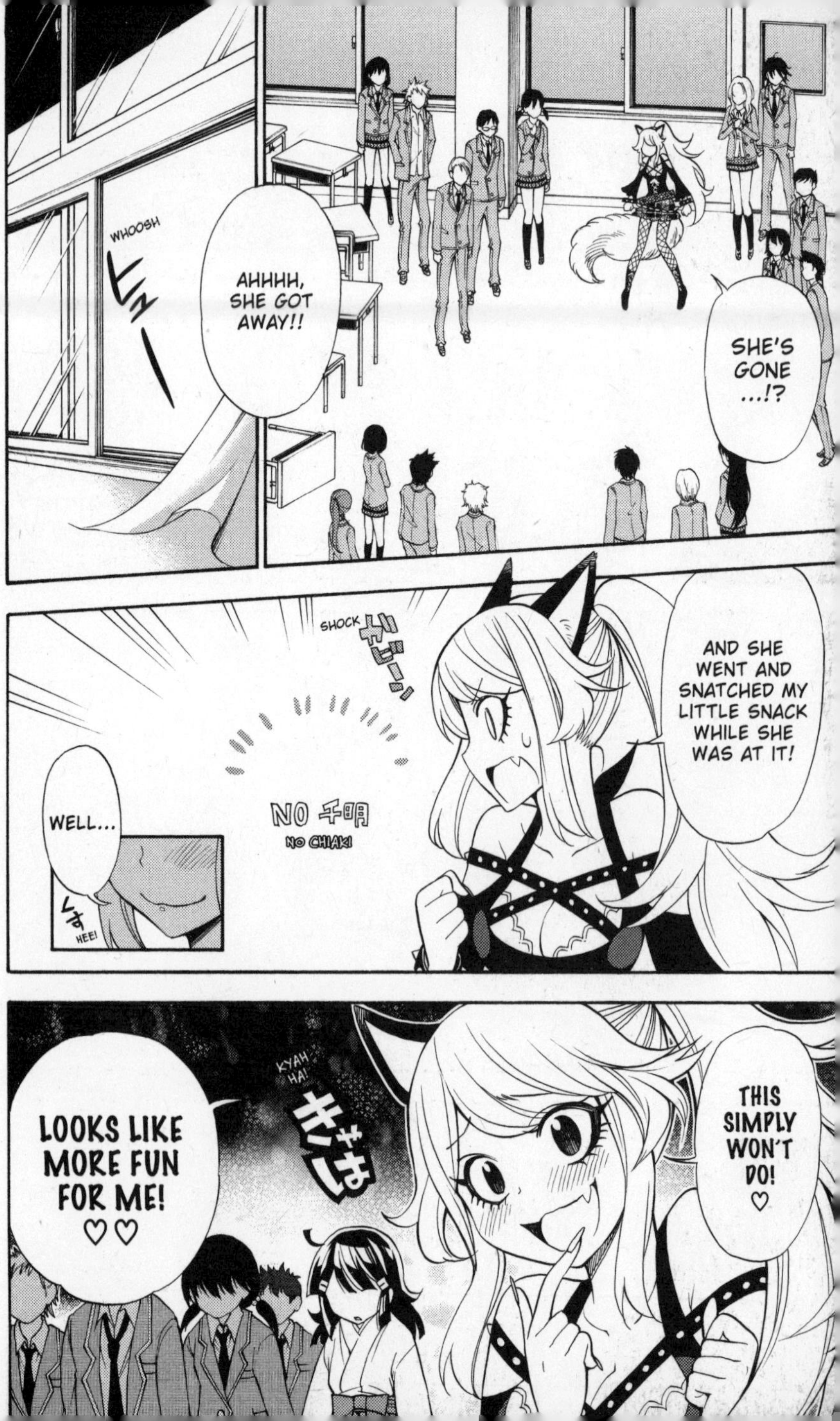
SHE'S GONE ...!?
AHHHH, SHE GOT AWAY!!
ヒュー
WHOOSH
AND SHE WENT AND SNATCHED MY LITTLE SNACK WHILE SHE WAS AT IT!
SHOCK
NO 千明
NO CHIAKI
WELL...
くす
HEE!
THIS SIMPLY WON'T DO! ♡
KYAH HA!
きゃは
LOOKS LIKE MORE FUN FOR ME! ♡♡

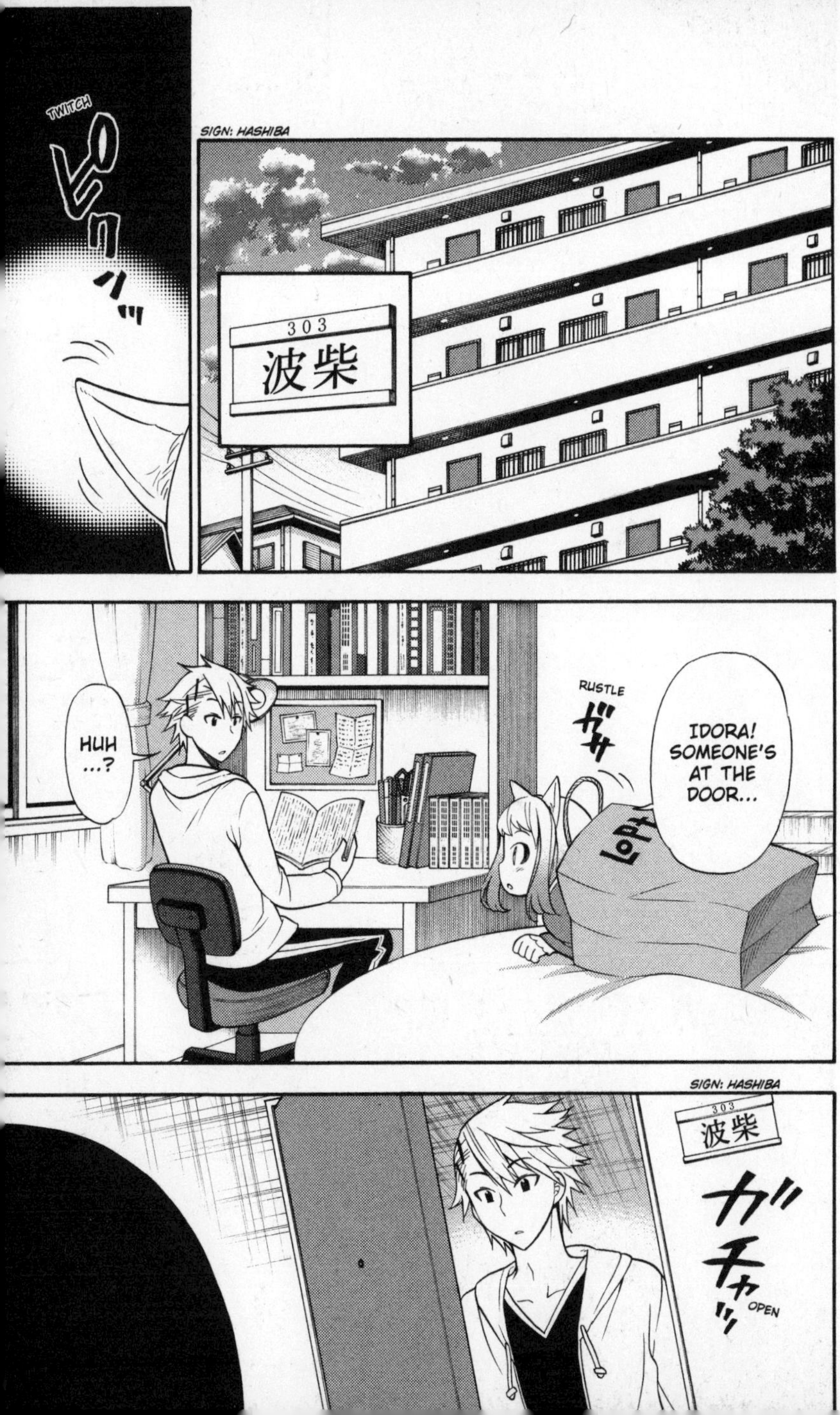
SIGN: HASHIBA
303
波柴
TWITCH
IDORA! SOMEONE'S AT THE DOOR...
RUSTLE
HUH ...?
SIGN: HASHIBA
303
波柴
OPEN

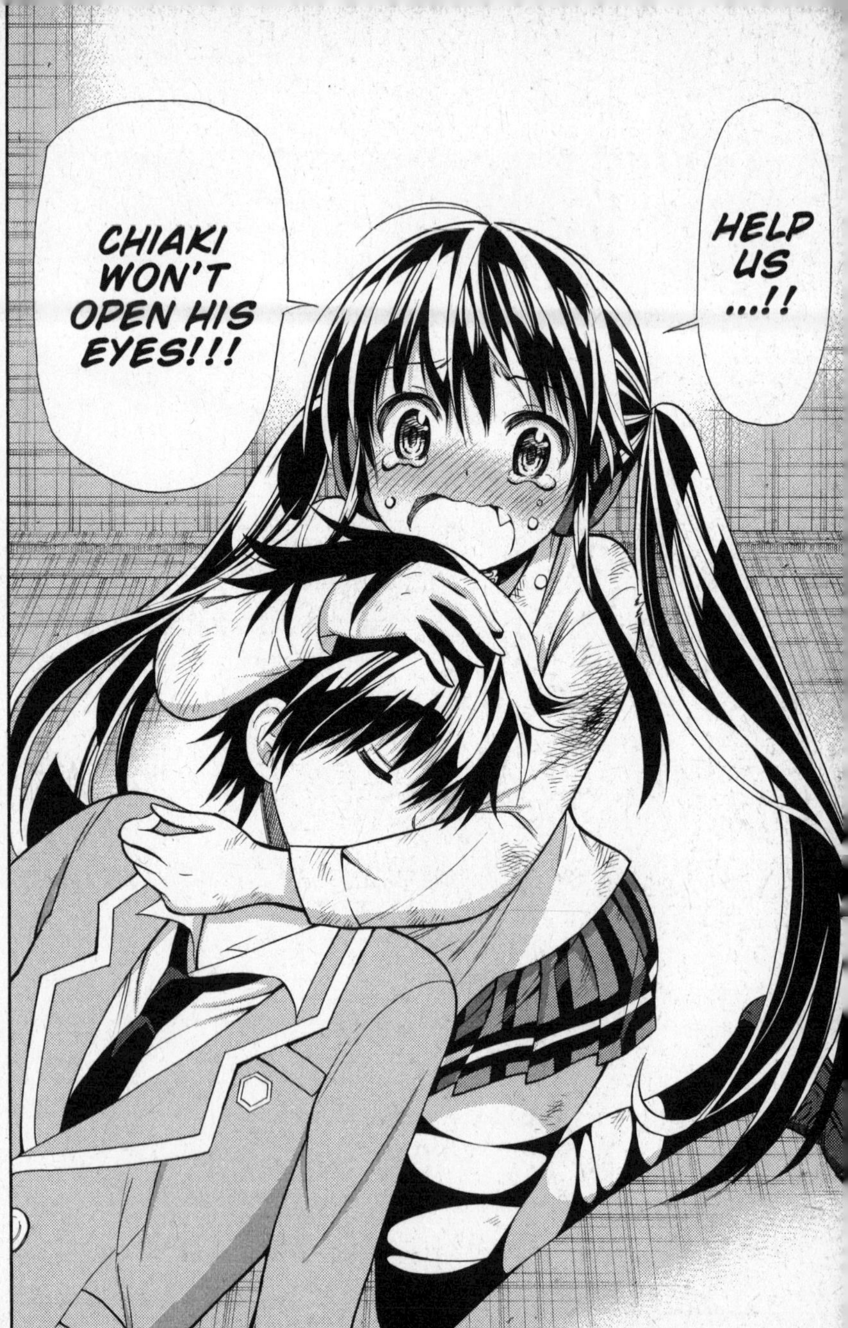
HELP US ...!!
CHIAKI WON'T OPEN HIS EYES!!!

TO BE CONTINUED IN **TODAY'S CERBERUS 3**!

TODAY'S CERBERUS-SAN

CHAPTER 5

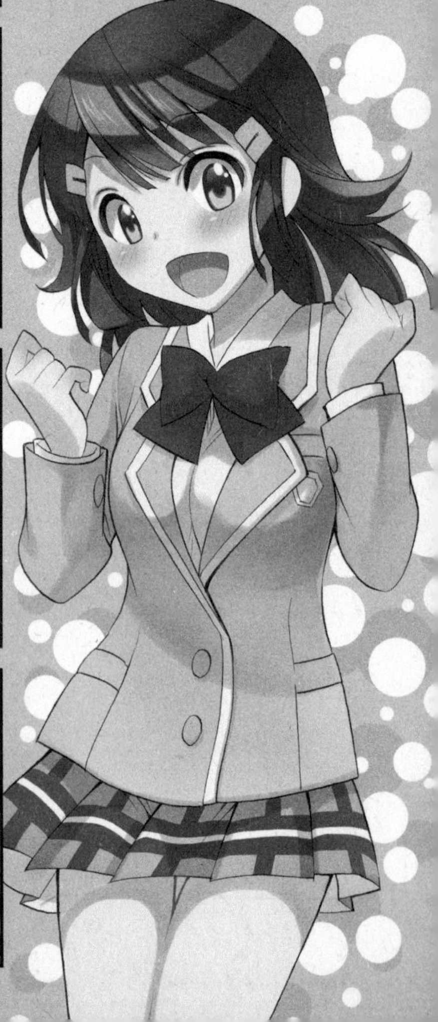

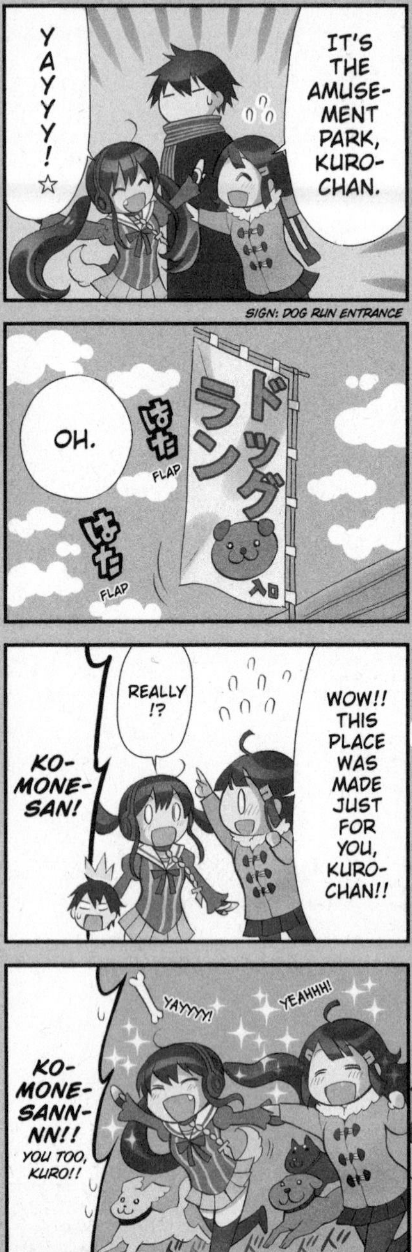
IT'S THE AMUSEMENT PARK, KURO-CHAN.
YAYYYY! ☆
SIGN: DOG RUN ENTRANCE
はた FLAP
はた FLAP
OH.
WOW!! THIS PLACE WAS MADE JUST FOR YOU, KURO-CHAN!!
REALLY !?
KO-MONE-SAN!
YEAHHH!
YAYYYY!
KO-MONE-SANNNN!!
YOU TOO, KURO!!
STOMP STOMP STOMP STOMP STOMP

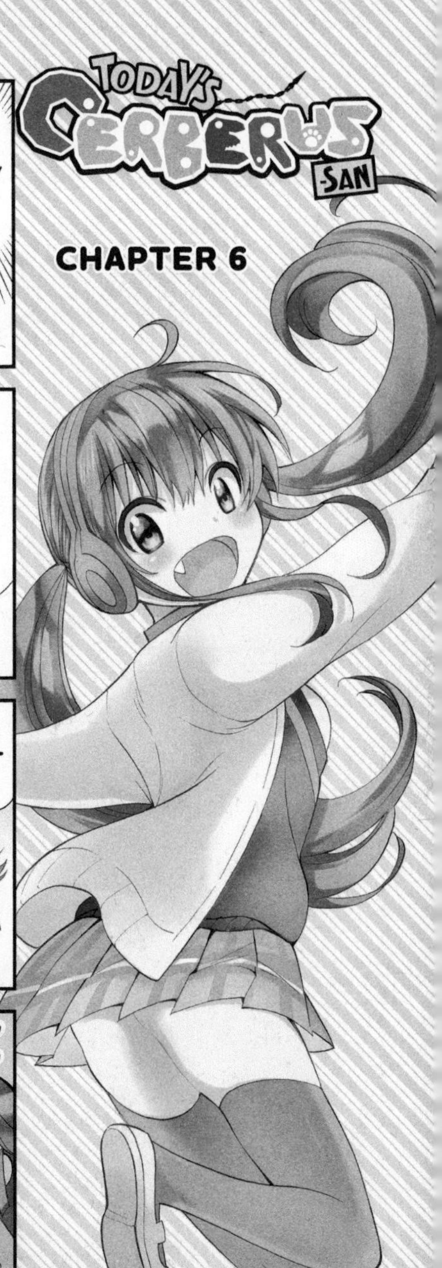
TODAY'S CERBERUS -SAN
CHAPTER 6

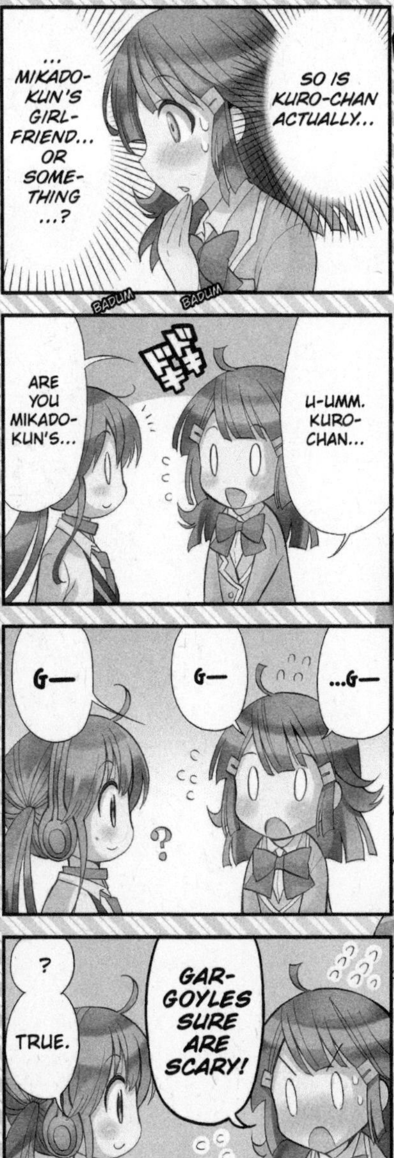
SO IS KURO-CHAN ACTUALLY...
... MIKADO-KUN'S GIRL-FRIEND... OR SOME-THING ...?
BADUM
BADUM
U-UMM. KURO-CHAN...
ドキ
ARE YOU MIKADO-KUN'S...
...G—
G—
G—
GAR-GOYLES SURE ARE SCARY!
?
TRUE.

TODAY'S CERBERUS-SAN

CHAPTER 7

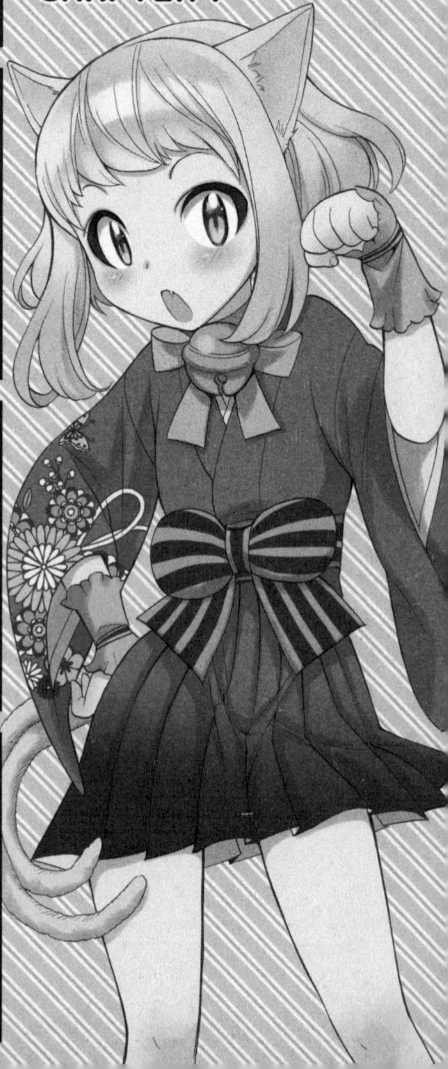

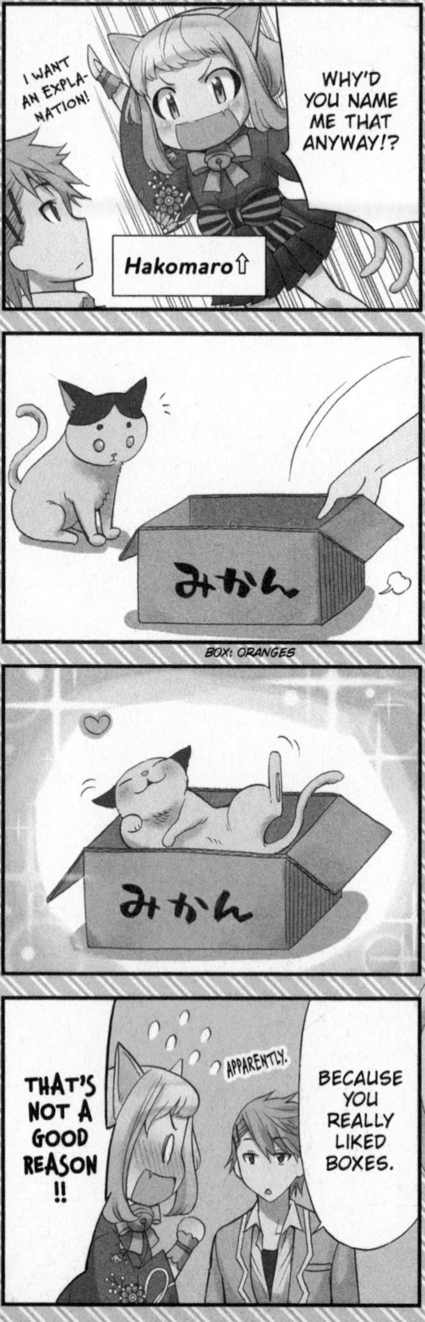
WHY'D YOU NAME ME THAT ANYWAY!?
I WANT AN EXPLA-NATION!
Hakomaro⇧
みかん
BOX: ORANGES
みかん
BECAUSE YOU REALLY LIKED BOXES.
APPARENTLY.
THAT'S NOT A GOOD REASON!!

TODAY'S CERBERUS-SAN

CHAPTER 8

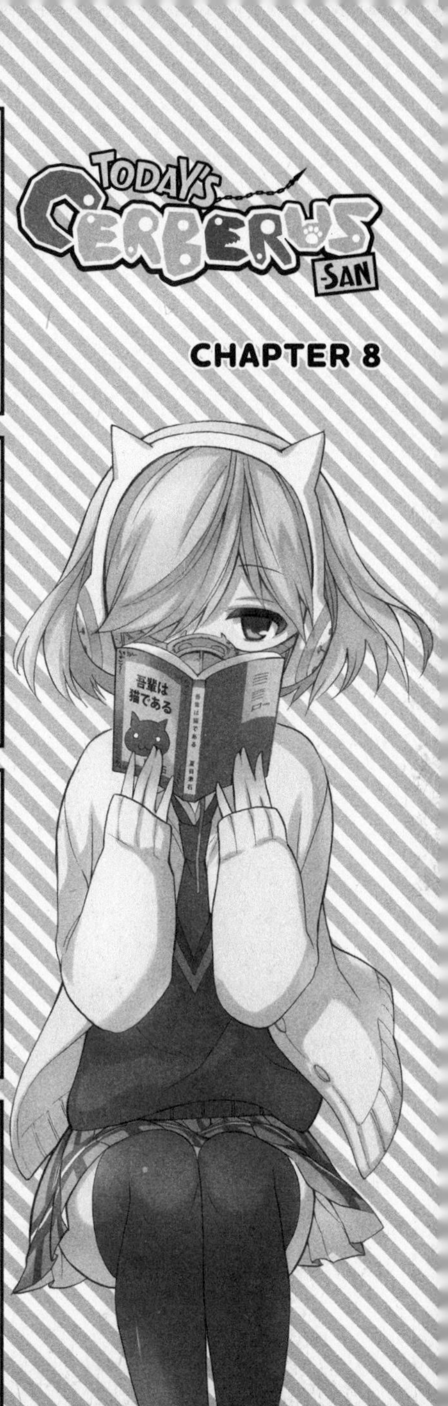
吾輩は猫である
BOOK: I AM A CAT

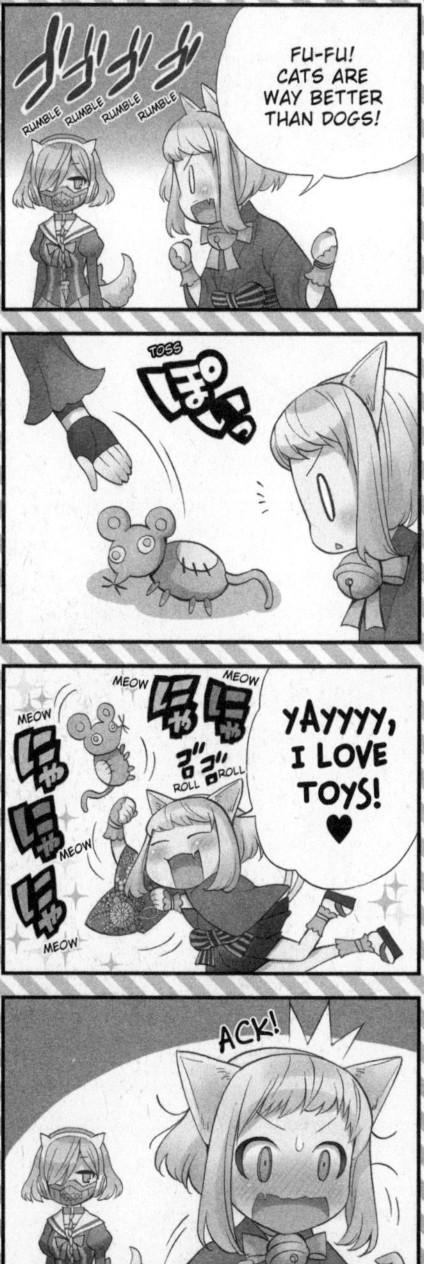
ゴゴゴゴ
RUMBLE RUMBLE RUMBLE RUMBLE
FU-FU! CATS ARE WAY BETTER THAN DOGS!
TOSS
MEOW MEOW MEOW MEOW MEOW MEOW
ROLL ROLL
YAYYYY, I LOVE TOYS! ♥
ACK!

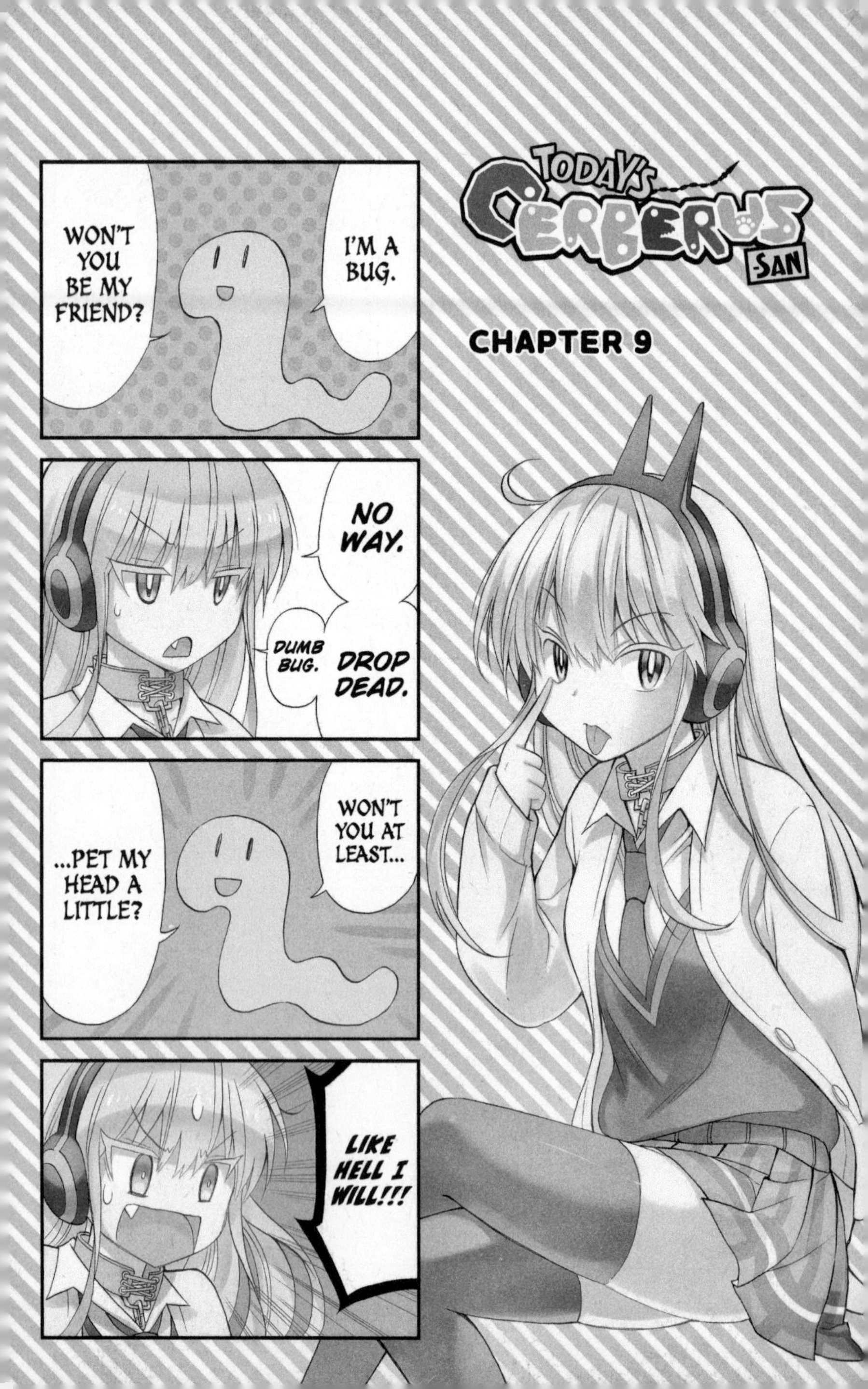
TODAY'S CERBERUS -SAN
CHAPTER 9
I'M A BUG.
WON'T YOU BE MY FRIEND?
NO WAY.
DROP DEAD.
DUMB BUG.
WON'T YOU AT LEAST...
...PET MY HEAD A LITTLE?
LIKE HELL I WILL!!!

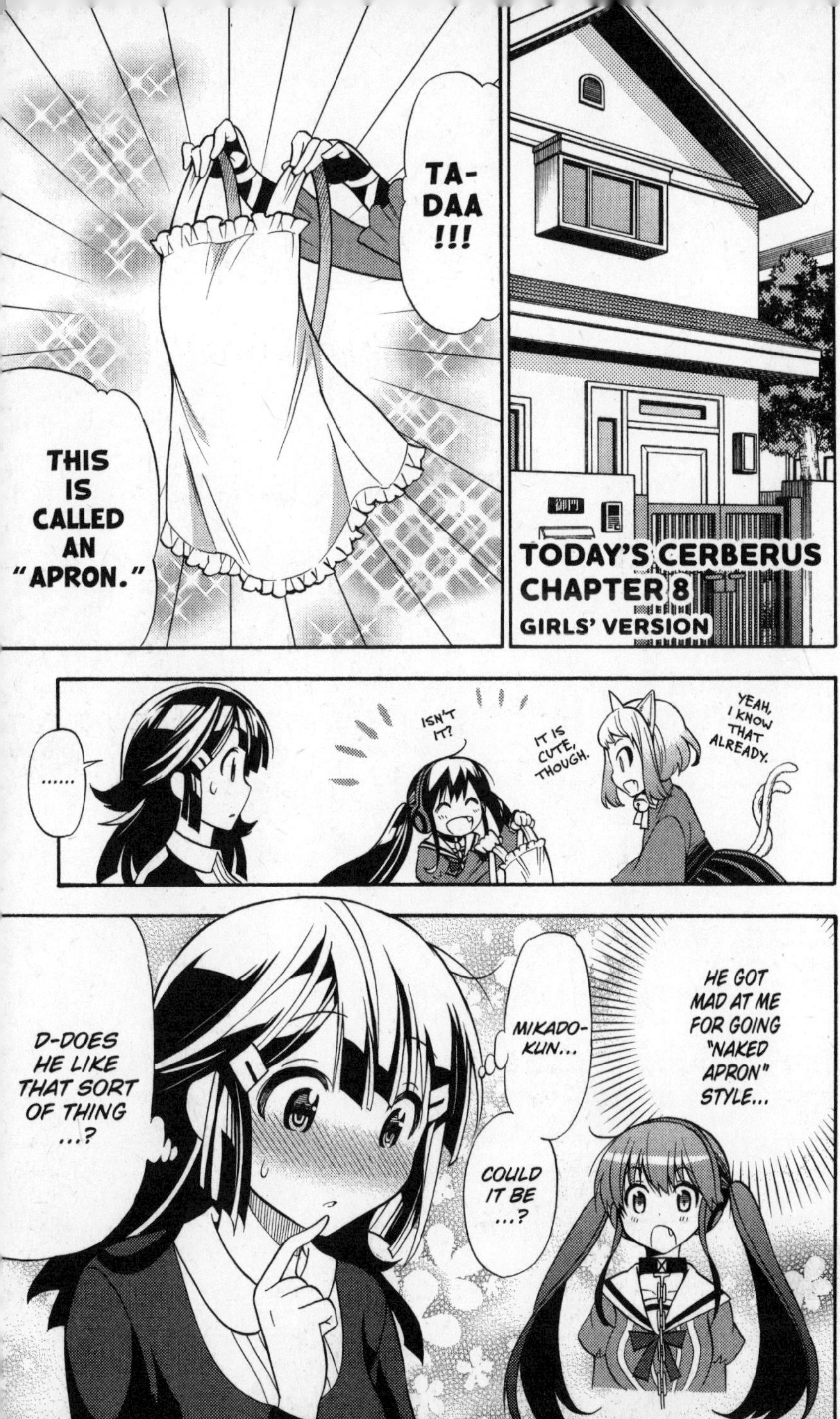
御門
TODAY'S CERBERUS CHAPTER 8
GIRLS' VERSION
TA-DAA!!!
THIS IS CALLED AN "APRON."
YEAH, I KNOW THAT ALREADY.
IT IS CUTE, THOUGH.
ISN'T IT?
......
HE GOT MAD AT ME FOR GOING "NAKED APRON" STYLE...
MIKADO-KUN...
COULD IT BE ...?
D-DOES HE LIKE THAT SORT OF THING ...?

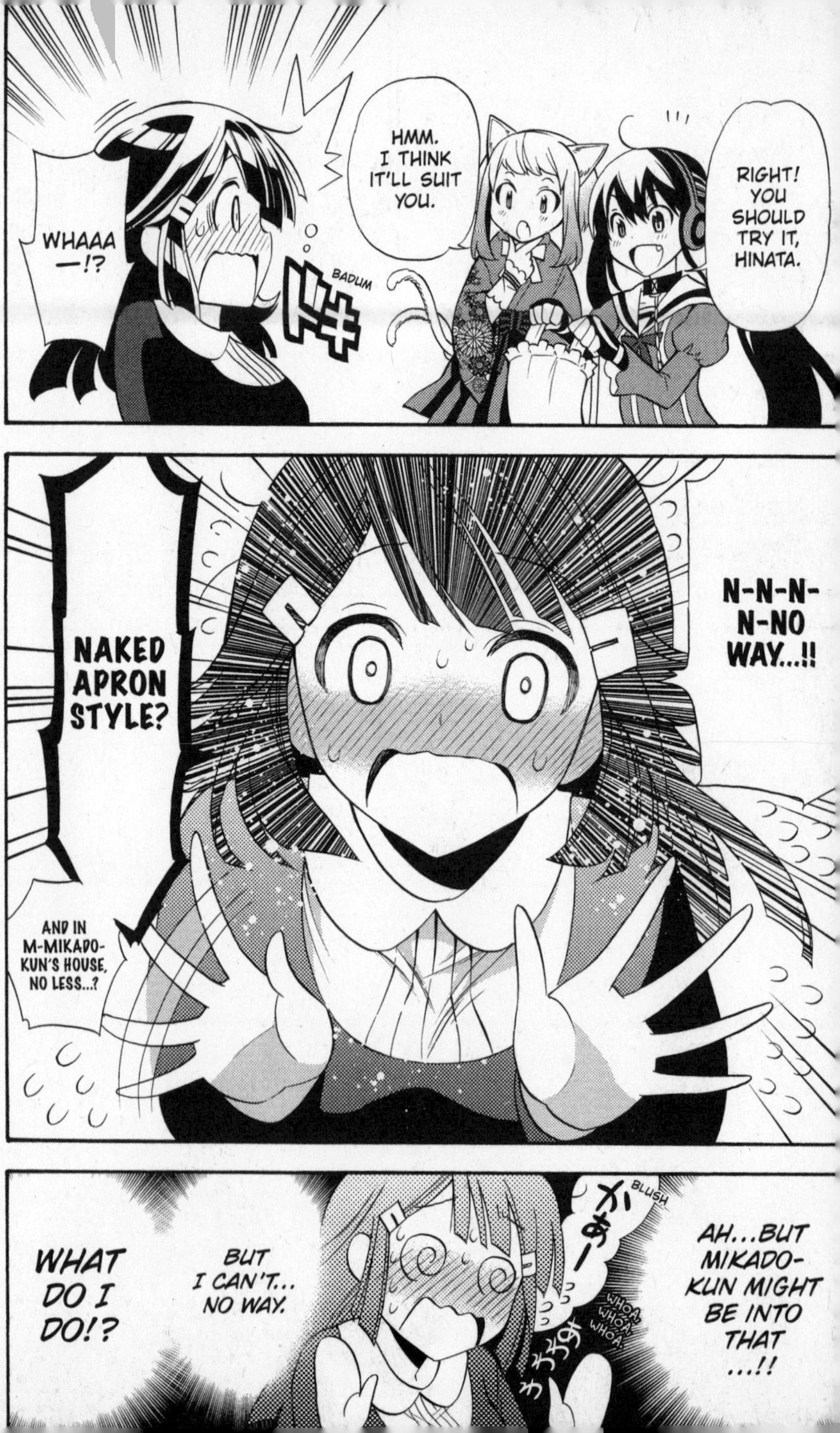
RIGHT! YOU SHOULD TRY IT, HINATA.
HMM. I THINK IT'LL SUIT YOU.
BADUM
ドキ
WHAAA—!?
N-N-N-N-NO WAY...!!
NAKED APRON STYLE?
AND IN M-MIKADO-KUN'S HOUSE, NO LESS...?
AH...BUT MIKADO-KUN MIGHT BE INTO THAT...!!
かぁー
BLUSH
WHOA WHOA WHOA
BUT I CAN'T... NO WAY.
WHAT DO I DO!?

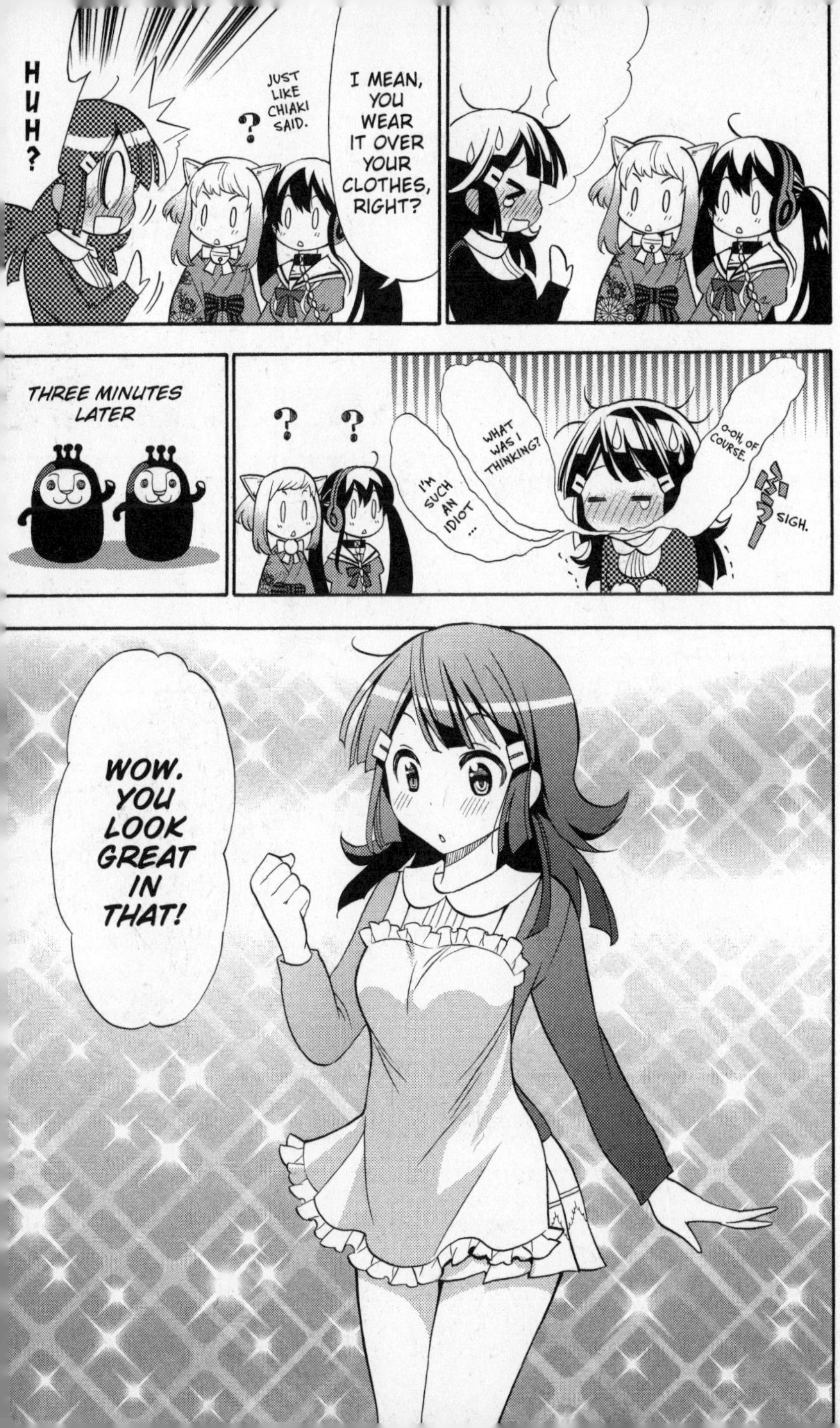

I MEAN, YOU WEAR IT OVER YOUR CLOTHES, RIGHT?
JUST LIKE CHIAKI SAID.
HUH?
O-OH, OF COURSE.
WHAT WAS I THINKING?
I'M SUCH AN IDIOT...
SIGH.
THREE MINUTES LATER
WOW. YOU LOOK GREAT IN THAT!

THIS APRON...
I FEEL REALLY FOCUSED WEARING IT...
LIKE I COULD ACCOMPLISH ANYTHING.
I... DON'T THINK I COULD GO FOR NAKED APRON STYLE YET. THAT'S TOO EMBARRASSING, BUT...
BADUM
BADUM
...MAYBE SOMEDAY I'LL WEAR THIS FOR MIKADO-KUN AND...
LET'S HEAR IT FOR THE APRON SQUAD (?)!!
YEAHHH.
RIGHT!!
WHETHER COOKING...
...OR CLEANING...
...OR SHOPPING, I CAN DO IT ALL!
OPEN

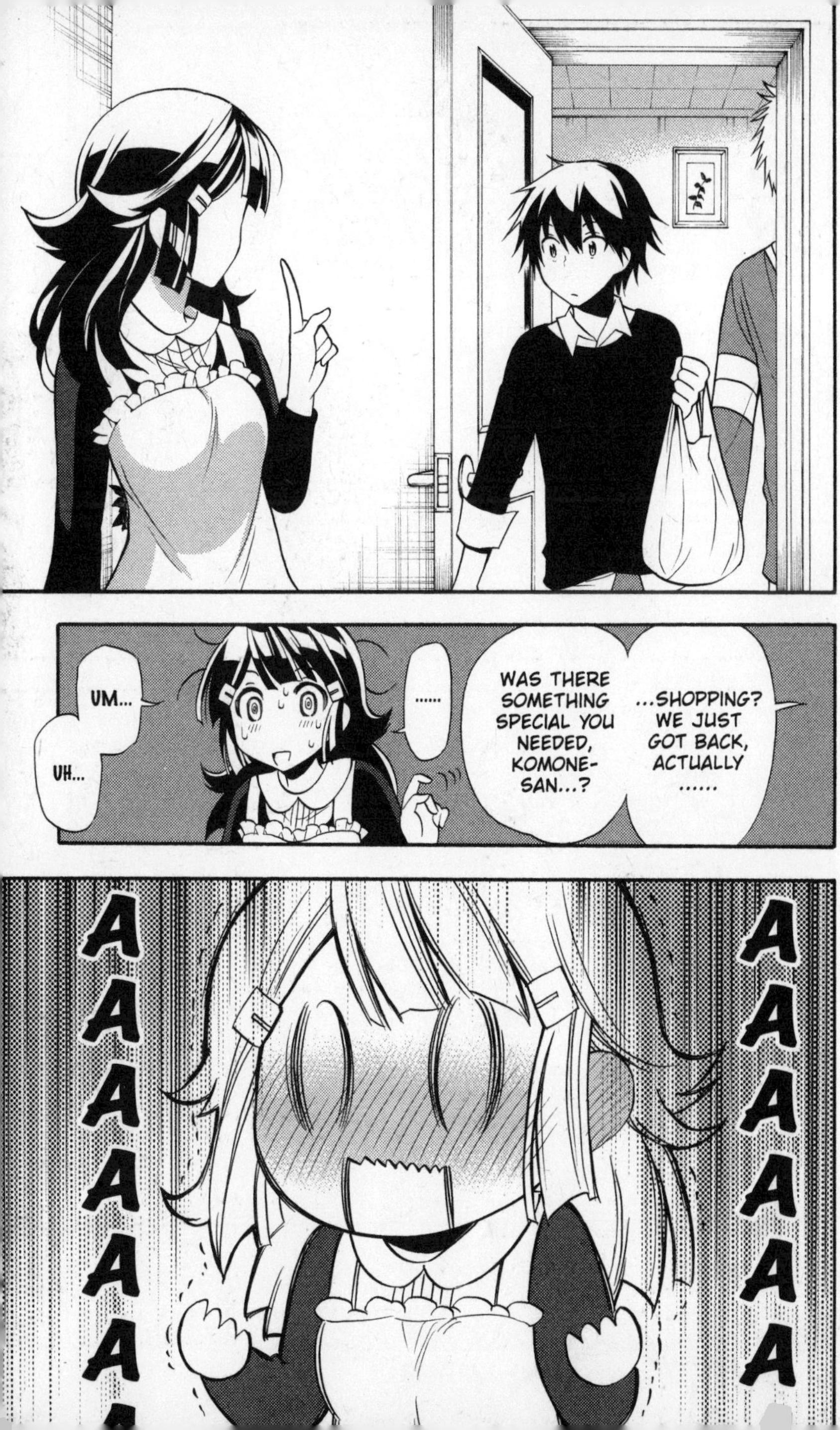
...SHOPPING? WE JUST GOT BACK, ACTUALLY ......
WAS THERE SOMETHING SPECIAL YOU NEEDED, KOMONE-SAN...?
......
UM...
UH...
AAAAAAAAA
AAAAAAAAA

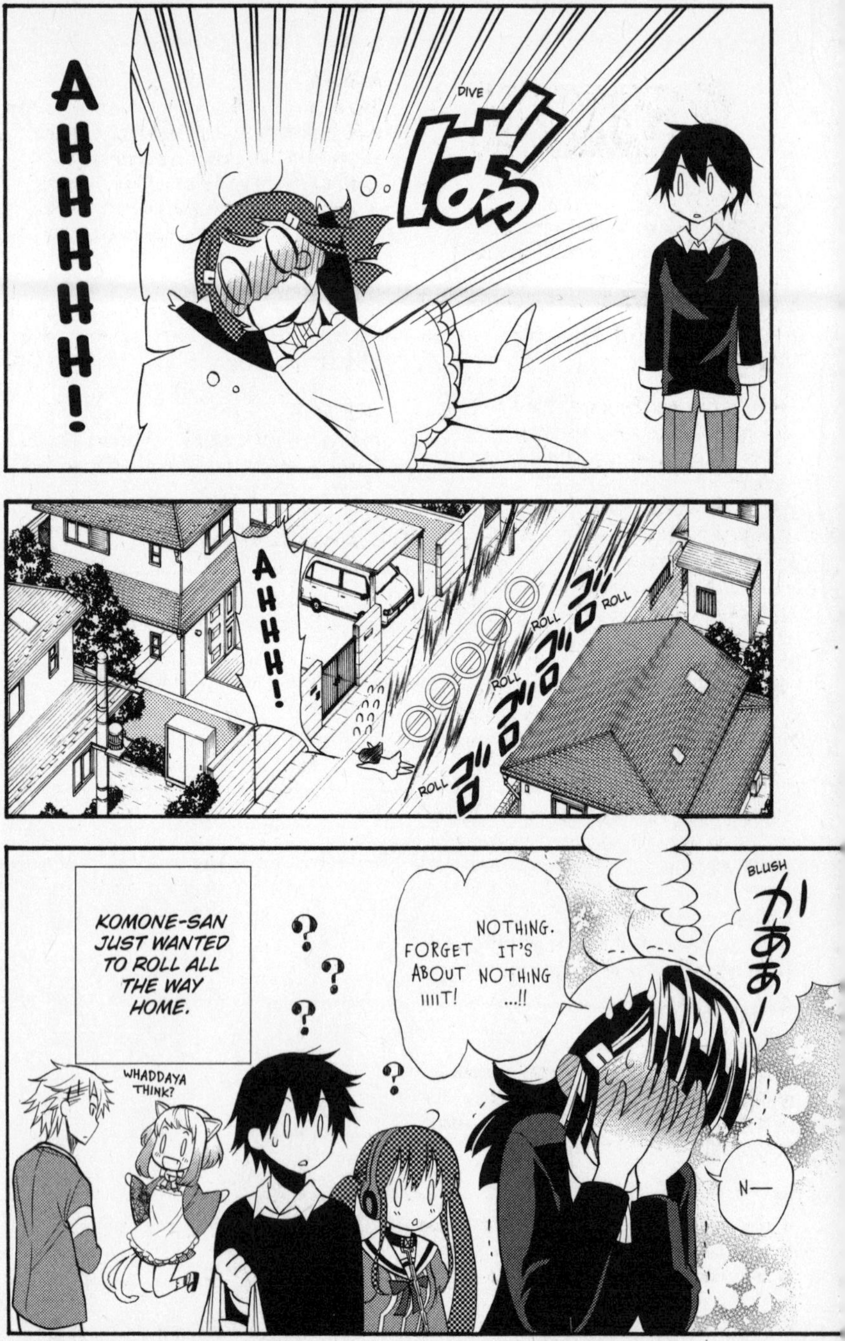
DIVE
ぱっ
AHHHHHH!
ゴロ ROLL
ゴロ ROLL
ゴロ ROLL
ゴロ ROLL
AHHHH!
BLUSH
かあぁー
N—
NOTHING. IT'S NOTHING ...!!
FORGET ABOUT IIIIT!
???
?
WHADDAYA THINK?
KOMONE-SAN JUST WANTED TO ROLL ALL THE WAY HOME.

STAFF-> MORI · GARAKUTA IMAYAMA · FUJIKO DOSEI · YUU JUNA · WATARINI FUNE

NOTES

COMMON HONORIFICS

no honorific: Indicates familiarity or closeness; if used without permission or reason, addressing someone in this manner would constitute an insult.

-san: The Japanese equivalent of Mr./Mrs./Miss. If a situation calls for politeness, this is the fail-safe honorific.

-kun: Used most often when referring to boys, this indicates affection or familiarity. Occasionally used by older men among their peers, but it may also be used by anyone referring to a person of lower standing.

-chan: An affectionate honorific indicating familiarity used mostly in reference to girls; also used in reference to cute persons or animals of either gender.

-sensei: A respectful term for teachers, artists, or high-level professionals.

PAGE 20
Hinata handing Chiaki a can of hot tea isn't as weird as it seems. Some vending machines in Japan dispense both hot and cold canned drinks.

Page 54
Chiaki thinks salty when Idora mentions *senbei* (rice crackers) because they're often salty and more of a savory treat.

PAGE 60
-maro is a common suffix for male pet names, which is why being called "Hakomaro" gets Hako so riled up.

PAGE 61
Nekomata is a type of Japanese *youkai* ("monster spirit") that is said to have a forked tail. Some legends state that ordinary house cats will transform into *nekomata* if they grow old enough.

PAGE 117
Hiyoko means "chick" (a baby bird) in Japanese, and the box brought by Hinata contains a famous brand of chick-shaped sweets that go well with tea.

PAGE 124
The kanji in Idora's name mean "power," "authority," and "tiger."

PAGE 143
Here we see a typical kanji quiz in Japanese language class. Students must write in the phonetic reading next to the indicated kanji. Kuro naturally gets question one right, as the kanji is "haji," meaning "shame," which she studied at length. She gets the other questions completely wrong, though...

PAGE 167
Fenrir is a giant wolf in Norse mythology. It's foretold that during the apocalyptic battle, Ragnarok, Fenrir will kill the god Odin.

PAGE 184
Knowing that *hako* means "box" in Japanese makes the origin of Hako's name make a lot more sense.

PAGE 185
Roze is reading *I Am a Cat*, a famous novel by author Natsume Soseki written from the perspective of a cat.

TODAY'S CERBERUS ❷

Ato Sakurai

Translation: Caleb Cook • **Lettering: Bianca Pistillo**

TODAY'S KERBEROS Vol. 2 ©2014 Ato Sakurai/SQUARE ENIX CO., LTD. First published in Japan in 2014 by SQUARE ENIX CO., LTD. English translation rights arranged with SQUARE ENIX CO., LTD. and Yen Press, LLC through Tuttle-Mori Agency, Inc.

English translation ©2015 by SQUARE ENIX CO., LTD.

Yen Press
1290 Avenue of the Americas
New York, NY 10104

Visit us at yenpress.com
facebook.com/yenpress
twitter.com/yenpress
yenpress.tumblr.com
instagram.com/yenpress

First Yen Press Print Edition: January 2017
Originally published as an ebook in July 2015 by Yen Press.

Yen Press is an imprint of Yen Press, LLC.
The Yen Press name and logo are trademarks of Yen Press, LLC.

The publisher is not responsible for websites (or their content) that are not owned by the publisher.

Library of Congress Control Number: 2016946072

ISBN: 978-0-316-50459-1 (paperback)

10 9 8 7 6 5 4 3

WOR

Printed in the United States of America